Morality and the Professional Life
Values at Work

Cynthia A. Brincat
Medical College of Wisconsin

Victoria S. Wike
Loyola University of Chicago

Library of Congress Cataloging-in-Publication Data

Brincat, Cynthia A.
    Morality and the professional life : values at work / Cynthia A.
Brincat, Victoria S. Wike.
        p.   cm.
    Includes bibliographical references and index.
    ISBN 0-13-915729-8
    1. Professional ethics.   I. Wike, Victoria S.   II. Title.
BJ1725.B75   2000
174—dc21   98-56099
                                                              CIP

Acquisitions Editor: Karita France
Editorial Assistant: Jennifer Ackerman
Production Editor: Jean Lapidus
Manufacturing Buyer: Tricia Kenny
Copy Editor: Michele Lansing
Cover Design: Bruce Kenselaar

This book was set in 10.5/12.5 New Century Schoolbook by Pub-Set, Inc.
and was printed and bound by Courier Companies, Inc.
The cover was printed by Phoenix Color Corp.

© 2000 by Prentice-Hall, Inc.
Upper Saddle River, N.J. 07458

Printed in the United States of America

10   9   8   7   6   5   4   3   2   1

ISBN 0-13-915729-8

PRENTICE-HALL INTERNATIONAL (UK) LIMITED, *London*
PRENTICE-HALL OF AUSTRALIA PTY. LIMITED, *Sydney*
PRENTICE-HALL CANADA INC., *Toronto*
PRENTICE-HALL HISPANOAMERICANA, S.A., *Mexico*
PRENTICE-HALL OF INDIA PRIVATE LIMITED, *New Delhi*
PRENTICE-HALL OF JAPAN, INC., *Tokyo*
PEARSON EDUCATION ASIA PTE. LTD., *Singapore*
EDITORA PRENTICE-HALL DO BRASIL, LTDA., *Rio de Janeiro*

Contents

Preface

Our current employment market has seen an increasing demand for ethically sensitive professionals. The thrust of this demand comes from employers who demand that their potential employees have some sort of ethics education. As the population being served by professional ethics courses grows, it is impractical to have a multitude of career-specific ethics courses (e.g., medical ethics, business ethics, engineering ethics, journalistic ethics, education ethics). This impracticality lies not only in terms of cost effectiveness but also in the way in which most professional ethical issues are relevant for a variety of fields. Consequently, ethics education has moved away from a career-specific approach toward an approach that stresses the way in which ethical issues are relevant for all professions. Unfortunately, the availability of resources for teaching professional ethics has not acknowledged this move toward generality. To address this void in available resources and to teach our own students, we have written this text, which takes a constructive or positive approach in teaching professional ethics, focusing on the values that are important to professionals. This text provides an approach to teaching professional ethics that is able to overcome the potential divisiveness across fields of expertise, thereby addressing perennial ethical issues in a context-specific format.

Currently available are numerous resources for teaching professional ethics, all of which have their strengths. After using a number of these resources, we found that we were utilizing their best aspects while at the same time incorporating our own inclusive, unified approach, grounded in fundamentals. By virtue of being inclusive, we accept the relevance of professional ethics for all of those who work or plan to work professionally, and not just its relevance to those in stereotypical professions, such as doctors, lawyers, and businesspersons. Thus, our text does not focus on several distinct professions but instead considers the shared ways in which professionals working at all kinds of jobs face moral problems. Accepting that how one does one's job is of greater moral relevance than what one actually does for their job is our keystone. Through this text, we encourage students to recognize the values fundamental to the experience of being a professional and to develop the skills for moral reasoning that allow these values to be interpreted. We have given students what they need to learn about professional ethics, namely, theoretical frameworks, interpretive skills, and practice in applying these, while at the same time we have provided teachers with what they need to teach the course, namely, a clear text, exercises, readings, and discussion questions.

A text such as this one is a product of many things: our own work experiences, the work experiences of our friends and colleagues, and the experiences we have had in the classroom with our students. We are both grateful to all of those who have generously shared their stories, comments, and criticisms, all of which improved and enriched this project. Needless to say, any remaining imperfections are the sole responsibilities of the co-authors.

Victoria Wike is grateful to Loyola University of Chicago for providing her with a leave in order to complete this book, and to Carole Heath, who helped with copyright permissions, and to Brian Chrzastek, who helped with proofing and the index.

Cynthia Brincat acknowledges Youngstown State University for release time to finish this project and the National Endowment for the Humanities for providing the opportunity to participate in a summer seminar for college teachers on literature and values, organized by John McGowan and Allen Dunn. She also is grateful to the professional ethics students of Youngstown State University for their enthusiastic responses and comments that helped make this text better. Without the work of Catherine Clagett and Kiki Eberth, the final stages of proofing and formatting the readings for this text would have been impossible. And finally, she thanks her parents, who taught her the meaning of many different types of work. She dedicates this book to them.

Acknowledgments

The authors thank the following reviewers for their helpful comments and suggestions: Professor James Massey, Polk Community College; and Professor John Abbarno, D'Youville College.

Cynthia A. Brincat
Victoria S. Wike

PART 1

Morality and the
Professional Life

Introduction

Professional ethics has come of age in a period of great change. Our conceptions of work and how it is to be done, let alone done well, are being challenged. In this dynamic climate, there is a great call for moral professionals. It is debatable whether or not everyone who works has a concern for morality, but it is certainly the case that the marketplace and society are requiring moral sensitivity in those they employ. Recognizing this need, we offer a treatment of professional ethics that, when actualized, will allow those who work to be more reflective as they face the unavoidable issues of morality in their professional lives.

As we begin to consider the issues of professional ethics, we can think of our goal as the development of ourselves as moral professionals. We can think of this text as something like a building project or construction project site which, through hard and conscientious work, will aid us in becoming professionals who know how to act morally. Like any sort of construction site, before the work begins, we must have a plan through which we organize our work into various stages. Most building projects begin with ground clearing, foundation laying, and infrastructure work. That sort of preliminary or "hard hat" work characterizes Part 1 of our text. Later, in Part 2, we fill in the infrastructure and build upon our solid foundations. This will leave us with a moral system that is complete enough to be useful and incomplete enough to be flexible to the nuances of situations in which we must deal with the moral issues of acting professionally.

Ground clearing can take a variety of forms. We begin our ground clearing work in professional ethics by breaking that very word apart. That is, we first examine what it means to be a professional. In chapter 1, we consider what a profession is and is not. One who practices a profession is not necessarily morally superior to one who does not practice a profession. Hence, a profession is merely a type of occupation that gains moral significance through the way in which it is accomplished, professionally or nonprofessionally. With this understanding of professions and professionals in place, we end this chapter by considering some helpful ways to gain insight into what one wants to do and how one would like to do it.

After breaking the term *professional* apart and clearing that conceptual ground, in chapter 2 we consider what it means to "do" ethics. Such considerations necessarily include an understanding not only of what ethics is but also what it is not. In chapter 2, we come to a prescriptive understanding of ethics. This understanding begins the articulation of what we mean by professional ethics insofar as it presents ethics as including a system of rules and values that are universal.

Eventually, the same thing happens in Part 1 of this text as happens in any building project. With things broken down, and the theoretical ground cleared, we begin, in chapter 3, to build things back up, that is, we put the terms *professional* and *ethics* back together and finally address what it is to "do" professional ethics. By examining the different manners in which professional ethics traditionally has been done, and the inherent advantages and disadvantages to these approaches, we move ahead in getting ready to build.

Once ground clearing work is done, some of the really rewarding hard hat work begins as we continue in chapter 3 to establish a foundation for our project of enabling us to be moral professionals. Professional morality is not a separate kind of morality but instead consists of the implementation of the morality that governs our lives in general. It is morality made manifest in our professional lives. This approach, in its holistic orientation, allows us to make real the underlying value commitments that are a part of what it is to be moral, professionally and otherwise. It is here that we can appreciate that we are really building something and not merely taking things apart.

With these value commitments of chapter 3 in place and artic-ulated, it is as though the foundation of our structure has been poured. This values approach is a firm foundation on which to build a professional morality and establish ourselves as moral profession-als. As we proceed, we fill in the structure that the values approach demands, with the specific values of integrity, respect for persons, justice, compassion, beneficence and nonmaleficence, compassion, and responsibility. Even with as much as we have already done, nothing yet in our structure is quite above ground. There are no beams or girders in place, but the preliminary stages that must be accomplished for their installation are done. After all of this plan-ning, ground clearing, and with the basic foundation of our project laid out, we can begin to actually build on it in the latter half of Part 1. In chapters 4 through 6 we install the infrastructure that is required to do a values-based professional ethic, and in doing so, we begin to see how our behind the scenes, hard work pays off.

The first stage or step in building on the values foundation be-gins in chapter 4 and consists of moral explanations. Here we estab-lish that moral explanations serve as the primary supportive beams of our professional moral framework. A commitment to values is use-less unless it results in actions, yet actions that arise out of a com-mitment to values will need to be justified and explained. This is accomplished through moral reasons, which explain decisions and actions and explain why it is we do what we do as well as why other people do what they do. Besides providing moral explanations, in this chapter we also assess moral explanations. Like the actions they seek to explain, moral explanations come in many shapes, sizes, and variations. Through giving and assessing explanations, we are able to understand and to begin to appreciate the connection between our value commitments and actions. Thus the work left to chapters 5 and 6 is filling in that support system, so that the rest of our structure can be built around it.

Once we understand moral explanations, we move on to chap-ter 5, where we come face to face with moral theories. Moral theories are an intermediary step between values and the rules for the actions which they seek to establish. In this chapter, we come to understand several of the different ways that this step can be taken as we con-sider the various moral theories organized by the headings of "doing theories" and "being theories," as well as how they are utilized. Through our moral theories, we interpret our value commitments and begin to make detailed moral explanations for our actions.

We continue to fill in the details of the infrastructure in chapter 6, where we develop a framework for moral analysis and a case resolution model. Here we make concrete the ways in which values lead to decisions, as values are interpreted by means of theories, which in turn articulate the rules that apply to situations. Together, these steps make useful our commitments to the various values, as they demonstrate the ways in which these commitments help determine our professional actions and explanations.

Even with all of these aspects of our construction in place, from ground clearing to foundation laying to the building of the infrastructure, our work is not done. We will have a structure for doing professional ethics, but admittedly, this structure will not be a finished product. In Part 2 of the text, we take our final steps toward filling in our structure and thus completing our project. Here, through taking a detailed look at the way values are put into practice in our professional lives, we will interpret and test all that we have accomplished in Part 1. With that understood, we turn to Part 1, to the beginning of our work.

1

What Professions and Professionals Are

Work is a central concept to the human experience. We "work it," "work hard for our money," "work out," and "work through things." Almost all of us will have to work for pay at sometime in our lives. Typically, we understand our work as what we are or what we will become. When we ask children about their future jobs and careers, we ask them, "What do you want to be when you grow up?" We don't ask them what they want to work at or what they want to get paid for doing. Instead, we equate their future being with what it is they will work at or get paid for doing. Even when meeting someone for the first time, we typically ask him or her, "What do you do?" We do not ask about relationships, commitments, or belief systems, but about occupations. Through this simple question, we relate to a person with whom we have never previously had contact. Work is a universal enough phenomenon to become a shared bond or an easy way for strangers to relate. Thus, work and working is a central way in which we define ourselves and others, and our relation to our world.

Even though we can point to this one thing that serves as a major way we define ourselves, in doing so we really have not done very much, that is, we do not know that much more about ourselves or others, let alone about work itself. Work and our relation to it is a very complicated issue. Like it or not, accepting that we define ourselves by what it is we "do" or "work at" is only the beginning of the story. We are still left to consider many other aspects of our relation to our work, such as its relative importance to other aspects of our life, the issues surrounding compensation, and the role personal satisfaction plays in our understanding of our work. This is to name only a few of the concerns relevant to our relationship with our work. In considering these issues, we are completely ignoring the question of whether or not defining ourselves by our work, or being defined by others through our work, is a positive thing. Fortunately, this complicated historical, social, and psychological question is not the focus of this book. Instead, in writing a book about professional ethics, we accept the centrality of work to the human experience, and we propose a way to examine and order that centrality so it reflects some basic values that are an inherent part of the experience of a working life.

Since the topic of this book is professional ethics, much of the concentration of the first half of the book will be on what we understand as ethics, while the second half of the book will concentrate on the way ethics relates to being a professional or the way taking part in a profession relates to a moral life. In examining ethics in the first half of the book, we will begin to realize how to express ourselves in moral situations, or the specific language used in discussing ethics. In the second half of the book, we will apply these tools to the moral situations professionals encounter. In doing all of this, it is helpful to start to look at the notion of what it means to engage in a profession. With that in mind, this chapter will explore what counts as a profession, what it means to be a professional or exhibit professionalism, as well as the relevant factors we consider as we choose a profession. From the starting point of what it means to be a professional and its related issues, this chapter will proceed by addressing how it is that the rest of this book gives us a framework for conceiving of the way in which we will engage in our professional activities.

What It Does Not Mean to Engage in a Profession

Considering the idea of a profession, being a professional and exhibiting professionalism is not as easy as it sounds. We can consider some of the criteria for what a profession is, and we will undoubtedly leave something out and include something that someone will not agree is germane to the issue of what a profession is. The same holds true for a professional and professionalism. Abstract terms that have changed over time are often like this, and it is best to remain flexible and adaptable in our attempts to define them.

One way to begin to examine the terms *professional, professionalism,* and especially the term *profession* is to look at something that they most certainly do not include. A profession does not include a greater moral value than a nonprofession. There is no way a person who practices a particular occupation is morally superior to someone who practices an occupation not deemed to be a profession. This would infer that someone is morally superior to another merely because of their membership in a group, their training, or their specific expertise, which is absurd. Yet it is not uncommon to make this assumption. It is even implicitly present in our understanding of moral behavior. We need not go far in our language to find an example; think about the way criminal behavior is described. Imagine a crime, then imagine a "white collar crime." Which sounds more harmful? Of course, a white collar crime sounds less harmful than a typical crime. It even sounds tidy, as though the criminals are wearing dressy clothes and clean up after themselves!

Likewise, engaging in a profession does not necessarily lead to a compromised moral status any more than not being a member of that particular profession. Lawyers should quickly come to mind. Currently, it seems that lawyers have become the moral scapegoats of our societal dissatisfactions with the justice system. Practically everyone knows a lawyer joke that portrays lawyers as being profit hungry, without scruples, and for sale to the highest bidder. But, merely in virtue of practicing his or her profession, a lawyer does not have a greater proclivity to an immoral character. In fact, it could be argued that as officers of the court, lawyers have a greater propensity to moral character, and that is why we notice those who deviate from the expectations of the profession. Some of the greatest civil rights victories have been accomplished in the courts, by lawyers. This goes to show that no profession or nonprofession, in and of itself, has any greater or lesser moral standing than another.

Another way that those engaging in professions have seemed superior to those engaged in nonprofessions is in terms of prestige. In society, it is a fact that most of us often value white collar workers over blue collar workers. Originally, the purpose of these terms was merely to differentiate types of work by the kind of clothing, protective or otherwise, that usually was required.[1] Currently, the terms not only include a prestige factor, but often a class distinction as well, one that typically reflects income and educational background.

The distinction between white and blue collar work says nothing about the sophistication or skills needed to practice the work, or the importance of the work itself. Furthermore, this distinction certainly contributes nothing morally relevant to the discussion about the relationship between these two categories. However, in society, we regularly prize professions over nonprofessions. This is an evaluative judgment that usually is based on economic and training factors—not moral ones. For example, if one were to take piano lessons from the neighbor down the street for ten dollars a lesson and then have an opportunity to take piano lessons from a concert virtuoso for ten times that amount, the services of the virtuoso could seem better than those of the neighbor, therefore the latter would be held in higher esteem. The virtuoso's services, in being more expensive, have a higher value than those of the neighbor's, at the very least, from an economic perspective. More specifically, the economic value we refer to here, the one that makes the virtuoso's services "better" than those of the neighbor's, is not a morally relevant better. We are not saying that the virtuoso is a better person than the neighbor. Instead, the better here refers to the increased value of the lessons coming from the virtuoso, a value that is probably made up by the training the virtuoso has undergone as well as that individual's musical repertoire and skill. It says nothing about which piano teacher is a better human being. In paying more for the services of one provider over another, we are deciding among criteria that are not morally relevant, but relevant merely to the quality of the service provided. Basically, just because someone performs a valued service, that in and of itself does not necessarily impact on his or her status as a moral individual. If a particular occupation is going to lead to a higher income and standard of living, as professions often do, we will think of this occupation as being inherently more worthwhile than something that leads to a lesser income and standard of living. It is important to note that this comparison of worth is only relevant to economic worth and that it says nothing about quality of life or level of satisfaction. It is important not to pack inappropriate meaning, moral or otherwise, into the baggage of our understanding of professions.

A simple way to begin to understand the notion of a profession and its related issues is to consider its key concept or most fundamental aspect. We have already established that one way to do this is to think about what a profession is not. To continue in this vein, one more thing a profession is not is leisure. A profession is not play, nor is it that which is the focus of our holidays or vacations. It would be nonsensical to say that you were going on vacation in order to practice your profession. Understanding a profession as not play or as not leisure is a limited negative definition and says nothing about our feelings toward leisure and its opposite, since we all know people who are not very comfortable with leisure, just as we all know those who believe that all work and no play make us dull. That is to say, so far we are making no judgments about the merits of leisure, holidays or vacations. So, following up on this limited negative definition, we come back to our original concern about what fundamentally a profession is, since it is not contentious to say that play and leisure are not work. It is thus possible to begin to understand what we will be considering when we consider a profession, if we consider what it is we mean when we talk about work. Through work, understood in the broad manner as not being leisure, we can begin to understand the characteristics that all professions minimally share. Primarily, a profession is work.

Work and Our Attitude Toward It

Work, like the concept of a profession and its related terms, is complicated and has come to mean different things throughout history. If we look at some of the more common and straightforward understandings of work, we will go far toward examining part of what it means to refer to something as a profession. So, in what follows, a brief history of work will be given so that we understand a bit about where our attitudes about work have come from, and quite possibly where it is they might evolve. The point of this discussion is not so much a history lesson as it is a chance for us to examine our own attitudes toward work and what has influenced them. In doing so, we can get closer to this shared aspect of a profession, hence, what it means to be a professional.[2]

One of the first references to work that has had a major influence on our Western theoretical roots comes from the Bible. Picture the Garden of Eden. Adam and Eve are frolicking, with no concern for their nakedness, or anything at all. This lack of concern for where their next meal is coming from, day care, and health insurance can, if nothing else, be considered leisure. Looking down on this scene, the Genesis story tells us that God, the major protagonist here, thought that everything that had been made "was very good."[3] So, in the beginning—so to speak—leisure was a good thing. Well, most of us know how the story ends. Adam and Eve get kicked out of the Garden of Eden, and as punishment they must toil and sweat for their sustenance.[4] In short, work is a punishment metered out to our mythic ancestors, through which they are denied leisure.

This idea of work as punishment has predominated throughout Western society. That is, anyone who is working has been punished and is thereby seen as having committed some great evil, while those who have a life of leisure have obviously been blessed in some way, since they have not been made to toil and sweat for their sustenance. Needless to say, this understanding of work could give some comfort to those who exploited the sweat of another's brow. Why worry about the toiling of your neighbor and your not needing to do so if this has all been preordained by divine decree? In short, work from the very beginning was loaded with moral meaning. Those who worked were somehow lesser persons than those who did not.

While the Western tradition began under the auspices of the Judeo-Christian framework, a different approach to work was present within at least one Eastern tradition. The Taoist tradition that understands humanity as being merely one minuscule part of the flow of nature, or the Tao, interprets work as an expression of this flow. In short, Taoism views work as one of the many ways a person is able to express himself or herself. Since we are supposed to be a part of the Tao, and work is a part of us, our work is supposed to aim toward a deeper unity with the Tao. Thus work is an expression of a person's place in the natural order. This place is not one of conquering, but of cooperating. Work, like living in general, becomes a way in which humanity can express the Tao. This is exemplified in the Taoist parable about Cook Ting. In this story, Chuang Tzu describes a famous cook who, in butchering the meat for his kitchen, never dulled his knife. This cook was able to keep his knife so sharp because he worked within the already present delineations of the carcasses, never trying to cut through bone, nor to go against the grain of muscle and sinew.[5] Although not a pretty tale for vegetarians, Cook Ting gives us a Taoist approach to work that demonstrates the way in which work can be integrated into a person's position in the world, a position that, in its practice, allows us to further our unity with the Tao. Work is therefore a further expression of a person's harmony with his or her surroundings.

We can think of present-day examples of work that are harmonious with one's position in the world, especially as we reflect on the way work is evolving to accommodate the many demands made on those in the workforce. Things like flex time and shared positions in a corporation allow employees to have their work not interrupt their lives, but become a part of them. Think also of the ingenuity of many self-employed individuals who have been able to make a living at a hobby or something they enjoy. Thus, Cook Ting gives us a metaphor that demonstrates the way in which we can work within prescribed limitations, creatively and flexibly, while ending up with the same product, without dulling our knives.

Returning to the Western tradition, which when we left it viewed work as a punishment for our iniquity, we are still left in a situation of despair. That is, in understanding work as a punishment and a necessity, we are never able to escape this stain on our humanity, since most of us have to work. As time went on however, work eventually became the way through which we could erase the preexisting condition of punishment that work entailed. We are indebted to the Puritans for this attitude toward work, an attitude that predominated in the seventeenth century and remnants of which can still be seen today. The Puritans realized that work was our punishment, yet if our work went well, the Puritans felt that divinity was smiling on them. Work going well was measured in terms of material success. Therefore, those with many material possessions began to be seen in a favorable moral light, while those with fewer possessions were seen as less moral, since their work, now not the expression of their punishment but the means to their salvation, was not going well. Things have certainly changed. Initially, work was seen as a punishment, but now it is seen as a salvation. Teasing out the underlying implications of this view, those who are not working are incapable of salvation.[6]

Once secularism took over and the idea of God was removed from the discussion of work, we were left with the notion of work which prevails today. This is much the same place the Puritans left us, with one exception. Instead of divinity being the ultimate arbiter of worth through work, work itself is the ultimate arbiter of worth. What we are worth, morally and otherwise, is measured by our work. Nowadays, a person has a good job, and if she excels at it, she is a good person; if she does not excel, then clearly she is not a good person. We unreflectively hold work in high regard. Doing so is not necessarily a bad thing, but as with any judgments, it is best to make them reflectively and without implicit assumptions. It would be a hard point to justify that work in and of itself was good or bad, and superior or inferior to not working. The brief historical discussion of our attitudes about work shows that our regard for work over leisure is contingent upon our cultural context. Consequently, we would also be hard pressed to hold any type of work superior to any other. Any statement of this sort, laden with unreflective judgments of merit, insignificance, or even instinctive emotional responses of favor or disfavor, would have to be justified relative to the criteria by which the assessment is being made. For example, an auto mechanic is superior to a university professor in terms of her earning potential, while a university professor is superior to an auto mechanic in terms of being able to keep his clothes clean.

With all of these caveats in place, we see that work has long been the central defining characteristic of who we are and how we are to think of ourselves and others. The way this keystone gets interpreted is often contingent upon societal attitudes and other criteria, all of which can be relative to particular interests. Thus, work has many interpretations, yet for our purposes we have highlighted only an unreflective moral interpretation of work as inappropriate. No occupation is morally superior to any other. Work in and of itself has no moral worth; it only gains or loses moral worth through its expression or the manner in which it is done. The moral expression of work or its lack is the subject of *this* work. This book is not merely investigating the moral professional, nor professional morality, but morality *and* the professional life. This approach understands morality and the practice of a particular occupation as being two distinct things that are hopefully, but not necessarily, related. Our goal is to see that they are related in a productive and positive manner.

Identifying and Describing a Profession and a Professional

Now that we have some understanding of what work is, we can consider what it means to be part of a profession and what professionalism entails. Although these terms may seem to be different parts of the same question, they are best understood as being two unique questions that are closely related. We have so far determined that a profession is at least work. Well, is all work professional? Here we already see confusion. We have professional work, professions, and professionals. The first term is an adjective describing the type of work being done, while the other terms are nouns, naming the kind of work and the kind of person who does their work in a certain way. In this section of the chapter, we will concentrate on nouns. This is not to say that the adjectives are not interesting, but instead that they are essentially derivative from their nouns. That is, the primary focus of our investigation will be those things that are named by the terms *profession* and *professional*. We are interested in those occupations that are professions and those people who are professionals. What makes them what they are?

To answer this question, we need a few more terms to help us keep things clear. Whenever we work at something, we are occupied. But all work does not entail an occupation. Today, all work is not even done by people. Often machines and sometimes animals perform the work. So, even though work is done, it is not always and necessarily an occupation—ask anyone who is a good friend or a good parent about the work that that entails. Friendship, parenting, and relationships of all sorts require a tremendous amount of work, even though none of these are considered occupations. All occupations, however, entail work, and the work they entail is work for pay. Pay need not be monetary, but occupations are compensated work. Of all occupations, not all are professions. Thus, not all workers practice professions. The issues raised by these concerns return us to a familiar question—what is an occupation and how is it practiced? Upon meeting someone, we ask them, "*What* do you do for a living?" They answer. With an analysis of that answer, we can determine whether their occupation fulfills some minimum criteria for being a profession. Continuing the discussion, we then ask the same person, "*How* do you do what you do for a living?" They answer. With an analysis of that answer, we can thus determine if they exhibit professionalism. If an occupation is done in a certain manner, it is done professionally, and the person who performs it exhibits professionalism. So, a profession refers to a certain type of occupation, while professionalism refers to the manner in which the occupation is done.

But what of the term *professional*? Strictly understood, if an occupation is an agreed-upon profession, and the person who performs it does so professionally, then that person is a professional. In short, to be a professional, one must not only do a certain type of work—a profession—but one must also do this work in a certain manner—professionally. But it seems that we use professional in a number of other less restrictive ways, none of which add very much to a critical understanding of the term. In an uninteresting way, at least for our purposes, one could be called a professional when he or she does a job for pay, or in a way that is not amateurish. Thus, anyone is a professional if he or she is paid for his or her work. The child who sells lemonade on a hot summer day is then a professional lemonade seller. Yet, we really are not too concerned with the moral questions that face this young entrepreneur. Along the same line, in another mundane, literal sense, any person who practices an established kind of occupation we commonly refer to as a profession is a professional, in the same way that someone who practices law is a lawyer, and someone who practices dentistry is a dentist. But when we say about someone, "You are a professional!" or "That was a very professional job you just did!" we typically mean more than that which is already contained in the title of his or her occupation. It is primarily because of this additional component that being a professional entails that the terms *profession* and *professional* will not be treated as simply entailing one another. Instead, we will look at these two terms separately.

Returning to our analysis, we previously referred to "what" (What do you do?) and "how" (How do you do it?) questions. Basically, these questions indicate *what* occupation a person practices and *how* he or she does so. These "what and how" questions will take us far, not only in determining what is and what is not a profession and a professional, but also in determining what occupation we would like to practice and the manner in which we would like to practice it. Take a look at the following chart, which breaks down what we consider *profession* and *professional*.

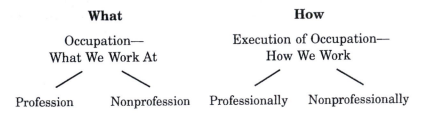

Here we can look at the terms *profession* and *professional* separately. Considering the term *profession*, in our ordinary usage, many things immediately come to mind; sexual commerce (deemed the oldest profession), professions of faith (expressed by clerics), and certain occupations that are identified by shared characteristics. In particular circumstances, it is appropriate to refer to each of these as a profession. However, we will limit our reference to those things that count as occupations and not as assertions, if only because this is a book about professional ethics. So, we have narrowed the discussion somewhat. Yet, in considering professions, are prostitution and medicine both professions? Some might say yes, but we would then have to determine what criteria they are applying to arrive at such an answer. In virtue of being work for pay, both of the afore-mentioned could count as a profession, since often in our ordinary usage we unreflectively deem something a profession merely because it is being done for pay. But, since we are treating the term *profession* in detail, let us try to specify the criteria by which something is a profession a bit more exactly.

In the preceding chart, we see that at the very least, a profession is what we work at. That is, all professions are occupations, but not all occupations are professions. Much of the literature on professions tries to come up with a few shared characteristics or qualifying criteria articulating what a profession entails. These are things like, "A profession requires extensive training." For each of these examples of what a profession is, there is always a counterexample. That is, something that we all recognize as a profession will not meet that particular criterion. Yet, with that understood, these categories are still helpful in pointing us toward one way of indicating what typically is recognized as a profession.

One of the primary criteria that underlie what occupations count as professions is group identification. A profession usually consists of a group of people who in their occupation all do the same thing. Of course, the profession can be executed with greater and lesser skill, but in its execution, the activity must be recognized. Try to imagine going to a symphony performance and looking over at the violin section—made up of concert violinists, a valued profession. Each member of the section is playing his or her violin, but one person in the section is using the violin to scratch his back. Back scratching, although possible with a violin, is not what is recognized or not what counts as a recognizable criterion for a concert violinist. Thus, the man who scratches his back with the violin is not a recognizable member of the concert violinist profession. One can imagine the other violinists not even wanting to claim this truant as their own. This itchy individual could still be a concert violinist, performing the actions associated with that career, but unless he displays the appropriate behavior, we would be hard pressed to recognize him as a member of that profession. Often professions are organized into societies of their own, centered around this ability to recognize one another. A criterion for this is often the body of knowledge that these groups share. These professional societies, such as the American Veterinary Medical Association and the American Institute of Certified Public Accountants, serve to identify the group, to give it support, and to often protect the interests of the members of the group. These groups identify the people that share relevant skills. We would not go to the Veterinary Medical Association to get our watch fixed. Truly, watch repair is a highly skilled occupation, with its own society, but the skills needed to fix a watch are not those that serve as membership criteria for the Veterinary Medical Association.[7] The Veterinary Medical Association has its own means to recognize those who practice its group's specialized skills.

In understanding a profession as an identifiable group that provides the same service, we are pointing to a regulated set of skills and knowledge that those members of the group have gained through requisite training. If a group has a unique, shared set of skills and knowledge by which its members recognize one another, it typically has a way of determining when someone has acquired this special information. For example, one is not a nuclear physicist just because he or she says so. To become a member of that profession, certain training and education specific to nuclear physics is required. This requirement for regulation in standards of skills and training has become more and more a part of the character of professions. This is particularly evident when we think about groups that are seeking to be recognized as professions, as was the case with the nursing profession. Over the past decade or so, this profession has made a greater move toward professionalization. Nurses are clearly an identifiable group, but in the past, often nurses' training took place in the hospital and did not require a four-year degree. Now, the nursing profession has standardized its training and requires board certification and continuing education to maintain certification. Thus, to become a member of that profession, certain requirements must be met, and the meeting of those requirements is monitored so that one who has not met them is not considered a member of that profession. In some cases, the requirements of regulated training come from the organization itself, while in other cases the criteria for the skills and knowledge the group has, and thus membership in that profession, comes from the government or another societal agency. Together, regulated training and the consequent regulation of skills provide another mark of a profession.

In addition to identifiability and regularity in training, a profession entails specific knowledge. One expects individuals who are engaged in a profession to deliver a service or to possess a skill that is not available just anywhere. If an occupation does not entail knowledge that is particular to that occupation, it usually does not count as a profession. For example, the person who makes cappuccino at the corner cafe is not engaged in a profession. Although it can be tricky, frothing milk and making espresso does not include occupation-specific knowledge. Nor do cappuccino makers have their own society or training requirements. We could imagine a society of people who love cappuccino meeting to discuss the relative merits of this or that variation, but we would be hard pressed to form a group that is organized solely around its knowledge of making cappuccino for pay.[8] When an occupation does not include knowledge that is a product of specialized training and skills, it typically is not referred to as a profession, whereas a board-certified psychologist, in treating patients, utilizes knowledge specific to his or her occupation. The knowledge and skills required for the practice of psychology are not skills that are acquired through daily living, but are specific to the occupation of a psychologist, and a product of the specialized training such individuals receive. Just as we would not go to the Veterinary Medical Association to find someone to repair our watch, we would not allow just anyone to fulfill the role of psychologist. The fulfillment of this role hinges on the specialized knowledge and skills that the psychologist possesses. In having such specific knowledge, the practice of psychology entails a profession.

As was previously pointed out, the definition and criteria marking something as a profession are problematic. For example, we could define a profession as something with a long tradition and clearly delineated responsibilities. Under those auspices, medicine would surely fit. The medical profession has a long history and some specifically delineated responsibilities. But what about a different career? For instance, what about a computer systems programmer? That occupation is certainly something we would all recognize as a profession, but it most definitely does not have a long history, nor does it have an agreed-upon set of responsibilities. Technology is changing, as is the world we live in, even as we are reading these words. Because of this, we need a definition and an understanding of profession and professional that is able to grow with these changes and developments.

Let us return to our original question. In considering what is and what is not a profession, we consider the oldest profession—sexual commerce. There currently is not a society or an organization of prostitutes in this country, nor is there a monitored or specific training process. The trade of sexual commerce does not entail knowledge that no one else has. In short, when we call prostitution the oldest profession, we do so incorrectly, at least according to the previous criteria.

Loosely characterized, a profession consists of primarily three things: a group identity—those in the profession can easily identify one another; some shared or agreed-upon education, training, or certification—those in the profession generally agree upon and recognize certain requirements needed to practice their profession; and a special kind of knowledge—those who have the knowledge are able to perform services for others who do not. Clearly, there is a good bit of interrelatedness among these characteristics. This is to be expected, since they depend on one another, to some extent, for their practice. For example, in identifying their members, professional societies might appeal to regulation in training and a group of specific skills everyone shares. Even with this interrelation, understanding these specific criteria for an occupation being a profession, with their weaknesses and strengths, we are in a position to apply them to some of the occupations in which we are interested.

Earlier we looked at the profession of medical physician. Clearly a physician is an occupation we would be quick to call a profession. There certainly is a group identity, from white coats in hospitals to the American Medical Association; physicians have an easy way to be identified and to self-identify. There exist requirements for education and certification, and a specialized service is at stake. Taking out someone's spleen or diagnosing the need for spleen removal cannot be done without some specific skills physicians share. In sum, the occupation of physician is a recognized, established profession.

What about other occupations? Some cases, in fact, most, are not as clear-cut as that of a physician. Many occupations are only beginning to emerge as professions, and in doing so, they do not necessarily fulfill all of the requirements we have articulated, nor do they fail to fulfill them. We call these occupations "emerging" professions, since we can safely surmise that they will eventually fulfill the criteria of a profession, and thus become recognized professions. Many, if not most, professions have gone this route.

The fields of law enforcement and the military are currently going through some discussion about potentially becoming professionalized. There are arguments both for and against the professionalization of both fields. Currently, neither field is understood as a full-fledged profession, and the controversy surrounding their professionalization centers on what would be lost if this did occur. How is it that law enforcement and the military are not professions? Let us first consider our guidelines for understanding what a profession is. With regard to group identification, few groups have as strong an identity as the military and law enforcement. Clearly, because of the inherent danger and unique nature of their occupations, loyalty, camaraderie, and so on figure into what it takes to do a job in these fields well. Thus both of these fields easily meet the first stipulation for what a profession is. With respect to regulated training, it seems that both fields qualify there as well. From the police academy to boot camp and officers' training school, there is a regulated and required training regimen for law enforcement and military personnel. But what about the third criterion? Do the military and law enforcement require any specialized kind of knowledge or skill that is not a part of what is regularly expected of citizens? The answer to this last question will distinguish whether these fields are viewed as professions. It could be that law enforcement and the military require different skills than those we expect from just about everyone. Or, it could be that law enforcement and the military only require a kind of concentration on particular skills that we all already possess, a kind of honing of particular aspects of our nature. Since this last criterion for what entails a profession is somewhat controversial, we consider these fields emerging or qualified professions, insofar as the question of whether they are professions is still unsettled.

When we consider whether something is a profession, and the question is not settled as in the aforementioned situation, we then must ask if it is a good thing for the question to become settled. That is, what is at stake if these fields become professionalized? What could be the positive and negative consequences of their becoming professions? Most of the arguments both pro and con for the professionalization of law enforcement and the military do not center around issues of training and group identification, but on what would be lost if these groups thought of themselves as no longer being a part of the citizenry from which their duties originate. For example, if a soldier or law enforcement official were given an order that clearly violated his or her common moral sense, as a member of the greater moral community, he or she would need to recognize his or her membership in the larger community and not obey an outrageous order. Think of cases of unwarranted police brutality. When an individual is subject to undue force at the hands of law enforcement officials, and no one who is aware of this action is willing to stop the behavior, it could be argued that the group identification among those officials is too strong. This notion that professionalism will lead to isolationism, a dangerous potential in these occupations, is a clear-cut argument against professionalism. Yet what about the inherent risk and even outright danger involved in these occupations? With professionalism typically comes greater financial rewards, and arguably, through the great risks that these individual men and women undertake, they are quite deserving of increased financial award. Furthermore, with professionalism, there often is an increase in the rigor and standardization of training. With training meeting higher standards, professionalization could ensure that quality individuals would fulfill the occupational positions of these fields and thereby eliminate the possibility of abused power. Thus we have clear-cut arguments in favor of professionalism in these fields.

So, with fields such as law enforcement and the military, professionalism is not all positive or negative. The professional status of these fields, although they have most of the characteristics of a profession, is not settled. Thus, it is not clear that law enforcement and the military are to be considered professions, thus to address their ambiguous status, we refer to them as qualified or emerging professions. In so doing, we exhibit a sensitivity to the issues and impending possibilities of professionalization, and we consider all aspects of the move both toward and away from professionalization so that any moves are done with an awareness of the potential outcomes for all of those involved.

Now that we have taken a look at a profession and an emerging or a qualified profession, what about an occupation? What is it that does not require any particular training, does not consist of group identification or include specialized skills? Occupations that are service based, consisting of tasks that we sometimes pay other people to do that we know how to do but choose not to, often are not professionalized. Think about owning your own business. In the evening, perhaps you are needed at home. In order to leave earlier, you have someone clean up your place of business for you (perhaps so you can go home and clean up your own residence). Cleaning, for pay, is an occupation. Cleaning is typically something that does not require specialized skills or training, as it is something that most of us do for ourselves for free.

The aforementioned examples are not exhaustive, but are merely some concrete ways to begin thinking about what is and what is not a profession, an emerging profession, and an occupation. But what about the term *professional*? We have some criteria for that, but where do they come from, and should they be maintained? In a previous chart, we determined that being a professional depends on exhibiting professionalism. Thus, of what does professionalism consist? Very simply, professionalism relates to the way a job is done. Any occupation, or even any work, can reasonably be said to be done professionally. Like the term *profession*, professional has been used in a variety of ways not helpful in our discussion. For the sake of this discussion, professionalism consists of a skill or quality component and a relational component. The skill component requires that a professional be competent in performing the tasks of his or her work, while the relational component requires that the work the professional does will not be harmful to persons or society. Each of these, when actualized, allows an individual to exhibit professionalism.

We ask someone how they do their job, and they respond that they do it very well. But what does it actually mean to say that one does a job well? Typically, this is, in part, a technical issue. If you are a brain surgeon or a carpenter or a dry cleaner, you do your job well when you perform the duties of your position so that you competently accomplish the tasks for which you are responsible. A brain surgeon would probably make just as poor a carpenter as a carpenter would make a brain surgeon, but each is able to do their job well when they maintain a level of competency that allows these tasks to be accomplished.

In executing their tasks, a person who exhibits professionalism not only does his or her job technically well, but also does not engage others in a harmful or negative manner. This other way of doing a job is not an aspect of the technical component. Here we are talking about something else, the relational component of doing one's job professionally. In fact, this relational component entails that a professional could be said to do his or her work in such a way as to perform a service, and not merely a task for pay. This issue becomes specifically relevant in places where one's role as a professional comes into conflict not with one's personal beliefs but with one's underlying responsibilities as a consequence of one's relationships with others. For example, when soldiers marched prisoners into death camps, an admittedly immoral act, they often defended themselves by saying that they were only following orders. Hence, these soldiers were doing their job well. Yet, the execution of their job, their maintenance of a level of competency, was tremendously harmful to particular individuals and to society. In being responsible for marching prisoners to their death, soldiers ignored the responsibilities or even minimal prohibitions that were in place between them and other human beings, namely the prisoners. Thus, these soldiers cannot be said to be professional according to this dual criteria.

So, when a job is done technically well and with minimal or no harm to others, and even positively in such a manner as to benefit them, we say that the job was done professionally. The person who performs this job is said to have behaved professionally or to have exhibited professionalism. Any occupations that count as professions and that are done professionally allow one to be a professional.

If we were to make a list of questions for what counts as a professional and behaving professionally, it would look like the following:

Q1: Is the work being done a profession? (What?)

If yes, go to Q3. If no, go to Q2.

Q2: Is the occupation being done well, both technically and relationally? (How?)

If yes, the occupation is being done professionally.
If no, the occupation is not being done professionally.

Q3: Is the profession being done well, both technically and relationally? (How?)

If yes, the individual is a professional.
If no, the individual practices a profession but is not a professional.

It should be evident from the aforementioned discussion that being a professional, and exhibiting professionalism, are good things. That is, although we have stressed that work in and of itself has no moral status, the execution of work or how it is done has moral status. This moral status comes into effect as we appreciate the way an occupation is executed relative to our criteria for judging action in general. Truly, our work often puts us into situations where we must bracket our personal commitments in order to uphold the commitments we have made to our work or our profession, but we still find the same things worth prizing; it is just that the criteria by which they are judged valuable is often more complicated in an occupational situation.

Consider this example. You are working in the quality control department of an auto manufacturer. Your job is to ensure that the products coming off of the production line are manufactured correctly and are safe. Your position is crucial. Although you do not often find assembly errors, any error you do find is a potential lawsuit at best for your company and a potential fatality at worst. You have been there several years and have a close relationship with one of your colleagues, Bart. You and Bart have socialized; you would even consider him a friend. Bart arrives at work intoxicated. You see that Bart has some coffee, then you arrange a ride home for him, talking him into taking a sick day. After a frank discussion, Bart confides in you that he has a history of substance abuse, but he thought that the problem was under control. Thus, he got carried away the night before and was not really aware of his condition when he arrived at work. The incident never happens again.

This is not a very dramatic case in professional ethics, which is why it is probably typical. Everyone values friendship, and this often includes the ability of our friends to do what they want to do with their lives, even when it is destructive. However, when Bart showed up at work, as his friend you realized that his intoxication would impair his performance and future at work. Insofar as you are an employee, working at an occupation, you realized that your responsibility, of making certain that the assembly work was done properly, would be sacrificed by Bart's impairment. So you arranged for Bart to not work and for someone to cover for him. In doing so, you valued your position and your relationship with Bart. In this instance, the conflict was not so great. Perhaps if Bart's problem had continued, the issue of friendship and responsibility would have conflicted in a more abrasive manner.

In dealing with Bart, you acted professionally. By looking at the criteria for what professionalism entails, we can see how this is the case. You fulfilled your duties technically well, by making sure that the job that was at stake was done and the performance of that job was not impaired. Job performance would have been clearly impaired if Bart had remained on the job. By sending him home and getting someone to cover for him, maybe even yourself, you followed through on the technical aspect of your job. Furthermore, in following through on the responsibilities of your job, you did so with sensitivity to the relationships that are a part of that job. You were sensitive to the relationship dynamic between you and Bart insofar as you covered for him and remained sensitive to the underlying issue of why he showed up at work intoxicated. You also were sensitive to the people who would later be purchasing cars, thereby overseeing the production of car parts that will eventually be depended upon in their cars. You have a relationship with the people who will be driving these cars, however peripheral that relationship might be. Granted, you are not expected to send them a birthday card or call them on Mother's Day, but you have a minimal responsibility to them as purchasers of your company's automobiles. Your occupation as quality control manager is not morally loaded. However, the way you perform this occupation has moral implications. When you perform your occupation technically well, then you have exhibited one aspect of professionalism; when you perform it with an eye for its relational component, you have exhibited another. With both of these aspects in place, you display professionalism.

Choosing a Profession—Some Things to Consider

Since we have spent all of this time considering what a profession is and how to be a professional, we would be well served to consider the profession or occupation in which we would like to engage. With this understanding of work in place, we can look at why we decide to do what it is we decide to do. Keep in mind throughout that there is no one particular career or no one exclusive place that is singularly right for each of us. Our interests and priorities change as the different circumstances and influences on our lives change, as do our attitudes and approaches toward them.

Many times when we meet someone, we ask, "What do you do for a living?" It was pointed out that this central question is an important way for us to understand ourselves and others. But this question also points to a way of distinguishing the categories of doing that are a part of our lives. When we choose our work, we decide what it is we will do. This "what" question and its answer can take us far, not only in understanding what we will do but also why we will do it—or even if we want to engage in a profession or an occupation.

Consider this "what" question. "What do you want to do?" Answer it for yourself. For the purpose of this thought experiment, an answer to this "what" question will consist of an occupation. Of course, there are many ways to answer the question. You might want to watch TV, read a book, or go bowling. However, try answering the question specifically with an occupation, the one toward which you are leaning. Do not panic. This is not binding, but a simple exercise. You can change your mind before the end of this paragraph. But for now, answer what you want to do, where that doing is an occupation of some sort.

With some further analysis, we can discern whether this occupation is a profession. Notice the use of the term *occupation*. An occupation is something that occupies you. It is not loaded with moral meaning, nor does it distinguish various types of positions from one another. So in answering this question, make sure your answer is a "what" answer and not a "how." For example, when asked about the above, you may say, "I want to be an architect." Hence, an architect is what you want to do with your life. Or you may say, "I want to be the person who carries around the pepper mill at fancy restaurants and puts pepper on people's salads." You might even say, "I want to take a nap." Either of the first two answers indicate that these are occupations. Certainly one requires more extensive training, regulation, and certification than the other. The third answer, napping, does not work with this exercise.

Think again. What do you want to do with your life? This time, give an answer that is an occupation. For example, maybe you want to be a napper by profession, sleeping in the window of mattress companies. This sort of mercenary napping counts as an occupation. We can now assess these occupations and see if they fulfill our criteria of what a profession is. Yet before deeming any of the aforementioned as professions, let us consider another question, the "why" question. "Why do you want to do what you do?" This question, like the earlier one, also will have some constraints. The "why" here will refer to the manner in which your profession will affect your lifestyle, thus the "why" question will require you to consider how you want to live. Again, for the sake of this thought experiment, consider the way you want to live your life, not merely why you want to perform your occupation, but how you want to live and why this occupation fits into that picture. Perhaps your answer to this question rests on a desire to help people. Perhaps your answer centers around a desire for a high standard of living. Maybe you want to live fast, and that is why you want to do what you do. Once again, be careful about not adding moral baggage to what is merely a description of a lifestyle. Hopefully this is not the first time you have considered this question, but if it is, spend some time with it and let your imagination run wild.

With the "what" and the "why" questions answered, at least preliminarily for the sake of this exercise, the issue to concentrate on here is the relationship of your answers to the "what" and "why" questions. Together, these answers give us another criterion for determining whether something is only an occupation or an occupation that aims to be a profession. When the expression of why we want to do what we do is closely tied to what we have chosen to do, then our occupation certainly can be considered a profession, and perhaps more interestingly, we can be considered a professional. This is the case because one's career choice is then inextricably tied to one's notion of self.

For example, if the why you want to do what you do stems from a desire to be on a flexible schedule, utilizing your creative talents and with little commitment to one place of employment, perhaps freelance advertising is for you. That way you work for a specific client on a specific job and then your relationship with the client is over. Yet, in this instance, the why of why you have chosen to do what you do is not specifically tied to the what of what exactly you have chosen to do. Any number of occupations could fulfill this criterion. So your relationship to your occupation does not designate it as a profession according to our criteria, nor would you be a professional, although you could still act professionally.

But what about the other criteria, discussed earlier in the chapter, which designated a professional? Of course, some aspects of a profession are present here. A freelance advertiser does perform some specialized services and certainly could require special training. To date, though, there is no professional group centered around the group identity of freelance advertising. Often companies have their own advertising departments, which is a different kind of work than that which would be included in freelance advertising. In short, it is unclear whether freelance advertising, so described, would consist of a profession. More details would need to be supplied to determine the issue one way or another. If you feel strongly about this, supply the details. Regardless of its designation as a profession or as an occupation, a person who engages in freelance advertising can still do his or her job with technical skill and relational sensitivity. So, according to both of our criteria, the freelance advertiser is potentially both practicing a profession and potentially a professional.

Let us consider a different sort of why. Perhaps because of your personal history, you have determined that adolescence is a pivotal time in an individual's life. Because of this, why you want to do what you do will consist of helping adolescents understand themselves and make good decisions. Of course, this is not the only thing you will do with your life. Why you do what you do need not be the sole reason for someone's existence. Perhaps another part of your life would consist of a desire to have meaningful relationships, personally and professionally. You could even think that concern for these two kinds of issues might make the world a better place. This could certainly be the case, but living your life in order to make the world a better place is a pretty tall order, and even if this were within your limits, this desire is a kind of why that would require a bit more specificity. Recognizing the above whys, you have decided that the what you want to do with your life occupationally would consist of the occupation of school psychologist. In this instance, the what of school psychology fulfills and is inextricably tied to the why of aiding adolescents in their self-understanding and decision making. Thus, according to our criteria, school psychology would be a profession for the individual with these whats and whys.

Consider the other criteria discussed earlier in the chapter that designated a professional. In this case, it seems that all of our aspects of a profession are present here. A school psychologist does perform specialized services, requires special training, and shares enough characteristics with others in order to have group identification and professional societies. We can even suppose that the school psychologist described, with these specific why concerns, does his or her job with technical skill and relational sensitivity. So, according to both of our criteria, the school psychologist in this instance is a professional.

However, the additional consideration of the relationship between the what and why questions gives us something else to think about in terms of calling something a profession and the individual who practices it a professional. What the what and why questions point us toward is a commitment to one's occupation such that it is more than just a way of paying the bills. This is an evaluative or a qualitative way of determining something as a profession and someone as a professional. They are not definitive and exhaustive criteria for determining something as a profession, any more than are the criteria articulated earlier in this chapter. What these questions do provide is a different, more personal rubric for thinking about professions, so one can see where one's own desires lie. A profession is not for everyone. Work is probably for everyone, but a profession is not. Just because one is leaning toward a profession now does not require a permanent commitment. These questions might help articulate one's desires relative to work in such a manner that one can see the importance relative to the other concerns of one's life that the chosen occupation will have.

Now that we have considered the what and why questions, there are still others that are relevant to one's decision about choosing an occupation. Immediately, inquisitive personalities will consider the where, how, and with whom questions. When considering an occupation, how important is location? It would be poor planning to have a great desire to live near one's family in the Midwest and to want to be an oceanographer. Likewise, it would be difficult to love warm weather and want to be a ski instructor. Practical concerns like the demographics of employment prospects are certainly relevant should one have a need or great desire to be in a certain geographical area. If a city makes one nervous, one must consider their chosen occupation. Does it require the support that can only be provided by an urban area? Questions like these are integral parts of a commitment to an occupation, and it is not unreasonable to consider them relevant to one's career choice. Once this question is dealt with, one can consider the how of what one wants to do. The how of how an occupation is practiced requires more detail than the qualified technical skill and relational sensitivity answer we concentrated on for determining professional behavior. There is much more to the question, "How do you want to do what you do?" Are you in it for the money? Do you want to concentrate on a particular aspect of the profession over another? The what, why, where, how, and with whom questions about practicing a profession are all an implicit part of a choice of one profession over another, but an explicit consideration of these questions may be something one is compelled to do.

Consideration of the what and why questions provides a framework for beginning to think about what kind of occupation one sees oneself performing in the future, as well as the why of performing it. The other questions—where, how, and with whom—are relevant to this concern as well. Based on the previous discussion and with what follows, one should have a pretty good sense of one's desires, relative to work. The choices—whether one will be a professional, practice a profession, or work at an occupation—are limitless, and none of them are permanent.

So What Kind of Professional Do You Want to Be?

By now, you should have some indication of the profession or occupation for which you are training, or, at the very least, to which you are attracted, as well as an idea of what it means to practice it professionally. Yet there are still other questions about your occupation or profession that must be answered. What *exactly* do you want to do? In what exact form will you practice your occupation or profession? Maybe you have decided that you are going to be a teacher; maybe you have even decided that you are going to be a good and conscientious teacher, but in what exact form are you going to be a teacher—a first grade teacher, a special education teacher, or a university professor? Answering these questions will require more time and more reflection on the nature of your chosen occupation or profession, and on the specialized ways in which occupations or professions can be practiced.

So far we have distinguished a profession from behaving professionally. Thus, two kinds of occupations can behave professionally, professions and nonprofessions. With two groups behaving professionally, we can actually talk about two kinds of professionals. One group would be the professionals to which we have been referring throughout this chapter. This group practices an occupation that is a profession and does so in a professional manner. The second group we could refer to as occupational professionals. This group would consist of those who practice an occupation that is not a profession, but do so in a professional manner. This leaves us with the following two kinds of professionals:

Professionals	Occupational Professionals
practice a profession	practice a nonprofession
practice it professionally	practice it professionally

In this text, we will demonstrate a model of a type of professional and a type of professional behavior. This model has arisen as a consequence of much of what has not been a part of the discussion of professions and professionalism. That is, instead of discussing what can go wrong with the professional experience, this approach presents the way professionals can exhibit the best part of what they share as common moral commitments to certain human values.

Because of this approach, it is not central to our discussion to distinguish the different types of professionals to which we are referring. When reading the term *professional*, realize that it refers to an occupational professional as well as to what has typically been understood as a professional. Since the goal of this text is to encourage actions that exhibit the practice of particular values in one's occupation, and since this concern is one of professional ethics, a reference to this term made as inclusive as possible is most fitting with our task. This inclusion is in accord with our everyday understanding of the term. The dictionary definition of the noun "professional" tells us that a professional is:

1.   a person following a profession, especially a learned profession.
2.   one who earns a living in a given or an implied occupation.
3.   a skilled practitioner, an expert.[9]

Together, these three definitions and much more make up what we mean by a professional. It is important that one recognizes what has gone into the formation of our working definition and what it entails.

Conclusion

With this first chapter behind us, it should be apparent what approach this book will take in dealing with the ethical issues that are a part of our professions and our professional lives. We now know what a profession is and what it means to be a professional and to act professionally. Now we are ready to engage in some of the necessary work that is required to fill in the rest of our ethical landscape. Once this landscape is in place, we can introduce the values that are professed as being an important part of many professional lives.

EXERCISES

1. Consider each of the following approaches toward work. Give an example of work, professional or otherwise, that would instantiate the approaches.

   1. Work as a punishment
   2. Work as a part of the flow of the natural world and society
   3. Work as a salvation or liberation—spiritual, moral, material or otherwise
   4. Work as the defining characteristic of who we are (living to work)
   5. Work as a necessary part of life (working to live)

   Which of the above approaches toward work comes closest to your own view? Explain.

2. Which of the following are professions? Distinguish your answer by specifying whether the occupation is an established profession (ESP), an emerging profession (EMP), or something other than a profession (OP). List the primary factor that influenced your classification of the occupation.

1.	Naval officer	6.	Aeronautical engineer
2.	Commercial baker	7.	Factory farmer
3.	Teacher's aide	8.	Massage therapist
4.	Actor—intermittently employed	9.	Machinist
5.	Psychic	10.	Auto mechanic

3. Analyze the following occupations in terms of the what/why distinction (What do you want to do? Why do you want to do what you do?). Which of these have as a central component both the what factor and the why factor? Would you agree that they are all professions? Assume that each of the following is practiced in a professional manner. Explain your answers.

   1. Psychologist
   2. Electrical engineer
   3. High school teacher
   4. Florist
   5. Golf instructor

   Give three examples of your own, including a concrete, detailed example of how someone practicing each might act professionally and non-professionally. Be sure to include an analysis.

4. Consider at least two of your own future ambitions. Are they professions? Do they allow for professional expression? If so, which of the traditional characteristics of a profession do they exhibit? If not, what are the characteristics of your choice that distinguish it from a profession? Analyze your goals in terms of the what/how distinction. Analyze at least two of your future ambitions relative to all of the above criteria.

NOTES

1. *Webster's Ninth New Collegiate Dictionary* (Springfield, Mass.: Merriam Webster, Inc., 1983), 162, 1345. The term *white collar* came about in the 1920s, while the term *blue collar* came about around the time of World War II production (1946).
2. The organization of this discussion of work is indebted in part to the introductory essay of the longer essay "Work and Employment," vol. 29 in the *Encyclopædia Britannica*, 15th ed. (Chicago: Encyclopædia Britannica, Inc., 1991), 916.
3. Genesis, 1:30. The Holy Bible: New Revised Standard Version (New York: American Bible Society, 1989).
4. See Genesis, chapter 3.
5. See Chuang Tzu, *The Basic Writings*, translated by Burton Watson (New York: Columbia University Press, 1964).
6. The roots of the Puritan ethic were made famous in Max Weber's seminal work *The Protestant Ethic and the Spirit of Capitalism*. See Max Weber, *The Protestant Ethic and the Spirit of Capitalism*, translated by Talcott Parsons (New York: Scribner, 1958). As a consequence of Weber's work, rightly or wrongly so attributed, it is documented how poor people and those without jobs are seen not as a symptom of a great social problem but as being morally defective. This attitude is certainly reflected in our devaluing of those who are not employed, either by choice (e.g., stay-at-home parents) or not by choice (e.g., displaced steel workers). One who does not work is morally flawed.
7. See Jane Clapp's work, *Professional Ethics and Insignia* (Metuchen, N. J.: The Scarecrow Press, Inc., 1974).
8. Once again, a warning is needed. To say that cappuccino making is not a profession is in no way to say that it has any lesser moral value than a recognizable profession. As any coffee addict knows, there is nothing more valuable early in the morning than a cappuccino maker. Recognizing that making cappuccino does not constitute a profession is not to say that the occupation cannot be done professionally or in a professional manner. However, a cappuccino maker cannot be a professional while being solely engaged in that occupation, however important the societal service is that he or she is performing.
9. See the term *professional* in *The American Heritage Dictionary*, 3rd ed. (Boston: Houghton Mifflin Company, 1992), 1446.

2

What Morality Is

Let us begin by collecting our thoughts. We know that professionals are faced with making decisions about how to practice their occupations or professions, thus they deal with cases and situations. Professional ethics is about helping professionals decide what to do when they are confronted with a case or situation that raises a moral problem. Some cases raise questions that may confront members of only select professions, while others deal with issues confronting all professionals. All involve moral problems that must be solved by professionals.

What will these moral cases look like? Some will be simple, while others will reflect a complex array of issues. There are several reasons why cases become complex. Cases get more complicated as more people are involved. A simple case might include only a few people; a complex case may concern the well-being of many people or may have attracted legal or public attention. Cases also get complicated because they raise the issue of *who* should decide in addition to the issue of *what* should be decided. Difficult questions arise in moral situations about who has the authority to decide. Cases are complex because there is a history to the situation in question, and there is a future to be worked out in the situation. Cases have pasts and futures. The past must be made known and accounted for, just as the future must be planned for and predicted. Any discussion of a case in professional ethics will look at the people involved in the situation and their roles in it and what led up to and might follow the situation in question.

We will consider here how to recognize a moral problem. We will learn a strategy for identifying when a claim or situation is "in the realm of morality," that is, when moral claims or questions are being asked as opposed to other sorts of claims or questions, for example, questions about information, advice, or legal counsel. In chapter 1 we considered what a profession is and what a professional is. In this chapter, we look at what ethics is and what it presupposes, and we consider various ways of "doing" moral thinking, though our focus will be on prescriptive ethics. We need to look at the questions that confront professionals, both because we may become professionals at some point and because we will certainly encounter professionals when living our lives.

There are many questions to be asked and answered about even a fairly simple case. Before we can reach a decision about issues like those raised earlier, we need to consider more precisely why a case raises moral problems.

Definitions of Ethics

First, let us define "ethics." Ethics is, simply put, the philosophical study of moral behavior, of moral decision making, or of how to lead a good life. Ethics involves the analysis of moral language and the study of the process of moral deliberation and justification. Put another way, doing ethics requires a person to reflect on what is good and what is bad and what is right and what is wrong.

There are three points to make about this definition. First, ethics concerns both right and wrong and good and bad, although these two distinctions are not synonymous. So, for purposes of clarification, let us understand that the terms right and wrong apply to one group of objects and the terms good and bad apply to another group of objects. Right and wrong apply only to actions, while good and bad describe not actions but motives, intentions, persons, means, ends, goals, and so on. Hence, actions are not good or bad, just as motives and consequences are not right or wrong. The language of ethics treats actions in different terms than it treats persons, ends, and intentions.

Second, there is a technical distinction between the terms ethics and morality. Morality is the activity of making choices and of deciding, judging, justifying, and defending those actions or behaviors called moral. Ethics, on the other hand, is the activity that studies how choices were made or should be made. It considers and reflects on how we judge, justify, and defend our moral choices. In short, ethics is the study of morality, the study of what we do. Morality could exist without ethics (if no one investigated how morality is done), but there cannot be ethics without morality (we cannot study morality unless there is morality). We do morality and engage in moral behavior, whether we reflect on it or study it. Thus morality is like eating; it is an inevitable part of everyone's life. Ethics, on the other hand, is like nutrition.[1] It is crucial to living a good life, but it is not an inevitable part of living or an activity engaged in by all.

However, this is not a distinction that we pay much attention to in day-to-day life. We tend to use the terms interchangeably when we say, "That was ethically wrong" and "That was morally wrong." So we will not hold ourselves to distinguishing between "moral" and "ethical," but it should be clear from the presence of this distinction that our task will be to do both ethics and morality.

Third, there are different ways to do ethics, as we see in the aforementioned definitions of ethics. These differences are due to the fact that some approaches to ethics emphasize certain parts of the moral situation, while other approaches stress different parts. Because there are many understandings of what ethics is, there is no single agreed-upon definition of ethics.

What Ethics Is Not

Let us explore a bit further the definition of ethics by considering what ethics is *not*. First we consider the relationship between ethics and other philosophical disciplines, and second, we look at why ethics is different from other disciplines such as law, religion, economics, and etiquette.

Ethics is different from philosophy in general because its task is more narrowly defined as having to do with questions about morality. Philosophy is the love of wisdom[2] or the pursuit of knowledge concerning human nature and meaning, the natural world and society, and first principles, God, or ultimate reality. Philosophy includes other specialties besides ethics. These are some of the most common topics philosophy treats.[3]

1. *Ethics*
2. *Aesthetics*: the nature of art
3. *Logic*: methods for distinguishing good from bad reasoning

4. *Social and political philosophy*: the justification and limits of government; moral problems with social dimensions
5. *Metaphysics*: criteria for determining what sorts of things are real
6. *Epistemology*: the nature and scope of knowledge
7. *Philosophy of religion*: the concept of God
8. *Philosophy of science*: the logic of scientific evidence; the quest for scientific knowledge
9. *Philosophy of language*: the nature of meaning; theories of language learning
10. *Philosophy of law*: the nature of law

These are not particularly relevant to our discussion of professional ethics. However, most treat issues that have some theoretical or practical bearing on the questions of ethics. For example, the laws of logic give us rules for rational reasoning, which must be followed as much by ethical thinkers as metaphysical thinkers. Furthermore, if an epistemologist (a philosopher of epistemology) knew how to distinguish knowledge from belief, then that would be of use to a moral thinker in evaluating whether the claim of another is a matter of knowledge or belief. Likewise, if the philosophy of law can tell us the theoretical basis for law or the relationship between law and justice, then ethics would have a better sense of what grounds its interpretation and application of justice. Ethics is a philosophical specialty separate from but not unrelated to other philosophical specialties. There are issues which cross specialties, and the question of how the specialties relate to each other is continually discussed.

Since ethics is a philosophical specialty, it is not the same as law, religion, economics, or etiquette. None of these endeavors aim at the philosophical study of moral behavior. All of these studies aim at regulating behavior, but there are two reasons they are not the same as ethics. Like ethics, they prescribe behavior, though unlike ethics,

1. they do so not for the purpose of doing what is morally right, but for the purpose of satisfying others.
2. they put forward their rules not by requiring persons to use their own capacities, but by appealing to the authority of others.

Ethics operates by prescribing rules for what is morally right and by requiring persons to use their own capacities to make decisions. It appeals to an internal authority (one's own capacities) and not to an external authority (someone else's opinion). While ethics respects the authority of others, it does not allow the authority of others to replace the processes of justification provided by an individual. Ethics is unlike other philosophical disciplines and specialties, though they treat related questions, and ethics is unlike the fields of law, religion, economics, and etiquette, though all of these offer rules of conduct as well. These fields differ from ethics in that they aim at purposes other than doing what is morally right, and because they appeal to the authority of others to justify actions.

Let us show exactly why law, religion, economics, and etiquette are not the same as ethics.

Ethics Is Not Law

The law does provide rules for behavior. Many moral conflicts are resolved by judges and the courts. The law is not irrelevant to morality, though it does not replace morality. The purpose of laws in regulating behavior is to ensure order and protect life. Laws can be based on the same moral goods as morality. But laws can also be unjust and violate moral goods. Witness the segregationist laws of the 1960s or, some would argue, the present policy of the Illinois Department of Corrections in enlisting licensed physicians to insert the catheter used to kill prisoners by lethal injection.[4] The physicians in one Illinois case were granted anonymity by a U.S. district judge. The law may be wrong about what is necessary to ensure order or protect life. Given this, the standard of morality is separate from the standard of law. What is legal may or may not be moral; what is illegal may or may not be immoral.

Also, a person making a moral choice is told what to do by the law and offered as a reason for doing it "because it is the law." An appeal to law locates the authority for behavioral rules in a source external to the individual's own capacities. In law, a person looks outside of himself or herself in order to justify an action. An appeal to an external reason (here, to the authority of the law) carries weight in moral deliberations but cannot by itself be the basis for moral action.

Ethics Is Not Religion

For many persons, religion overlaps with ethics in that their religious beliefs dictate certain actions and prohibit others. Some people claim that they know what is right and wrong, due to the teachings of Jesus or Buddha or Mohammed, or to the writings in the Bible or the Torah or the Koran. We are not denying that religious beliefs frequently play a part in a person's moral grounding, or in the choice of a moral theory. A devout Christian or Jew will find that the Ten Commandments offer powerful moral guidelines. Yet religion teaches us mainly what God's will is and how to accomplish it, and not what is right and how to do it. The religious life is the goal of religion, not morality as such. It is possible that the dictates of religion may conflict with morality, or that the dictates of morality may disagree with religion. Witness, for example, a holy war that morality judges to be unjust. A war engaged in to convert the heathen or to defend God's elect may involve actions that morality determines to be maleficent, unjust, or unduly cruel. Or, look at a physician's practice of aborting defective fetuses, which some religious rules prohibit.

Religion does not make ethics dispensable. It prescribes behavior, and it may do so in part for the purpose of doing what is right, but it also does so for other reasons. When religion details what actions a person should take, it is not always clear whether we are interested in morality for its own sake or whether we are viewing morality as a means to infinite reward and pleasing God.

Ethics Is Not Economics

Economics is also sometimes allowed to substitute for ethics. When we read that an insurance company has refused to pay for an employee's needed liver transplant, we know economics is at work, but not necessarily ethics. It is tempting in many areas of professional life to resolve moral problems by considering what is most cost effective and not by what is right. Money is a much easier variable to quantify than rightness. But what is more economical or useful is not necessarily what is right.[5] It may be economical for companies that have contracts with government agencies to reward the employees at those agencies with gifts, dinners, and trips, but it may not be morally right. It may be that the gifts do not just reward but are intended to bribe and influence the way in which the agency conducts its business.[6] Similarly, it may be uneconomical and even useless for physicians to perform cardiopulmonary resuscitation (CPR) on patients over age seventy, but there may be times when it is still right to do so, for instance, when the patient or family requests it, or in times of emergency.[7]

Certainly the question of money or more generally of costs and benefits is relevant to ethics. We will treat the issue of proportionality or cost-benefit analysis and its place in discussions of beneficence

and nonmaleficence in chapter 11. However, while costs and benefits are always relevant considerations in moral problem solving,
they are not the exclusive considerations. In looking to economics for
answers to problems, we focus on satisfying others, or on efficiency
and profit, not on what is right. Economics also can be seen to presuppose a strict listing of costs and benefits and a calculative
process used to arrive at rules for behavior. It appears as though a
moral decision can be reached objectively, logically, and in the same
way by all who can do the mathematics and add up the costs and
benefits. This economics-based approach ignores the values implicitly at work in deciding what are costs and what are benefits, and
in weighing and comparing costs and benefits.

Ethics Is Not Etiquette

Etiquette is, of all of the aforementioned studies, least like
ethics. While etiquette is aimed squarely at the regulation of behavior, its goal is to maintain the social standards deemed necessary
for pleasant or harmonious social interaction. Etiquette is about
manners, about the customs handed down in a particular country or
social class. The standards are not the same across social classes
or countries, nor are they justified by anything more than "this is
the way it has always been done." Etiquette is aimed not at doing
what is morally right but at doing what is accepted as appropriate
in certain social situations. Etiquette no doubt contributes to
amenable human relationships, but it is justified simply by precedent. Ethics, on the other hand, determines which duties and rights
define human relationships, and it is justified by careful reflection
on human goods, knowledge of human nature, and so on, and not by
simple precedent. In addition, the rules of etiquette are accepted on
the authority of others; that, in fact, is part of the point ("According
to Miss Manners . . .").

Presuppositions of Ethics

Before we start doing ethics, several presuppositions or prerequisites of ethics and moral thinking must be acknowledged. First let
us consider what a presupposition or prerequisite is. It is something that must be assumed as being true or must have happened
in order for something else to happen. It is something that has to

be done prior to and in order for something else to be done. Think of a prerequisite in an ordinary context. We know, for instance, that Accounting 201 (Introductory Accounting I) is a prerequisite for Accounting 303 (Intermediate Accounting I).[8] This means that students cannot take Accounting 303 unless they have already taken Accounting 201. Intermediate and advanced courses, like Accounting 303, need not begin at the beginning; they can assume that students have learned basic concepts from their introductory courses. In the same way, doing ethics is like an intermediate or advanced course, and some beginning concepts or presuppositions must be recognized before we can continue.

Some prerequisites or presuppositions are useful, and some are more than useful—they are necessary. Accounting 201 is a useful prerequisite for Accounting 303, but it is not absolutely necessary to take it before taking Accounting 303. We all know of cases where prerequisites have been waived. It is possible that there might be a sufficiently good reason to bypass a prerequisite of this sort. For instance, a department might allow a good student to enroll in both Accounting 201 and 303 at the same time in order to enable the student to make steady progress in his or her course work when Accounting 303 is offered one semester but not the next. Thus a prerequisite of this kind is useful but not absolutely necessary.

The prerequisites of ethics we are going to consider are prerequisites in the stronger sense of being necessary. They are claims necessary to assume in order for us to do ethics. Without taking for granted these presuppositions, we cannot do ethics. Hence, these prerequisites of ethics cannot be waived. They certainly are open to discussion, but for our purposes, we will merely assent to these presuppositions in order to get on with the discussion of professional ethics.

The presuppositions of ethics are assumptions about what people are like and what it is to be a human being. Reflecting on these presuppositions points to the limits of ethics. It also points to the ways in which ethics is related to other studies. Although these prerequisites will not be proved by ethics, they are argued for by other disciplines and philosophical specialties like psychology, philosophy of human nature, and so on. The prerequisites or presuppositions of ethics are:

* People are free.
* People want to do what is right.
* People can make conscious, thoughtful, and reflective decisions.

The first presupposition of ethics is that people are free. This means that people have real alternatives and that they can make choices. It means that people are not determined, psychologically or biologically. They are not controlled by their hormones, their genes, or their upbringing. Philosophers speak of freedom as having two components: freedom from and freedom to. On the one hand, freedom requires the *freedom from* controlling influences. These controlling influences might be biological, physical, psychological, or social, such as the following:

1. If you are compelled by the genes in your chromosomes to be an aggressive, take-charge, noncooperative person, then you, in your role as a company manager, are not free.
2. If you are forced at gunpoint to cut off life support systems to your patient, then you, in your role as a nurse, are not free.
3. If you are so pressured by your need for self-esteem and acceptance that you accede to every wish of your friends, including dispensing prescription drugs without a prescription, then you, in your role as a pharmacist, are not free.
4. If you can make decisions only by appealing to your membership in a certain family, or a certain religious or social group, then you, in your professional role, are not free.

If you are not free, you cannot be moral. So we must be able to conceive of ourselves as being separate from the genes in our chromosomes, the families in which we live, the social groups in which we belong, and so on in order to be ethical thinkers.

On the other hand, freedom requires the *freedom to* be self-determining. It necessitates the power to take charge of one's life and to be capable of stepping into the role of decision maker. Persons have the ability to do independent thinking and to make their own choices. They are free to be self-governing. "Freedom to" means that persons have the capacity to determine their own futures. Not only are they not forced by something to make a certain choice, they can, by themselves, choose. If the conditions under which one works allow one to make choices about how to practice one's occupation, then one has the freedom to be self-determining.

No doubt there are still difficulties and questions here. No one is completely, absolutely free. All of us are influenced by others and by outside factors. None of us are able to completely determine by ourselves how to practice our occupations. Even with the freedom to be self-determining, there are limitations, imposed by professional societies, government regulations, and client expectations, to our freedom to practice our occupation as we choose. We are not claiming or looking for a rugged individualist who acts alone in making moral decisions. We are insisting that ethics and morality are grounded on the assumption that persons can act in opposition to the influences of their desires, the wishes of their families and employees, and so on. Do not worry; not everything about freedom has been said. We will return to freedom and autonomy in chapter 7.

A second presupposition of ethics is that people want to do what is right. That is, it matters to people whether they do what is right or what is wrong. People are not indifferent in regard to moral questions. If no one cared about doing the right thing, there would be no point to the questions of ethics or to this book. If a particular person was not interested in acting morally, there would be no possibility of engaging in moral discourse with him or her. If no one ever cared about doing the right thing, there would not be ethics. So, in order to do ethics, we presuppose that people have a moral sensitivity.

Again, we will not take time to justify the claim that people want to do what is right. Our experience in the world suggests that not everyone always wants to do what is right. We have Hitler, John Wayne Gacy, and many others to remind us that there are persons who seem to not care about doing what is right. Some people just seem to be evil or immoral. On a less dramatic scale, even children and normally good adults occasionally do something they know is wrong.[9] So our experience does not obviously confirm the truth of this assumption.

We might appeal to sociologists, psychologists, theologians, and philosophers for help in proving this assumption. There may be ways of showing that the assumption is true, even in the face of the contradictory evidence of our experience. For instance, perhaps Hitler and Gacy wanted to do what was right and simply misunderstood what right was.[10] But from our point of view, what is important is not the proof of the truth of this assumption. What is important is the relationship between this assumption and ethics. Ethics needs to make this assumption in order to have something to do, so we will take the desire to do what is right as a given to make possible the working out of a professional ethic.

A third prerequisite for ethics is the capacity in persons to make thoughtful, reflective choices. Ethics and moral thinking will require us to use our own capacities to sort through facts, evaluate alternatives, and justify conclusions. Moral decision making and ethics require thoughtful reflection and careful consideration.

We will not prove this assumption that persons can use their own reflective abilities to arrive at conclusions. We will take it to be a given in order to move on in our understanding of the ways in which ethical thinking can be done.

Ways to Think about Ethics

There are three ways to think about morality that we must distinguish in order to have a better idea of what ethics includes and what our account of professional ethics aims to do. The three ways are:

1. descriptive thinking;
2. prescriptive thinking; and
3. metaethics.

Let us consider each in turn.

Descriptive Thinking

Descriptive thinking, relative to morality, is concerned with the description of moral behavior or moral decision making. It describes what people are doing and how they are deciding to do it. Descriptive thinking makes no evaluative judgments. It simply reports the facts. So, for instance, when a sociologist or an anthropologist such as Margaret Mead observes and records the moral thinking and practices of a person or group of persons, that is descriptive moral reporting.[11] The following statements could be made by an ethicist doing descriptive thinking:

"The nurse decided not to cover up the medical technician's action."
"The defense attorney ignored his client's private admission of guilt."
"Pastors tend to be social activists on issues such as fair housing and
    gambling."

Descriptive thinking tells what the case is, what has been decided on, or what has happened.

Prescriptive Thinking

Prescriptive thinking makes the moral judgments that descriptive thinking does not. It goes beyond noting the behavior of others to judging the behavior of others. Prescriptive ethical thinking is concerned with what should be the case and not simply with what is the case. These statements could be ascribed to an ethicist doing prescriptive thinking:

"The nurse was right when she decided not to cover up the medical technician's action."
"The defense attorney should not have ignored his client's private admission of guilt."
"Pastors ought to be social activists on issues such as fair housing and gambling."

Typical of prescriptive moral thinking is the language of right, should, and ought, and their opposites—wrong, should not, and ought not.

Descriptive Facts/Prescriptive Evaluations

These two ways of thinking about morality are theoretically quite distinct. The descriptive thinker notes what the case is, what has happened, and what the facts are. The prescriptive thinker judges what ought to be the case and what should have happened. Ethicists refer to the difference between these two approaches as the fact/evaluation distinction or the is/ought discrepancy. It is important to be able to distinguish facts from evaluations, so let us take a closer look.

A fact is an account of a certain state of affairs. It is a claim about the way things or people are. A fact can be true or false. It is true or false, for example, that there is life on Mars. A fact is subject to empirical or sociological justification.

Fact

- includes terms like these: do, is, has, do not, is not, has not
- describes a decision or opinion already reached
- reports the opinion of someone

An evaluation or a judgment is a statement about what ought to be. It is a claim about what some person or group of persons ought to hold dear. It is a claim about what the good is, of what is valuable. We evaluate when we say, "Scientists should try to find out whether there is life on Mars," and when we say, "Knowledge is valuable." A judgment cannot be true or false. It may be true or false that specific persons agree with this judgment, but the judgment itself is not subject to the categories of truth and falsehood. Persons might be judged good or bad for making the judgments they make, but the judgment cannot be deemed true or false. An evaluation or a judgment is a claim about what ought to be the case, regardless of whether or not it presently is the case.

Evaluation

- includes one of these terms: should, ought, right, should not, ought not, wrong
- tells of a future state of affairs to be brought about or avoided
- judges what someone should have said or done
- involves comparative judgments like more important, less important, better, worse

So a statement can be factual, that is, descriptive or evaluative, that is, prescriptive. Some examples follow:

Facts

1. Most physical therapists value confidentiality.
2. Nobody takes a verbal agreement seriously.
3. In our society, we do not know and do not trust the people with whom we do business.
4. According to my veterinarian, the family who takes care of an animal is as much the veterinarian's client as the animal.
5. An accountant has both an employer and clients.

Evaluations

6. Physical therapists should value confidentiality.
7. It is a good thing that nobody takes a verbal agreement seriously.
8. In our society, we should not trust those we do not know but with whom we do business.
9. The animal, and not the animal's human caregivers, ought to be the veterinarian's only concern.
10. Accountants should try to please both their clients and their employers.

Keep in mind that the clues for recognizing facts and evaluations, discussed before the examples, are not by themselves infallible ways of distinguishing a fact claim from an evaluative claim. Note that number 7 reports how people act, yet it is an evaluative claim. It does not just summarize how people act, it judges how they act and evaluates their acting. Number 1 includes the word "value," but it is a factual claim since it is only reporting what physical therapists do and not prescribing what they ought to do. Thus these clues may help, but we must still test a claim carefully to judge whether its intention is to describe a state of affairs or to prescribe a state of affairs.

Now, with all of these tools for considering a case, let us jump right in.

> *David Grant, a farmer, had experienced months of abdominal and gastrointestinal pain. His local doctor could find nothing wrong. Finally, his wife Louise called a major research hospital, which agreed to evaluate him.*
>
> *David was having a severe bout of pain when the Grants arrived for his appointment. The doctor who examined him, Dr. Miles Finch, decided that David's appendix had burst and prepared him for immediate surgery.*
>
> *Several hours later, with David still in the recovery room, Dr. Finch came out to speak to Louise. Dr. Finch appeared to be nervous and kept his eyes averted from Louise as he spoke. The surgery had revealed a burst appendix, but also discovered an inoperable abdominal tumor the doctor believed to be malignant, although that would have to be confirmed by lab tests. Dr. Finch recommended radiation treatments to shrink the tumor and possibly control the cancer.*
>
> *Louise listened quietly but did not cry. She then told Dr. Finch not to tell her husband about the possible malignancy of the tumor. She recommended that he be allowed to believe that the reason for the radiation treatments was to shrink the tumor. She reported that her husband was a very emotional man, an almost obsessive worrier, and frightened of medical talk.*
>
> *Dr. Finch's policy was to tell patients what he judged that they needed or wanted to know. As he listened to Louise characterize her husband, he wondered what he should say to David.*

We now wonder, what questions does this case raise? Some of the most obvious follow:

1. Was Dr. Finch right to go to Louise first with the news of her husband's inoperable and possibly cancerous tumor? In other words, did he have David's approval to first bring the news to Louise? Did he need David's approval? Has he violated David's confidentiality or privacy?
2. Is Dr. Finch correct about David having a malignant tumor?
3. Should Louise be the one to decide what her husband is told? That is, is Dr. Finch obligated to carry out her wishes and not inform her husband of the possible malignancy of his tumor? Or is it up to Dr. Finch to decide what to disclose to David? Is Louise a good judge of how her husband will deal with the medical news? Will it in fact be possible to keep the information about the possible malignancy of his tumor from

David, given that he may undergo radiation treatment? Is it fair to let David agree to undergo treatments if he does not fully comprehend what the treatments are for?

4. Does not disclosing information to David violate his trust or harm him? Is not disclosing the whole truth to David the same as lying to him? Does disclosing the whole truth to him harm him or ruin his remaining life?

5. Are Dr. Finch's feelings of nervousness in communicating with Louise appropriate? Are his feelings relevant to his decision of what to tell David?

6. Is Dr. Finch's practice of deciding what to tell patients on a case-by-case basis a good or an appropriate practice?

7. Is Dr. Finch a good doctor? How does his membership in the medical profession guide, influence, or determine his course of action?

This list of questions is not exhaustive. You may think of others to ask about this case. Even so, let us consider a few points regarding what these initial questions indicate. A number of informational and moral concerns must be clarified. Some questions are moral, some are not. Part of the job of ethics is to tell us how to distinguish between moral questions, like question 4, and nonmoral questions, like question 2. Both kinds of questions may need to be answered in resolving a case, but they are important in different ways. Answering the factual questions will not resolve a moral problem but, on the other hand, resolving a moral problem well depends on having good information and accurate facts.

We will focus on the moral judgments that Louise and Dr. Finch have made or will make. Perhaps if we were making the decisions, our moral judgments would not be the same as theirs. But first we must learn to describe the facts of the case and to recognize the evaluations made by those in the case.

Finally, let us note several points about the relationship of descriptive thinking to prescriptive thinking. The first point is that descriptive thinking is not very interesting to ethicists. It can provide a historical record of what people believe and do, but it cannot resolve any questions people have about what they should believe and do. A second point is that prescriptive thinking builds on descriptive thinking. In order to judge a person's behavior, we must have correctly assessed the nature of his or her behavior. To arrive at the best solution to a moral problem, we must first have understood the situation that generated the problem and we must have all of the facts. Prescriptive thinking does not leave descriptive thinking behind; rather, it uses descriptive thinking to provide the information and facts that inform a moral judgment or resolution. A third point is that in actual practice, it is sometimes hard to separate descriptive from prescriptive thinking. It is difficult for sociologists and, for that matter, most of us, to describe the behavior of someone without judging it.

Now that we can identify descriptive and prescriptive thinking, let us briefly define the third type of moral thinking, metaethics.

Metaethics

Metaethics involves the logical analysis of moral language. It aims to make precise the meanings of moral terms and the logic of moral argumentation. Its goal is not to dictate action but to provide clarification on the nature of moral language. So a metaethicist analyzes the moral claims and judgments of the prescriptive ethicist, not to evaluate their moral correctness but to judge their logical correctness.

Earlier we used the examples of a nurse who was right, a defense attorney who should not, and pastors who ought. The metaethicist questions what we mean by using the terms, "right," "should," and "ought." For example, the metaethicist asks whether these terms have objective meaning or subjective meaning. In calling the nurse "right," do we mean to say that rightness is an objective property that the nurse possesses, like she might possess the property of tallness? Is rightness something the nurse has? Or do we mean by rightness merely to confer subjective approval on the nurse we are calling right? Perhaps right is a shorthand way of saying we approve of her action. In this case, the nurse does not possess anything in being right, although she is supported by our claim and the recipient of our congratulations and approval. So a metaethicist aims to discover the connotations of moral terms that allow us to make claims of praise and blame.

Although the questions of metaethics are relevant to the pursuit of prescriptive accounts of ethics, they should not replace them. It would not be appropriate to allow our uncertainty about the meaning of moral terms to keep us from making moral claims or reaching moral conclusions. We should work to be clear in defining terms and constructing arguments, but we must keep in mind that moral language is meant to be used to explain, account for, and judge moral experience. Our focus is on prescriptive ethics, although we will take seriously both the need for factual descriptions (descriptive thinking) and the need for clear and precise language (metaethics). To finish with our Milos Finch example:

- It is important to have a description of what he and Louise have done, and when, why, and to whom they have done it (descriptive thinking).
- It is important to know how we are using words like "possible malignancy" and "obsessive worrier" (metaethics).
- But finally, it is for the purpose of determining what he should do (prescriptive thinking) that we engage in the collection of facts and the analysis of terms.

More on Prescriptive Ethics

Prescriptive ethics, we have said, has to do with the making of moral judgments. It is the realm of ethics in which persons judge actions and other people as well as make moral choices and defend them. We must reflect in more detail on what it means to do this judging, choosing, and justifying. When a prescriptive claim is made, for instance, "Teachers ought to keep their promises," there are two noteworthy features of this claim.

1. Prescriptive claims involve a system of rules and values.
2. Prescriptive claims are universalizable.

The first feature of prescriptive claims, a system of rules and values, is simple to understand. We will in chapters 3 and 6 define the terms *rules* and *values* more specifically, but for now, they refer to those moral directives and moral goods that persons try to follow or manifest in their actions. For instance, always tell the truth, and little white lies are acceptable are both rules. Integrity is a value; so is nonmaleficence. Rules and values are related to each other, as we will see. They are the machinery of prescriptive ethics. They work together more or less smoothly to facilitate the judging, choosing, and justifying of ethical choices. Without an understanding of what rules we are following or should follow, and of what we value or should value, we cannot engage in normative ethics.

The second feature of prescriptive claims, universalizability, is not as easy to understand. It refers to the fact that moral claims are generalizable, that is, that there is a commonality in moral judging and choosing. It means that in prescriptive ethics the person who is judging or choosing is judging or choosing for others, and not only for himself or herself. Judgments and choices apply generally, not just to this particular case but to others like it. By universalizing choices, we are speaking not just for our particular selves but for others as well, and we are speaking not just of this case but of others like it.

There are various ways that prescriptive ethics can be universalizable. Not all of the ways are equally credible. One way there could be universalizability is if all persons ought to do the same thing. So there is universalizability in saying, "No person ought to take credit for another's ideas." Here we are reaching a conclusion about all people, a universalized group. There also is universalizability in the claim, "I in my position of authority ought not take sole credit for my subordinates' ideas," since in saying "I," I mean anyone like me or anyone in my situation. It is not the format of the claim that is crucial, it is the intention. The claims of prescriptive ethics apply to more than particular people and unique situations.

The main point is that a prescriptive claim cannot refer only to a single person or situation. By definition, it aims at being able to judge others and decide for others. It may make a claim about all persons (everyone), or it may make a claim about a class of persons (all managers, all politicians who desire to be respected). To understand the ways a normative claim can be universal, consider the following possibilities. A normative claim asserts both that something is universal and that it is universal to some.

1. What is universal?
    A. Values; what we hold to be good.
    B. Actions; what we do.

2. To whom is it universal?
    A. All people.
    B. Some group of persons.

Given this, there are four ways in which a normative claim can be universal.

	All	Some Group
Values	1	2
Actions	3	4

Consider the following examples:

1. Everyone ought to value honesty.
2. Politicians ought to value honesty.
3. No one should lie or deceive when asked a straightforward question.
4. Any politician who wishes to be respected should not lie or deceive when asked a straightforward question, unless there is considerable risk to him or her or others if the truth is told.

Some of these types of universality are more reasonable than others. It is harder to prove that everyone ought to do something (number 3) than it is to prove that some specialized group of persons ought to do something (number 4). It is harder to prove that everyone ought to value something (number 1) than it is to prove that some specialized group of persons ought to value something (number 2). Possibly we can agree that honesty ought to be valued by persons, but we will surely disagree over which types of situations require complete truth telling and which allow for deceptions or lies. Perhaps other conclusions can be drawn about which of these types of universalizability are easier or harder to prove. However, let us not lose sight of the main point. Prescriptive ethics involves making ought claims that are universalizable in one or more of the four senses listed earlier. Prescriptive claims require one of these kinds of universality, not all.

Conclusion

Prescriptive moral thinking is a complex enterprise, and to engage in it we must be well acquainted with the definitions and concepts of ethics. This chapter aimed to describe what morality is. It considered the case of Dr. Finch and the questions involved in his decision-making situation. Ethics was defined and distinguished from other philosophical disciplines and the fields of law, religion, economics, and etiquette. Several presuppositions of ethics were pointed out. Descriptive, prescriptive, and meta-ethical ways of thinking about morality were contrasted and the differences between facts and evaluations and the way both have a role to play in moral situations were considered. Finally, the way in which prescriptive ethics involves a system of rules and values and is universalizable was examined. Now, with this understanding of what ethics is, professional ethics will be discussed in chapter 3.

EXERCISES

1. Identify which of the following statements are descriptive, namely,
    statements of fact (D) and which are prescriptive, namely, evaluative
    statements (P).

D   **1.**   It is no longer possible for an employer to openly discriminate
             against homosexuals.
P   **2.**   It should be legal to provide marijuana to glaucoma patients.
P   **3.**   Birth defects need to be prevented.
P   **4.**   Fraud is wrong because it undermines trust.
P   **5.**   If there are two equally qualified candidates for the job and one
             is a man and one is a woman, preference should be given to the
             woman.
D   **6.**   A company that does work overseas is frequently expected to fol-
             low local custom and offer bribes to secure partnerships.
D   **7.**   The families who have pets expect to have their wishes about
             their pet's treatment carried out by their veterinarians.
P   **8.**   A nurse should not withdraw from a case that requires actions that
             violate his or her conscience without first securing a replacement.
D   **9.**   The accountant's obligation is to his or her employer, and not to
             the client.
P   **10.** Newborns more than eight weeks' premature should not be given
             extensive medical treatment.
P   **11.** Personal responsibility should be the highest good.
D   **12.** Gene therapy practiced by well-trained scientists is a safe, reli-
             able method for correcting genetic diseases.
P   **13.** A priest who passes on information learned in the confessional
             should be relieved of his duties.
D   **14.** Fraud causes harm to the client, the practitioner, the company
             that tolerates it, and society at large.
P   **15.** Lawyers must not cooperate in fabricating evidence no matter
             what their opinion of the law in question.
P   **16.** Some jobs are not worth having.

2. Reflect on the following cases and questions:

CASE 1: THE LAWYER AND THE WELFARE RECIPIENT

*Mr. Smith, a public interest lawyer, represents a welfare recipient who
has five children, who makes $60 a week babysitting, and whose family
barely survives. She has not reported this income to the welfare agency,
as it would disqualify her as a recipient. Her action constitutes criminal
fraud. Mr. Smith must file reports of all income in a court in which she
is suing for divorce, and these reports may well be forwarded to the welfare agency. What should he do?*[12]

Some questions to consider:

1. Who is the lawyer's employer?
2. Who is the lawyer's client?
3. What is the lawyer's job? Is it to get the best possible divorce settlement for the client? Is it to truthfully represent his client's divorce case and work toward the best settlement for his client? Is it to protect his client? Is it to protect society, or uphold the law, or act as a servant of the court?
4. What laws or standards of the profession apply to the lawyer's situation?
5. How did the lawyer discover the babysitting earnings? Can he pretend that he never heard this information?
6. Is it likely that others or other agencies might also discover the babysitting earnings?
7. Are the two cases—the divorce case and the welfare fraud case—related?
8. Does the lawyer's participation in one case have implications for the other case?
9. Does the divorce case have an impact on the welfare fraud question? In other words, will the fraud be discontinued if there is a divorce settlement? Will the need for the extra money no longer exist?
10. How badly is the extra money from the babysitting needed?
11. Is the welfare law just?
12. How many cases of welfare fraud are followed up, prosecuted, and convicted?
13. Must the lawyer withdraw from the case in order to not report the babysitting earnings?
14. Can the lawyer withdraw from the case and advise the client to not disclose the babysitting earnings to her next lawyer?
15. Is babysitting money "income"?
16. Does the amount of the babysitting earnings make a difference?
17. Are there other questions you consider crucial? Which ones? Why are they crucial?

CASE 2: THE NURSE AND THE SIXTEEN-YEAR-OLD PATIENT

Beth Miller is a sixteen-year-old girl who came with her mother to have a physical in preparation for going away to summer camp. After the physical, Beth's mother left the examining room to have the camp forms completed by a nurse, and the doctor left to see another patient. A nurse came in to give Beth a tetanus shot. Beth asked the nurse to please have the doctor write her a prescription for birth control pills and to please do it in a way that would not alert her mother. The nurse knew that Beth's mother was just down the hall and that the doctor was not expecting to return to Beth's examining room. The nurse wondered what to say and do.

1. List the questions, answer them, and reach a conclusion.
2. What are some descriptive statements or facts about the case?

3. What are some prescriptive statements or evaluative statements raised by this case?
4. In what way is your conclusion universalizable? Explain.

NOTES

1. This analogy is borrowed from Lawrence M. Hinman, *Ethics: A Pluralistic Approach to Moral Theory* (New York: Harcourt Brace Jovanovich, Inc., 1994), 1–6. Hinman also uses it to make additional points.
2. This definition is offered first under the heading of "Philosophy" in *The Encyclopedia of Philosophy*, Vols. 5 and 6 (New York: Macmillan, 1967), 216.
3. These philosophical fields are selected from a broader list provided in *Philosophy: A Brief Guide for Undergraduates*, published by the American Philosophical Association, 1982. The definition of each field is adapted from the descriptions offered in the above work on pages ii–v.
4. This is reported by Beverly Merz, "Physicians Assist in Illinois Execution By Lethal Injection," *American Medical News* (September 21, 1990), 3, 50–51.
5. Jeremy Bentham and John Stuart Mill propose versions of a theory called "utilitarianism" in which utility is offered as the standard for what is right. See Jeremy Bentham, *An Introduction to the Principles of Morals and Legislation*, 1789, and John Stuart Mill, *Utilitarianism*, 1861. Mill also made an attempt to show that justice is the same as utility (*Utilitarianism*, chapter 5).
6. See, for example, the MSI trial, where Management Services of Illinois, Inc., was accused of fraud and bribery for gifts it provided to employees at Public Aid (Rick Pearson, "MSI Gave Out Gifts, Not Bribes, Jury Told," *Chicago Tribune*, August 7, 1997, MetroChicago section) 1, 8.
7. See George E. Taffet, M.D., Thomas A. Teasdale, M.P.H., Robert J. Luchi, M.D., "In-Hospital Cardiopulmonary Resuscitation," *The Journal of the American Medical Association*, Vol. 260, No. 14 (Oct. 14, 1988), 2069–2072.
8. This particular course numbering and sequencing comes from the accounting department at Loyola University of Chicago (*Undergraduate Studies Catalog*, 1996–97), 155.
9. Witness Augustine's analysis of his act of stealing pears as being especially wrong because he knew he was choosing and doing wrong (*Confessions*, Book 2).
10. This is probably how Socrates would assess the situation, since he believed that virtue was a kind of knowledge, hence that vice (doing wrong) was due to ignorance (*Republic*, I).
11. Margaret Mead (1901–1978) was an anthropologist who began her field work in 1925 when she studied adolescent girls in Samoa. She worked in the Admiralty Islands and in New Guinea and focused on problems of education and culture, cultural change, and crossnational relationships.
12. This case appears in Alan H. Goldman, *The Moral Foundations of Professional Ethics* (Savage, Md.: Rowman & Littlefield Publishers, Inc., 1980), 104, although he credits the case to Gary Bellow and Jeanne Kettleseon, *The Mirror of Public Interest Ethics* (unpublished manuscript), problem 3.

3

What Professional Ethics Is

Because you have picked up this book, and because you have made it to this chapter, you have some interest, however peripheral or mandated, in being a professional, or behaving in a professional manner. Having articulated in chapter 1 that behaving professionally has a significant moral component and then in chapter 2 spelled out what a moral component is and is not, we will now discuss the ways in which one can begin to make morality actual. Of course everyone, or most everyone, wants to be moral. Why not? But the actual doing of moral behavior is a lot more complicated than the simple desire. If a desire to be moral were equivalent to being moral, then the world would probably be a much more livable place.[1]

Even the term *moral* is not simple. For our purposes, when we make a moral reference to behavior, we are saying that it is capable of being judged as being praiseworthy or blameworthy, and right or wrong. Yet some behavior is morally neutral, like sleeping or getting dressed in the morning. But even these behaviors, which in and of themselves have no moral component, gain such a component through the context in which they are enacted. For example, we would find nothing morally problematic in sleeping after a hard day of honest labor. But suppose you are a shepherd, sleeping on the job while you are supposed to be keeping an eye on sheep that have been stalked by a neighborhood wolf. Within that context, the sleeping behavior has a moral component. The moral component, in this instance, stems from your not only failing to fulfill a professional duty to protect the property—the sheep—but also your putting another being—the sheep—at a risk that could be avoided. So, when we are concerned with morality, we are concerned with behavior that has either a positive or negative moral component. Thus, when we are concerned with the behavior that primarily takes place when we are doing our work, we name a concern for that behavior a concern for professional morality. In virtue of it being a concern for professional morality, that is, a concern with how moral choices are made (or ought to be made) in our professional life, we are involved in doing professional ethics. This notion of morality is based on the distinction between morality and ethics that we discussed in chapter 2. To summarize:

Morality: What We Do	Ethics: The Study of Morality
What we do in our occupational life	The study of what we do at work
What we do in our nonoccupational life	The study of what we do at leisure

Since we are concerned with not only what decisions are made in our professional life but how they are made, we are engaged in professional morality and professional ethics. With this in mind, this chapter will consider some of the different ways that we can approach the sorts of questions professional morality and ethics raise, and concentrate on the approach that is indicated by many professionals through the codes established by their societies and that we find most helpful for approaching morality and professional life.

Professional Ethics Compared to General Ethics

As we begin our discussion of professional ethics and the various approaches to the moral problems it raises, it would be helpful if we considered the relationship of professional ethics to ethics in general. How are the questions and issues raised in professional ethics any different from those encountered in any sort of ethical situation? If you are a good person, are you not going to be a good person while you work? What is to be gained by considering the moral issues of our work life? Why do we need a separate field of study for the moral problems we encounter at work? These are certainly valid questions, which will be treated as we continue. Yet, even if this book were to not distinguish ethics from professional ethics, it is a fact that many colleges, universities, and even high schools have courses in ethics and also courses in professional ethics, business ethics, health care ethics, engineering ethics, and so on. Thus, the distinction between ethics and professional ethics is already in place. Even so, these latter courses have been in existence for only twenty-five years or so. With this relatively recent establishment of a separate treatment for the questions of professional ethics, it is worthwhile to consider why these courses and these specialized fields have come into existence.

Why we have an increase in specialized ethics education is at least partially answered by pointing to the increased specialization in the jobs of the working world. At a very pragmatic level, as technology has increased and the world has changed, ethical issues have been raised that are quite specialized. It is not important for all of us to decide if we would recommend that an organ donation be procured for an individual with advanced alcohol-related cirrhosis of the liver, nor is it important for all of us to decide in the days of greater access to communication what exactly is constituted by insider trading, nor do we all need to appreciate the subtleties of the relevance of DNA testing as evidence. These specific ethical questions for the fields of medicine and commodities and genetics and law will not concern all of us. Underlying them though is the general ethical concern that we all typically have with issues of justice and integrity. In short, as various professional fields are becoming more specialized, the ethical problems and issues that they face are likewise becoming more specialized. Because of this, traditional ethics education has not been helpful enough, so more particular, professional, field-specific ethics education has been implemented.

Another reason professional ethics has appeared in order to deal with the increasingly more complicated moral issues faced in our occupations comes from the efforts of professional societies to develop ethical codes. In developing these codes, groups of like employed and trained individuals are trying to give themselves some guidance in handling their occupationally specific moral concerns. In doing so, each occupational group further differentiates its ethical concerns and standards from those of general ethics. Remember, we have not said that the ethical codes of groups come into conflict with our traditional understanding of ethics. Rather, occupational groups have come together to discuss and suggest some ways of dealing with the moral issues and problems that members of their organizations face. Thus the American Psychological Association gives its members guidelines on being respectful of patient confidentiality, while the American Bar Association gives guidelines to its members on dealing with attorney-client privilege. Both statutes are dealing with what certain professionals can and cannot repeat when told to them by their patient or client. However, each group deals with this problem in a very different way, based on their members' understanding of how they should relate to that other person as their patient and client.[2]

As professional groups are differentiating the moral problems their members face, and technology and change are further dictating specialization in the various moral problems faced in occupations, there is at the same time an increased governmental and a legal regulation of professions, occupations, and those who practice them. This is nothing new. Government has often stepped in to monitor safety and labor practices in various occupational fields.[3] That is, in the face of some seeming challenges to our understanding of ethics, value, and occupational standards, government has stepped in to not only monitor but also to regulate the way in which certain professions are practiced. These three contributing factors have all led to a greater need for more specialized ethics education so that it is more context and content specific and sensitive to the various occupationally related moral problems of our time.[4]

With this understanding of the growth in the specialized field of professional ethics, a second question we must try to answer is how these courses and specialized fields relate to ethics in general. That is, for the longest time, college and often secondary curriculums have included ethics education. Well, what is it and what has it left out? Likewise, what is in it that the field of professional ethics has retained and should retain? What has professional ethics further developed and augmented? In considering the tools we need for both professional and general ethics, we see that many of the definitions, distinctions, and even cases that we treat in professional ethics also are or could be treated in general ethics. Both fields of study discuss the same sorts of things like respect for persons, justice, and honesty. They also both consider the same sorts of issues like personal integrity and social well-being. Yet there are some differences between the two studies. Noting these differences will help us recognize what is distinctive about professional ethics.[5]

A primary difference between general ethics and professional ethics is the audiences at which they are aimed. Professional ethics, for some of the reasons mentioned in the beginning of this section, aims to reflect on the morality of those serving in professional capacities. The moral information it contributes is job- or role-specific morality. It recognizes that there are both similarities and differences among the professions, hence that although we expect all those engaged in occupations to engage in moral behavior (or at the very least not to engage in immoral behavior), there are some particular moral expectations for certain occupations. Meanwhile, unlike professional ethics, general ethics is aiming to provide a moral framework for everyone, not only those in the professions. Contrary to the specificity of professional ethics is the broader audience of general ethics. General ethics aims to speak more universally. Ethics in general does not focus on the individual as a member of a profession, but instead focuses on the individual as a member of a greater moral community that shares in the moral benefits and obligations in which all of humanity participates. General ethics does not distinguish between one's working or professional status and one's status as a member of the larger moral community. In recognizing that we are members in various moral communities such as humanity, families, friends, and occupations, general ethics gives us a common framework for appreciating these communities. As long as we are human, we can do ethics—we do not need to be employed in any capacity.

Another way professional ethics differs from general ethics is in terms of the topics or issues it treats. Even though this is a valid difference between the two ways of doing ethics, here it is hard to insist on any absolute distinction. The topics of promise keeping, confidentiality, and fair hiring practices are just as important to general ethics as they are to professional ethics. But the importance of these issues to general ethics is the importance that stems from their reliance on general ethical commitments that we all typically share. For example, we keep a promise to someone when we are honest, have integrity, and value someone's ability to make decisions based on what we have promised to do. Thus promise keeping is something that stems from a general ethical concern for integrity. Yet we know that in cases involving various occupations and professions, promise keeping can hold even more practical importance as it appears in a particular context where more is at stake. If you are a mathematician who specializes in statistical analysis and you are serving as an expert witness in a product liability case, your promise is very valuable, monetarily and otherwise, to a number of people. Hence, when you swear to tell the whole truth in court, the keeping of your promise becomes a professional concern. This sort of case could be one way that we consider promise keeping in professional ethics, however, it is not the only sort. Of course we treat cases involving doctors, managers, and social workers in professional ethics. However, professional ethics does not have an exclusive right to these cases, since they could of course be used to illuminate various concerns in general ethics as well.

Appreciating that cases involving professionals are often fair game for both professional and general ethics, we also appreciate that there are some issues typically treated in general ethics that are not considered in professional ethics, and vice versa. For example, general ethics will discuss the issues of the morality of various sexual relations, the propriety of abortion, euthanasia, war, and censorship, while professional ethics does not specifically treat these issues in and of themselves. Professional ethics is concerned with the questions that arise in the practice of one's professional life, relative to the ethical concerns that are important to all of us. These questions may include issues such as the propriety of having sex with one's co-workers or clients, or the acceptability of participating in abortion or euthanasia cases, given one's professional and personal standards. They may be questions about how nurses should understand their jobs when serving in the military during a time of war, or how school administrators should respond to the school board's decision to censor students' reading materials. Thus professional ethics considers only the moral issues that arise in one's professional life, and while a part of that discussion considers how one's professional and personal lives come together, the main goal of professional ethics is to help persons serving in professional capacities think and act in morally responsible ways. Traditionally, the field of general ethics does not explicitly recognize that the moral questions faced by practicing professionals need to be distinguished from the moral questions facing all individuals generally. In not making that distinction, general ethics concerns all of the pertinent moral questions and issues that can arise in the course of the life of anyone, not contingent upon what they do for a living. In short, general ethics concerns a broader range of issues than does professional ethics.

The final way of articulating the difference between professional and general ethics is in their methodologies, or modes of operation. Professional ethics is typically grounded in concrete cases. Professionals come to understand the expectations and moral difficulties confronting their professions after finding themselves in situations that raise questions. The theory and codes of professional ethics are a response to the complex cases in which professionals find themselves. The method of professional ethics in being so squarely case oriented can be described as a "bottom up" method. That is, professional ethics typically starts right on the ground, in the middle of a problem, and from there it develops ways and means to proceed. In general ethics, the method of moral reasoning is not always case oriented. Moral theorists formulate moral rules and guidelines based on accounts of human nature, religious beliefs, or philosophical assumptions. These rules and theories are then taken to be applicable to concrete cases. The work of relating these rules, principles, or theories to cases generally happens last in ethics. General ethics, in starting with rules and theories, can be seen as a "top down" method. It starts off with a conceptual framework that is often not originally rooted in the concrete, but rather in something more abstract. Put simply, general ethics begins with rules and theories and then applies them to cases, while professional ethics begins with cases or experience and uses them to understand or to help develop rules and theories.

One thing to keep in mind here is that this discussion has primarily differentiated professional ethics from general ethics, or ethics in general. Take a look at the following chart:

ETHICS

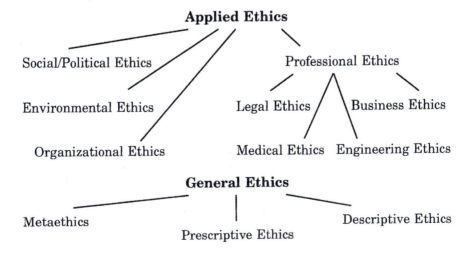

Applied Ethics

Social/Political Ethics

Professional Ethics

Environmental Ethics

Legal Ethics   Business Ethics

Organizational Ethics

Medical Ethics   Engineering Ethics

General Ethics

Metaethics

Descriptive Ethics

Prescriptive Ethics

Our discussion thus far has concentrated on the ways in which general ethics is different from professional ethics. But the field of ethics includes many specialties, some more abstract and some more applied. There are plenty of other fields in applied ethics than just the professional one, and any listing of or dividing up of the subspecialties of ethics inevitably reflects some minimal bias. Yet, as it stands for our purposes, ethics has a general and an applied side. Under the general side are all of the ethical concerns like meta-ethics, the history of ethics, prescriptive and descriptive ethics, and the like. Under the applied side, we have all of the ways ethics comes out to meet the world. There is the ethics that comes out of our concern for the environment, and then the fields that this discussion concentrates on: professional ethics. In referring to it here, professional ethics includes all of the subspecialties of things such as legal, business, medical, and engineering ethics. But a case might be made, although we reject it, that those specific fields do not share enough in common to be grouped under professional ethics. Instead we argue that the professions and professionals in all of these fields share similar value commitments and can thereby profit from being treated together. It is not important to name everything that is *not* professional ethics, but it is more important to understand that ethics includes both general and applied fields.

With this discussion behind us of what professional ethics shares and does not share with general ethics, we are ready to get down to what professional ethics actually is. We have distinguished the field of general ethics from the more specified, occupationally related field of professional ethics. Since the topic of this book is professional ethics, we would be well served to delve into this topic a bit further. As has been said, professional ethics studies the way in which we make decisions in our occupational life. Professional ethics considers the morality of our professional choices. In short, by virtue of doing professional ethics, we are going to talk about the process of how we make the moral decisions in our work life as well as the actual decisions that we make in our work life.

Approaches to Professional Ethics and Moral Lives

The one thing that we seem to have established minimally is that professional ethics deals with the moral actions that take place in our working life and the surrounding issues that this includes, while the tradition of general ethics deals with moral actions that take place in our life in general and thus all of the ethical issues with which we deal. With that very broad approach to the issues of professional ethics, we are going to have to narrow things down a bit. One way to do this would be to build on what we have already established. That is, we have talked about how ethics in general seeks to make universal judgments and how professional ethics seeks to make more particular judgments. But now we will consider the way in which these judgments are made relative to one another. Is there a relationship between these two groups of moral judgments? Of course there is some sort of relationship between the two, since to have no relationship is to have some kind of a relationship. Let us examine two of the more predominant ways of thinking about how it is that general ethics, or our overarching moral commitments, relate to professional ethics, or our professional commitments.

In talking about the aforementioned, we are considering one of the primary questions of the nature of our moral self. That is, in the root of all of our action—our moral self—what is the relationship between our ethical life, professionally and in general? We have said that professional ethics concerns what we do in our occupations and general ethics concerns all of our general ethical concerns. We can think of the way in which these two are related in primarily two ways. We can think of ourselves as consistently holding to one integrated moral self or moral life, regardless of what we are doing, or we can think of ourselves as holding on to diverse moral selves, pulling out the one that is most appropriate, depending on what it is we are doing. For the sake of our discussion, we will refer to these two modes of thought as holism and separatism, respectively.[6]

When we think of the praiseworthy aspects of our moral selves, such as helping people, and then we make that concrete by thinking of the way in which we help people who are carrying heavy parcels, we do not typically think, "Wow! I sure am a good parcel carrier!" Instead, we typically think of the behavior of helping someone carry parcels as coming from an underlying desire in us to help people which, if a part of the way we act, is a part of our moral self or life. So our moral actions can be thought of as the concrete parts of our moral selves. Likewise, when we think about aspects of our personality that we would like to change, do we think as we sit at home watching our favorite sit-coms, "I am some rotten sort of community volunteer! The community volunteer in me is really just a lazy slug!" As in our first example, the fact that you are not community volunteering is not a product of that part of your personality that is trying to be a couch potato, but instead it is a product of your failure to enact or embolden yourself in your role as a community volunteer. Instead of thinking of ourselves as a failed community volunteer when we stay home and watch TV, we typically think that we would like to encourage that part of our moral selves that is community minded. Becoming a community volunteer would then require us to develop that part of our moral self or life, which would direct us to act on our impulses of civic spirit. This moral self is that which relates the general and applied ethical sides of us insofar as it relates our overarching moral commitments to our moral life, professional and otherwise. Now we are left to consider how it is that this moral character is to relate.

When we discuss that aspect of ourselves of which we are particularly proud, perhaps the carrying of heavy parcels, do we think of the desire to engage in that behavior as a part of us different and separate from the other parts of our moral personality? Under holism, we would have a commitment to helping people who are carrying heavy packages. This commitment would hold regardless of what role we might play in our life. Granted, if you worked for a packing and shipping company, your professional life would more easily support this commitment. But, under holism, your professional life need not be centered on your moral commitments, but your moral commitments must remain consistent regardless of what you are doing. Thus when we think of a part of our personality, such as helping, that part of us leads us to behave in one manner or another. The thinking that would emanate from this approach might be something like, "Wow! I am awfully good at helping behavior, and when I carry parcels for people who find them difficult to manage, at work or in my neighborhood, I am exhibiting the best parts of my helping self."

Under separatism, we would thereby think of an aspect of oneself in helping behavior with heavy packages as a behavior reflecting a moral commitment that changes contingent upon the circumstances under which one finds oneself. Assisting people with heavy parcels is a kind of action that comes from a particular version of one's moral self, distinct from the other, different manifestations of one's moral self. This kind of action becomes acted upon contingent upon the moral self that one is committed to at a particular point in time.

As we have discussed, these two ways in which to speak about how we think of our moral selves or lives are likewise ways of approaching professional ethics. If we fill them into the chart we started out with, the chart will grow to look like the following:

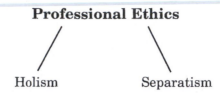

Professional Ethics

Holism   Separatism

Holism and separatism give us two ways of approaching the problems of professional ethics that are parallel to the examples of an analysis of a moral self given earlier. In short, holism says that we are committed to the same moral rules and responsibilities, whatever sort of behavior we are engaged in and whatever situations and relationships in which we find ourselves. Thus our moral self remains the consistent and integrated source of our moral decisions and actions. Separatism consists of an approach to professional ethics that says we are committed to one type of moral rules and responsibilities while engaging in one type of behavior—professional, and another type of rules and responsibilities while engaging in the other aspects of our life. Thus our self has more than one manifestation. Under separatism, our moral self is the consistent source of our moral behavior, but we have more than one moral self operating, and one self may make a decision that is contrary to a decision that another self in different circumstances may have made.

Going back to another prior example of behavior that we would like to encourage in ourselves, suppose you are living your life and you want to work in a domestic abuse shelter or at the very least feel bad about not taking the time to do such a thing. This sort of response is a reflection of your moral self or life. If you found the holist approach persuasive, you would have this response at home or at work, in whatever situations you find yourself in. In the separatist or role approach to professional ethics, in your role as a professional you would not have the same moral concerns and commitments that you would have while you are not engaging in your profession. Thus a concern for community volunteering may not be appropriate relative to the commitments you have made in your professional role; that concern is not present or even a part of you in the context of your work life. We can create a chart to illustrate the difference between a holistic and separatist approach to professional morality.

Under the rubric of holism, you make a commitment to the kind of moral individual you would like to be, and the kind of moral

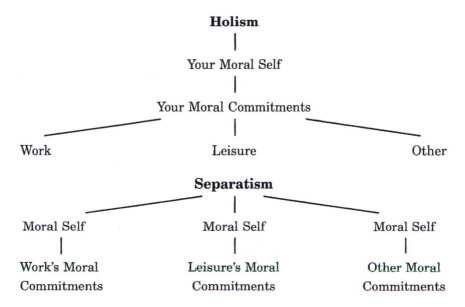

life you would like to have, which is then your morality. This then plays itself out in your work life, in your leisure life, and in every other aspect of your life. The moral actions that come from these commitments are coming from one unified group of value commitments. Under the separatism rubric, you do not make a commitment to any comprehensive view of a moral self, but you do make a commitment to a morality within a particular context. When at work, you operate under your commitment to the kind of professional you would like to be. During leisure and other times, you operate under a different set of moral commitments that are then reflected differently in your decisions.

Imagine this case: You are at home after a long day of work. While there, your spouse arrives a bit later, after stopping off on the way home from work to get his or her hair trimmed. The effect of this minor alteration is pretty awful insofar as it is a butchering. Your spouse is insecure about the haircut, and turns to you with the famously loaded line, "What do you think?" After a thoughtful pause, you respond that the haircut looks fine. Miraculously, that is the end of the conversation. In a nutshell, you lied, or more generously, you did not tell the truth. The haircut looked terrible and in order to spare your spouse's feelings and avoid trouble, you "stretched the truth." Before you relax, the case is not yet over. The next day, as a part of your job with the drug enforcement agency, you catalog evidence. You realize that some evidence, namely two kilos of cocaine, is missing. When your supervisor comes by and asks if everything is okay, you do not respond, "Fine." Instead, you report the missing evidence.

In this instance, you are seemingly a separatist and not a holist. That is, in your personal life, you hold to the rule that it is alright to lie, while in your professional life it seems like you do not hold to the rule that it is alright to lie. Granted, a haircut and a drug bust are quite different, with very different things at stake, but through this exaggerated example the difference between holism and separatism should be clear. The actions in each of the instances were significantly different. At one point, the commitments in which your action is rooted held that lying is an acceptable type of moral behavior. In the second instance, the commitments in which your action is rooted held that lying is not an acceptable type of moral behavior. This then goes into your moral character— which then holds that lying is not alright. We now have two contradictory moral commitments. Under separatism, this is no problem, since you admit that you have a different set of moral commitments in your work life than you do in your personal life. That is, you have a moral self that governs your work life and one that governs your home life.

Even under holism, this situation still might not present a problem, although this would be a harder point to maintain and would require some deep self-reflection. That is, you could still say that you are committed to one set of moral rules and responsibilities that consist of telling the truth, but in this case you went against your own moral commitments. Perhaps you felt that not hurting your spouse's feelings was worth some moral transgression, or perhaps you felt that there were other mitigating circumstances at play. Whatever your reason in this justification of holism in the face of apparently contradictory commitments, there is a certain danger. When we expand or qualify our commitments enough, we risk their becoming meaningless, thus a consistency of commitments is a goal for holists. Of course, no real instance is as clear as our example of bad haircuts and missing cocaine. But by introducing this example, you will hopefully start to think about where you stand on the issue of holism and separatism.

Often the way in which separatism is described as a way of thinking about our moral selves and lives is understood in terms of role morality. That is, in honor of our professional roles, we have different sets of moral commitments. These professional moral commitments might allow us to do some things that would not be allowed in our personal life, or they might prevent us from doing some things that would be allowed in our personal life. We can use this approach to professional morality to explain our haircut/cocaine example. Because of your professional role as an agent of the drug enforcement agency, you are not allowed to perpetuate falsehoods. However, in your role as a spouse, you are allowed to perpetuate falsehoods in order to spare feelings. In role morality, we have still a different set of moral commitments for our professional life and our personal life. The differences between the moral commitments primarily consist of the relation of the moral commitments to the function of the role.

One key aspect of role morality is its implicit support of the general norms of society. Role morality says that with respect to our professions, we have to interpret the general norms of society in very specific ways.[7] These interpretations are to not contradict what our general morality commits us to, but to specify it functionally. To not conflict with our general societal norms, separatism or role morality presupposes another level of commitment where our moral self is unified insofar as that self allows us to uphold the general values of society. These general values of society become the moral commitments that ground our moral self. This leaves us with the assumption of a sort of qualified or postponed holism. Even without the added stipulation role morality gives to separatism of not allowing its moral norms to conflict with our general societal norms, there needs to be some unifying moral ground that allows for the multiple moral grounds of separatism. That is, in appreciating that we have more than one moral self at work in separatism, the level that we appreciate that in ourselves requires a unified moral stance.

Disparate moral commitments lead to disparate moral lives. Consider this example: You are still cataloguing evidence for the drug enforcement agency. After reporting the two missing kilograms of cocaine and receiving your supervisor's approval, your supervisor says to you, "So, what do you think of my haircut?" Unbeknownst to you, your supervisor and your spouse both use the same person to cut their hair, an error in aesthetic judgment on both of their parts. Now what do you say? According to a separatist or role-determined morality, you would have to tell your supervisor how awful you actually consider the haircut. Remember, according to your separatist position, you have determined that lying is inappropriate on the job. Therefore, you cannot lie to your supervisor about the haircut. But if you maintain your holist perspective, you could respond to your supervisor that you thought the haircut was "fine."

This holism assumes a commitment to not hurting the feelings of others when such action can be avoided without harm. This is a moral commitment to which you remain committed, regardless of the circumstances.

In this text, we will maintain that the professional's life is not to be differentiated in terms of moral commitments from his or her personal life. If you lie under certain circumstances in your personal life, those sorts of moral commitments will follow you in your professional life as well. In the case of the terrible haircut, hopefully you would maintain a level of consistency in your answer, both personally and professionally. Furthermore, this example indicates the ways in which a person's personal interests are often interspersed with the professional, and it is an artificial separation to draw a line between one set of commitments and another. In our most foundational moral commitments, it is inconsistent to hold conflicting positions. Thus, in what follows, we will present a way of filling in the foundational moral commitment in such a manner as to allow for the greatest consistency and moral integration.

Two Common Ways of Articulating Holism

Understanding these two ways of viewing the claims of professional ethics, and accepting that our approach adopts a holistic framework to an ethical life (understanding a holistic framework as merely a commitment to one singular moral self), we can examine the ways in which this holistic framework can be articulated. We have talked about ethics as a discipline in chapter 2, and we have differentiated professional ethics from the study of general ethics. Now we will continue to fill in the chart we have been working from by distinguishing the ways of articulating the holistic framework of professional ethics.

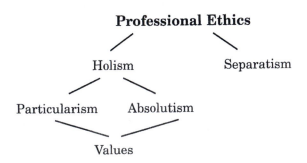

In this third section of the chapter we will be focusing on two common ways to approach moral problems, specifically the problems of professional ethics, and in the next section we will consider the third way of interpreting holism. Approaches to ethical issues are different than ethical theories, which would come next in our chart. The approach to an ethical issue comes before our theory, insofar as it assumes and points to the things we find important that our theories seek to uphold. Basically our ethical approaches ground our theories by pointing to the most key aspects of moral life in such a manner that we see how it is possible to begin to make them relevant in the world. Our ethical approaches allow us to interpret our general moral commitments. This section of the chapter will concentrate on two approaches or ways of interpreting our moral commitments: particularism (case-based reasoning), an ethical approach that works from the bottom up; and absolutism (principle-based reasoning), an ethical approach that works from the top down. The next section will treat values, that which serves as the conceptual backdrop for both particularism and absolutism.

By looking at these three approaches, we will see that both particularism and absolutism are problematic unless they assume some sort of a backdrop of moral issues that they plan to interpret. That is, in virtue of working to uphold certain important aspects of our moral commitments, both particularism and absolutism assume the importance of particular moral values, yet they fail to do so explicitly. This leads to confusion, conceptual and otherwise. In what follows, we will look at both particularism and absolutism, demonstrate how they assume the importance of a value-based approach to professional ethics, and then highlight the values approach itself.

As a society, we seem to lack a shared singular moral worldview, and this is not some sort of ethical dysfunction. That is, the fact that we do not all agree is not some sort of failure, but perhaps it is even some sort of success insofar as we allow many different viewpoints. Yet the plurality of moral opinions specifically relative to the professional life will not go away. Nowadays, it seems that when we talk about issues in professional ethics, we do so in the context of our current societies and their collective views on these topics. One approach to professional ethics that takes into account this plurality of opinions and highlights particular aspects of certain situations is particularism. Particularism seeks to discover our general moral commitments by considering the particular context of our moral situations. It is evident in approaches to problem solving that use the method of case analysis. Case analysis has become a prevalent trend in problem solving in that it looks at the particulars of situations, concentrating on the context involved, and from that develops moral rules to guide our actions.[8] In so doing, through particularism we exhibit a great sensitivity to the diverse and multiple manifestations of our ethical life, professional or otherwise.

In particularism, our moral perspective is not then presumed before we deal with a moral situation. It is worked out from the context of the situation itself and the social norms that are seen to be evident in that context. This is what makes particularism an approach to moral problems and not a moral theory itself. According to particularism, it is through case analysis that we come up with a moral theory. We do not have a moral theory independent of any particulars, thus particularism is especially sensitive to our social norms. Currently, many of our moral codes come about as a consequence of our society. Case analysis capitalizes on this by identifying the source of our moral rules—ourselves and our society. This position sees no value in an approach that begins with a moral theory which determines the ways in which moral decisions are to be made.

So now that we understand a bit about what makes up the particularist approach, let us consider how it works. Suppose you have the following simple moral problem:

> *It is Monday morning. You are not feeling great. It could be physical or it could be psychosomatic, but you have gone to work and felt worse. However, on this particular Monday, you have a big presentation to give for a client who you are hoping will contract with your company. You really have two choices here, with several nuances involved: go back to bed and call in sick, leaving it to your assistant to deal with all of the rescheduling details; or go into work and give the presentation, knowing it could be improved if you were to have a few more days to work on it, illness or not.*

What is to be done here? How can a solution be reached when there are so many things seemingly at stake? The method of case-based analysis suggests a manner that allows those with differing backgrounds—academic, religious, philosophical, or otherwise—to reach a consensus on the matter at hand. This is possible, since all of the major differences in viewpoints are bracketed, and the individuals involved in solving a moral problem go right to the problematic situation itself. The solution of concrete moral problems through compromise and consensus, working with the social norms that are already in place, is the keystone of particularism. Analysis of a particular instance begins with setting up a paradigm case.

That is, when faced with a professional problem, you set up an instance where the solution is clear—with a positive outcome; then you set up another instance where the solution is clear—with a negative outcome. Then, in looking at the case in question, you determine which paradigm case it is closest to, and therein lies the solution to your problem.[9]

Returning to our case of the individual with the Monday morning blues, we can set up two paradigm cases, each with a different outcome. First, if you are deathly ill, then you should not go to work. Next, if you are not deathly ill, and you are not ill enough to have your performance compromised, then you should go to work. In considering this, which of these paradigm cases is ours closest to? It looks as though you are going to have to get out of bed and go to work. We see that this is true by looking at the particular details of the case and realizing that you have gone to work feeling worse. It must be noted, nonetheless, that even though you are going to work, you can still try to reschedule your presentation, or even work on it some more. All the particularist approach helps us with is the specific outcome of this particular case by comparing it to paradigm cases that you have constructed out of the circumstances of your situation. The way this outcome then gets played out in all of its ramifications is still very much up for grabs.

Now that we have taken a look at particularism, we must admit that it seems like a perfect way for dealing with all of the multiple understandings of morality in our society. It allows us to just "jump into" a situation while bracketing all of the difficulties caused by our moral commitments. The proponents of particularism practice case analysis in a way that is supposed to be theory and principle neutral. This approach works out what is and what is not valuable within the context of a particular case. It assumes nothing about what ought to be valued by people or how people ought to live out their values. It allows the situation to determine the solution as well as what moral commitments to act on.

So what could the problem be here? When we look at cases, it seems that we are not as theory neutral as we claim. Not everything is determined out of a social context. In determining that values and principles arise out of cases, the theory neutral particularism of our method does not account for what informs which cases are chosen in the first place and the theoretical preconceptions behind those choices. That is, in setting up the paradigm cases, why did we concentrate on the employee's illness and not on the presentation that was to take place that day, or on any other particular detail? We may have had a different outcome if we had framed the cases with a different sort of sensitivity and slant. For example, what if we had concentrated on the role of the assistant in the case? How responsible would it have been to have left the assistant responsible for rescheduling the presentation? This aspect of responsibility is secondary to that of following through with the presentation itself. The aspects of the case that become central to case-based analysis do not do so without reason. Those who highlight one particular detail over another reveal what it is that is seemingly important to them. This importance is not determined in a vacuum. It assumes that the individual coming to the case has some predispositions of one sort or another, thus the theory and principle neutrality of case-based analysis is compromised.

What if we then went on to consider the case of the Monday morning blues in another way. In doing so, we would need to forget all that we had already concluded about the case. What if this same employee, after going into work, and giving her presentation, got salmonella poisoning from the luncheon served after the presentation. We would then have to decide on Tuesday if she would be going into work. It is not in any way clear how a person using particularism can move from case to case without holding an idea of some sort of overarching ethical principle or value by which he or she could direct his or her choice of cases. This choice reflects bias or at least reflects an underlying moral commitment at work. Hence, without any dominating theory that can be appealed to in comparing cases, we are not able to competently judge between competing claims or interpretations of our common practices. So even though we are developing our moral commitments out of a shared social context, we could come up with different interpretations of this context, and if all we have is this context, we have no way to determine what is a better or worse interpretation of the situation.

More troubling than a failure to arrive at a consensus is what can potentially go wrong when through particularism we articulate our shared social meaning without sensitivity or attention to the economic and power relations that shape our social consensus. If we let moral commitments arise solely out of our shared social context, then we risk perpetuating the oppressive relations that are a part of our society. Think about it. If we were to come up with our moral commitments about things like the inherent right of women to earn equal pay, freedom to engage in consensual sex, and the equality of individuals regardless of race, all based on our shared norms that come out of our social contexts, we could be in big trouble. Much of the content of our conclusions would depend on the social group with which we were involved as the origin of our shared social meaning. Even so, particularism gives us no theoretical distance from which to criticize the aspects of our society that can lead to oppression.[10]

Particularism does give us sophisticated contextual sensitivity in our moral approach, but at the price of ignoring underlying theoretical commitments that allow us to move between cases. Furthermore, it does not give us tools for developing moral consensus, and in practicing it, we risk perpetuating the worst and most oppressive aspects of our social norms. In the face of this sort of anything-that-society-says-goes relativity, many people turn to a more absolute moral approach such as that put forth in absolutism.

As an antidote to particularism, there is another moral approach known as absolutism. This approach assumes principles, that is, guides for action, then uses these principles to solve moral problems. According to the proponents of absolutism, it is an approach to the interpretation of moral commitments that is compatible with all ethical theories. This is the case because all ethical theories, insofar as they seek a good outcome, must presuppose a concern for the kinds of principles that this system espouses.

In and of itself, absolutism is not a moral theory. It is a means to approach and generate moral theories. It allows us to order our important commitments into a rubric for application to a moral situation. This application can be done with a sensitivity to any number of moral theories. Absolutism, in using guides for action, adheres to the principles on which these guides are based. Furthermore, these principles are not to be violated. Not violating principles is easy, under ideal circumstances, but that condition rarely exists. Consequently, we are left to balance our principles within the limits of our situation. The most famous proponents of principlism come out of the bioethical tradition and use principlism to solve moral problems in that field. For our purposes, we will be looking at a principled approach to problem solving in the professional field. However, it is important to recognize the four principles that are typically at work in this sort of an absolutist approach. They go as follows: Autonomy: respect a person's decisions and values; Beneficence: help people; Nonmaleficence: do not harm people; Justice: treat equals equally.

When faced with a moral problem, the goal is to uphold the principles. The goal of the principles is to provide guides for our action that tell us what to do in certain situations. Clearly, it is rarely possible to consistently uphold all four principles in any situation, even when considering a simple case. Oftentimes, in bringing about a good outcome, such as cutting costs, you are harming someone through layoffs and cutbacks. Thus, nonmaleficence is sacrificed for beneficence. So recognizing that it is difficult, if not impossible, to uphold all of the principles, the absolutist approach requires that principles be balanced with prudential limitations such as minimizing the infringement on any given principle as well as minimizing the negative effect the infringement will cause.[11]

Now that we understand a bit about what comprises the absolutist approach, how does it work? Let us return to our original, simple moral problem.

> *It is Monday morning. You are not feeling great. It could be physical or it could be psychosomatic, but you have gone to work and felt worse. However, this particular Monday, you have a big presentation to give for a client who you are hoping will contract with your company. You really have two choices here, with several nuances involved: go back to bed and call in sick, leaving it to your assistant to deal with all of the rescheduling details; or go into work and give the presentation, knowing it could be improved if you were to have a few more days to work on it, illness or not.*

Here we see that if we are to uphold your autonomy, you should be able to choose whatever you would like to do on this Monday morning. However, given beneficence, what would it mean to do good in this situation and to whom? The same goes for nonmaleficence. What would it mean to cause harm in this situation? Then there is the question of justice. If you call in sick, what about your assistant and his need to deal with the fact that you really did not feel prepared for your meeting? Absolutism shows us how each of these principles are absolutely related to this situation, but we do not seem to be very close to a solution to the problem.

So what could be the harm? Who could possibly object to autonomy and the rest? This absolutist approach does thoroughly provide us with normative guidelines for morally right action. That is, although absolutism might not solve our problem, it clearly articulates what this perspective holds as the relevant principles for moral discourse. But what is missing is that which will serve as our guidelines for the interpretation of these guidelines. That is, within absolutism, the meaning of the principles themselves is not clear, nor is the content of the principles in any way apparent. Absolutism works through the subsuming of ethical context under principles, enabling us to ascertain our obligation to act in a certain way. But the key aspect of applying the principle, how it is to be applied in this particular situation, never gets filled in by the absolutist. In short, how to figure out how to apply a particular principle in a particular circumstance is not included in the principle.

Furthermore, absolutism assumes an unquestioning acceptance of the principles that it recognizes. The question, "Why these principles and not others?" is never asked.[12] That is, even if we have some minimal conditions for the application of the principles, there is not a persuasive argument ever given for the initial acceptance of the principles themselves.

Absolutism ignores the dissent that comes about as a result of normative differences with regard to what is right or wrong and good or bad. Truly, those wielding the principles are out for the moral good, but it is their notion of moral good that they are out for, which is what allows them to apply the principles in a particular situation, in a particular way. Yet, not only do we not all agree as to what is right or wrong and good or bad, but we also do not agree as to what these terms mean. Good and right are no longer held unanimously. Furthermore, if good and right ever were held unanimously, universal allegiance to such norms was probably brought about by coercion. The absolutist approach insists on a sameness and absolute uniformity in moral experience and ignores the plurality and diversity of moral life.

Articulating Holism through the Values Approach

In the previous section, we considered two approaches to holism that provide ways of expressing our moral commitments. Neither was very satisfying. Particularism fails because it leaves us to relativism and potentially to the perpetuation of all of the worst aspects of our society's norms. Particularism points to a set of values behind its sensitivity to the particular details of a situation. Those values are the norms that allow us to move from case to case, highlighting specific aspects of the cases we are actually considering upon which to build our problem-solving paradigm cases. Likewise, absolutism fails. It leaves us with an absolute commitment to certain principles, but neither defends making an initial commitment to them, nor provides much clarity on figuring out the content of the principles. This approach makes it tough to be sensitive to the way in which these principles are to be played out in our moral situations. With that said, we now turn to what it is that seems to be lurking behind both of these moral approaches. That is, insofar as particularism has implicit theoretical commitments and absolutism is unable to ground its principles, we see that a values approach, in making an unselfconscious appeal to values as a means of expressing our moral commitments, allows for the most viable way to proceed.

The values of integrity, respect for persons, justice, compassion, beneficence and nonmaleficence, and responsibility are nothing new. In fact, we see echoes of them in each of the above approaches to doing professional ethics holistically. This is due to the fact that our values are always around. It seems too simple, but consider this. Whenever we make moral decisions, we have all sorts of things going on. From the aforementioned, we saw that some of the things going on were situational or context related. Other things going on were not situational, but absolute, and they thereby have held, regardless of the situation. What a values approach to doing professional ethics allows us to do is to adopt the best parts of both absolutism and particularism. This unlikely combination, like oil and vinegar, is possible when we see that every time we approach a moral problem we are assuming that certain things are good—absolutely. In trying to bring about any sort of solution or outcome to our problem, we are implementing these goods. But when we implement the goods, and do so well, we do so with a great sensitivity to the context in which we are engaged. Thus we need both an absolute adherence to values, but also an aggressive sensitivity to the contexts and situations in which they will be implemented. How is this possible?

Perhaps we would be well served to take a close look at values and what is required in order for them to be usefully enacted. We have seen that certain goods, as things that we eventually have to appeal to, are behind both particularism and absolutism. What does this tell us about our moral situation? Eventually, our moral commitments come down to taking a stand on some issues. By taking a stand, we do not mean an unreflective posturing for any old thing. Instead, we are advocating that as individuals interested in actualizing a professional life, we turn to the guidelines given to us for professional life, and we see that they point us to certain values that are to be consistently upheld across all professions.

If we look at the guidelines for things that are typically recognized as professions, that is, if we analyze professional codes, certain themes emerge. These themes to a greater and lesser degree all hold something, or even various things, as valuable. These valued things are often in the background of our consideration of an issue, but they inform that consideration. For example, in requiring that their members have a sensitivity to issues that involve conflicts of interest, the *Statement from the Professional Standards and Ethics Committee* of the American Society for Public Administration demonstrates that *integrity* is important. That is, a professional code typically holds that a conflict of interest is not a good thing. The reason it is not a good thing is because we have an underlying commitment to persons that requires us to deal with them in a loyal, honest manner. This is integrity, insofar as we are remaining integrated in such a manner that we are not in conflict.[13]

The aforementioned is a pretty clear example of the way integrity is related to the practice of a profession. We can think of other clear examples quite easily. Consider the way in which the value *respect for persons* is made manifest. When we demand confidentiality as an integral part of the practice of a profession, as many professions like law and psychology do, confidentiality is important because we have a fundamental commitment to respect people. Part and parcel of this respect is maintaining the rights that we accord persons. But what about our other values? How does a value like compassion become enacted in a professional life? If we look at the *National Association of Social Workers Code of Ethics*, we see that there is a commitment to "promote the general welfare of society."[14] To determine what constitutes the general welfare of society, and to believe that such a thing should be promoted, a commitment to the value of compassion is assumed. An appreciation of the situation of others and attention to how it can be improved would be impossible without being compassionate.

Appreciating that we have a commitment to certain values that are enacted in our professional life is not so radical. Through these rubrics, which can provide the grounding for what a professional life requires, we are just supporting our ordinary understanding of what professional morality requires. Certainly an argument could be made that a commitment to these values is also a part of the living of a moral life outside of its occupational expression. In fact, such arguments have been made throughout the history of ethics.[15] Fortunately, for our purposes, we need not rehearse them all here. For now, it is enough to appreciate the way values work to anchor our professional actions which, in virtue of being classified as professional, already include a commitment to our six values; namely, integrity, respect for persons, justice, compassion, beneficence and nonmaleficence, and responsibility.

Where We Are and Where We Go from Here

Since we have an idea of what a values approach to professional ethics problem solving includes, now what? We seemingly are no closer to how to actually solve any kind of problem that we might run into in our professional life. Of course, just because we have recognized a practical and an efficient way to approach moral situations, our work is not over. If it were, this book would be a lot thinner. With the recognition of six fundamental values for living a professional life and arguably for living a moral life when not practicing a profession, we have a lot to do. We have stressed that values are the backdrop of any moral approach and its expression, but these values must be made concrete through action in our professional lives. This is possible through an interpretive structure which includes a moral framework that allows us to implement our values.

In the second half of this book, we will concentrate on each of these six values and give them some content so we can have a sophisticated understanding of what it is that a commitment to them requires. We will not do this in an abstract manner, but we will consider the way each value is expressed in the professions, its potential conflicts with other values, and some ways to deal with these conflicts. These six values are those things that our everyday professional (and even nonprofessional) lives are constantly appealing to for meaning. When we demand responsibility from our professionals, including ourselves, we do so because responsibility is a good thing. When we then offer reasons, we must ask why those reasons for responsibility being a good thing are good, and then we must ask why the next set of good reasons are good. Eventually, if we do not fall asleep, we see that at some point we have made a commitment to responsibility, basically just because it seems central to our moral selves and lives. Who we are is not absolute, but that we are certainly is. Our commitment to our values is contingently absolute. By absolute, we understand that the values that inform our experience and ground our commitments are the ground of our professional morality, and they are so absolutely. By contingent, we understand that the values that ground our actions absolutely only become meaningful through being understood in a particular context. Hence their meaning and significance is contingent on the arena in which they are enacted. That kind of qualified absolutism is defensible through an appeal to our situation and a pragmatic recognition of what is required to practice a profession. As we continue to appreciate and describe the implementation of these values in professional life, we will see that this contingent absolutism is more than enough for us to proceed.

With a commitment to integrity, respect for persons, justice, compassion, beneficence and nonmaleficence, and responsibility, we are not guaranteed moral behavior. But an underlying commitment to these values defines a moral professional and can lead to actions that uphold our values in such a manner that we actualize our professional potential.

Conclusion

In this chapter, we bridged the gap between the professions, discussed in chapter 1, and ethics, discussed in chapter 2. In doing so, we discussed how our professional morality relates to our general morality and how holism provides the framework for making our professional life actual. After considering various ways to approach making manifest our moral commitments, we settled on a values-based approach as that which undergirds the other two approaches, particularism and absolutism. Through understanding values as the underlying commitment that supports all of the work we want to do in professional morality, we will avoid the problems involved in a commitment to particularism or absolutism. Furthermore, through values, we now have a positive way to approach morality and the professional life.

EXERCISES

1. In this chapter, we have distinguished professional ethics from general ethics because of differences in audience, content, and method. Give an example of a way in which the following concerns are relevant to us generally and to a particular profession. That is, give an example of a way in which justice is a concern to everyone (general ethics) and then how justice is a concern in a particular profession by means of discussing justice relative to audience, content, and methodology (professional ethics).

    1. Integrity   4. Compassion
    2. Respect for persons 5. Beneficence and nonmaleficence
    3. Justice   6. Responsibility

2. Determine if you are a holist or a separatist for the following commonly understood moral goods. First, answer if you are a holist or a separatist. Next, give an example of how the value would be held to or violated in both your professional and personal life (holist), or give an example of how the value would not be held to or violated in both your professional and personal life (separatist).

1. **Truth telling**
2. **Loyalty**
3. **Generosity; material and/or nonmaterial**

3. Analyze the following cases to determine if you have a split between your professional and personal morality. That is, would you do things differently in your professional life than you would in your personal life?

CASE 1: RECYCLING AND THE OFFICE

Drucilla Rogers works at a software company in the product develop-ment department. She has been there for one year. Recently out of grad-uate school, Drucilla took some time in between beginning her corporate career and finishing her education to work for a nonprofit nuclear waste watchdog organization. She was deeply struck by the effect of nuclear waste and waste in general on the environment. Since that time, she has been active in promoting recycling in her community.

Drucilla was required to relocate for this job. She was surprised at the low level of recycling that was going on in the community to which she relocated. Since her arrival, Drucilla has encouraged the city plan-ners to promote recycling and areas for recyclables to be dropped off. Two weeks ago, the community held a major recycling drive, led by Dru-cilla, and it was a great success.

Drucilla's picture was in the paper for this, and several of her friends saved copies of the paper for her and commented on the picture, in which Drucilla was surrounded by garbage. She took all of the teasing good-naturedly, until her supervisor at work asked her about being involved with the recycling project. Drucilla responded, "I'm glad you asked me about it. I thought we could implement some of the same programs here. Nothing too major to begin with. Perhaps we could start with some paper recycling and bins for people's polystyrene, aluminum, and plastics."

Drucilla's supervisor looked uncomfortable. She then said, "Frank-ly, I need to speak with you about your work on this project. One of our major software contractors is the local waste hauling corporation. Every bit of recycling that is done in this town gives business to their com-petitors. Should they realize that you have been generating business for their competitors, they might pull their business away from us, and we need this account." As her supervisor continued, Drucilla felt miserable. "What you do on your own time is your business, but we can't have an overt move toward recycling in this office."

CASE 2: PERSONAL AND PROFESSIONAL

Harrison Thomas was one of the most promising new hires at an urban architectural firm. Only thirty-three, Harrison had been with the firm for one year and had distinguished himself right away. When he arrived at his new job, his supervisor, Martin Cambriole, was impressed by the accounts that followed him, unsolicited, from his prior job. Recently he had been chosen as one of the key architects for a major city project. Consequently, Harrison and several of his associates were being introduced and honored at a city dinner showcasing new projects.

Martin is often worried about Harrison's future with the firm. Six months ago, he invited several of the new younger associates and their spouses to his home for dinner. At that time, Harrison came into his office, sat down, and said, "Martin, I'd like to talk to you about your dinner party. I've thought about this very carefully, and I want you to know that I plan to bring my partner, Jason Langen." Although surprised, Martin continued without missing a beat. "Please feel free to bring whomever you like to my home." Although he was not close friends with any gay men, Martin's ex-wife's brother was gay, had often been to Martin and his ex-wife's home, and Martin was not uncomfortable with the issue.

In this most recent visit to his office, Harrison informed Martin that he planned to bring Jason to the city dinner. Although only a mid-sized operation, Martin's and Harrison's firm has a respectable client roster and the opportunity to secure more business through this new, high-profile project. Martin was aware that many potential clients and many of the area's most influential political and business leaders were expected to attend the upcoming dinner. All of this raced through Martin's mind as he asked Harrison, "Why do you want to do this? Why do you want to mix your personal and professional lives?"

CASE 3: CONFLICTS IN A SOCIAL WORKER'S SOCIAL CONSCIENCE

You are a licensed clinical social worker employed by a municipal government to, among other duties, supervise the admission and retention of clients in a long-term shelter for homeless families. The people who come to your facility usually have spent at least six weeks moving around among various overnight shelters or even living in the streets. Because low-priced rentals are extremely scarce in your area, when clients are given rooms in your building their average length of stay is fourteen months. Families of up to four persons are assigned single rooms. Larger families are given two rooms. Two-thirds of your residents are children under the age of fourteen.

According to local law and federal guidelines, preference for admission to your facility is to be given to single-parent families with young children. And because the demand for shelters is so great, all of the 200 families in your building are nominally headed by single females. But many of the frequent visitors to the facility, all of whom must *sign in with a guard at the entrance, are obviously the husbands of women and the fathers of children in residence. Most of these men live in the streets or in overnight shelters, working at unskilled jobs when they can find them, and contributing whatever they can to support their children.*

What, if anything, should you do about this situation? If you identify these men as being legally involved with your clients, many of the women and children will have to leave the shelter. But if you ignore the problem, you will be condoning illegal activity within your area of responsibility and run some risk of losing your job. What do you do? Analyze your response in terms of the absolutist approach.[16]

4. Analyze three professional codes of your choice. List three values that they all share. In arriving at these values, be sure to define them in such a way that would be compatible with all three codes. Are you coming up with any values left out of the primary six that have been presented here? If so, what are they and what do they add to the discussion?

NOTES

1. This inability to follow through on one's own desires is termed *akrasia* by Aristotle, and means weak willed. In virtue of our will not being able to keep us on the right track, it is weak.
2. See the section entitled "Client-Lawyer Relationship, Rule 1.6," in the *Model Rules of Professional Conduct*, © 1983 by the American Bar Association; see also "Principle 5: Confidentiality" in *Ethical Principles of Psychologists*, © 1981 by the American Psychological Association.
3. Consider some of the newly formed organizations for overseeing various professional practices, such as the Occupational Safety and Hazard Agency (OSHA), which monitors hazardous materials to which we can become exposed at work, from asbestos to nuclear waste. Several agencies also exist for accreditation of various institutions, from hospitals and universities to those that license and inspect tattoo parlors.
4. From child labor laws and strict procedures governing the use of human subjects in research to the "V-Chip" to monitor the controversial things that are shown on television, often there has been government regulation of the ethical aspects of professions. Specialized ethics courses and training help professionals meet these relevant criteria.
5. Tom L. Beauchamp and James F. Childress, for example, distinguish general normative ethics from applied normative ethics by claiming that in the latter, while we are not dealing with an independent field, we are applying general moral principles to a specific area of human activity (*Principles of Biomedical Ethics, 2nd ed.*, New York: Oxford University Press, 1983, 8–9). They also note that general moral codes apply to everyone, while professional moral codes include derivative moral rules that apply to a particular group of persons

(ibid., 9–10). We might challenge their claims that professional ethics is not an independent field or that its codes are derivative. Yet they recognize, in distinguishing general from professional ethics, both "content" and "audience" differences. Deborah G. Johnson, on the other hand, answers the question of why professional ethics is "special" (different from general ethical theory) by pointing to what distinguishes professionals from moral agents in general. She also notes the "audience" difference between the two fields (*Computer Ethics, 2nd ed.*, Englewood Cliffs, N.J.: Prentice Hall, 1994, 39–41).

6. Other texts and approaches refer to this approach in any number of ways. Most often, what is referred to here as separatism is referred to as role morality, when moral frameworks are contingent upon the roles being undertaken.

7. This is a gloss on the role morality of Michael Bayles. See Bayles, *Professional Ethics*, (Belmont, Calif.: Wadsworth Publishing Company, 1981), chapter 2, for a more detailed and nuanced discussion of role morality.

8. Even though case-based reasoning (or casuistry) is particularly popular now, especially in bioethics, its heyday was in the seventeenth century, and there it met with some controversy. One of the most famous polemics against casuistry was written by Pascal, which has permanently given casuistry something of a tainted moral status. Regardless of Pascal's abuse and the Jesuits' misuse, case analysis is enjoying a new resurgence in popularity, both in the classroom and in the clinic, formally and informally.

9. For a more detailed and infinitely more nuanced discussion of case analysis, see Albert R. Jonsen and Stephen Toulmin, *The Abuse of Casuistry* (Berkeley, Calif.: University of California Press, 1988).

10. These criticisms of case analysis are discussed clearly by John D. Arras. See his article, "The Revival of Casuistry in Bioethics," *The Journal of Medicine and Philosophy*, 16 (1991), 29–51.

11. For the most famous and well-articulated instance of principled absolutism, see Beauchamp and Childress, *Principles of Biomedical Ethics* (New York: Oxford University Press, 1979, 1983, 1989, 1994).

12. This criticism of absolutism is discussed quite well by Soran Reader. See his article, "Principle Ethics, Particularism and Another Possibility," *Philosophy* 72 (1997), 269–291.

13. This example is pulled from a statement edited by Herman Mertins Jr., and Patrick J. Hennigan in the *Professional Standards and Ethics Committee, American Society for Public Administration*, © 1982 by the American Society for Public Administration.

14. This example is from Section VI of the National Association of Social Workers, Inc. *Code of Ethics of the National Association of Social Workers*, as adopted by the 1979 *NASW Delegate Assembly*, effective July 1, 1980.

15. Many examples of virtue or value theorists are a part of the philosophy canon. From Aristotle to MacIntyre, there have always been proponents of values as a way to proceed in our moral commitments.

16. Case adapted from Peter Y. Windt, Peter C. Appleby, et al., *Ethical Issues in the Professions* (Englewood Cliffs, N.J.: Prentice Hall, 1989), 346.

4

Moral Reasons and Explanations

In this chapter, we expand our account of the language of morality in order to improve our understanding of what moral thinking is and to sharpen our ability to do and to evaluate moral thinking. We need to be able to identify and describe moral thinking, and we need to be able to do and assess moral thinking in order to be moral professionals. Our goal is not only to recognize moral thinking when we see it but to do moral thinking, and to do it well.

We already know some things about moral thinking from the first three chapters. We know that it is prescriptive moral thinking that enables us to make judgments about what should or should not be done. We know that the approach of holism effectively allows us to connect our personal and professional lives. We have also seen that values are at the heart of moral action and moral decision making, because to make a moral decision we must know what we are committed to or what is valuable to us. Now, in this chapter, we will see that several more moral tools are necessary for us to be able to use values to arrive at concrete "shoulds" and "oughts."

What are these tools that make possible prescriptive moral thinking and the expression of values in the world? When we make or defend a decision or judge a decision someone else has made, we necessarily give reasons. We choose a course of action or make a judgment, and we offer an explanation for why we did so. For now, we will begin by figuring out what reasons and explanations are and then finish by discovering how to evaluate moral reasons and explanations. Along the way, we also will learn to recognize moral dilemmas, the thorniest of moral problems, in which we must choose between various moral reasons or explanations, and hence in which we cannot act on all of the moral reasons or explanations at hand. In chapter 5, we will develop more specific names for the parts of a moral explanation, but for now it is enough to learn to identify moral reasons and explanations and to evaluate them.

Reasons and Explanations

Most of us do not think too much about what reasons and explanations are. Yet, in the course of a typical day, we both give and listen to all kinds of reasons and explanations. The teacher hears that the student's homework is not turned in because the dog ate it. The boss hears that his employee is not coming to work today since it is a religious holiday. The mother tells her child that he cannot watch any more TV and when he asks why she answers, "Because I said so!" In all of these cases, explanations are given and reasons are offered. We use reasons and explanations to make our own decisions, and we discover the reasons and explanations of others by listening to what they say about their decisions. But not all reasons and explanations are strong, and not all are moral. Leaving aside questions of strength and morality for the moment, let us consider what reasons and explanations are.

A reason is an "explainer"; it is given in order to explain something. The dictionary defines a reason as "the basis or motive for an action, decision, or conviction; a declaration made to explain or justify an action, decision, or conviction."[1] A reason explains how something came to be or came to happen. A reason may describe a cause or it may refer to a motivation. A reason is something that contributes to the making or defending of a decision. Reasons can be stated independently of the actions or decisions they explain. "I said so!" is a reason that could be used to justify any number of actions and decisions. So, by itself, a reason, though it is an explainer, is not necessarily tied to any particular thing being explained. Reasons are transferable; they can be used in many different contexts, even at the same time.

Now, when a reason is used to explain a particular decision or action, it then becomes part of something larger than itself, namely, an explanation. The dictionary says that an explanation is "that which serves to explain or to account for something."[2] An explanation occurs when a reason or many reasons are used to explain something. An explanation is the sum of all the reasons offered for some decision and, in it, reasons are not just hypothetical explainers that could be used to explain any decision. They are actual explainers used to explain some particular decision. In other words, with an explanation, we have the whole picture. We have all of the reasons that are directed toward justifying a decision. The following schemes show how reasons can work:

1.   Reason   Reason

                     Reason   Reason

       Reason

2.   Explanation

              Reason + Reason ...   ⟶   Decision

In the first scheme, reasons are hypothetical explainers; they are not yet used to explain something, thus there is no explanation. So far, reasons are merely free-floating, since they are not yet being used to justify anything. Potentially, these reasons can be used to justify many different decisions.

In the second scheme, reasons are used to explain a decision, thus there is an explanation. Reasons are now connected to a decision and serve as its justification. We might further illustrate the nature of reasons and explanations by using a linguistic analogy. A reason is like a word, on its own meaningful, but not particularly interesting. Yet words can come together and be used to make up different sentences that communicate many different messages. Likewise, a reason can be used in many different contexts and can be used to support many different decisions. An explanation is like a sentence. A sentence is a collection of words used to communicate a particular message, and an explanation is a collection of reasons (or sometimes only one reason) aimed at justifying a particular decision.

Often there are certain key words that help us identify that there is an explanation being given. A reason is frequently preceded by the words "since," "because," or "for." The decision or course of action may be preceded by "thus," "therefore," or "hence." In an explanation you might find one or more of these key words, or you might not. For instance, consider these explanations:

I became a social worker since I want to help people live better lives.
I want to help people live better lives, hence, I became a social worker.
It was because I want to help people live better lives that I became a social worker.
Wanting to help people live better lives, I became a social worker.

In these examples, the course of action is "I became a social worker," and the reason is "I want to help people live better lives." These sentences are explanations because a reason is used to justify a certain course of action. An explanation can include one reason or many reasons, depending on how much evidence is given to back up a decision. Consequently, an explanation can take place in one sentence or may require many sentences. Sometimes explanations are difficult to recognize because the decision may be only implied or the reasons may be only hinted at. As we go on to analyze and evaluate explanations, we will have to judge how well an explanation works, but for now it is enough to know what reasons and explanations are.

Moral Reasons

Now, for the sake of moral thinking, we must turn our attention to a particular kind of reason, namely, a moral reason. A moral reason must satisfy certain criteria in order to qualify as such. In this way, we are distinguishing moral reasons from nonmoral reasons. If a reason fails to satisfy any of the criteria of a moral reason, then it is not a moral reason. Nonmoral reasons still count for something; they are not worthless. In many areas of life, we are content with giving nonmoral reasons, like when a parent says, "I said so!" But in the realm of professional morality, moral reasons are what we are after and only moral reasons contribute to the defense of a decision or course of action.

Let us look at what comprises a moral reason.

A Moral Reason

- is universalizable—not contingent.
- is thoughtful and reflective—not based on natural instincts, gut feelings, outside pressures, or the desires of authority figures.
- expresses concern for others—not selfishness.
- expresses a moral value—not an economic, a legal, or a social value.

Remember that a reason must meet all four of these criteria in order to count as a moral reason. As the above suggests, sometimes it is easier to recognize or define a moral reason in terms of what it is not than in terms of what it is. Even so, let us explain each of the four criteria in turn before looking at some examples.

First, a moral reason is universalizable, that is, it is not unique to a particular person or applicable to only one specific situation, but applies generally. In a sense, a moral reason sets a policy for persons in similar situations. As we saw in chapter 2, universalizability is one of the properties of prescriptive ethics, thus it is not surprising that universalizability must be evident in any reason that is to count as a moral reason.

Second, a moral reason is thoughtful and reflective. A reason is not moral if it is based on natural instincts or on a gut feeling or if it appeals simply to the authority, opinion, or desires of another. A moral reason needs to be the product of a person's own thinking. Certainly we are influenced by our instincts, gut feelings, and the opinions of others. These instincts, feelings, collected opinions, and influences are important to who we are and the way we live. But moral thinking requires more than simply acting on feeling or instinct, because there is nothing especially moral about feelings and instincts.[3] Cats and dogs have feelings and instincts but they cannot give moral reasons. A moral reason reveals the thoughtful, reflective views of the person putting forth the reason. Furthermore, it is not enough to express someone else's thoughtful, reflective views. Giving a moral reason requires that we make a commitment and that we decide for ourselves how much the opinions or authority of others ought to count, and then that we give our own moral reasons, having taken these things into account. We can decide to agree with the opinion of another, but in doing so we are agreeing with the opinion and thus committing to the same view.

Third, a moral reason shows concern for others. It cannot be simply selfish. Of course, survival, self-preservation, and self-interest also count in the realm of prescriptive ethics, just like the opinions of others. Self-interest is of value to persons. It is a universalizable value in that each of us is interested in our own self-interest. However, a moral reason requires that more than self-interest be taken into account. Self-interest is not the only value, and it is not necessarily always the highest value to individual persons. Witness the religious martyrs who gave up their lives rather than deny their faith, or the Red Cross workers who in World War II risked their lives to give aid to those who were suffering. For these people, self-interest was not the highest value. A moral reason must acknowledge the interests and well-being of others. A reason that does not consider the interests of others is not a moral reason. A reason that reveals concern for self as well as concern for others is still a moral reason. As long as others are considered, it is acceptable to consider self-interest as well.

Fourth, a moral reason expresses a moral value. It identifies something as being morally valuable, worth doing or having. It urges that some action be taken or some decision be reached in order to bring about or take into account what is morally valuable, and not what is legally, economically, or religiously valuable. A moral reason points to a moral value, like justice, integrity, and so on, as that which should be upheld. We said in chapter 3 that moral values are what ground moral actions and decisions. Hence, a moral reason must be grounded in one of the six values: integrity, respect for persons, justice, compassion, beneficence and nonmaleficence, and responsibility.

Now that we have described the four criteria for a moral reason, let us look at some examples of reasons. Our aim in providing these examples is to give you a chance to test your ability to identify moral reasons. There will be other such chances in the examples and cases to come, but for now, consider which of the following reasons are moral reasons, and which are not, and why.

We start with a situation.[4] Suppose you are on a hospital ethics committee that is discussing the fate of Baby Joe, an abandoned newborn who has Down's syndrome and an intestinal blockage. If surgery is performed, he will live; if not, he will die. Those at the ethics committee meeting all argue for the same decision. They all believe that the surgery should be done. Their decision is: *Do the surgery on Baby Joe.* Everyone at the meeting also offers an explanation for why the surgery should be done, and each explanation contains one or many reasons. In listening to the committee members' explanations, you discover that there are four separate reasons at work. Some committee members appeal to one of the reasons; others appeal to several of the reasons. You also judge that some of the four reasons are moral reasons, while others are not. The four reasons follow. Which of them are moral?

1. Not to treat him would be against the law.
2. We have treated babies with similar problems in the past, and it would not be fair to not treat Baby Joe.
3. He has a good chance at having a reasonably good quality of life, so death is not in his best interest.
4. We want to continue to have a good reputation in the community, which we will need in order to raise funds for a new addition to the hospital, and the community would not look favorably on a decision not to treat.

If you said reasons 2 and 3 are moral reasons, you are correct. Reasons 1 and 4 are not moral reasons. Let us briefly consider why each reason is or is not moral.

Reason 1 is not moral even though it is universalizable, since it can apply to more than Baby Joe's case, and even though it shows concern for others, since something beyond the committee's self-interest is valued. The problem with it is that it expresses only a legal value, namely, a concern for upholding the law, and not a moral value. Also, the reason is not thoughtful and reflective. Instead, it appeals to a law, to an authority outside of the committee members as justification for the decision. As it is, the reason that results from this appeal does not count as a moral reason because it does not show the thinking and reflective judgment of the committee.

Reason 2 is moral because it meets the four criteria. It is universalizable in that it can apply to others in similar circumstances. It is thoughtful and reflective, since it reveals the thinking of the committee and not feelings, instincts, or the opinions of others. The reason acknowledges and considers the interests of others, since it is looking beyond the interests of the committee and it expresses a moral value, namely, justice.

Reason 3 also is moral. It too is universalizable, since it can be applied to all babies who have a good chance of having a reasonably good quality of life. It is thoughtful in that it is based not on feelings, instincts, or the opinions of others, but on the committee's own careful views. Reason 3 shows concern for another, namely, Baby Joe. Finally, the reason is grounded in a moral value, namely, beneficence and nonmaleficence.

Last, reason 4 is not moral, although it meets most of the criteria. It is universalizable, thoughtful, and reflective. It might even be argued that the reason expresses a moral value, integrity, or beneficence and nonmaleficence. But the reason is not moral because it is exclusively selfish and it does not acknowledge or consider the interests of others. It reflects only the self-interest of the committee in worrying about the public's perception of the action the committee takes and its effect on fund-raising. As it is, the reason is not moral.

Quite possibly, reason 4 could be developed into a moral one. We could show that the addition to the hospital is necessary in order to meet the health care needs of the community, and thus to further beneficence and nonmaleficence. In this way, the whole community has a stake in the public perception of the hospital and its practices. Under this interpretation, it is not just the committee's or the hospital's reputation that is central to this reason, but rather the good of the community. Harm is avoided and good is done to many when the hospital can raise the money it needs to build more facilities to serve the public. Hence, the hospital's reputation or its standing in the community may not be just a matter of self-interest but a matter of interest to the whole community, since it affects the kind of care the public will receive, the willingness of other medical professionals to work with hospital staff, and the willingness of bankers and the public to fund the hospital's expansion. According to this interpretation, if we develop and add to reason 4, it could be a moral one.

Thus a reason counts as moral only if it satisfies the four criteria just discussed. Nonmoral reasons are a part of life and can play a role in decision making, but not in *moral* decision making.

Moral Explanations

We have seen that moral decision making involves giving moral reasons in support of some decision or action. We first identified what a moral reason is, and now we will consider moral explanations. With what we have already said about reasons and explanations, our task is considerably simplified. We recognized early on that an explanation is just a collection of reasons offered in defense of a decision. So, where the reasons at stake in an explanation are moral reasons, we have a moral explanation, and where the reasons at stake in an explanation are not moral, we do not have a moral explanation. Moral explanations can include nonmoral as well as moral reasons. If some or at least one of the reasons in an explanation is moral, then we still have a moral explanation by disregarding the reasons that are not moral. In sum, a moral explanation occurs when at least one of the reasons offered to explain or justify a decision is a moral one.

Consider this example. Let us suppose that Fred is a manager who decides to lay off one of the members of his department. He might have decided on this course of action because he promised upper management that he would increase profits by paring down his overstaffed department, and he believes in keeping his promises. This is a moral explanation, because it includes a moral reason for a decision. Fred's reason is universalizable, thoughtful, not selfish, and expresses the values of integrity and beneficence. Or, Fred might have decided to lay off the employee because he caught her submitting fraudulent expense account reports, and he expects his employees to be honest. Here again, the explanation is a moral one, since it contains a moral reason. The reason is universalizable, reflective, not selfish, and expresses the values of integrity and justice. Or, to consider one more possibility, Fred may be letting his employee go because he never really liked her to begin with. It should be obvious by now that this is not a moral explanation, because the reason contained in it is not a moral one. The reason Fred is giving—"I never really liked her"—is based on an unreflective emotional reaction, thus it is not a moral reason. Plus, in order to be a moral reason, it would have to express a moral value, and this reason does not. So, since Fred's reason is not moral, his explanation cannot be a moral explanation.

Thus it is easy to identify a moral explanation. No new set of criteria besides what is in place for moral reasons needs to be introduced. If you can recognize an explanation and a moral reason, then you can judge whether an explanation counts as a moral explanation. Note that we are not yet evaluating moral explanations, we are only identifying them. We are not in a position to judge whether moral explanations are weak or strong. All we are claiming is that a moral explanation is one that includes at least one moral reason, while an explanation that has no moral reasons is not a moral explanation. Before we begin to consider how to evaluate moral explanations, we will look at situations where not all of the moral explanations can be acted on. We have learned how to identify moral reasons and explanations, and now we will look at what happens when moral reasons and explanations lead to incompatible decisions. Finally, we will consider how to assess moral reasons and explanations.

Moral Dilemmas

In some situations, all of the reasons point toward the same course of action. In the example of the hospital committee and Baby Joe, all of the reasons supported performing the surgery. But there are other situations in which the reasons lead to different decisions, thus in trying to decide what to do, a person is forced to choose among the reasons. In Baby Joe's case, there could have been some reasons that justified doing the surgery and other reasons that favored not doing the surgery. In deciding which action to perform and which decision to make, a committee member would then be confronted with reasons that lead to incompatible choices. This is called a dilemma, and it is because decision making requires us to resolve and, if possible, to avoid dilemmas that we need a way to deal with the reasons that lead to competing decisions in a dilemma. We will begin by defining dilemmas and moral dilemmas, and then we will learn how to resolve all kinds of dilemmas.

A dilemma is a fairly broad term that refers to any particularly perplexing situation or problem. It also can refer to a situation in which a person has to choose between two equally balanced alternatives.[5] The word comes from the Greek "di," or "two," and "lemma," or "assumption or proposition." In a dilemma, a person is faced with two assumptions or beliefs or reasons for acting, which lead to two opposite courses of action. These two assumptions make it hard to decide what to do. In a dilemma, a person is torn between doing one thing or another because there are persuasive reasons to do both, but doing both is impossible. For instance, you face a dilemma when you have to decide whether to work late to finish the project you said you would have done, or to go to a party because you enjoy parties and would have fun. If you cannot both work late and go to the party at the same time, these are two incompatible courses of action, although both are backed up by reasons. Building on our earlier scheme, a dilemma looks like the following:

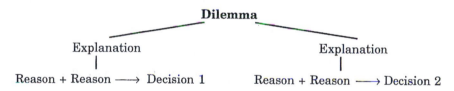

A dilemma, like the above, may be a real dilemma for someone but, from the point of view of morality, it is not a difficult dilemma because it is not a *moral* one. In the above dilemma, the worker has two explanations for action that lead to opposite courses of action. The reason in one explanation—"to finish the project you said you would have done"—is a moral reason. It is universalizable, thoughtful, not based exclusively on self-interest, and expresses a moral value, integrity, or responsibility. The reason and the explanation are moral. The reason in the other explanation—"you enjoy parties and would have fun"—is not a moral reason because it does not acknowledge or consider the interests of others, and it does not express a moral value. This reason and explanation are not moral. In this dilemma, there are not two *moral* explanations leading to incompatible decisions, hence a *moral* professional will know right away that it is morally right to act on the moral explanation and hence to finish the project. This dilemma is easy to resolve because there is only one *moral* choice, namely, that backed up by a moral explanation.

Moral dilemmas are more difficult to deal with than other types of dilemmas because the decision maker is faced with choosing between two alternatives, both of which are backed up by moral reasons (and thus moral explanations) and both of which cannot be done.[6] It is a kind of moral, no-win situation. Whatever choice is made in a moral dilemma, and a choice must be made, some of the moral reasons will be acted on, but others will be ignored. One course of action will be pursued, and one will be left behind. Moral dilemmas force moral decision makers to choose between incompatible alternatives and, in doing so, to choose between moral explanations. Thus, a moral dilemma looks like the following:

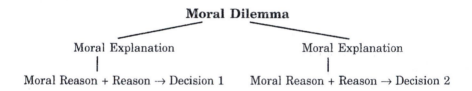

Moral Dilemma

Moral Explanation   Moral Explanation

Moral Reason + Reason → Decision 1   Moral Reason + Reason → Decision 2

Luckily, true moral dilemmas are rare. False moral dilemmas, however, are very common. Usually what seems at first glance to be a moral dilemma on further reflection turns out not to be. Sometimes what we thought was a moral dilemma is only a dilemma, since there are not in both instances moral explanations between which we must choose. And sometimes what we took to be a moral dilemma because it had two opposite alternatives both backed up by moral explanations is not a real moral dilemma, because it can be creatively solved in a way that does justice to both moral explanations and outcomes. That is, often it is possible to find a way to resolve what is taken to be a moral dilemma. Maybe there is a third alternative that is supported by both moral explanations. Maybe there is a way to creatively and imaginatively connect the opposite alternatives, or to act on one first and then the other. The point is that we should not give up hope when we come across what seems to be a moral dilemma. Many so-called moral dilemmas can be thoughtfully reconciled in a way that somehow acknowledges and takes into account all of the moral reasons.

The classic example of a moral dilemma is presented by Jean-Paul Sartre. He relates the story of a boy who came to him for advice.[7]

> *The boy had an older brother who was killed in the 1940 German invasion of France. His father, who tended to be a collaborator with the Nazi occupiers, was on bad terms with his mother. His mother lived alone with the boy and lived only for him. The boy was faced with the choice of leaving for England and joining the Free French Forces to avenge the death of his brother and to work for the well-being of the French community or staying with his mother and helping her to carry on.*

The boy has two choices; he can go or he can stay. He cannot do both. Each course of action is supported by a moral reason or a moral explanation. If he goes, he aims to realize justice, beneficence, and nonmaleficence toward the community. His action is universalizable, thoughtful, not selfish, and it expresses a moral value. Similarly, if he stays, he does so out of respect for persons, compassion, and beneficence and nonmaleficence to an individual. Again, his action is universalizable, thoughtful, not selfish, and it expresses a moral value. This is a *moral* dilemma, and not just a dilemma, because the boy faces two incompatible alternatives, both of which are supported by moral reasons. In short, there are two moral explanations leading up to two opposite courses of action, between which a decision must be made.

But let us think more carefully about this moral dilemma. Is it a true moral dilemma where the alternatives are irreconcilable, and so an either–or choice between the moral explanations is necessary? Maybe it is possible to find a creative solution to this moral dilemma or a way of avoiding it.[8] Granted, the boy cannot both go and stay at the same time. But he could perhaps stay for a bit, while he prepares his mother to cope with his going, or he could stay and find a way to work at home for justice and beneficence and nonmaleficence toward the community. The moral explanations at stake in this moral dilemma are not themselves mutually exclusive; only the actions which bring them about are. Looking for creative solutions helps us as we try to find ways to resolve what appear to be moral dilemmas.

Consider next the dilemma of a TV anchor and journalist. Let us determine whether it is a moral dilemma.[9]

A new manager, with a national reputation as an innovator in tabloid television news, is hired by an NBC-affiliate TV station. The new manager hires Jerry Springer, a talk-show host, to deliver nightly news commentaries. Springer is hired to create more interest in the news, and the manager insists that what Springer does on his talk show (tawdry topics and ambushing guests with shocking news) is not relevant to his credibility as a news broadcaster.

Carol Marin, long-time news anchor and award-winning journalist at the station, objects to the hiring of Springer. She believes that news journalism requires credibility and that Springer has forfeited his credibility. Hiring Springer, she claims, undermines what she and the news station do and is disrespectful to news staff and viewers alike. But Marin has a contract with the station. What should she do?

Carol Marin certainly faces a dilemma here, if not a moral dilemma. There is a conflict, and Marin is unhappy and finds herself in a difficult position. But is this a moral dilemma? We know that for it to be a moral dilemma, Marin would have to be faced with two incompatible choices, both backed up by moral explanations that include moral reasons. Let us analyze Marin's choices and explanations in order to decide whether her dilemma counts as a moral one.

Looking first at Marin's alternatives, perhaps it is not clear what her two incompatible choices are. Look at the situation more closely. Marin objects to Springer's hiring, but she has a contract. Is the conflict over whether to make known her objections to Springer? Or is her dilemma about how to make her objections known, or to whom she should relay her objections? Since her contract with the station is mentioned, we will view her two incompatible alternatives as quitting her job or not quitting her job. Now, given these incompatible decisions—to quit or not to quit—we need to consider the nature of the explanations offered in support of the decisions in order to determine whether we have a moral dilemma. Are there or are there not *moral* explanations that back up each alternative?

On the one side, Marin's alternative is to quit her job. For this decision, she gives a moral explanation. She claims that hiring Springer is disrespectful to her and to viewers, it undermines the credibility of the news team, and it is inconsistent with what she and the news station do. This explanation includes several reasons. If we apply the criteria for moral reasons to these reasons, we discover that they are moral reasons. The reasons, and hence, the explanation, are universalizable, thoughtful, and acknowledge and consider the interests of others. These reasons, and thus the explanation, also exhibit moral values, such as respect for persons, and integrity. On this side then, in favor of quitting her job, there is a moral explanation.

On the other side, Marin's option is to not quit her job. In support of this decision, the case reports that "Marin has a contract with the station." It is possible that there is a moral explanation lurking behind this statement. Marin may believe that she has a responsibility to the station and to her agent and to herself to fulfill her contract. She may view the contract as a sort of promise and may feel that her integrity can be upheld only if she abides by the contract. If this is her view, then Marin's explanation for not quitting is moral. It includes reasons that are universalizable, thoughtful, unselfish, and that express moral values such as responsibility and integrity. But it may be that Marin's only explanation for not quitting is a legal one, namely, that she is legally bound to work for the station. In this case, her explanation is not moral because her reason is not moral. She is not presenting a reason that expresses moral values, rather she is only following the authority of the law because it is the law. On this account, Marin does not have a moral explanation in favor of not quitting.

Thus there is this uncertainty about Marin's explanations. We cannot say for sure that she has moral explanations to support both of her incompatible choices. If she did have a moral explanation to justify quitting and another to justify not quitting, then this would be a moral dilemma. But, as it is, since we cannot determine what lies behind her concern for her contract with the station, we do not positively have two moral explanations at stake, thus we do not have a moral dilemma.

We might also look at whether the station's senior management faces a moral dilemma. They are in the middle of a conflict between two of their employees, both of whom, they seem to think, are valuable to the station. They have an award-winning, long-time employee who is objecting to a decision made by the new manager they hired. They also have a new manager hired precisely to make some innovative changes to the programming. Should they support their award-winning anchor and override the new manager's decision to hire Springer and risk having the new manager quit, or should they support their new manager's decision and overrule the anchor's objections and risk having the anchor quit? There are moral explanations that could be given to support both alternatives. On the one hand, by letting Springer go, they express respect for persons and beneficence and nonmaleficence, especially to Carol Marin and maybe to the public as well. They respect Carol Marin by honoring her judgment of what is appropriate and responsible news broadcasting. Carol Marin benefits by not losing her job and by having her experience and seniority valued. Even the public may benefit if Marin is correct, in that the old style of news reporting is the best. On the other hand, by keeping Springer, they also show respect for persons and beneficence and nonmaleficence, especially to the new manager and maybe to the public here as well. The new manager's decisions are upheld, and his rights as a manager to hire new staff and propose changes are respected. Springer is respected by not being fired before he has had a chance to prove himself. The new manager benefits by not having his authority undermined by senior management, and the public may benefit from a redesigned news format and news commentators with new skills.

The following happened in the Carol Marin case:[10]

> Carol Marin first tried to talk management out of hiring Springer. When that didn't work, her lawyer began talks with senior management to get her out of her contract. Finally, with Springer due to start work, she was allowed to resign. She stated, "I don't want anyone to think this is me abandoning the profession. It's me embracing the profession. It's me explaining the profession. I tell journalism students, 'If you're gonna come into this business you have to be prepared to leave where you are if you feel it's a matter of principle.'"

We concluded that in Carol Marin's case, it is not clear that she faced a *moral* dilemma. A dilemma, yes; a *moral* dilemma, maybe. And even then, this may not have been a true intractable dilemma. The solution Carol Marin reached is evidence of our creative solution approach to moral dilemmas. She did not simply view her situation as one in which she had to choose between quitting or not quitting her job. She recognized that there were other alternatives, alternatives that might allow her to keep her job, yet realize the moral explanations and moral values at stake in the other alternative (the respect for persons and integrity realized by quitting her job). Hence, she took steps to bring about these creative solutions. First she tried to convince senior management not to hire Springer. Had this worked, she would have kept her integrity, her contract, and her job. When that failed, she worked to get senior management to release her from her contract. This solution worked, and she was released from her contract and was able to maintain her integrity and respect for persons, though she lost her job. From her statement, it is clear that the main issue for Marin was the matter of professionalism and the values it includes. As she saw it, she could not have realized her values and kept her job. The conflict forced Carol Marin to choose between two actions—give up her job or not give up her job—but she found a way to express her moral values and still keep to the legal constraints of her contract, which at first seemed impossible. Thus, although Carol Marin's situation is not yet a moral dilemma unless she recognized a moral reason to uphold her contract, it does help us learn how to recognize moral dilemmas and how to begin to resolve them.

Evaluating Moral Reasons and Moral Explanations

So far in this chapter, we have focused on the task of identification. We have considered how to identify a moral reason, a moral explanation, and a moral dilemma. Moral decision making, we have shown, involves giving a moral explanation, that is, giving reasons for having reached some decision or taken some action. We have seen that moral situations often but not always involve a moral dilemma, namely, a choice between alternatives backed up by moral explanations, hence, by moral reasons. Now we turn to a much harder task, that of evaluation. Evaluating a moral reason or a moral explanation means judging how strong the reason or explanation is, and this requires that we distinguish between strong and weak moral reasons and explanations.

You might be wondering why this second task is necessary. Why is our job not over, now that we can recognize moral reasons, moral explanations, and moral dilemmas? The answer is a simple one if we think about it for a minute. If we take a look at our moral experience, we discover that not all moral reasons and explanations are equally good. Some moral reasons and explanations are better; some are worse. Even if a person gives a moral reason for acting a certain way, there may be stronger moral reasons to support not acting that way or to support acting in a completely different way. It also happens that one person's moral explanation for reaching a certain decision may be better than another person's, even though both persons made the same decision. In moral dilemmas, we are forced to compare moral explanations and to assess which moral explanation is stronger or overriding in a particular situation. Hence, to resolve moral dilemmas and to facilitate the assessing of moral explanations, we must find some way of evaluating which moral reasons and explanations are strong and which are weak. It is this way of assessing moral reasons and explanations that we will develop here.

In the early sections of this chapter, we discussed moral reasons first, and then we turned to moral explanations. Now we will follow the same format. Since a moral explanation is simply the collection of moral reasons given for a decision, it is obvious that there is a close relationship between moral reasons and explanations. It seems likely that the strength of a moral explanation will be affected and quite possibly determined by the strength of its moral reasons. For instance, it appears unlikely that you could give a strong moral explanation if your moral reasons are weak. Yet, in spite of this connection between moral reasons and explanations, it will not always be easy to move from reasons to explanation. In what follows, we will consider more carefully the relationship between moral reasons and explanations, but we will start by treating them separately.

Consider first moral reasons. Moral reasons are better or stronger insofar as they more effectively support a decision. They support a decision better when they are focused. That is, the main property of a strong moral reason is that it is focused squarely on the problems, persons, and values involved in the decision being made. A moral reason is stronger when it is more focused on the variables involved in the decision, and it is weaker when it is less focused on these variables. We evaluate moral reasons in the following way:

Strong Moral Reasons	**Weak Moral Reasons**
1. Are relevant to the decision made.	1. Are irrelevant to or only vaguely relate to the decision made.
2. Take account of the person or persons most affected by the decision.	2. Are indifferent to the person or persons most affected by the decision.
3. Consider the values most central to the situation rather than the less central values.	3. Consider the values less central to the situation and thereby fail to act on central values.

So a strong moral reason is a focused moral reason. It is relevant to the decision made in that it in fact justifies the decision and is not simply extraneous or incidental. It considers the relevant persons affected by the decision and not simply those far removed from the situation. Finally, it focuses on the values of central importance in the situation and not on values that are remote or peripheral. A moral reason is stronger to the extent that it satisfies more of the characteristics of a strong moral reason. A moral reason becomes progressively weaker as it fails to satisfy each of the characteristics of a strong moral reason.

Now that we have seen how to distinguish strong from weak moral reasons, let us move on to evaluating moral explanations. Moral reasons, we have said, must be focused in order to be strong reasons. But does a collection of focused, that is, strong, moral reasons make a strong moral explanation? The answer is, not necessarily. It would be great if strong moral reasons made a moral explanation strong, because our work would be simpler. But this easy way of evaluating moral explanations, which would make their strength dependent entirely on the strength of their moral reasons, will not hold up. In order to see why strong moral reasons do not necessarily add up to a strong moral explanation, we need to return to a consideration of the relationship between moral reasons and explanations.

Remember that moral explanations are the sum of all of their moral reasons. Explanations are wholes of which reasons are parts. And as the old cliche goes, "The whole is greater than the sum of its parts." Now what does this mean for evaluating moral reasons and explanations? It means that sometimes, even if the moral reasons are strong, that may not be enough to make the moral explanation strong. What we need in a moral explanation is something more than we require in a moral reason, but it can only come from moral reasons, since a moral explanation is just a collection of moral reasons. One strong moral reason can motivate us to act, but by itself probably does not provide a strong moral explanation. To put it another way, a moral explanation may be weak, not only when all of its moral reasons are weak, but even when some of its moral reasons are strong.

What we need in a strong moral explanation besides a strong moral reason is comprehensiveness. A strong moral explanation must not only be focused, due to its moral reasons, but it must also be comprehensive. This means that a better moral explanation will comprehensively consider all of the perspectives that help us apply values in the situation, all of the persons affected by the decision, and all of the values at issue in the situation. In other words, a strong moral explanation is probably bigger than a single or even a few strong moral reasons, because it must exhibit a comprehensiveness that usually is not found in one or even a few strong moral reasons. We evaluate moral explanations by judging whether they are comprehensive, that is, by judging whether their reasons are not only focused but, when taken together, also are comprehensive. We evaluate moral explanations in the following way:

Strong Moral Explanations	**Weak Moral Explanations**
A. Use several perspectives to interpret and apply values (e.g., may consider consequences, motives, rights, virtues, relationships, and life stories).	A. Focus single-mindedly on one perspective to interpret and apply values (e.g., may consider only consequences and ignore motives, rights, virtues, relationships, and life stories).
B. Take into account all persons affected by the decision.	B. Are indifferent to some of the persons affected by the decision.
C. Consider more values rather than fewer values.	C. Consider at least one value, but in doing so ignore other values.

Thus a strong moral explanation has at least one strong moral reason, and it is comprehensive. A weak moral explanation has only weak moral reasons or, even if it has one or more strong moral reasons, it is not comprehensive. To satisfy the requirement for comprehensiveness, a strong moral explanation will probably have to have several strong moral reasons, not just one. It is very hard for a single strong moral reason to provide the comprehensiveness needed for a strong moral explanation. Strong moral explanations take a broad view of moral situations. They make use of several perspectives to interpret and apply values instead of relying on just one. In chapter 5, we will discuss these perspectives, which we will come to call theories. Basically, what a perspective does is decide whether values are to be enacted by focusing on consequences or motives or rights or something else. When we choose a perspective, we choose a way of putting values into practice. A strong moral explanation makes use of several perspectives for applying values, rather than just one. A strong moral explanation also considers all of the persons who stand to be affected by the decision being made, and not just one person or group. And it considers more values rather than fewer values. Thus, the focus of the moral reasons that make up a moral explanation is important in evaluating moral explanations, but so is the comprehensiveness of the moral reasons taken altogether.

In concluding our discussion of how to evaluate moral reasons and explanations, we issue two reminders. First, recall that all of the reasons and explanations we are evaluating here are *moral* reasons and *moral* explanations. They have passed our tests, and we have determined that they are moral and not nonmoral. What we are now comparing are the various moral reasons and the various moral explanations in order to distinguish between those which are better and those which are worse. Next, the second point to remember is that no chart or list can give us conclusive proof that a moral reason or a moral explanation is strong or weak. So, what we are doing in speaking about strong and weak moral reasons and moral explanations is using a flexible comparative measure, and not an ironclad definitive measure. Think of moral reasons and explanations as being measured against a kind of scale that extends from the weakest moral reasons and explanations to the strongest ones. Somewhere in between here are reasons and explanations that are strong, those that are weak, those that are stronger than the alternatives in this case, and so on. Our lists of characteristics can be helpful guides, but they are not dogmatic rules. If you find a moral reason or an explanation that according to our list of characteristics is strong, but you believe is weak, defend your evaluation of the reason or explanation. And if you believe that the best moral reason or explanation in a case is one that according to our list of characteristics is weak, make a case for it.

Next, let us see if we can use what we have discussed here. Can we evaluate moral reasons and explanations? Can we distinguish when reasons and explanations are strong and when they are weak? If we cannot do this, we have not only wasted a lot of time, but we will be unable to resolve moral dilemmas. In our ordinary moral experience, we distinguish between better and worse moral reasons and explanations, and unless we can use what we have discussed here, we will have no basis for these better and worse evaluations.

Consider the following moral explanations and the moral reasons contained in them:

1. *Reverend Giannini talked with a troubled teenager from his congregation who stopped by after church. Later in the week, the teenager's mother came by and asked if the Reverend would approach her child and help discover the source of the child's troubles. Reverend Giannini told the mother that he had already spoken with the teenager and that he thought the teenager's problems were not serious but typical teenage problems. He decided this course of action would relieve the mother's worry.*

2. *Reverend Giannini talked with a troubled teenager from his congregation who stopped by after church. Later in the week, the teenager's mother came by and asked if the Reverend would approach her child and help discover the source of the child's troubles. Reverend Giannini told the mother he had already spoken with the teenager and that he thought the teenager's problems were not serious but typical teenage problems. He decided on this course of action primarily because he believed not only that the most good would come from this qualified disclosure, but also that he could maintain his promise to the teenager to keep the conversation confidential. The teenager's confidentiality was maintained, although his visit with Reverend Giannini was disclosed, which reassured his mother. Finally, Reverend Giannini believed that his primary goal as pastor was to help individuals, thus this decision allowed him to care for and respect the teenager at the same time he cared for the teenager's mother and respected her need for reassurance.*

In case 1, Reverend Giannini told the teenager's mother about his talk with the teenager because he wanted to relieve the mother's worry. Reverend Giannini's moral explanation includes only one moral reason, which is, "He wanted to relieve the mother's worry." Applying our list of characteristics to this reason, we learn that it is a weak moral reason in support of his decision to talk to the teenager's mother. It is weak and less focused because it fails to meet all of the characteristics necessary in a strong or focused moral reason. Reverend Giannini's reason is relevant and pertinent to the decision he makes (see characteristic 1), and it does highlight the values of beneficence and nonmaleficence, which are central to Reverend Giannini's situation (see characteristic 3). But the reason is indifferent to one person, namely, the teenager, most affected by his decision of what to tell the teenager's mother (see characteristic 2). Thus, Reverend Giannini's moral reason is weak and less focused.

Now, what about Reverend Giannini's moral explanation? Since he offers only one reason for his decision and that reason, we have said, is weak, it follows, according to our list of characteristics of moral explanations, that Reverend Giannini's explanation also is weak. His moral explanation is already not focused, since its only reason is weak. But, in addition, his moral explanation is not comprehensive, since for one thing it utilizes only one perspective for applying values, namely, looking at consequences (see characteristic A). Also, his explanation fails to take into account all of the persons affected by his decision, namely, himself and the teenager (see characteristic B). And it considers only one value, beneficence and nonmaleficence, and ignores other values, like integrity and respect for persons (see characteristic C). Thus, Reverend Giannini's moral explanation is weak, because it is neither focused nor comprehensive.

In case 2, Reverend Giannini again decides to tell the teenager's mother about his talk with the teenager, but this time he gives a different explanation. This time his moral explanation includes several moral reasons. They are: "He believed the most good would come from this qualified disclosure," "He could maintain his promise to the teenager to keep the conversation confidential," "His goal was to help individuals," and "He could care for and respect the teenager and care for the mother and respect her need for reassurance." Each of these moral reasons has to be measured separately against our list of characteristics to determine whether it is a strong moral reason. For the sake of brevity, we will do this in an abbreviated way. All of Reverend Giannini's reasons are relevant to his decision of what to tell the teenager's mother (see characteristic 1). All of them seem to take into account the persons most affected by the decision, namely, the teenager and his mother (see characteristic 2). Some of the moral reasons meet this characteristic better than others, in that some consider both the teenager and his mother, while at least one—"He could maintain his promise to the teenager to keep the conversation confidential"—considers only the teenager and not his mother. Perhaps this reason is less focused or weaker than the other reasons, although all of the reasons consider the teenager, arguably the person most affected by the Reverend's decision. In many cases such as this one, there may be uncertainty regarding which persons are most affected by a decision. But we are not going to get distracted by that question here. All of Reverend Giannini's moral reasons take into account at least one of the persons who has the most to gain or lose in this situation. Regardless of this complication, all of Reverend Giannini's reasons consider the values that are most central to his situation (see characteristic 3). His reasons express concern for beneficence and nonmaleficence, integrity, and respect for persons. His reasons for telling the mother are strong moral reasons, in that they are relevant to the decision and focused on the persons and values central to the situation.

Now, what about Reverend Giannini's moral explanation in case 2? This time, he gives a strong moral explanation. He has offered several strong moral reasons for the decision he made, thus his reasons are focused, and his moral reasons, taken collectively, are comprehensive. His moral explanation makes use of several perspectives in order to interpret and apply values (see characteristic A). Reverend Giannini is looking at consequences, but he is also upholding duties, acting virtuously, and aiming to care for persons and relationships. In addition, his explanation shows concern for all those who have a stake in his decision of what to tell the teenager's mother, namely, the teenager, the mother, and himself (see characteristic B). Finally, his explanation considers more rather than fewer values. His reasons seek to express beneficence and nonmaleficence, integrity, respect for persons, responsibility, and compassion. Given all of this, Reverend Giannini's explanation is comprehensive. Since it is comprehensive and the moral reasons he provides are focused, his moral explanation is a strong one. This time, in contrast to case 1, Reverend Giannini offers both stronger moral reasons and a more comprehensive moral explanation which together result in a strong moral explanation.

As these examples show, we can evaluate moral reasons and explanations by judging the degree to which they are focused and comprehensive. The task of evaluating moral reasons and explanations is not easy, but it is an important part of a moral life. Acting morally requires discriminating between better and worse reasons and stronger and weaker explanations. To work well with colleagues and clients, to maintain self-respect, and to be part of a community, professionals, and for that matter, all moral thinkers, must not accept all moral reasons and moral explanations as though they are of equal merit. Skill in evaluating moral reasons and explanations is necessary to a good professional practice and to a moral life.

Conclusion

In this chapter, we looked particularly at how to recognize and evaluate prescriptive moral reasoning. We defined a moral reason and looked at examples of reasons that are moral and reasons that are not moral. We also discussed how to identify moral explanations and dilemmas, and we developed some initial strategies for how to resolve moral dilemmas. Last, we considered how to evaluate moral reasons and explanations. Prescriptive morality requires both recognizing moral reasons and explanations when we encounter them and assessing which are strong and which are weak. In the next chapter, we will continue our discussion of moral reasons and explanations by looking in detail at the various perspectives for applying values (theories) that can be used in a moral explanation. These perspectives or theories are employed by moral reasons and explanations and, as we have seen, when a moral explanation takes into account several such perspectives, it fulfills one of the characteristics of a strong moral explanation.

EXERCISES

1. Give a moral and a nonmoral reason that supports each of these decisions.

   1. It is unacceptable for advertisers working for cigarette companies to target teenage audiences.
   2. Government employees are expected to publicly express only those views that are consistent with the policies of the government.
   3. Where possible, employees should be monitored to ensure that they do not use the telephone for personal business.

2. In each of these paragraphs, state the decision reached and the explanation given for it. Then decide if the explanation is a moral explanation or not. Explain why or why not.

   1. Bribery of foreign officials by international corporations should be prohibited, since it gives an unfair advantage to those corporations who do it.[11]
   2. Lawyer Jim, a partner at Smith and Jones, is billing his client at his rate of $150 per hour, even though the bulk of the research is being done by Lawyer Julie, an associate, who has lower rates, because that is the policy at Smith and Jones.
   3. Engineers in large firms have an ethical responsibility to do their jobs the best they can, and to report their observations about safety and improvement of safety to management. But they do not have the obligation to insist that their perceptions or standards be accepted. They are not paid to do that, they are not expected to do that, and they have no moral or ethical obligation to do that.[12]
   4. Company property is not for personal use, according to company regulations.[13]

3. In each case, discuss what decisions or courses of action are possible. Explain whether there is a moral dilemma at stake. If it seems as

though there is, is it a true one or are there any ways to creatively solve it? Describe some of these creative solutions, if any. Determine what the best decision is, in your opinion. Explain why you feel it is the best decision. Work to develop strong moral reasons and a strong moral explanation when supporting your decision.

CASE 1: THE NURSE AND THE PATIENT'S PRENATAL TEST

Theresa Kim is a nurse employed in the obstetrical practice of Dr. Elaine Fishman. Dr. Fishman performs prenatal tests on fetuses, including amniocentesis, and she performs abortions in some cases.

Susan Jones has arrived to have an amniocentesis to determine the sex of her fetus. She and her husband have a healthy, normal daughter, and they would like to have a son to round out their family.

Dr. Elaine Fishman believes the Jones's have the right to request amniocentesis. But Theresa is uncomfortable with the idea of doing the test, solely to determine the sex of the baby. She is worried that the Jones's may decide to abort the fetus if it turns out to be female.

Theresa expresses her concerns to her supervisor but her supervisor tells her to carry on as usual. At this point, it is inconvenient for the rest of the staff to cover for her, and it also inconveniences Dr. Fishman and the patient.

CASE 2: THE MOONLIGHTING SUPERVISOR

J. P. is a supervisor at a large branch of the U. S. Immigration and Naturalization Service (INS). He works flextime and is not always at his desk during normal business hours. He is also a lawyer and moonlights as a criminal defense attorney, specializing in the defense of juvenile gang members. Some of his law business is conducted during regular business hours. The state's attorney complains to J. P.'s boss about his moonlighting. He wonders if J. P. is meeting the requirements of his INS job and, for that matter, if J. P.'s juvenile clients are getting sufficient attention and representation. He questions how J. P. can be loyal both to the INS and his clients.

CASE 3: THE SCHOOL PSYCHOLOGIST AND THE CLIENT'S PARENTS

Chi Chung is a school psychologist at Streeter Junior High. Mary Monroe, age fourteen is referred to her because Mary is becoming increasingly depressed and socially withdrawn. Ms. Chung finds Mary somewhat inhibited by her overbearing parents, while working to de-

velop a sense of her own identity and autonomy. Over several months of meetings, Ms. Chung believes that Mary is making good progress. But then Mr. and Mrs. Monroe begin telephoning Ms. Chung and expressing concern that Mary is becoming too assertive and independent, and that she is spending more time with her peers than with her family.

4. In the following statements, state the moral explanations. List each reason in the explanation. Then decide if the moral reason given is weak or strong, less focused or more focused. Explain why. Then decide if the moral explanation given is weak or strong, less comprehensive or more comprehensive. Explain why.

    1. Police officers ought to be allowed to jail traffic offenders on sight, since doing so would contribute to the overall safety of those who abide by the laws.
    2. On principle, John's spouse must be told about the fact that John has changed his will, so I (their lawyer) will call and inform her.
    3. Young people ought to choose their own professions and not be pressured by their family's preferences. This way, they will take more responsibility for their choices and be more invested in their professions, hence, will do a better job at them.
    4. School counselors should provide support for classroom teachers and take over some care for unruly students, since that benefits the teachers and the school as a whole.
    5. Magdalena did not take office supplies home from work, although she knew many other managers did, because she felt it was stealing, thus wrong in itself, and because she thought it ended up costing the company money that might otherwise have been used on salaries or benefits.

NOTES

1. *The American Heritage Dictionary of the English Language* (New York: American Heritage Publishing Co., 1969, 1970), 1086.
2. Ibid., 462.
3. Aristotle believed that ethics is about feelings, in addition to actions and virtues, but he claimed that reason must guide feelings. Reason must determine when and how and for what reason to exercise anger or love (*Nicomachean Ethics*, Book II, Chapters 5–7). Jean-Paul Sartre also is critical of using feelings to guide actions. He points out that people cannot distinguish true from false feelings, thus cannot reliably trust their feelings as reasons for action (*Existentialism and Human Emotions* [Secaucus, N.J.: Citadel Press, Inc., 1957], 26–27).
4. This situation is embellished from one given in Tom L. Beauchamp and James F. Childress, *Principles of Biomedical Ethics* (New York: Oxford University Press, 1979), 15, and some of the reasons stated therein are paraphrased here.
5. *The American Heritage Dictionary of the English Language*, 360

6. Some authors consider moral dilemmas to be part of what is tragic in human life. Since human knowledge and resources are limited, there is opacity in many situations, in that no matter what choice we make, serious moral concerns are left unresolved (Thomas M. Garrett, Harold W. Baillie, and Rosellen M. Garrett, *Health Care Ethics: Principles and Problems*, 2d ed. [Englewood Cliffs, N.J.: Prentice Hall, 1993], 7, 11).

7. Summarized from Jean-Paul Sartre, *Existentialism and Human Emotions*, 24–28.

8. See Anthony Weston, *A Practical Companion to Ethics* (New York: Oxford University Press, 1997), 30–32, who argues that Sartre's example of the boy is a false dilemma and that other options, besides the two recognized, need to be explored. Weston also details several other options.

9. This case involving Chicago journalist and TV news anchor Carol Marin and talk-show host Jerry Springer was reported in the *Chicago Tribune* (page 1, front-page story by Steve Johnson, "Carol Marin Quit WMAQ Over Jerry Springer," and page 1, MetroChicago section commentary by Mary Schmich, "Marin's Decision to Step Down Puts Her a Step Up"), Friday, May 2, 1997.

10. *Chicago Tribune*, Friday, May 2, 1997.

11. This statement is modified from Peter A. Facione, Donald Scherer, and Thomas Attig, *Ethics and Society*, 2d ed. (Englewood Cliffs, N.J.: Prentice Hall, 1991), 11.

12. See Richard T. DeGeorge, "Ethical Responsibilities of Engineers in Large Organizations: The Pinto Case," *Business and Professional Ethics Journal* 1:1 (1981), 5.

13. Taken from Peter A. Facione, Donald Scherer, and Thomas Attig, *Ethics and Society*, 2d ed., 11.

5

Moral Theories

People in their professional and personal lives adopt different kinds of ethical perspectives. We can see this in the emerging profession of the police officer. When faced with a suspect who is refusing to cooperate, some police officers think first about what the rules are, what the suspect's rights are, and how to bring about the best consequences for the officer, the suspect, and the community. Other police officers think of how to be a good officer, how to care for the suspect and the community, and what has happened in the case to lead the suspect to adopt such an unruly attitude. The responses of these two types of police officers reflect different types of ethical theories and commitments. The officers address moral situations in different ways. For instance, the first kind of officer is aiming to do what is best by considering rules, rights, and future consequences. The second kind of officer is trying to be the best officer by focusing on the character of the police officer, and how the officer ought to care for others and consider the suspect in light of his or her own history and the history of the situation in question. The first type of officer aims to do good; the second aims to be good. In short, they put values into practice according to different strategies.

In adopting different types of theories, neither officer is right or wrong. Both are employing good moral systems. Yet their understanding of what counts as relevant in a moral situation, or of why a certain act is right or wrong, differs. They may do the same thing (for instance, immobilize and gag the suspect) but the reasons they have chosen this action will differ. The first will say she did the action because it conforms to police procedure. The second will say he did the action because it was the only way a conscientious, caring officer could have acted. This difference in perspective illustrates a key difference between types of moral theories.

Moral theories vary insofar as they manifest different senses of why some action ought to be done or left undone, or of what aspects of a given moral situation must be tended to. A moral theory interprets our underlying values and is the way in which we provide a scheme to determine which values take priority in any given situation. In this chapter, we will consider what moral theories are, and we will offer a way of classifying types of moral theories. As we will explain, some moral theories focus on what a person does, "doing" theories, while others focus on who a person is, "being" theories. By the end of this chapter, you will be able to analyze and appreciate the use of moral theories in particular situations, such as in the aforementioned example of the two types of police officers. This is important because our moral theories are the means by which we interpret and apply our values in the world.

What Moral Theories Are and How They Are Classified

A moral theory is a perspective on moral situations. It is the way in which a person's values are acted out in the world. A moral theory is the way one chooses to live out and interpret one's values, or to put it in other terms, it is the way a professional puts into practice the choices made about what is valuable in his or her profession or occupation.

A moral theory has two tasks. First, it must provide an orientation toward moral situations. A theory involves a set of claims or assumptions about how moral situations ought to be addressed, and which component of a moral situation takes priority. So a theory determines if consequences matter most, or intentions or relationships or something else.

Second, a moral theory must resolve conflicts among rules and values. When rules come into conflict or when competing values cannot both be acted on, a moral theory bites the bullet insofar as it provides a hierarchy of one's values. In sum, it must enable one to resolve moral dilemmas and defend the solutions reached.

Thus a moral theory is the broad perspective a person brings to his or her moral experience, to the living of his or her professional and personal lives against the backdrop of a commitment to values. For our purposes, we will not discuss how a person forms or learns a moral theory. This is treated by a separate discipline called moral development, or moral education. Philosophers have recognized and utilized a number of moral theories. Let us first consider a scheme for classifying moral theories before we examine each in detail.

MORAL THEORIES

Doing

Consequentialism	Rights	Duties
Future of Community	*Rights of Individuals*	*Duties of Individuals*

Being

Virtue	Care	Narrative
Character	*Relationships*	*Past History and Future Plans*

First let us acknowledge that other schemes for organizing moral theories are possible. However, this scheme is our interpretation of how the main types of ethical theories especially relevant to professionals can be characterized and related. In this scheme, there are six major types of ethical theories: consequentialism, rights, duties, virtue, care, and narrative. They are organized into two classes. The first class includes consequentialism, rights, and duties, which are theories that focus on doing, on determining what a person ought to do. In order to figure out what a person ought to do, these theories use reason to calculate and assess the proper course of action. For them, ethical theory aims at ensuring that we do the right thing. The second class includes virtue, care, and narrative theories, which focus on being, on who the moral agent is, and on what kind of person he or she is or wants to be. These theories are interested in the status of moral agents, and not so much interested in the consequences or even the nature of actions. Certainly action is the result of what a person chooses, and a right action is one that is a true reflection of who the moral chooser is, and of the relationships, history, and plans that characterize the chooser's life. Still, the person choosing is the central concern of these theories, and the action chosen by the person is of secondary concern.

In order to reflect on the differences among the theories, consider this case. In what follows, we offer responses to the case that reflect the way a person might use a particular theory to interpret his or her underlying value commitments. No theory is perfect. Each has strengths and weaknesses. We conclude our discussion of each theory with an assessment of its strengths and weaknesses.

> *Suppose you and fifteen other new hires (ten men, five women) are part of a one-year management training program at a large accounting firm. Every three months you report to a different supervisor and do a different type of work. After the first three months, you are rotated to Bob Fritz's group. At the end of the first week, you have observed that Bob treats the women trainees differently than the men. He refers to the women as "girls," "gals," and "chicks," and he winks at them when he makes jokes. From what you can tell, the women trainees have not visibly reacted to this or said anything, and you have not asked them about it. Should you do anything about it?*

Doing Theories: Consequentialism, Rights, Duties

We know what doing theories have in common; namely, a focus on action, on determining what persons should do. We now turn to how doing theories differ. We discuss three types of doing theories, beginning with consequentialism.

Consequentialism

Some examples follow of how a person with a consequential theory could respond to the case involving Bob Fritz:

1. "I bet my future at the firm would be in jeopardy if I say anything, and my family will be disappointed if I mess up on my first real job."

2. "Probably the women have decided that more good comes from ignoring the comments (since it is only a three-month stint) than would come of making a big deal out of them."
3. "I'm going to speak to someone in the Human Resources Department about this since in the long run the company and everybody who works under Bob Fritz is hurt by his sexist treatment of women."

Note that these consequential responses do not all arrive at the same conclusion. We do not know whether a consequentialist would do nothing, speak with the women trainees, go to the Human Resources Department, or anything else. We do know that a consequentialist would decide what to do by assessing the future consequences of the possible options. The consequentialist would compare how much good and harm comes from doing nothing to the amount of good and harm that comes from speaking to someone in Human Resources, and pick the action that, according to him or her, realizes more good than harm. All of these responses are attempts to use reason to decide which action will bring about the greatest amount of good. Consequentialism aims at realizing the best consequences.[1] It is future oriented; it is looking to bring about the best possible ends. We can summarize consequentialism this way: According to consequentialism, an act is right only if it tends to produce more good consequences than bad consequences for everyone concerned.

Consequentialism sounds simple: Perform the action that maximizes more good consequences than bad for all concerned. Suppose you are faced with the Bob Fritz situation and you want to make use of the consequential theory. You must first consider what options are available. Then your consequential theory requires that you list what particular persons are affected, either positively or negatively, by each option. So, for example, doing nothing has an effect on you, it has an effect on the other women and men trainees, and it might even have an effect on the company as a whole. Talking to someone in Human Resources has repercussions for you, the other trainees, Bob Fritz, Bob Fritz's boss, the Human Resources staff, the company as a whole, and maybe your family. Next, you, the consequentialist, must judge how much good or harm comes to each of the persons under each of the options. This could be accomplished by quantifying the worth or even by assigning a numerical figure to the good or harm that comes to each person. This quantification could be a number on a scale of 1 to 10, or it could be pluses and minuses on a scale of 1 to 5, or something else. Last, you total the amount of good and the amount of harm that each option would result in and pick the right action, namely, the one that brings about more total good than harm.

Now, following this consequential calculation, you probably are left with some questions. Maybe some of these occurred to you. How do we figure out exactly which people are affected by a certain option? How do we know whether choosing a certain option will result in good or bad consequences to a person? And how do we know how much good or harm will come to a person from choosing a certain option? There are no easy answers here. Employing consequential theory means we thoughtfully anticipate what follows from a certain course of action, but sometimes consequences turn out to be something other than what we expected. Consequential theory makes use of a calculative process, but it involves individual subjective assessments and predictions about the future that cannot be absolute.

Taking all of the above into consideration, the most important strengths and weaknesses of consequentialism follow:

Strengths	Weaknesses
It has a comprehensive procedure for calculating what is right.	It cannot determine with certainty what the consequences will be.
It values each person's good equally.	It sacrifices individual goods and rights for the sake of the larger good of the community.

As we have seen, one strength of consequential theory is its logical, comprehensive procedure for decision making. The procedure is systematic, orderly, and inclusive, in that it takes into account anyone's interest that might be affected by the moral situation. A second strength is that the procedure is designed to be fair, since every affected person's interest is counted, and no one person counts more than any other. The good and harm to every person affected by the decision is weighed and added in the final calculation.

One drawback to consequentialism is that it requires us to predict consequences that in fact are never certain. Also, by being so comprehensive and inclusive, consequential theory focuses on realizing the greatest amount of total good for all, regardless of to whom the good accrues. Consequentialism works to benefit the group, the community at large, and in doing so, it overlooks or is willing to sacrifice individual goods and rights.

Rights

Next, let us consider another type of doing theory, namely, a rights theory. Ways in which a rights theorist might respond to the Bob Fritz case include:

1. "All employees have the same right to be treated respectfully."
2. "I probably ought to just keep out of the situation, since the women's right to privacy ought to be upheld."
3. "Since Bob Fritz is our training supervisor, he's got the right to decide how to deal with us except if he goes so far as to violate our constitutional rights to life, liberty, and the pursuit of happiness."

Often, as in this case, there may be many rights at stake. In the Bob Fritz case, you have rights, as do Bob Fritz, the women trainees, Bob Fritz's boss, and in fact everyone in the firm. A rights theorist might have to decide whose rights should be met first or what rights are more fundamental than others. Are Bob's rights as the supervisor more basic or more overriding than the women's rights to privacy or respectful treatment? The main point is that a person using rights theory believes that an action is morally right when it respects rights and wrong when it violates rights.[2]

Let us consider what a right is. It is a morally or legally justified claim on someone else. It is the prerogative of the rights holder to claim (or demand) something from someone else (the individual or society that recognizes the right). A right to privacy would require that social workers not reveal details from cases to interested family members or neighbors. A right to equal treatment would require that employers not discriminate against women, minorities, those with AIDS, and so on. Rights theory takes the view that the most important aspect of any situation is the rights of the individuals present in the situation. We can summarize rights theory this way: According to rights theory, an act is right only if it upholds rights.

Suppose in addressing the Bob Fritz situation, you decide to use a rights theory. As a rights theorist, you will consider what rights are at stake. In this case, there are rights to integrity, privacy, and equal treatment. You will also consider whose rights are at issue. Bob Fritz has rights as a supervisor, and you have rights as an employee of the firm, as do the women trainees. Plus, Bob's boss and the Human Resources Department may have rights to set policies or to be kept informed of management practices. Then you will determine how to preserve and uphold these rights. It may not be immediately obvious which option is best in terms of upholding rights. You may need to assess which rights are overriding or whose rights take precedence. One way or another, you will use your reflection on the situation and the persons involved in it to arrive at the alternative that does the best job of honoring rights.

It is hard to say what a rights theorist would do in this case. The rights theorist would have to decide whose integrity or privacy ought to count more and which rights are more fundamental. Is the right to integrity more basic than the right to equal treatment? Which rights must be satisfied first? For that matter, how do we know what rights persons have? After all, a person may claim to have a right to something that she does not in fact have. Who decides what rights we have, and where do rights come from? These are difficult questions facing rights theorists. With these in mind, consider the following strengths and weaknesses of the rights theory:

Strengths	Weaknesses
It respects the value of the individual.	It cannot determine with certainty what rights individuals have.
It is compatible with Western society's political theory.	It sacrifices the larger good of the community for the sake of individual rights.

On the positive side, a rights theory recognizes the intrinsic worth of each individual. It accords each individual standing and authority merely in virtue of their being human. Rights theory sees that moral decisions about right and wrong grow out of one's understanding of persons as the bearers of rights, which are granted to them by God or by nature or by society. Modern Western societies also have modeled political systems based on this view of persons possessing rights. The United States Constitution has a Bill of Rights (1791) and the English Parliament long ago enacted a Bill of Rights (1689). For many of us living in modern society, thinking about human rights is a common and natural way of addressing moral situations.

On the negative side, a rights theory faces certain problems involving its justification and application. We have seen that there are questions about what rights we have, which rights are basic rights, and where rights come from. Rights theorists also have to deal with the question of whether persons can lose their rights. These difficult questions must be answered by a rights theory. Also, critics of rights theory object that while rights theory focuses on individual rights, it ignores the good of the whole community. This is essentially a consequential objection. Rights theory, unlike consequentialism, makes the choice to define what is right in terms of individual moral prerogatives instead of good consequences for all. In so doing, it is willing to sacrifice the good of the community for the sake of ensuring individual rights.

Duties

Now let us turn to duty theories. The following are some possible duty-based responses to the Bob Fritz case:

1. "I'm going to find out if there is a company policy prohibiting sexual harassment."
2. "As a matter of principle, I have a duty to right wrongs where I can, so if there is something I can do to stop this wrong treatment of the women trainees, then I must do it."
3. "My assignment is to do well on the work Bob Fritz assigns me. I have no special obligation to the other trainees, since none of them has asked me to get involved, so I will stick to my assignment."

Note that a person using duty theory is not bound to any particular conclusion. A duty theorist may decide to take some action, or to do nothing. We cannot tell what duty theorists would decide, but we do know why they would pick their decision. We know that they will reach a decision by considering what to do, and especially by considering duties, and not consequences or rights. A person using duty theory may pick the same action as that picked by a consequentialist or a rights theorist, but the duty theorist will reason toward this course of action in a different way. For duty theory, the rightness or wrongness of an action does not depend solely on whether it produces good or bad consequences.[3] A duty theorist wants to do the right thing, regardless of the consequences. For example, talking to someone in the Human Resources Department may have many bad consequences, but it may still be the right thing to do, according to a person using duty theory. A duty theorist believes that certain things like keeping promises and upholding commitments made in the past are right, regardless of whether the consequences of doing so are good or bad.

The duty theory is unique insofar as it looks at the motive or intention of the person choosing, the means by which the act is accomplished, and the nature of the act itself. Hence, duty theory considers many aspects of a moral situation—motives, means, the act itself, rights, consequences—and never decides what to do solely on the basis of the consequences or the rights at stake. According to duty theory, an act is right for at least one of the following reasons: It is done for the sake of duty, it has a good motive, its means are acceptable, and/or the nature of the act itself is good.

Let us consider how a person using duty theory would approach the Bob Fritz case. First, you, the duty theorist, will consider your alternatives in light of the various duties at issue. You would not think primarily about consequences or rights. It is not very important what might happen to you, the trainees, Bob Fritz, or the company, or what rights each has. Instead, you, the duty theorist, will consider the duties, rules, commitments, promises, and contracts that might obligate you. You will reflect on whether you have duties to Bob and the firm, duties to fellow employees, and duties to your own sense of self or conscience. You, the duty theorist, will decide which alternative best accomplishes your duties and good intentions. It may very well be that you will have to decide which duties to act on or which commitments and promises supersede others.

In one sense, the duty-based decision-making process is easier than the consequential, but in another sense it is harder. It is easier because there is no prolonged process of calculating future consequences, assigning values to each consequence, and totaling up good and bad consequences. The duty-based process is simpler because it is not a detailed, calculative affair. On the other hand, its process is harder than the consequential one, for just this same reason. It has no easy way to compare the various duties at issue and contrast the nature of one act to another. The duty-based process depends more on intuitive or supposedly self-evident claims. For instance, a duty theorist might say that an act that inflicts harm is by nature more wrong than an act which avoids inflicting harm. A duty theorist may find it hard to explain why one duty is more pressing than another.

Consider the following strengths and weaknesses of duty theory:

Strengths	Weaknesses
It recognizes the complexity of moral situations—motives, means, ends, and the nature of the act are all important.	It sometimes ignores consequences.
It respects the value of the individual.	It sacrifices the larger good of the community for the sake of individual duties.

The duty theorist counts as relevant many aspects of a moral situation, such as the motive, the means, the nature of the act, and even, for some duty theorists, the consequences. It is valuable to look at all of the aspects of a moral situation before deciding which aspect of the situation is overriding. Duty theory also respects the dignity of individuals and the obligations owed to them. It does not endorse permitting the good of all to always supersede the good of a particular individual. For duty theory, a duty or promise to a single person can be more morally compelling than good consequences to a whole community. Our experience backs up the duty approach by acknowledging situations in which the good of a single person is more important than the good of a whole community. Witness, for example, psychiatrists and investigative reporters who refuse to divulge information about clients and sources, even when faced with arguments claiming that the good of the community depends on having that information.

The main problem with duty theory is twofold. First, some versions of it exclude any consideration of consequences. This seems rather extreme. Given its attempt to be attentive to the complexity of moral situations, it seems only reasonable to assess consequences along with the other variables in the situation. We know from our experience that there are times when the consequences are clear, predictable, and certain, and it would be foolish to ignore that sort of information in deciding what to do. Second, duty theory may underemphasize the communal aspect of our lives by allowing individual duties and promises to supersede our concern for the effects of our actions on others. If human experience is necessarily social and shared with others, then, critics fear, duty theory is dangerously isolationist. Duty theory permits persons to use their own reasoning to identify duties, recall promises, and so on, and it does not require that persons assess how their actions will affect others. This is seen as a weakness, particularly by those who believe strongly in the connectedness of persons and the communal nature of our lives.

As we have seen, all moral theories have strengths and weaknesses. We will differ in terms of how serious the weaknesses seem to us. Your evaluation of each moral theory will depend on whether you agree or disagree with the assumptions it makes about the nature of human persons and human actions. We also must hold open the possibility of combining several theories so that the weaknesses of one can be offset by the strengths of another. Let us now leave the "doing" theories with their emphasis on dictating action and turn to the "being" theories and their concern for the person acting.

Being Theories: Virtue, Care, Narrative

We know what being theories have in common: a focus on who the acting person is or wants to be. Let us look at the differences among them by treating each being theory in turn, beginning with virtue theory.

Virtue

The following are some responses to the Bob Fritz case that indicate a virtue theory:

1. "What sort of person would I be if I do nothing?"
2. "My family and education have taught me that a good person never uses belittling language."
3. "One of the marks of persons of character is that they never interfere in the lives of others unless asked."

In the responses to the Bob Fritz case, the virtue theorist is aiming to discover what a good person would do. If a good person never uses belittling language, then Bob Fritz is not a good person. That may be a step in helping us decide how to act toward him. If a person of character never interferes unless asked, then the virtuous response in this case is to do nothing. On the other hand, it may not be obvious to us what a virtuous person would do, so we may need to start by considering whether this action is one that could be done by a virtuous person. Does doing nothing in this case reflect a good or bad character? A virtue theorist is not tied to any particular outcome in this case or in any other. The only requirement is that the person acting must act virtuously, must act for the sake of virtue, or must act in the way a person of virtue would act. The standard for moral action has nothing to do with consequences, motives, rights, and so on. Instead, the standard for action is the virtuous person or the virtues themselves.

Virtue theory maintains that the good person does right actions.[4] Hence, to know what is right, we must first see what a good person is and then what a good person does. A virtue is a good character trait or disposition. It is a tendency to act in a way that promotes the human good or human flourishing. The opposite of virtue is vice. A vice is a bad character trait or disposition. It is a tendency to act in a way that fails to promote the human good or human flourishing. For example, justice is a virtue, as is friendliness and benevolence. Their opposites—injustice, a lack of friendliness, and malevolence—are vices. According to virtue theory, an act is right if it reflects virtue or good character, that is, if it is the sort of act a virtuous person would do.

For a virtue theorist, many virtues might be acted on in the Bob Fritz case, such as justice, benevolence, loyalty, friendliness, and courage. The moral decision maker may act on the basis of any or all of these virtues. Speaking up about Bob Fritz might manifest the virtues of benevolence, justice, and courage, while doing nothing might promote loyalty and benevolence to Bob. The task of a virtue theorist is to outline what virtues are at stake in a situation, consider how each option would or would not realize the virtues, and then pick the course of action that expresses either more virtues or the more important virtues.

Unfortunately, there is no automatic way of knowing whether benevolence and loyalty to your superior or benevolence and justice to your colleagues is a better choice for a virtue theorist. For some, a virtue whose expression affects more people is preferable to the expression of a virtue that affects only one. The acting out of benevolence to many people would thus be preferable to acting out of benevolence to one. Also, a choice that expresses many virtues may be preferable to a decision that realizes only a few virtues. In this way, consequentialism may provide a service to virtue theory. Consequentialism tells the virtue theorist that realizing more virtues is better than realizing fewer virtues, and that those virtues that have an effect on more people are more important than those that have an effect on fewer people.

Yet, a virtue theorist need not accept the help of consequentialism. A virtue theorist may decide that it is not always better to realize more virtues rather than fewer. Maybe the few virtues are more important than the many. In other words, virtue theory can develop ways that are not consequential to decide which virtue to act on, or which action best expresses the virtue. A virtue theorist can rank the virtues or decide that on grounds of certain relationships the virtues must be expressed first toward some persons and only later toward others. For example, virtue theorists can claim that we must pay back a loan before giving gifts to our friends, and that we must act to benefit our parents before we act to benefit ourselves or our friends.[5] Finally, however, a decision between two alternatives sometimes comes down to a choice between this virtue or that one.

With all of this in mind, let us summarize the strengths and weaknesses of virtue theory:

Strengths	**Weaknesses**
It is person centered, not rule centered.	It does not explain how to move from a virtue to right action.
It is flexible, since it can recognize differences among persons and circumstances.	It cannot be universally applied, since definitions of virtue vary from person to person and culture to culture.

The attraction of virtue theory is that it is focused on persons, not rules, hence it can be flexible. It is a holistic, humane approach, since it evaluates the whole person and not isolated actions. It is flexible in that it allows that virtue be practiced differently toward family than toward friends. Virtue theory is praised for not requiring us to treat each person identically or each situation the same.

On the other hand, critics claim that virtue theory is not practical, since there is no easy or clear way to translate traits of character into concrete actions. It is possible that good persons may have no idea of what to do in complex situations, where all they have to go on is their good character. Also, there is a problem with the universality of the virtues. Without consensus on what the virtues are, there is relativity among virtue theorists. If we cannot be sure what the virtues are, or we cannot agree with others about what the virtues are, then virtue theory seems to be little more than a subjective way of solving problems.

Care

Let us next turn to care theories. The following responses to the Bob Fritz case reflect a care theory:

1. "My relationship with my mentor, Bob Fritz, requires me to speak with him privately about how his comments and actions might be interpreted by others."
2. "Caring for my fellow interns means doing what they are comfortable with, so I'll ask them privately whether they think I should do anything."
3. "In order to support both Bob Fritz and the other trainees and not embarrass either by a public confrontation, I'll speak confidentially to the Human Resources Department."

In these responses, the aim is clearly to act in a way that supports other persons and relationships rather than in a way that undercuts persons and relationships. Your goal as a care theorist in the Bob Fritz case is to figure out how to express care for others. To do this, you need to have an understanding of the nature of your relationships with Bob Fritz, with the other trainees, and maybe with the Human Resources staff and Bob Fritz's boss. For whom do you care? What best expresses this care?

For a moral agent who approaches situations from a care perspective, the moral action is one that allows the agent to express care for and be in a supporting relationship with others.[6] A theory based on care emphasizes the way persons in friendships, families, and communities mutually support and care for each other. According to a care theory, there is no right or wrong, independent of persons, situations, and relationships. There is instead the caring thing to do in this situation, which is the right thing to do, and the uncaring thing to do, which is the wrong thing to do. Acts are right or wrong insofar as they manifest or undercut caring for and about others. According to care theory, an act is right if it expresses care for another or is done to maintain or further a caring relationship.

In our case, using a care theory would mean trying to find the alternative that best allows the expression of care. You would consider your relationships to Bob, the women trainees, other employees, the company, and so on, and would look for a way to manifest care and sustain relationships. You would probably want to avoid causing any embarrassment that might occur if there was a public confrontation. You would look for ways to improve the women's situation and for ways to help Bob be a better manager and have a better relationship with the trainees. This in turn might help others in the company who have relationships with Bob or the trainees. In short, using care theory means looking for alternatives that realize the most care or that express care toward the greatest number of people, or perhaps toward the people that most need or deserve care.

No doubt there are still questions that can be raised about a care approach. Is it better to express more care or to express some care toward more people? Do some people deserve more care than others? Who exactly should we care for? Another problem with care theory is that in its early forms it was modeled on the mother figure, who seems to many to exemplify the caring, nurturing person. But as a result, there were questions about the universalizability of care theory. To be really useful as a moral theory, care theory must adopt a new model, since mothers are not the only ones who care, and women are not the only ones who care.

Keeping these questions in mind, we will summarize the strengths and weaknesses of care theory:

Strengths	Weaknesses
It is person centered, not rule centered.	It does not explain how to move from caring to right action.
It stresses the communal and emotional nature of human lives.	It cannot be universally applied, since definitions of care vary from person to person and culture to culture.

Like virtue theory, a theory of care is rooted in persons and our relationships to them. For care theory, moral decisions are made by focusing on persons, especially on our relationships with them, and not by attending to actions, duties, consequences, and so on. This is a strength because it is a humane and personal approach to decision making. The care ethic also accords significance to our emotional attachments to others. It looks at the total person—emotional, spiritual, physical, rational—and claims that the basis of moral action is our caring relationships with others. This inclusive view of the person is at least one reason an ethic of care is such a persuasive moral theory.

On the negative side, the care ethic suffers from the same defects as virtue theory. As of yet, the care ethic has no clear and detailed account of how one should translate care into actual practice. More work needs to be done on what it means to care concretely. In addition is the problem spoken of earlier, the universalizability question. Can we assume that care is or should be the universal standard for women and men, for persons of different cultures, and so on? We need to be able to provide reasons for thinking that the care theory is universal, and not merely situational. Critics worry about the insufficiently developed details of the care ethic and about the subjectivity and relativity inherent in caring. Should we only care for those we care about, or should we also care for those we may not even know and those we do not care about?

Narrative

Finally, let us consider the last of the being theories, narrative theory. The following responses to the Bob Fritz case reflect a narrative approach to moral situations:

1. "Bob Fritz's comments are probably due to the fact that he is an older employee, 'from the old school,' and not used to working with women."
2. "I've gotten to know others in the firm and the new trainees pretty well in the last few months. I feel that I have a history at the firm and with my colleagues and therefore any behavior that impacts one of us affects all of us."
3. "Ever since I was a child I was shy, although my parents encouraged me to speak my mind and stand up for what I believe. During high school and college, I spoke up for some unpopular causes and was ridiculed by my peers. Those experiences have made me cautious about what I say. I'd like to avoid getting into a situation where I am unpopular and ridiculed for what I say."

It is difficult to reach a conclusion about what a narrative theorist would do in the Bob Fritz case. Each of the above responses fits with a narrative approach, in that each reflects what a possible person might make of the Bob Fritz situation, based on that person's goals, history, and views of Bob and the firm. We cannot say that a narrative theorist would choose one response over another, because we do not know where any particular narrative theorist is in the course of her or his life, goals, and story.

All of the responses are grounded in a narrative theory, because they focus on the persons who are involved in the case and on the unique histories and pasts of those persons. The responses reveal that moral decision making is done by particular persons who are at a particular point in the story of their lives. Our decision on how to evaluate Bob Fritz's sexist remarks will depend on what we know about the story of Bob's life, the story of the decision maker's life, the history of the mentoring situation, the histories of all of the individuals involved in this training group, and the traditions and cultures of these persons.

Narrative theory insists that morality is about the unfolding of a life within a culture, and not about character or caring.[7] It is contextual and attentive to individual histories and social traditions. The aim of narrative theory is thus to enable persons to make choices within the particular context of who they are, what they care about, and what they have done, instead of requiring persons to act for the sake of the more abstract virtues or to care. Narrative theorists use the story—the idea of a narrative in time—to make sense of moral situations and moral decision making. According to narrative theory, an act is right if it reflects the ongoing story of a person's life and the culture and tradition within which he or she lives it.

In applying narrative theory to a particular case, such as Bob Fritz's, the narrative theorist needs to understand the context of the situation and the histories and beliefs of the persons who find themselves in the situation. The narrative theorist will consider questions such as: What is Bob Fritz's history as a manager and as a person? Could his comments to the women trainees be due to some illness or stress in his life? What is the decision maker's history? For example, how have you, the decision maker, dealt with cases like this before? What do you value, and how do you feel about your job? How are the women trainees responding to Bob's actions? What do you know about their histories, beliefs, and values? Finally, what is the history and working climate of the firm? Have other supervisors been like Bob? What are the laws, traditions, and cultural practices within which this firm does business and these persons live?

Answering these questions provides information about the context of this moral situation and about the life stories of the characters in it. From a narrative approach, the more information we have about individuals' lives and cultural traditions, the better decisions we will be able to make. Assuming however that we do not have any special knowledge about Bob or the women or the history of the company, we will have to act on the basis of what we do know.

In aiming to apply narrative theory, problems arise. The idea of life as a story fascinates philosophers. However, it is not clear how the idea of life as a narrative can be used as a moral theory, or how it sets a moral standard. In other words, how does understanding a person's history and goals tell us what we ought to do in a moral situation? Or, in situations where there are many persons, each with his or her own history, how do we find a solution that takes into account each of their unique histories? There also is the problem of how the narrative theory, which recognizes the unique stories of individuals' lives, can be universalizable. How can it make use of general rules if it claims to take into account unique persons and histories? Perhaps narrative theory is part of a moral theory, but not the only part. These problems suggest that narrative theory is in need of further development and clarification.

With all of this in mind, let us sum up the strengths and weaknesses of the narrative approach:

Strengths	Weaknesses
It is person centered, not rule centered.	It does not explain how to move from narrative to right action.
It stresses the consistency and wholeness of a person's moral life.	It cannot be universally applied, since every narrative is unique.

On the positive side, narrative ethics is focused on persons. It sees actions and decision making as part of the continuum of a life and a culture. It takes the choices a person makes as part of the ongoing saga of the person's life and culture. As an ethical theory, it provides a sense of wholeness and continuity to both individuals and to cultures, and for this reason, it may be preferable to other theories.

On the negative side, it is not clear how to use narrative theory to decide what to do. It is not evident that by seeing our lives as stories we will know when faced with a moral dilemma what to choose. Narrative ethics may be more of a technique for describing a moral situation than a theory that explains how to know what to do. If the best that narrative theory can do is say, "Look at your ongoing story and the ongoing story of your tradition," then it does not tell us whether our story or tradition is good or bad. It does not set a moral standard. We need some standard or some goal that is separate from "life as a narrative" in order to have a basis for making choices within that narrative. There also is a concern about the universalizability of narrative theory. If every narrative is unique, then how can there be universality in narrative theory? Certainly there is no other person exactly like me, with my same life history, facing the exact same Bob Fritz. Yet all prescriptive theories must be universalizable, thus narrative theory, to count as a prescriptive theory, must somehow evidence this universality. Finally, narrative theory has not shown us either a standard for moral evaluation or universalizability, and these remain problems for the theory.

How to Use Moral Theories

Now it is time to step back and inquire about the point of this detailed discussion of moral theories. We have considered moral theories because we believe that your moral thinking as a professional and private person can be informed and clarified by moral theories. There are several ways moral theories are useful in the field of professional ethics.

The first way is that they give us insight into the moral thinking of ourselves and others. We can learn what approach to a situation a person will take by looking at the person's theory. If you know that your employer is a consequentialist, then you can be sure that consequential reasons will be especially compelling to her. Theories differ not because they tell us to adopt different courses of action but because they advise us to adopt different reasoning approaches to situations. Theorists are distinguished not by what they do but by how they decide what to do. You will not be able to recognize a consequentialist or a care ethicist by what they do. You will need to know why they decided to do what they did in order to tell them apart.

The second way theories are useful is that they explain our relationship to values. Theories both illuminate values (point them out) and interpret values (put them into practice). Theories support and interpret values, but they do not replace them. If we know a person's moral theory, then we probably know which values are especially important to him or her. A consequentialist values in particular beneficence and nonmaleficence, that is, benefitting and avoiding harm. A care ethicist especially values beneficence and compassion. In addition, if we know a person's moral theory, then we know why they hold the values they do. Theories resolve value conflicts by ranking values and developing arguments in favor of choosing one value over another. In short, theories are related to values in three ways: they highlight values, they interpret values, and they resolve value conflicts. All of these tasks are crucial to persons whose personal and professional lives are governed by values.

The third way they are useful is that, in addressing moral situations, they provide different models for how to deal with them. Sometimes moral theories can work together, although they do not always. You are free to choose among these theories. You need not be a duty theorist for life. You may discover that certain value conflicts are best dealt with by a duty approach, while other moral situations call for a consequential theory. We have seen in our discussion of the theories that some are compatible with others and can work together. A duty theorist can consider consequences as well as duties. A narrative theorist needs a virtue theory or some other theory in order to have a standard or goal for persons to strive toward in their life stories.

Conclusion

In this chapter we have discussed moral theories, which we have defined as tools that aid in the process of moral decision making. A theory provides a moral mind-set, a way of addressing and resolving moral problems. Each theory offers a way of thinking through and deciding about cases, and in this chapter, we used the theories to deal with the Bob Fritz case.

We recognized two types of moral theories: doing theories and being theories. Doing theories develop rules for action, while being theories depend on the moral agent expressing his or her character, relationships, or life. Doing theories include consequentialism, rights theory, and duty theory. Being theories include virtue theory, care theory, and narrative theory. As we have seen, no theory is perfect. Each has its good and bad points. The choice of a moral theory is left up to you, that is, it is left in the hands of individuals. Choose a theory, and use it consistently in all of your moral decision making. Or, decide to use different theories in different situations when the circumstances make one sort of approach better than another. Or, finally, combine theories and, by incorporating different perspectives, build on the strengths of the different theories.

EXERCISES

1. First, identify in each paragraph whether the reasoning manifests a doing theory (Do) or a being theory (Be), and second, whether the reasoning reflects consequentialism (Co), rights (R), duty (D), virtue (V), care (Ca), or narrative (N). Explain why.

1. "A professional needs tenacity and self-discipline to meet the arduous technical and practical demands of the work and a firm set of values and humane spirit to discharge the duties in practice. While altruism is not a necessary condition for expert work, we are able to trust the occasional selfish professional because he or she works within a social network of ethical persons."[8]

2. "It can happen that your very absorption and avid participation in life can become what keeps you from hearing that still small inner voice that distinguished right from wrong. . . . As Barbara Jordan put it in her powerful voice, 'What is right is right is right.' Ethics does not change, only the ethical environment changes. To hear we must listen, to ourselves."[9]

3. "Parental requests for children to write home, visit and offer them a reasonable amount of emotional and financial support in life's crises are well founded, so long as a friendship still exists. Love for others does call for caring about and caring for them. Some other parental requests, such as for more sweeping changes in the child's lifestyle or life goals, can be seen to be insupportable, once we shift the justification from debts owed to love. . . . What is relevant is the ongoing friendship that exists between parents and children. Although that relationship developed partly as a result of parental sacrifices for the child, the duties that grown children have to their parents result from the friendship rather than from the sacrifices."[10]

4. The father of the gravely ill child was a retired military leader. He was belligerent and arrogant with the hospital staff, and strict and dictatorial in his behavior toward his wife and other children. He refused to speak with anyone but the doctor of his ill child. The doctor kept all of this in mind as she entered the room to spell out the prognosis of the ill child.

5. "Drug use cannot be considered in a vacuum. We must understand it within the context of crime, violence, corruption, prostitution, multinational cartels, adverse health consequences, enormous social costs, and the collapse of our cities."[11]

6. "So great moreover is the regard of the law for private property, that it will not authorize the least violation of it; no, not even for the general good of the whole community."[12]

7. "I have urged that we should think of the ideal as the idea of what professionals should *be* rather than as a catalogue of what they should *do*. . . . What a person is, however, displays itself in what he or she does. Professionalism as a fundamental formation of personality and character is only a disposition until it is released in a stream of actions. Actions actualize and reinforce dispositions and dispositions are valuable just because they shape actions."[13]

8. "Suppose someone is holding another's property in trust (a deposit) whose owner is dead, and that the owner's heirs do not know and can never hear about it. Through no fault of his, the trustee's fortunes are at lowest ebb. He sees a sad family around

him, a wife and children disheartened by want. The man is kind and charitable, while those heirs are rich, loveless, extremely extravagant spendthrifts, so that this addition to their wealth might as well be thrown into the sea. And then ask whether under these circumstances it might be deemed permissible to convert the deposit to one's own use. Without doubt, anyone asked will answer "No!"—and in lieu of grounds he can merely say; "It is wrong!", i.e., it conflicts with duty. Nothing is clearer than that."[14]

9. "A medical student explains the decision not to turn in a proctor who violated the school rules against drinking on the grounds that turning him in is not a good way to respond to the problem, since it would dissolve the relationship between them and thus cut off an avenue for help."[15]

10. "Business has now become the most powerful force in society. We cannot solve social problems unless business accepts a leadership role. That in turn requires business to act in the interests of the common good. This is a very new role for business—one it is not used to or prepared for. The norm has been for business to be a special interest, and adversarial to the rest of society."[16]

11. The company president is deliberating about whether to send Petra Schultz, company VP, to close a deal with a firm in Brazil. On the one hand, Petra is fluent in the language and has already made several trips to the Brazilian company. On the other hand, on her last trip, Petra was sent to Japan to finalize arrangements for the purchase of Japanese computer components. The Japanese were shocked and unhappy to discover that Petra was a woman, since in their country women do not handle top-level business negotiations. They also expected to "wine and dine" Petra, but she refused, since as a recovering alcoholic and vegetarian she had particular mealtime needs. Last, although Petra handed over the gifts which always accompany a business transaction in Japan, she faxed a letter to the company president indicating her unhappiness with this part of the arrangement. She felt the gifts amounted to a bribe, and that handing them over might constitute a breach of U.S. trade law.

12. "Absent a compelling state interest (such as protecting a child from unfit parents), it certainly would be an intolerable invasion of privacy for the state to take children from their parents. But Baby M has two parents, both of whom now want her. It is not clear why only people who can give birth (i.e., women) should enjoy the right to rear their children."[17]

2. As we did earlier, give three responses to the situations, as a consequentialist, rights theorist, duty theorist, virtue theorist, care theorist, and narrative theorist. Is one or more of these responses better than some other responses? Why? Is one or more of these responses worse than some other responses? Why?

CASE 1: THE SUSPICIOUS LAWYER

You are a lawyer and have accepted as a client a couple who is trying to recover a child that the wife gave up for adoption several years ago. At that time, the couple was not married and the father did not know that he had a child. Now that they are married and he is informed, they want the child back. You believe they have a good case, which is bolstered by the fact that the adoptive family is not wealthy and presumably cannot afford expensive counsel. You believe that you can win the child back. But later you become suspicious that the couple uses drugs. The child has no legal representation. What should you do?

CASE 2: MINORITY FRANCHISING

"There are companies that do a good job of minority franchising. Unfortunately, Ben & Jerry's is not one of them. . . . McDonald's record is the best: 4.6 percent of their franchises are Latino owned, and 11.9 percent are owned by African Americans. McDonald's minority franchise program is designed to include Latino, African-American, Asian, and female franchisees in numbers that mirror the company's consumer base. Toward that end, they try to identify, then eliminate, traditional barriers. . . . Of Ben & Jerry's 156 U.S. scoop shops, only two are owned by African Americans. We're hoping to do much better in the future."[18]

CASE 3: THE SPEEDY WORKER

In the movie Big, *Tom Hanks plays a character who is working as a computer specialist. On his first day of work, he is progressing so quickly that the person in the next carrel leans over and says something like, "Slow down! Pace yourself, you want to make the rest of us look bad?" Suppose a computer professional starting a new job finds that he or she can finish the assigned work more quickly than the other employees. What should the computer professional do—slow down, keep working at the same pace, or something else?*

CASE 4: CLIENT ACCESS TO THE PSYCHOLOGIST'S RECORDS

You are a psychologist who has on two separate occasions treated Isabel Ruiz. Isabel was raised by her aunt and uncle since her parents died when she was a year old. When she was sixteen, her uncle died and she suffered a reactive depression. After six months of psychotherapy, she successfully recovered from the loss and went on to finish high school, then went away to college. A few years later her aunt died, and Isabel returned to you for a few sessions. She has expressed some interest in reviewing her records in regard to her prior treatment. In your file is a developmental history given by Isabel's aunt and uncle when she was sixteen, which reveals the information, still unknown to Isabel, that her mother was shot to death by her father, who later committed suicide. How should you handle Isabel's request?[19]

NOTES

1. There are many kinds of consequentialism. Some philosophers classify egoism (the theory that what is right is what produces the best possible consequences for me) as a type of consequential theory (see, for example, Lawrence M. Hinman, *Ethics: A Pluralistic Approach to Moral Theory* [Fort Worth, Tex.: Harcourt Brace, 1994], 156; and Jacques Thiroux, *Ethics: Theory and Practice*, Fifth edition, [Englewood Cliffs, N.J.: Prentice Hall, 1995], 40–48). The most well-known type of consequentialism is utilitarianism, formulated by Jeremy Bentham and John Stuart Mill (see Jeremy Bentham, *An Introduction to the Principles of Morals and Legislation* [1789], John Stuart Mill, *Utilitarianism* [1861], and contemporary works such as Paul Edwards, ed., *Utilitarianism and Its Critics* [New York: Macmillan, 1990] and Amartya Sen and Bernard Williams, eds., *Utilitarianism and Beyond* [New York: Cambridge University Press, 1982]). A theory called "situation ethics," defined by Joseph Fletcher, also is a kind of consequentialism aimed specifically at maximizing more good (defined as Christian love, *agape*) than harm for all (Joseph Fletcher, *Situation Ethics: The New Morality* [Philadelphia, Penn.: Westminster Press, 1966]). Consequentialists differ in terms of how they define the good that consequentialism aims at realizing.
2. On rights theory, see Ronald Dworkin, *Taking Rights Seriously* (Cambridge, Mass.: Harvard University Press, 1977), and Robert Nozick, *Anarchy, State, and Utopia* (New York: Basic Books, 1974).
3. There are many kinds of duty theorists. Some, like Immanuel Kant, believe that the agent's motive is the most important factor in determining what is right. Kant claimed that a person is acting rightly only if he or she acts for the sake of duty, that is, only if the rule he or she is following is in accord with the moral law and was chosen in order to act for the sake of the moral law (Immanuel Kant, *Groundwork of the Metaphysic of Morals* [1785], Chapter 1). Other duty theorists focus on the intrinsic nature of the act itself and thus discover acts that are inherently evil or good (for example, St. Thomas Aquinas, *Summa Contra Gentiles*, Book III, and John Finnis, *Natural Law and Natural Rights* [Oxford: Oxford University Press, 1980]). Some types of duty theorists allow the consequences to count as one factor in determining what is the right thing to do, while others exclude consequences all together.
4. There are many examples of virtue theorists, both ancient and contemporary. Plato (428–347 B.C.) and his student Aristotle (384–322 B.C.) were virtue theorists (Plato, *The Republic* and *The Meno*; Aristotle, *The Nicomachean Ethics*). Contemporary philosophers like Alasdair MacIntyre and Philippa Foot are

virtue theorists (Alasdair MacIntyre, *After Virtue*, 2d ed., [Notre Dame, Ind.: University of Notre Dame Press, 1984]; Philippa Foot, "Virtues and Vices," in her book *Virtues and Vices and Other Essays in Moral Philosophy* [Berkeley and Los Angeles, Calif.: University of California Press, 1978], 1–18). Even the general public seems interested in virtue theory as evidenced by the popularity of William J. Bennett's books, including *The Book of Virtues* (New York: Simon & Schuster, 1993). One issue that divides virtue theorists is the question of what the virtues are. Aristotle developed a long list of virtues. Some are rather obvious—justice, friendliness, truthfulness—but others are more controversial—courage, gentleness, magnificence (*Nicomachean Ethics*, Books III, IV, V). William J. Bennett considers work and faith to be virtues (*The Book of Virtues*, Chapters 5 and 10). Thus, there will be as many different types of virtue theorists as there are people developing lists of virtues.

5. Aristotle makes these two points in his *Nicomachean Ethics*, Book IX.

6. Many but not all of those who espouse a care ethic are women. See, among others, Nel Noddings, *Caring: A Feminine Approach to Ethics and Moral Education* (Berkeley, Calif.: University of California Press, 1984); Rita C. Manning, *Speaking from the Heart: A Feminist Perspective on Ethics* (Lanham, Md.: Rowman & Littlefield, 1992); and Lawrence M. Hinman, who identifies Martin Buber's work, *I and Thou*, translated by Ronald Gregor Smith (New York: Scribner & Sons, 1960), as one that reflects the care ethic (Hinman, *Ethics: A Pluralistic Approach to Moral Theory* [Fort Worth, Tex.: Harcourt Brace Jovanovich, 1994], 353). The beginning of the care ethic can be traced back to Carol Gilligan's work in the 1970s. In her book, Gilligan claims that girls have a different moral attitude than do boys. Girls tend to focus on relationships and on how others would feel, while boys tend to hold more strictly to the rules and what is just (Carol Gilligan, *In a Different Voice: Psychological Theory and Women's Development* [Cambridge, Mass.: Harvard University Press, 1982]).

7. Narrative theory is a phenomenon of the twentieth century and is connected with philosophers such as Alasdair MacIntyre and Paul Ricoeur. See Alasdair MacIntyre, *After Virtue*, and Paul Ricoeur, *Time and Narrative*, 3 vols. (Chicago, Ill.: University of Chicago Press, 1985–1989). Also, see narrative theory used in an introductory textbook in Nina Rosenstand, *The Moral of the Story: An Introduction to Questions of Ethics and Human Nature* (Mountain View, Calif.: Mayfield, 1994) and narrative theory used in medical ethics in *Stories and Their Limits: Narrative Approaches to Bioethics*, edited by Hilde Lindemann Nelson (New York: Routledge, 1997).

8. From John Kultgen, *Ethics and Professionalism* (Philadelphia, Penn.: University of Pennsylvania Press, 1988), 95.

9. Nan Hutchins Bailey, "Learning: There Is Always Room for More," *Vital Speeches of the Day*, Vol. LXIII, No. 20 (August 1, 1997), 640.

10. From Jane English, "What Do Grown Children Owe Their Parents?" in *Having Children*, edited by Onora O'Neill and William Ruddick (New York: Oxford University Press, 1979), 355–56.

11. Barry R. McCaffrey, "National Drug Control: Reducing Drug Use and Its Consequences in America," *Vital Speeches of the Day*, Vol. LXIII, No. 20 (August 1, 1997), 623.

12. William Blackstone, *Commentaries on the Laws of England*, Book I, Chapter I (Oxford: Clarendon Press, 1765; rpt. Chicago, Ill.: The University of Chicago Press, 1979). The quote is on page 135 of the Chicago reprint.

13. Taken from John Kultgen, *Ethics and Professionalism*, 346.

14. Abridged from Immanuel Kant, *On the Old Saw: That May Be Right in Theory But It Won't Work in Practice*, E. B. Ashton, trans. (Philadelphia, Penn.: University of Pennsylvania Press, 1974), 53.

15. Adapted from Carol Gilligan, "Moral Orientation and Moral Development," in *Women and Moral Theory*, edited by Eva Feder Kittay and Diana T. Meyers (Totowa, N.J.: Rowman & Littlefield, 1987), 24.

16. From Ben Cohen and Jerry Greenfield, *Ben & Jerry's Double-Dip: Lead with Your Values and Make Money, Too* (New York: Simon & Schuster, 1997), 33.

17. Bonnie Steinbock, "Surrogate Motherhood As Prenatal Adoption," *Law, Medicine & Health Care* 16, No. 1–2 (1988), 48–49.

18. From Ben Cohen and Jerry Greenfield, *Ben & Jerry's Double-Dip: Lead with Your Values and Make Money, Too*, 119.

19. Adapted from a case in Patricia Keith-Spiegel and Gerald P. Koocher, *Ethics in Psychology: Professional Standards and Cases* (New York: Random House, 1985), 71.

6

Moral Analysis
and Case Solving

The purpose of this chapter is to tie together all of the pieces from the previous ones. This will give us the big picture, which will include the analysis of moral explanations and case solving. We will do this by following up on the language of morality, which we have already considered (reasons, explanations, values, theories, and more), and fitting together these pieces of moral decision making. Our aim is to provide you with a comprehensive picture of how a moral professional analyzes moral explanations and does moral decision making.

So far we have laid out many pieces to the picture called "the life of a moral professional." We have looked at who professionals are and what morality is. We know that the professional life is governed by values and that morality is about using moral reasons, and even better, strong moral reasons, to make decisions. We have looked at how professionals assess and evaluate moral reasons and explanations. We have seen that moral reasons express values and reflect the perspective of a certain ethical theory, whether consequential, care, or some other. Now we want to look comprehensively at how moral professionals make decisions. Moral professionals do two things: they analyze moral explanations given by others; and they develop moral explanations in the process of deciding what to do in moral situations. Therefore, moral professionals need to be skilled at analyzing moral justifications and at thinking through moral situations and giving moral justifications. These skills are acquired by putting together the pieces we have outlined so far, namely, moral reasons, explanations, values, and theories.

You may be wondering why moral professionals need these skills. The answer is simple. From the viewpoint of professional ethics, the professional's life centers around decision making. Professionals make decisions and respond to the decisions of others. Knowing everything there is to know about ethics will not help the professional unless this knowledge can be directed toward clarifying the processes of analyzing and making moral decisions. Professionals work with and for others—clients, employers, colleagues, and the public. There is a relational component to being a professional. Hence, part of the moral activity of professionals is understanding the reasons given and the decisions made by others. Sometimes professionals must be able to do this analysis of another's decision before being able to make their own decisions. From the point of view of professional ethics, decision making and case solving are the key activities of professionals.

This chapter completes our account of what morality is and our view of what professional ethics is. Upon completion, you will have the skills to analyze moral explanations and do moral decision making.

Introducing the Moral Framework

To begin to put together the pieces of the big picture, we will describe a moral framework that identifies four distinct parts in a moral explanation. Recall that a moral explanation is an account or a justification for a decision that includes at least one moral reason. An explanation is the sum total of the reasons offered in defense of a decision. The framework presented here offers a straightforward, simple way of analyzing what has gone into the making of a moral decision.

Let us first consider what the framework can and cannot do. The moral framework can provide a useful tool for discovering the internal structure of our moral explanations and for analyzing the moral explanations of others. It can help us recognize when we have a thorough, well thought out moral explanation. The moral framework cannot tell us if a moral decision is right or wrong. It cannot evaluate or judge a moral decision or explanation. For that we would have to turn to our discussion of strong and weak moral reasons and explanations in chapter 4. The moral framework can only help us understand what is involved in moral justification, what comes into play in the agent's moral thinking, and how the justification is framed. In allowing us to analyze the parts of a person's moral thinking, a framework is an organizing tool.

Is the framework presented here the only possible way of analyzing moral explanations? Of course not. There are other possible frameworks.[1] Is it the perfect structure? That would be hard to prove or describe, but it works well and can be applied equally well, whether a person is offering a consequential, narrative, or some other type of moral explanation. The framework enables us to see how an explanation is constructed, regardless of what type of theory it uses or what values it invokes. By locating several distinct parts in any moral explanation, the framework thus clarifies all types of moral explanations. In this way, the moral framework is proven to be useful, even if it cannot be shown to be the perfect or only possible way of clarifying moral explanations.

Now, knowing what the moral framework can and cannot do, let us describe it. The framework identifies four parts of a moral explanation.[2] In order to make a *decision*, a thorough moral explanation requires appealing to a *rule*, using a *theory*, and applying a *value*. Each part has its own degree of specificity and universality, and each part is related to at least one of the other parts. Each part is defined both in terms of what it is (what form it takes) and what it does (what its job is in relation to the other parts).

Let us take a look at each part of the framework. A decision is a concrete choice made in a particular situation. It is the most obvious piece of a person's moral thinking because it often is a public event, usually a choice or an action. A decision is what we see. Decisions are stated in the particular, although they are universalizable to others in the same situation. At the level of a decision, only the resolution reached, the choice made, is reported.

With the decision being what we see, how about the other three pieces of our framework that provide the moral explanation? Each of the other three parts aims at giving evidence for why the decision was reached. Each of these parts has a universality not obvious in the decision. While the decision is particular, the other parts of the explanation refer not specifically to this decision but to ways of approaching decisions generally. They look for ways to justify this decision by relating it to other decisions or to universal directives or goals.

A rule is a statement about the rightness or wrongness of a class of actions. It is stated more generally than the decision that follows from it or appeals to it for evidence. Rules are guidelines, or directives, about what ought or ought not to be done. A rule's job is to explain a decision. It accounts for the decision by showing that the decision falls into a broad class of decisions that are designated as right. When we settle on a rule, the rule can be applied over and over. A rule subsumes the particular decision into a larger class of right decisions, thus justifies it through its inclusion in this broader class.

The next part of the framework is theory, which we described in chapter 5, and which refers to a broad moral perspective. A theory is a way of interpreting and applying values. We identified six major types of theories: consequentialism, rights, duties, virtue, care, and narrative. A theory gives us a way of expressing values and a method for prioritizing values. It provides a framework for the application and living out of values. Theories also generate rules, hence give us a way of translating values into specific behavioral guidelines. Rules follow from theories, which have different mechanisms for putting values into practice.

The final part of the moral framework is value, which as we have seen in chapters 3 and 4 refers to a claim about what is worthwhile, what is good. A value is a single word or phrase that identifies something as being desirable for human beings. Values are acted on and applied by theories and then rules. We have guidelines about what types of decisions are moral because we have identified certain things as being good, which these decisions seek to uphold. Values are those goods that our theories, rules, and decisions work to bring about in the world.

To summarize, a decision is explained by a rule that is formulated in the context of a theory which both generates rules and interprets and applies values. This is our moral framework for understanding what goes into a moral explanation. We will use it to analyze the moral explanations of others and to help us clarify our own moral justifications. Since we use the framework as a tool for understanding the organization of a moral explanation, it usually makes sense to begin with the decision part. Ordinarily, what we see first is a decision, and then to understand the reasons for it, we work toward rules, theories, and values. Sometimes, however, the framework is used to organize an explanation for a decision that is in the process of being made. Then it makes more sense to begin with values and to work toward theories, rules, and a decision as we develop our reasons for a decision. Later we return to this use of the framework for decision making, expanding it into a full-fledged case resolution model. For now, we use the framework solely for analyzing decisions already made.

Moral Framework

<table>
<tr><td align="center">**Analysis**
(Decision Already Made)
⟶</td><td></td><td></td><td></td><td align="center">**Decision Making**
(Decision to be Made)
⟵</td></tr>
<tr><td align="center">Decision</td><td align="center">——</td><td align="center">Rule   ——   Theory</td><td align="center">——</td><td align="center">Value</td></tr>
</table>

The Framework Applied to a Case

Consider now how the framework enables us to analyze decisions that have already been made. With the framework we are able to diagram the parts of a person's explanation and thereby judge whether each part is clear and well thought out. After analyzing the structure and clarity of a person's explanation, we can then go on to assess the strength of the person's explanation. So, in the example that follows, we look at a decision that is already made, and we see how the decision maker arrived at that conclusion by analyzing the decision maker's rule, theory, and value.

> *Having recently completed her Ph.D. in chemistry, Georgine has not been able to find a job. Her family has suffered from her failure. Since they are short of money, her husband has had to take on a second job, and their small children have been subjected to considerable strain, uncertainty, and instability. An established chemist can get Georgine a position in a laboratory that pursues research in chemical and biological warfare. Despite her perilous financial and familial circumstances, Georgine feels that she cannot accept this position because of her conscientious opposition to chemical and biological warfare. The older chemist notes that although he is not enthusiastic about this project, the research will continue whatever Georgine decides. Furthermore, if Georgine does not take the position, it will be offered to another young Ph.D., who probably would pursue the research with alacrity and promptitude. Indeed, the older chemist confides, his concern about this other candidate's nationalistic fervor and uncritical zeal for research in chemical and biological warfare in part led him to recommend Georgine. Georgine's husband is puzzled and hurt by her reaction, since he sees nothing wrong with such research. He is mainly concerned about the instability of their family and their children's problems.*[3]

Granted, there are a number of moral issues that this case raises. One is biological and chemical warfare. What about the morality of war and, in particular, biological and chemical war? What about a person's participation, however peripheral in an organization, whose work contributes to biological and chemical warfare? Another related moral issue centers on the responsibility of individuals for the state of society or for institutional direction. Are specific individuals responsible for promoting biological and chemical war just because they happen to work at research institutions that study this? Are particular individuals responsible for wars or casualties that might at some future time follow from whatever use is made of their research? Finally, the case raises the moral question of how to balance work and family. Is there a way for professionals to live out their moral commitments at work and at home? Or, if those moral commitments compete, how should they reconcile them? All of these issues and questions may be on our minds as we look at Georgine's decision and her explanation. But we will not address all of these questions. We will only apply the moral framework to Georgine's case in order to describe the parts of her explanation.

Decision:

Georgine has decided to not take the job in the lab that pursues chemical and biological warfare. She also has decided to not count her husband's view that tolerates research on chemical and biological warfare and to not count the older chemist's view that her cautious stance on this subject makes her a better candidate for the job than the other candidate, who approaches the research with zeal.

Rule:

One of Georgine's rules is that chemical and biological warfare is wrong. She believes that she (and others) should not take jobs that promote chemical and biological warfare. Her rule is: People ought to follow their consciences and not do things that they are conscientiously opposed to. Another rule she holds that conflicts with her prior one is: People should get jobs and help support their families.

Theory:

Georgine is thinking at least in part like a duty theorist. She will not give up her sense of what is right, even to realize good consequences to herself, her family, and others. It may be that more harm comes to society if the other candidate takes the job, but Georgine is not primarily interested in producing good consequences, but in remaining true to her beliefs. She is, for reasons of conscience, opposed to chemical and biological warfare, regardless of the consequences of her opposition.

In addition to duty theory, Georgine is possibly using virtue theory or narrative theory. She is aiming to lead a good life as she understands it and to have her actions reflect her character. Or she might explain this decision in a narrative way by relating it to the ongoing story of her life, to other decisions she has made, to other experiences she has had, and to other commitments she has made.

It seems less likely that Georgine's theory is a consequential, rights, or care theory. Probably the reason Georgine is opposed to chemical and biological warfare is because she values beneficence and nonmaleficence and respect for persons. She does not want to cause harm or act in ways that fail to respect persons. But she does not say this, so to see her action as reflecting a concern for consequences is a bit of a stretch. Neither has Georgine said anything about rights or moral claims, so there is no evidence that points to a rights theory. Similarly, Georgine has not said anything that leads us to believe that she is manifesting a care ethic and choosing through her action to exhibit her caring relationship with the whole earth and future generations. While Georgine's theory could be a duty theory, virtue theory, narrative theory, or all three, we can eliminate consequential, rights, and care theories since there is no sign that she is making use of them.

There are two other points that can be made about Georgine's theory. First, since theories generate rules or, put in another way, since rules are formulated in the context of theories, there should be some connection between Georgine's theories and rules. Because her theory seems to be based on duty, virtue, and narrative, we know that her rules will be stated in terms of duties and obligations, character, and life story. Georgine's rules must reflect the theory or theories she employs. Second, since theories interpret and apply values, it is up to theories to rank or prioritize values if that is necessary in a case. As we see with Georgine, her theories have led her to conclude that integrity is more important to her than beneficence and nonmaleficence toward herself and her family. She is willing to let their uncertainty and suffering continue, at least temporarily for the sake of what to her is a greater good. This ranking of values is accomplished by the interpretive powers of a theory, hence when choices and hierarchies are made among values, we know that there is a theory at work.

Value:

Georgine can be seen to be valuing several goods. She has not enumerated her values, so we are doing some detective work to discover them. We can find Georgine's values reflected in her actions, decisions, rules, and theories. She values integrity as reflected in her unwillingness to act contrary to her beliefs or her sense of what is right. She values beneficence and nonmaleficence to herself and her family in that she is trying to get a job to help support the family and because she recognizes the stress and financial difficulties of her family. Georgine also values responsibility. She recognizes that she is responsible for her actions and for the results of those actions. She is in part responsible for her family, so she is job hunting in order to meet that responsibility. But at the same time she will be responsible for whatever work she does, and it is because of this sense of responsibility that she is cautious about deciding what work to do. She decides she will work only at a job where she can in good conscience accept responsibility for her work. Thus, integrity, beneficence and nonmaleficence, and responsibility are all valued by Georgine.

Issues When Using the Framework

Now that we have taken a look at a case, we can note several points about applying the moral framework. These points can be taken as cautions. Each draws our attention to some aspect of the framework and cautions our expectations for the framework. Thus, each caution reminds us that the framework is only an organizing tool for moral analysis and decision making. Would it not be easy if the framework could be applied in the same way by all of us and we would all arrive at the same answer? But not all moral thinkers use it in exactly the same way and, even if they did, the framework cannot provide the best moral explanations. What it can provide is the building blocks for moral decision making and moral explanations.

Caution 1: One value can ground or give a reason for many different theories, rules, and decisions.

There is no one-to-one connection between a value and a particular theory, rule, or decision. The same value, for instance, integrity, can be at work in two very different theories, for example, duty and care. No theory has exclusive possession of any value. In fact, all of the theories recognize to some extent all of the values. While beneficence and nonmaleficence may be more central to a consequential theory than they are to a rights theory, no value is identified solely with a single theory.

The same point can be made about the relationship of values to rules and decisions. Although two professionals share the value of loyalty, they may act on very different rules. Does loyalty mean loyalty to one's employer, loyalty to one's client, loyalty to one's colleagues, loyalty to the profession's code of ethics, loyalty to one's familial responsibilities, or what? To take another example, one of the values is respect for persons. When applied to severely handicapped newborns, some people believe respect for persons gives rise to the rule that all medical professionals must do everything possible to save the lives of handicapped newborns. Other persons believe respect for persons sanctions a rule that gives medical professionals the right or even the responsibility under certain conditions to let severely handicapped newborns (and others) die. Still others who value respect for persons may judge that severely handicapped newborns are not persons, thus they may claim that there is no rule regarding the treatment of handicapped newborns by medical professionals that follows from the value of respect for persons. For example, the Nuer tribe in Africa considers severely handicapped newborns hippopotamuses, born mistakenly to human parents. Consequently, the appropriate rule they follow is to allow these baby hippopotamuses to be rejoined with their families by placing them in the river.[4]

Knowing that someone values respect for persons does not tell us if he or she will decide to save handicapped newborns or let them die. The same value can give a reason for many different decisions. Thus identifying a person's values does not automatically show what theory or rule a person will follow or what decision a person will make. In the case of Georgine, the chemist, her values include integrity, beneficence and nonmaleficence to herself and her family, and responsibility. Based on this alone, we do not know if she will choose a consequential theory, a virtue theory, or some other theory. We do not know if she will develop a rule that furthers family accord and the well-being of her own children at all costs or only under certain conditions. And we do not know if she will decide to take the job or not. Values can be interpreted in different ways and can be used to justify multiple, and even competing, theories, rules, and decisions.

Caution 2: Some examples of moral decision making skip a part in the framework.

Since these parts of the moral framework together analyze a decision and its moral explanation, we can expect in general to find all four parts whenever we have a decision backed up by a moral explanation. But since our framework is not an air-tight system that can force all explanations to be constructed in exactly the same way, sometimes decision makers skip a part of the framework. There are two exceptional sorts of cases in which decision makers do not use all four parts of the moral framework. In one sort of case, the part that is left out is the rule. Some types of theories skip rules for philosophical reasons.[5] In other cases, persons simply may not need rules to interpret their values. They may be able to move directly from theory to decision. Georgine, the chemist, may have been able to move from her values of integrity, beneficence and nonmaleficence, and responsibility, and her duty, virtue, or narrative theory directly to her decision to not take the job. For her, the values and theories may have dictated her action without the need for any intermediate rules. So, remember, rules are not always a part of the moral framework, although they generally are a helpful part of the decision-making process.

In a second sort of case, the part that is left out is the decision. Sometimes a moral explanation is provided for a rule and not for a particular decision. Sometimes persons are only aiming to arrive at rules or policies, and they need not make a particular decision or yet apply the rule. In this type of situation, a moral explanation justifies a rule but does not have to reach a decision.

Caution 3: Values, theories, and rules can compete with themselves or each other.

The framework is not meant to suggest that the process of moral decision making and decision analysis is simple, tidy, and perfectly linear. In most cases, moral reasoning is not a straightforward process of moving from values through theory to rule to decision. If it were, our moral landscape would look very different. More likely, a decision maker has a collection of values loosely ordered and interpreted by a not very explicitly thought out theory. Maybe in a moral situation only one of these values will be called into question, but more likely several will be. Then the moral thinker has to decide how to deal with these several values, which exert competing demands. Even worse, the moral thinker also has to decide which theory to use to interpret the values and which rules are formulated by the theories. For instance, Georgine may have recognized several theories and rules that are relevant to the resolution of her situation, all of which reflect goods she values. Yet it may be impossible to act on all of the theories and rules. Maybe in this case Georgine cannot act on two of her rules: People ought to follow their consciences, and people ought to support their families. Thus, in a moral explanation, there are frequently several competing rules, theories, and values in evidence. And if the framework somehow suggests that a value is applied by a single theory that translates into one rule which gives a reason for one decision, then life itself is quick to correct that impression. Most moral decision making involves balancing the claims of competing values as they are acted out in theories and rules.

Caution 4: Even if we agree on values, once a decision is reached, there may not be agreement on how the values ought to have been implemented.

Decisions frequently reflect the fact that choices have been made to act on this value and not on that value, this theory, not that theory, and this rule, not that rule. Other persons may very well disagree with these choices. Even if they agree on the values, they may not agree on how the values are implemented. When we make decisions, some values are taken as central or overriding in this case, while others are taken as secondary, at least in this case. The same values will not be central all of the time. When you make a decision, you implicitly or explicitly decide to which values or theories or rules you are committed. Inevitably there will be disagreements over the ranking of rules, theories, and values which is evidenced in a person's moral decision. Decision making requires making these kinds of choices and rankings, though we are of course allowed to question each other's decisions and evaluate each other's moral explanations.

So, for example, we might disagree with Georgine. We may think that her family's well-being ought to count for more. Her family's well-being is an immediate good and one that Georgine is especially responsible for in her role as spouse and parent. She also can do much to bring about this good, and it is a good that affects many. We may feel that Georgine's integrity is a more abstract good, and while it affects her sense of well-being, it has no effect on others. Georgine of course could respond by claiming that her integrity affects more than just herself. If she upholds her integrity, she will set an example for her children and others to follow, and by being at peace with herself, she will be better able to be at peace with her family and others.

Or, perhaps we think that as a professional, Georgine has obligations to society that overrule her personal commitments. Perhaps she ought to do something to stop the other candidate, who is rumored to be filled with nationalistic fervor and enthusiastic about biological warfare, from getting the job. Maybe she ought to work with the professional groups that monitor the labs doing chemical warfare research or lobby other chemists or political leaders to put a halt to this kind of research. The point is, some would argue, as a professional, Georgine must be concerned not just with her personal aspirations and beliefs but also with the goals and beliefs of her profession, of the community of professionals of which she is a part, whether or not she takes this job.

In sum, we have noted four cautions to remember when using the moral framework.

1. One value can give a reason for many different theories, rules, and decisions.
2. Some examples of moral decision making skip over rules or decisions.
3. Values, theories, and rules can compete.
4. Not everyone will agree on how the values ought to be implemented by theories, rules, and decisions.

The moral framework helps us see the building blocks of moral explanations. But we cannot assume that the framework will be used the same way by everyone, or that it makes the analysis of moral explanations simple. The job of the framework is to provide a tool that clarifies how values, theories, rules, and decisions relate to each other in a case. The cautions remind us that the framework cannot determine how values ought to be implemented by theories, rules, and decisions.

Case Resolution Model

Finally, with all of the work we have done, it is time to formalize the process of resolving cases. We have already considered a case in which a decision was made. We have used the moral framework to expose the structure of a moral explanation. Now we turn to situations in which decisions need to be made, but are not yet made. In these cases, as we said earlier, we can reverse the four parts of the moral framework, and thus work from values through theories in order to develop rules and reach decisions. To be clear about the process of moral decision making and to be efficient in doing moral decision making, in what follows we are going to expand our four parts into eight parts and refer to them together as the Case Resolution Model (CRM).

Analyzing decisions is a bit easier than making decisions. When you analyze a decision already made, the person who made the decision, not you, has recognized a moral situation, collected the facts, considered the options, and made a decision. They also, more often than not, have to deal with the results of their decision. What remains for you to do is to isolate what the decision maker decided and how he or she used rules, adopted theories, and expressed values. In making a moral decision, things are different. Now all of the work is done by you. You are the one who has to recognize the moral situation and collect the facts. Doing so requires using the moral framework in reverse to make a decision and reflecting on the adequacy or appropriateness of your decision, not to mention dealing with the results of your decision. The CRM presented here provides a step-by-step procedure for working through a situation that raises moral questions in order to arrive at a defensible decision. We will use this model from now on to guide us in resolving cases.

There are eight steps in the CRM.[6] These steps can be seen as part of a three-stage process.

Stage I.

1. (*P*)resent the problem.
   Identify the issue, define the moral situation.
2. (*C*)ollect information.
   List the relevant facts.

Stage II.

3. (*L*)ist the relevant values.
4. (*E*)xplore the options and the ways in which the theories apply and interpret values.
   Consider the alternatives. Be sensitive to the possibility of solutions beyond the obvious. Look for a middle-of-the-road solution, a compromise, or a third choice where only two have been acknowledged.
5. (*A*)ssess the rightness and wrongness of various outcomes.
6. (*D*)ecide.
   Reach a solution.

Stage III.

7. (*D*)efend.
   Justify the decision. Give reasons that explain your decision. Assess whether they are strong reasons.

8. (R)eflect.

Consider first whether anything was lacking in the resolution of the case or in the defense of the decision. Discuss objections that might be raised to the decision reached or to the reasons offered. Then consider how this problem or situation could have been avoided. Suggest strategies for avoiding future cases like this one. For instance, could policy changes, better communication, and so on prevent cases like this one from arising?

First, in Stage I, (P) and (C) ask for the moral situation to be identified. Here the problem is stated and relevant data is collected and listed. These steps provide the background material necessary for moral decision making. In analyzing a decision already made, we do not need to do these two steps.

Next, in Stage II, (L), (E), (A), and (D) do the real work of our moral decision making. The four steps make use of the background material from Stage I in order to do moral problem solving. These four steps are the same as the four steps of the moral framework, but now in reverse: (L) calls for the recognition of values; (E) asks us to look at how theories put values into practice; in (A) we formulate rules and judge the rightness and wrongness of these various options suggested by the theories; in (D) we make a decision.

Finally, in Stage III, (D) and (R) conclude the process of moral decision making. They provide a kind of "wrap-up" through which we can rethink the decision we have reached and the defense we have offered for it. Here we reflect back on the whole process of resolving the case in order to assess whether the decision reached and the defense offered are in any way lacking and whether the problem could be avoided in the future.

There is one more point to note about the way the CRM works. The eight steps in the Model, (P), (C), (L), (E), (A), (D), (D), and (R) are not all equally taxing or equally time consuming. Some of them are fairly easy. (P) and (C) ask only for summarizing the situation and the facts evident in the case. Some of the steps are hard. (E) may be difficult, in that many different alternatives may have to be assessed and compared. (D), the decision step, does not need much explanation in the model, but it may be the step that requires the greatest amount of reflection and emotional energy. Do not expect each of the eight steps to be accomplished in the same amount of time. Also, steps that go simply or quickly in one case may be difficult and take longer in another case. You may, in one case, run through (P), (C), (L), and (E) quickly and then work for a long time on (A). In another case, you may work the hardest or longest on (L), in identifying the main values, or on (E), in elaborating the possible options. The steps in the CRM may be more or less difficult due to the circumstances of the case in which they are applied.

Now that we have articulated the CRM, let us see how it is used to arrive at a decision where one has not yet been made.

> *Abdul Khan, with an undergraduate degree in computer science, has his own consulting business. He is now designing a database management system for the personnel office of a medium-sized company that manufactures toys. Abdul has involved the client in the design process, informing the CEO, the director of computing and the director of personnel about the progress of the system and giving them many opportunities to make decisions about features of the system. It is now time to make decisions about the kind and degree of security to build into the system. The information they will be storing is extremely sensitive, because it will include performance evaluations, medical records for filing insurance claims, and salaries. With weak security, it may be possible for enterprising employees to figure out how to access this data, not to mention the possibilities for on-line access from hackers.*
>
> *Abdul has described several security options to his client, and the client has decided to opt for the least secure system because the system is going to cost more than they had planned. Abdul feels strongly that the system should be much more secure.*
>
> *He has tried to explain the risks to his client, but the CEO, director of computing, and director of personnel are all willing to accept a system with little security.[7]*

Stage I.

 1.   (*P*)resent the problem.

The main problem seems to be how to resolve the conflict between Abdul's recommended plan for the system's security and the client's unwillingness to compensate him for the more secure system. Hence, in contrast to Abdul's recommendation, the client decides to go with the less secure system.

 2.   (*C*)ollect the facts.

Abdul is a computer specialist. He is hired to design a database management system, and he has involved his clients in the design process. They have decided, for cost reasons, to go with the least secure system. Abdul feels that this is a mistake and that they ought to choose a more secure system. A more secure system is less likely to compromise employee confidentiality, whereas

As a virtue theorist, Abdul would aim to act in a way that expresses good character, that is, in a way that reflects the ideal professional he aspires to be. Again, it is not obvious what a virtue theorist would choose. On one account, Abdul acts virtuously by allowing his client to make the final decision on which system to select. In this way, Abdul is shown to be a just and benevolent person. On another account, virtue is expressed by further educating the client or even by threatening to quit. With this view, Abdul might believe that, as a virtuous professional, he must live up to his own and the profession's standards. Acting virtuously may require living up to personal and professional standards, even at the cost of losing a job or facing a client's displeasure. Thus, if Abdul uses a virtue theory, then he is likely to stress the values of beneficence and nonmaleficence, respect for persons, and integrity.

Abdul might decide to use care theory and to act in a way that expresses care and preserves relationships. One option suggested by care theory is to further educate the client about the pros and cons of the systems. This alternative cares for the client by continuing to work with him to arrive at the best alternative. It also reflects care for the client, not only as a management group but for all of the client's employees in seeking to find ways to protect their confidentiality and privacy. A second option proposed by care theory is to go along with the client's wishes and install the less secure system. In this way, the relationship between the client and Abdul is preserved. Perhaps it is up to the client, not Abdul, to decide how to best care for the employees. As a care theorist, Abdul is concerned with beneficence and nonmaleficence and respect for persons.

Using narrative theory, Abdul would look for an option that best reflects the ongoing story of his life and of his relationship with the toy manufacturer. In his history with this client, has he told them or led them to believe that they will be the ones to make the decision about the security system? Do they understand the professional standards, and do they understand how important it is to Abdul to have his professional judgment respected? Will Abdul be able to live with himself if the company chooses not to install the more secure system? Abdul may decide, in keeping with the narrative theory, to do what the client chooses, to further educate the company, or to quit or threaten to quit unless the company accepts the more secure system. Here Abdul is appealing to the values of beneficence and nonmaleficence, integrity, and responsibility

5. (*A*)ssess the rightness and wrongness of various outcomes.

Abdul might consider rules like these: It is right for a computer systems designer to adhere to the profession's standards; Clients ought to choose the most secure systems possible for their own protection; Clients ought to have the final say in selecting design features for a system; and It is not right for designers to pressure clients to accept the design features that they think should be chosen.

6. (*D*)ecide.

Abdul should look for some creative ways to further educate his client about the pros and cons of the security systems.

Stage III.

7. (*D*)efend.

Given the options, this decision is best because it allows for a continuing relationship of cooperation between Abdul and his client. It recognizes that up until this point, Abdul and his client have been working together to make decisions, and that it is in both the client's and Abdul's interests to have this relationship continue. All of the moral theories support this decision. Abdul can further the greatest good, uphold rights and duties, and still care for others, act virtuously, and act in ways that are consistent with the ongoing lives of the persons and the company in question. Perhaps the client does not really understand the level of risk involved in the less secure system. Abdul can educate him. Perhaps Abdul does not understand the financial costs to the client of installing the more secure system. The client can educate him. Maybe the company will have to wait a year to upgrade to a more secure system, when it is better able to bear the costs. At least Abdul can help the client see the risks in a less secure system, can work to reduce the cost of the more secure system, and can, by acting competently and with integrity, encourage the company to rehire him to do the upgrade when they can afford it.

The other options—acceding to the client's wishes or quitting or threatening to quit—are not supported by all of the theories. They fail in part because they are not sensitive to the working relationship between Abdul and his client. These options that fail view Abdul and his client as being independent of each other and as opposing possible sources of a decision. In fact, Abdul and his client are connected, and they share many of the same values. Both have a concern for beneficence and nonmaleficence, respect for persons (employee confidentiality and privacy), and professional integrity and responsibility (Abdul's ability to do a competent, responsible job). They may not agree entirely on how much emphasis or priority each of these values should have, but the alternative that allows them to work for their common values and to discuss their different senses of the importance of each value is preferable to those that do not recognize shared values. Here we can preserve dialogue, relationships, and community. With the other options, we could not.

8. (R)eflect.

As we reflect back on the decision made, we want to consider both the decision and the defense offered for it, and the situation that led to the need for a decision. In this case, the decision and the defense provided are well supported. Abdul found a decision that is backed up by all of the moral theories, hence one that realizes all of the relevant values. Obviously there are other ways of using the theories that could have led to different decisions. For example, a consequentialist could object that Abdul is wrong and that more good comes from giving in to the client's wishes, or a rights theorist might claim that Abdul is wrong because the client's rights take priority over both the employees' rights and Abdul's rights. There will always be objections to decisions made and defenses offered but, in this case, the objections are not serious or unforeseen.

There are two points about the situation itself that might be clarified in order to help Abdul and others avoid having to make decisions like this one. First, Abdul has involved the client in the design process and has let the client make decisions about features of the database system. In the future, Abdul could specify in advance what decisions will be the client's to make and what decisions will be his. He might explain in his consulting contract who has the final say on a decision. If he feels strongly about the security issue, he could inform clients in advance that he always uses the more secure systems and that he will not design a system with insufficient security, even at a client's request.

Second, the system has ended up costing more than the client planned. Is this Abdul's fault or the client's? If it is Abdul's, he should make sure to do better budget planning in the future. It is not fair to require a more expensive security system when the project is already over budget. Even if the bad planning was the client's fault, for example, if they did not accurately budget how many hours of time Abdul would need to design the system, Abdul could still help avoid having this happen in the future by offering clients estimates of the time and costs required to complete a job.

You may find additional points to raise. Do you have objections about the decision reached by Abdul? Or are there ways of avoiding Abdul's situation that have not yet been mentioned? If so, consider them here.

The CRM enables us to describe the situation facing Abdul Khan, explore its possibilities, reach a conclusion and defend it, and reflect on ways to avoid similar situations. In all cases, it gives us a procedure to follow in making moral decisions.

Competing Values

Both the moral framework and the CRM show us how a professional identifies values and ultimately acts on them. There are cases, though they are rare, like Abdul's, when all of the values can be acted on at once. It is more likely however that cases will involve moral dilemmas, that is, situations where values come into conflict, and not all of them can be put into practice at the same time. In and of themselves, values do not conflict. But in situations where they are enacted and used to support different rules and decisions, they can seem to conflict because the interpretations that follow from them conflict. In these cases we need a simple way of determining what to do when values compete.

One way of resolving value conflicts is to develop an absolute hierarchy of values so that the professional knows in advance the relative worth of each value. In what follows, we dismiss this idea of an absolute hierarchy of values as being contrary to good moral decision making. Instead, our way of dealing with value conflicts asks the professional in a particular case to first clarify the values and then to harmonize them and, only if all else fails, to rank them. In this way, competing values are recognized as being equally worthy, even though, in certain cases, choices must often be made among them.

Suppose that we first tried to establish an absolute, unchanging hierarchy of values in order to deal with moral dilemmas. For example, a medical professional might determine that beneficence to the benefit his client but not at the cost of compromising his integrity. An obvious first step is clarification. Look at the situation again. Reassess the facts and the values at stake. Is the conflict only an apparent conflict, or is it a real conflict? Is there a need for further information or communication? Would the apparent conflict dissolve if more information was available? Next, assuming that there is a true conflict of values, look for ways to integrate or harmonize the competing values. Is there a third alternative, a middle-of-the-road compromise, or a creative solution that would allow both values to be maximized? Is a win-win solution possible where both values can be taken into account? Or, by taking a long view instead of a short one or a broad view instead of a narrow one, can both values be realized? Is there a way to be sensitive to the claims of both values? Maybe both values are not realized to the same degree or at the same time, but maybe both can be realized in part.

If the harmonizing proves to be impossible or no creative solution can be discovered, then the only remaining way to resolve the dilemma (short of an arbitrary method like drawing straws from a hat) is to pick an overriding value and defend the choice of this value as overriding. Choose which value seems to you to be the greater value, and offer an explanation in defense of it. Pick the alternative that will bring about more good or the more important good or the good to the more important person in the case. In short, decide which value is more important in this case and provide reasons why. Sometimes there is just no way to avoid having to choose among competing values. In a specific case, a certain value is chosen, even if other values are thereby sacrificed. The ranking of values is an inevitable consequence of having to choose some values to act on while others are left aside. So a hierarchy of values may be the product of resolving a case where values compete and cannot be harmonized. However, this hierarchy is situational. It cannot be used in every case where these particular values conflict, nor can it be used to prevent competition among values.

Conclusion

In this concluding chapter of Part 1, we outlined a moral framework (Decision—Rule—Theory—Value). We considered how the framework is used, and we answered questions about the relationship of its parts. We discussed the Case Resolution Model, which operates in three stages and includes eight steps (P, C, L, E, A, D, D, and R). The CRM is used for solving cases and defending solutions to cases. Finally, we considered what to do in situations where there are competing values and decisions must be made. Given conflicting values and lacking any absolute hierarchy of values, we propose that the decision maker ought to clarify, harmonize, and rank. All of these tools will contribute to making one's moral explanations clear, precise, comprehensive, thoughtful, and well argued.

EXERCISES

1. In each of these passages, an explanation is given. A conclusion is stated in the form of a decision or a rule, and reasons are offered for it in the form of rules, theories, and values.

    1. Identify the conclusion. Is it a decision or a rule?
    2. Use the moral framework to analyze the explanation. If the conclusion is a decision, what rule, theory, and value justify it? If the conclusion is a rule, what theory and value justify it?
        A. Sybil, the paper's political reporter, has chosen to do an in-depth investigation of Mr. Jones, a candidate for a Senate seat, and for that matter, of all candidates for the empty Senate seat. She believes that in order to protect the citizens, newspapers should do what they can to inform people. Although some gossip is stirred up and candidates may be harmed by such exposure, society at large and citizens in particular can only be protected when they can fully comprehend the advantages and disadvantages of voting for each candidate.
        B. The working environment and culture ought to be made more democratic. If our aim is to achieve justice, then we must create more equality among those who work side by side. For instance, secretaries and lawyers, hourly workers and salaried workers, must be treated more equally. It is not only their right to equality that demands changes in the workplace but also our duty to ensure fairness.
        C. Professional landscapers, like all professionals, take pride in their work and in their level of competence and expertise. They do not just aim to do the job well; they also aim to do it in a way that is thoughtful and sensitive to those around them. Given all of this, professional landscapers should not use gas-powered leaf blowers early in the morning.

2. In the following case, several decisions have already been made by Frank, and he is in the process of making another decision. Answer the following questions:

    1. Use the moral framework to analyze the decisions Frank has already made. In other words, what were Frank's decisions? There is

CASE 4: THE BUSY BIOLOGY TEACHER REVISITED

Consider if and how you would deal with the above case differently if the last two paragraphs read as follows:

You surreptitiously look at your watch. In a half hour you are due to teach your advanced biology class and you hoped to use this time before class to review your notes, check your slides, and generally get organized for the class.

It seems unlikely that the student will be done talking to you in the next few minutes unless you do something to cut her off.

NOTES

1. For instance, Immanuel Kant thinks that moral reasoning is about testing maxims against the law of universalizability (*Groundwork of the Metaphysic of Morals*, Chapter 1); and Aristotle believes moral reasoning is accomplished by practical wisdom (*Nicomachean Ethics*, Book VI).

2. This framework bears some resemblance to but finally is fundamentally different from a scheme developed by Tom L. Beauchamp and James F. Childress. They list four levels of justification: particular judgments, rules, principles, and ethical theory. In their model, judgments are explained by rules, rules follow from principles, and principles are grounded in theories (*Principles of Biomedical Ethics*, 4th ed. [New York: Oxford University Press, 1994], 15). In our framework, theories are not the final explanation for actions, but values are. In their scheme, theories explain principles and values. In our model, theories are various ways of interpreting and applying more fundamental and self-evident values.

3. Adapted from "Case 38" in Tom L. Beauchamp and James F. Childress, *Principles of Biomedical Ethics*, 3rd ed. (New York: Oxford University Press, 1989), 454.

4. From Tom L. Beauchamp and James F. Childress, *Principles of Biomedical Ethics*, 3rd ed., 159.

5. See, for example, act-utilitarians like J.J.C. Smart, "An Outline of a System of Utilitarian Ethics," in J.J.C. Smart and Bernard Williams', *Utilitarianism: For and Against* (Cambridge: Cambridge University Press, 1973), and those who question the value of rules and instead practice casuistry, a case-based approach, such as Albert R. Jonsen and Stephen Toulmin, *The Abuse of Casuistry: A History of Moral Reasoning* (Berkeley, Calif.: University of California Press, 1988) and Baruch Brody, *Life and Death Decision Making* (New York: Oxford University Press, 1988).

6. Other texts in professional ethics offer their own versions of models for solving cases. For example, see Thomas Donaldson, "The Case Method," in *Case Studies in Business Ethics*, 2d ed., edited by Thomas Donaldson and A. R. Gini (Englewood Cliffs, N.J.: Prentice Hall, 1990), 13–23; John B. Matthews, Kenneth E. Goodpaster, and Laura L. Nash, *Policies and Persons: A Casebook*

in Business Ethics, 2d ed. (New York: McGraw-Hill, 1991), 2–7, 623, 627; David C. Thomasma and Patricia Marshall, *Clinical Medical Ethics: Cases and Readings* (Lanham, Md.: University Press of America, 1995), 11–12; and Patricia Keith-Spiegel and Gerald P. Koocher, *Ethics in Psychology: Professional Standards and Cases* (New York: Random House, 1985), 19–21.

7. Adapted from the case called "System Security" in Deborah G. Johnson, *Computer Ethics*, 2d ed. (Englewood Cliffs, N.J.: Prentice Hall, 1994), 38.

8. See, for instance, Statement F in the *Code of Ethics* of the National Association of Social Workers, which claims that the social worker's "primary responsibility" is to clients.

9. See, for example, Section I. Fundamental Canons, 1, and Section II. Rules of Practice, 1, in the *Code of Ethics for Engineers* of the National Society of Professional Engineers.

10. See also Lawrence M. Hinman, *Ethics: A Pluralistic Approach to Moral Theory* (New York: Harcourt Brace Jovanovitch, 1994), 347–52, on living with moral diversity; and Anthony Weston, *A Practical Companion to Ethics* (New York: Oxford University Press, 1997), Chapter 4, on resolving value conflicts.

11. Adapted from a case in Vincent Barry, *Personal and Social Ethics* (Belmont, Calif.: Wadsworth, 1978), 366.

12. Adapted from the case "Weldon Gates," credited to Professor Clinton L. Oaks, Brigham Young University, 1980, quoted in *Case Studies in Business Ethics*, 2d ed., edited by Thomas Donaldson and A.R. Gini (Englewood Cliffs, N.J.: Prentice Hall, 1990), 167–68.

13. Adapted from a case in Richard A. Wright, *Human Values in Health Care: The Practice of Ethics* (New York: McGraw-Hill, 1987), 122.

PART 2

Values at Work

Introduction

Doing thorough work in ethics, general or professional, requires a lot of ground clearing and foundation laying. This sort of work, although not the most exciting part of building something, is necessary for a successful outcome. Having this work behind us, we can turn to Part 2 of our text, where those things we have established, implemented, and learned in Part 1 will be applied. In applying them, we will be subjecting them to the most rigorous and important of tests. Namely, in Part 2, we will assess whether the guidelines, classifications, and methods we have come up with thus far provide help in working through, formulating, and living morality and the professional life.

If we continue to think of this text as something like a building or construction project site, now that we are in Part 2, we are able to fill in the infrastructure and build on our solid foundations. In Part 1, we established these foundations through our "hard-hat," ground clearing work. In our work thus far, our ground clearing basically allowed us to discover where we are coming from and where we are going. This started by breaking apart the term *professional ethics*. We examined what it means to be a professional in chapter 1, and what it means to do ethics in chapter 2. Having accomplished that, in chapter 3, we put the term back together and addressed what it is to do professional ethics. With these important foundations laid, in chapter 4 we examined the moral explanations necessary if the work presented in chapter 3 is to be done. Then, in chapters 5 and 6, with the additional material of moral theories, we built up our framework for moral analysis and the CRM. With all of this work done, we now have a moral system that is complete enough to be useful and incomplete enough to be flexible to the various ways in which we must deal with the moral issues of acting professionally.

Since we have cleared the ground, laid the foundation, and set up a skeleton framework of our moral system, it is time to see how well this systematic structure stands up to some wear and tear. Now that we have an understanding of morality and the professional life, and the way in which it is predicated on values, in Part 2 of our text we will put those values to work. This will allow us to give a detailed presentation of each of the values, that together serve as the most fundamental foundation of our moral framework, and by doing so we can work through their implications. We will do this in order to determine whether a moral system based on the values will stand the test of time and be effective. This testing and determination will be accomplished as we address the meanings, implications, and problems that arise relative to our value commitments, as well as the conflicts that are an inevitable part of recognizing and holding values valuable.

As we test the values approach and see how a value is to be enacted in professional life, we will see what it means and how it is to be understood in various contexts. This will allow us to be better able to fill in our infrastructure. Hence, each chapter will provide an understanding of what the value at stake is, as well as the related theoretical points involved. Each chapter also will include a discussion of a case, relative to the value being considered. In addressing a case, we will use the framework for moral analysis, or the case resolution model to clarify the nuances of what a value is about in being made actual. This will allow us to appreciate the potential problems and conflicts in understanding and practically interpreting the value.

We start off with chapters 7 and 8, which consider the values of integrity and respect for persons. These values are both centered on relationships, with ourselves (integrity) and others (respect for persons). In chapters 9 and 10, we continue with the values of justice and compassion, which are both concerned with some of the concrete consequences of our values in the world. We then conclude with chapters 11 and 12. There, in considering beneficence and nonmaleficence, as well as responsibility, we deal with some of the core issues of why our values matter to our professional life.

Our appreciation of the way in which a value is interpreted will be enhanced as we look at the ways in which others have interpreted the value. After two chapters, there is a collection of readings. Thus the readings follow the chapters on integrity and respect for persons, then those chapters on justice and compassion, and finally readings follow beneficence and nonmaleficence and responsibility. The readings in each group have been selected to highlight some of the issues involved with either or both of the values previously discussed. The readings are organized into a fiction selection and a theoretical selection, with the remaining two readings dealing with a problem particular to a profession that falls under the value at stake, or the particular way in which a professional interprets this value.

With all of these aspects of our construction in place, from ground clearing to foundation laying and the building of the infrastructure, you might wonder whether our work is done. That is, we have built up a structure for doing professional ethics, but admittedly, it is still a skeletal structure. After all of the interpreting and testing that occurs in Part 2, this structure will be seen as practical and sound. However, what good is it if it is not finished? Where are the doors and the windows? How will the skeletal foundation be filled in? These questions are not going to go away, and that is a strength of a morality built on values. As we laid our foundation, we discussed the limitations of an absolute morality and the limitations of a morality that is too particular or relative. Consequently, we decided that a values-based morality, established on a commitment to values that are to be interpreted relative to the particular context where they are to be enacted, is the best way to proceed. So each time we interpret our values in a particular context, which we get lots of practice at doing in Part 2, we are filling in the doors, walls, and windows of our moral structure. We can thus personalize our moral commitments by the way we enact values, although the values themselves are constant and stable. Our construction site is no longer under work, but completed. As moral professionals, we are able to contextualize what is ultimately absolute, namely, our commitment to values in our professional lives.

7

Integrity

Values are appealed to by everyone, from politicians to parents to advertisers. Family values, value for your dollar, and moral values all figure prominently in our social scenery.[1] In the prior chapters, although we have explained how values will fit into a moral system, we have yet to explain specifically how it is that each of the values to which we will appeal is defined. Even though we use values in many different ways, and do so often, when it comes to defining values and discussing explicitly what we mean by them, we often are at a loss. While this is true for all of our values, it seems particularly true for the value with which we begin—integrity.

Even a cursory appeal to the way integrity is utilized in professional codes is indicative of its myriad meanings. We are required, in our professional life, to respect the integrity of our clients, to maintain the integrity of our professions, and to keep high our own personal standards of integrity. Clearly, many issues are involved in defining this value and maintaining a commitment to it, perhaps so many that we may lose sight of the common core of what integrity requires. Put simply, integrity is that value which denotes commitment. Thus, integrity is a commitment to commitments. This is, of course, more or less complicated, contingent upon what it is that we are committed to. In this instance, relative to morality and the professional life, the commitment required is a commitment to the values described in this values-based approach to professional ethics.

Understanding integrity as not only a value in its own right but also as a commitment to a broader group of values, we recognize how it is that integrity is a value of a different sort than the other values of this system, such as respect for persons or justice. Integrity is a keystone value that is implied in virtue of our holding to the others. That is, integrity is the name we have for the value that indicates why it is important for us to remain true to all of our values. Likewise, the concrete interpretation of our values has implications for the value of integrity. In this manner, a commitment to integrity requires of us very real and necessary things. This necessity manifests itself in global and local interpretations of integrity, which we will discuss throughout this chapter. Globally, we are committed to integrity insofar as we are committed to values themselves, since they are the commitments to which we are committed. Locally, we are committed to integrity as we express what integrity uniquely requires of us, as one of the specific values to which we are committed. As a consequence of this dual aspect, integrity introduces us both broadly and narrowly to the values to which we are committed, and so it starts us off.

Thus, in this chapter, we will work toward understanding how it is that a professional is to honor and express his or her commitment to commitments. That is, the topic of this chapter is the value of integrity, what this value means, what it involves, and what it requires of professionals. This task will be aided by considering the way integrity is used by us and by our professional codes. In addition to seeing how it is that particular professions interpret integrity in their codes, our investigation will consider the ways in which integrity gets played out in a concrete case. Through an analysis of this case by means of our Case Resolution Model (CRM) we will see the ways in which a professional, grounded in the value of integrity, behaves. All of this will leave us with some guidelines to help us interpret the value of integrity. Finally, we will consider the conflicts that can arise among our commitments and the related issues involved therein.

What Is Integrity?

Think about the people you consider to have integrity. Perhaps politicians, your favorite teachers, or a relative comes to mind. Now think about the structures you consider to have integrity. Do you imagine the Golden Gate Bridge, the Sears Tower, the Empire State

Building, or your residence? Okay, now think about the products or institutions that you consider to have integrity. Do certain products have integrity to you? What about certain stores, companies, or sports teams? Integrity is a term bandied about without too much differentiation of its meanings. Just in the three above examples you might have thought about a person having personal integrity in virtue of their consistent commitment to a particular set of standards, a building having structural integrity insofar as it is well built and not liable to collapse, and products or institutions having integrity insofar as they are whole, integrated, or the same throughout. This is not even to mention any combination of these three understandings that you may have come up with in the meantime. These three meanings of integrity give us a place to start in order to concentrate on establishing a working meaning that allows us to be flexible and appreciate the way in which integrity is to be actualized in various situations.[2]

From the aforementioned, we can see how it is that a person can have integrity and how it is that a building or institution can likewise have integrity. Clearly, for the sake of our discussion, we are much more concerned with the integrity that is attributed or expressed by persons than that of a structure. But, in a way, all of the terms involved in defining integrity are related. We can begin broadly and then hone in on the more subtle aspects of this value. When an individual has integrity, he or she is consistently committed to a particular standard. Yet, for our purposes, just any standard will not do. If this were to be the case, an excellent pickpocket would have integrity, since such a person would be consistently committed to the standards of efficient and skilled pickpocketing. In a qualified way, such a skilled individual would have integrity, but not the sort of integrity we would desire to emulate. Instead of a commitment to *any* sort of standard, we are here concerned with a consistent commitment to *moral* or *ethical* commitments. Furthermore, these moral and ethical commitments should be structured so they reflect our valuing of values. Thus, a moral professional reflects integrity when he or she is committed to his or her value commitments. For now, this is a sufficient definition, but of course we will soon consider what such a definition requires of us in our actions.

Before we consider what integrity requires, what of its other definitions? What about integrity as structural, whole, or integrated? We have said that integrity is a commitment to a specific standard or commitment. However, since that is the case, we have determined that the commitments required need to be more than just commitments to anything. Instead, here we are concerned with moral integrity, which is a commitment to moral standards or commitments. A standard is understood as a moral or an ethical one insofar as such a commitment to it is morally laudable. We thereby exhibit moral integrity in that we remain committed to morally laudable standards. This is the case in our own values approach, a commitment we have spent much time determining as morally laudable. Thus, we have moral integrity when we stay committed to all of our values, including the value of integrity. This commitment allows us to maintain a sort of structural integrity insofar as our moral character is the same, whole, or integrated throughout. In sum, if there is to be moral integrity, the kind of integrity with which we are here concerned, there must be a consistent commitment to the moral standard which describes what we value. Hence, like a building with structural integrity, when we have integrity, our commitment to values will not collapse when things start getting stressful or challenging.

Given this definition of integrity as moral, we see that we cannot have conflicting, disparate, or opposite values at work in our system of moral values and still have integrity. If a building has a brick foundation but also has a wood foundation and a concrete foundation, it is going to be a big mess. The same goes for our moral commitments. Once we make a commitment to a certain set of standards, we cannot likewise be committed to a conflicting or competing set of standards. To maintain a commitment to both honesty and dishonesty would make maintaining a consistent moral system impossible, hence integrity would be impossible. If we are to maintain integrity, we must at a minimum have compatible value commitments.[3]

In short, integrity consists of a complete, thorough commitment to the moral values we have settled on for professional ethics. In valuing values, which include integrity, it is hard to determine which comes first. Do we value integrity, and thus we are committed to other values? Or, are we committed to values, including integrity? This sort of circular discussion could continue endlessly while serving little purpose. So instead of thinking of integrity as before or after a commitment to values, we would be well served to think of it as being two tiered. On one level, integrity is that value which indicates our commitment to the moral commitment at stake, the values described in our values-based approach to professional ethics. Once we are committed to our moral system and have thus displayed integrity on that sort of a global level, we move on to our second tier. On this more local level, we are left to interpret how this commitment to integrity will be played out in the world. We interpret integrity locally in this concrete and very practical manner by determining what it is that integrity means as one of the moral values to which we are committed. It can be confusing, but not if we note that there is merely one integrity, which manifests itself on two different levels. Neither alone is completely enough, but the former global commitment insofar as it requires us to uphold each and every value of our moral system takes us far in making morality real in our professional life. This is a making real which includes integrity as well as compassion, justice, and the other values in this latter, more concrete, and local sense.

What Integrity Involves

Like our other values, the primary problem with integrity does not come from recognizing a commitment to it, but instead in determining what a commitment to integrity requires. So now that we have defined integrity, we are left to consider what a commitment to integrity involves. Like many of our values, a commitment to integrity becomes most apparent when it is violated and is often more easily spoken of in terms of prohibitions than in terms of positive actions. However, mere prohibitions do not get us far when we are trying to figure out what to do. In order to figure out what to do instead of what not to do, we need to start positively, and from the simple overview of integrity that follows from our prior definition we can take a closer look at what it positively requires.

As usual, one place we can begin to interpret our definition of integrity as a commitment to values is through looking at the codes of several professions and how it is that they define integrity. Through their appeal to integrity we also can begin to see what it is that a commitment to integrity requires of us. The Association of Computing Machinery, in its "Canon 1" requires that "An ACM member shall act at all times with integrity."[4] That is not much help, unless there are some details to follow. Fortunately there are. Under this canon, there are both ethical considerations and disciplinary rules. By looking at the two together, we can get a better handle on what integrity is all about. For the most part, integrity requires positive honesty (e.g., "An ACM member shall not make deliberately false or deceptive statements . . .") as well as a negative or limiting honesty insofar as there is a requirement to disclose. That is, not lying is not enough. One must also tell the truth.[5]

Much the same definition of and requirements for integrity hold for the National Society of Professional Engineers in their *Code of Ethics for Engineers*. Here, under the category of professional obligations, it states that engineers, "shall be guided in all their professional relations by the highest standards of integrity." Like our prior example, this is not much help in and of itself, without some further guidance. Again, this guidance follows the claim of valuing integrity and is centered on requirements of honesty. Engineers are required to maintain honesty as a way of valuing integrity in that they "admit and accept their own errors" and "refrain from false or misleading pretenses" as well as advising their clients truthfully "when they believe a project will not be successful." Together, these requirements of integrity maintain the integrity of the profession.[6]

As we see in the codes of these two professional associations, included in any commitment to integrity is a commitment to honesty. Being honest is often associated with integrity in that we say of honest people, "They have integrity." The source of this implication is not too complex to trace. If we are to remain true to any sort of system, this requires us to remain honest, since approaching the world dishonestly would keep us from remaining wholly committed to honesty. This is not to say that when we are not completely honest we are unable to ever have integrity. Instead, valuing honesty and recognizing that dishonesty contravenes the intent of a commitment to integrity allows us to appreciate what is sacrificed when we are dishonest. In reality, we are all a little bit dishonest at times, even if that is merely telling your spouse you like his or her bad haircut, as in chapter 1. However, an underlying commitment to integrity requires us to carefully assess under what conditions we are dishonest, to recognize that we are being dishonest, and to recognize that it is wrong unless such action is taken for compelling moral reasons. Integrity requires being committed to honesty rather than partial honesty, even if sometimes there are moral reasons for not being completely honest.

Very close to a commitment to honesty is a commitment to promise keeping. Keeping a promise is a more relational-oriented way of maintaining honesty. A promise is a way that our honesty can be practical. It is the means through which we interact with others. Again, this implication of integrity is likewise not too difficult to trace. If we say something and mean something else, or say that we are going to do one thing with no intention of following through, we are then disparate in our commitments. Remaining integrated and committed to our commitments requires us to follow through on them. Thus, integrity requires us to follow through on our promises.[7]

If honesty and promise keeping are one aspect of integrity, that aspect which relates to our consistency in our truth commitments, then loyalty and dependability are the other aspect of integrity, that which relates to consistency in our action commitments. Just as with the honesty implications of integrity, we can see how the loyalty and dependability aspects of integrity are played out in a professional code.

The section, "Freedom and Integrity of Research," indicates how a requirement to be loyal is part of membership in the American Political Science Association. Its members, in securing funds for research, have a requirement to "avoid actions that would call into question the integrity of American academic institutions as centers of independent teaching and research." That is, political scientists should not do anything that would thwart the mission of their institutions. They should remain loyal to their institution's goals. Therefore, sponsoring "research as a cover for intelligence activities" would not be within the goals they are trying to serve as educators at academic institutions.[8]

Like honesty, it is not too difficult to trace how loyalty follows from the implications of a commitment to commitments. If we are part of an institution that has particular aims and goals, if we are committed to the institution, we are committed to their goals. This is the case, even if such a commitment consists only of not doing anything that would subvert these goals rather than doing something that would promote these goals. Think about someone who works for the police department and how affronted we are when that person is found to be guilty of wrongdoing. Think also of how controversial it becomes when an athlete is guilty of illegal drug use. Of course, if considered without concern for context, in both of these specific instances and in general, wrongdoing and illegal drug use are grossly problematic. Yet when these actions are done by those whose very occupation seems to stand for their opposite, law enforcement and personal physical excellence through sport, we are particularly troubled by this violation of loyalty which is a part of the requirements of integrity.

In the same way that promise keeping is one of the ways in which the honesty aspect of integrity is concretely practical, dependability is one of the ways in which our loyalty aspect of integrity, or our loyalty to our moral commitments, becomes concrete in the world. That is, by being loyal, we put our commitment to integrity into action. If we are loyal, there really is no way to know unless we display dependability and consistency in our actions. This does not mean that we unreflectively act the same when met with any situation. Instead, dependability means that in their manifestations, one's actions exhibit one's underlying moral commitments, including integrity, in a dependable, consistent manner.

By appealing to moral codes that require a commitment to integrity, we have shown that this value has concrete requirements of honesty, made actual in promise keeping, and loyalty, made actual in dependability. Now that we have this interpretation of the requirements of integrity, we move on to a concrete case upon which to practice the understandings we have gained thus far.

A Case Involving Integrity

Obviously the value of integrity manifests itself in different ways. Much of it we can discuss by considering the following scenario:

> Yolanda Biltmore is the fiction editor of a widely circulated and respected literary magazine. She came to the attention of the hiring committee of the magazine some years before through the kind intervention of a friend. This same friend has recently approached her with a story that his son has written. He then informed Yolanda that his son, who has always dreamed of having something published, is terminally ill. Seeing the story published would greatly please the son and of course the friend as well. Later that same day Yolanda read the story and determined that it is hardly up to the standard of the literary magazine. In fact, she is of the view that it is a hopelessly inferior piece of writing. Yolanda wants to publish the work, but feels a conflict about doing so. She values the respect her readers have for the standards of the magazine. Yolanda feels a responsibility to them, and she feels that they trust her to not publish what she would consider poor work. What should Yolanda do?[9]

Since there has been no decision in this case, we can use the case resolution model (CRM) to help determine how best to enact integrity. We begin with Stage I.

Stage I.

1. (P)resent the problem.

    Yolanda has been asked to publish a story that is not up to the standards of her literary magazine.

2. (C)ollect information.

The story Yolanda has been asked to publish is written by the son of a friend who may or may not have contributed to Yolanda getting hired to do her current job. The son of Yolanda's friend is terminally ill and, according to his father, has a heavy emotional investment in seeing his work published before he dies.

Stage II.

3. (*L*)ist the relevant value(s).

Integrity is the primary value at stake in this case. Other values certainly are relevant, but we will concentrate on a resolution of this case that will allow Yolanda to maintain her integrity. We are thus left to consider how Yolanda can maintain her integrity in this situation. A secondary value at stake is responsibility to the literary magazine. Compassion also is relevant here insofar as Yolanda feels compassion for her friend and what he must be going through as he deals with his son's imminent mortality.

4. (*E*)xplore the options and the ways theories apply.

If Yolanda were to act as a consequentialist, she would be left to consider who would gain the greatest good from publishing the story. Clearly the father would be pleased, as would his ill son. Quite possibly, Yolanda might also have a sense of satisfaction in having pleased these people. She also is left to consider the negative consequences of her action. The readers of the literary magazine would be disappointed in the quality of this work. Furthermore, in publishing work of a substandard quality, Yolanda's ability to do her job might be called into question.

As a rights theorist, Yolanda would need to consider who has rights in this situation. As no explicit contract or agreement has been entered into, the situation is a difficult one to assess. It probably would be fruitful to explore what rights Yolanda's friend thinks he has. Does he think he has the right to ask this favor of Yolanda? Likewise, what about Yolanda's rights? Does she have the right to refuse her friend's request?

According to a duty-based theory, Yolanda would have to determine where the greater duty lay. Should she fulfill a real or perceived obligation to help a friend, or should she fulfill her obligations to the magazine?

As a virtue theorist, Yolanda would aim to act in a manner that would best express her good character. This becomes complicated, as she must address how it is that she understands herself as a literary editor and a friend. On one account, a virtuous professional would maintain her standards of excellence in determining what counts as good fiction. On another account, a good professional would maintain flexibility in appreciating all of the different ways in which the public could become engaged in a piece of fiction, regardless of its literary merit. In short, how is a good character best expressed relative to this situation?

A care theorist would have much to consider in this case. How much care is actually being displayed toward Yolanda by her friend? What would be the best way to care for her friend? Yolanda is left to determine if being truthful or fulfilling her friend's wishes would best exhibit care. Would a caring friend actually put Yolanda in the situation she currently faces?

Like the care theorist, we would be hard pressed to consider everything that would be relevant in a narrative analysis of this case. What are the specific details of the story that dealt with Yolanda's involvement with this friend? How much influence did the friend actually have on Yolanda's getting this job? Likewise, is this friend prone to asking for big favors? What about the friend's story? Is he distraught? To whom does this overwhelming desire to be published really belong, to Yolanda's friend or his son? Perhaps the desire to fulfill the son's wish to be published comes from a sense of frustration in not being able to do anything about his failing health. Would a good friend publish the story or refuse it without dealing with these other underlying and perhaps more profound issues?

All of the above and more would be part of the options to be explored through each of the theories applied.

5.   (A)ssess the rightness and wrongness of various outcomes.

Yolanda could publish the story and violate her commitments to the magazine.

Yolanda could publish the story in such a manner that she explained to her readers the mitigating circumstances surrounding its publication.

Yolanda could not publish the story and feel that her friend was making an unfair, selfish request of her.

Yolanda could not publish the story and still work to be a caring friend in other ways.

6.   (D)ecide.

Instead of having an outcome for this case stated here, consider it yourself. Relative to the CRM, what would be the best decision for Yolanda and for all of those concerned?

Stage III.

7. (*D*)efend.

Defend and justify the decision that you came to in step 6. Give reasons that explain your decisions. Are they moral reasons? Are they strong or weak reasons?

8. (*R*)eflect.

Reflect on the decision you just defended. What could Yolanda have done to have prevented this situation, short of curing the son's illness and teaching him how to write? If she were to publish the story, what sort of objections to that course of action could be raised? Likewise, if she were to not publish the story, what would be the objections in that instance? What if the literary magazine were to have a group of people that decided which stories were to be published? Would such an editorial organization prevent Yolanda and others in her profession from being put into the difficult situation she now faces? What strategies would you suggest for preventing this sort of situation or for resolving it?

With a consideration of this case and the way it could be resolved through a sensitivity to integrity, we still see that there is much to do in interpreting the value. Integrity appears in a variety of ways in our professional lives. Often, when we consider the value, we need some rules to help us act on it.

Interpreting Integrity: Guides to Help

Now that we have considered integrity generally and in a specific case, consider the following guides that help us translate integrity into action. If these guides do not hold up, the pressure is on us to articulate why they are not valid and to do so with strong moral reasons.

Rule of Honesty

Be consistently honest, with yourself and others.

We have determined that honesty and its practical consequence of promise keeping is a part of a commitment to integrity. Thus our rule for honesty consists of honoring this commitment, although not doing so blindly and unreflectively. We should maintain honesty, unless strong moral reasons implore us to do otherwise. This is certainly the case with Yolanda. If she were to be honest, both with her friend or with his son, she could avoid putting herself in the difficult situation of having to fabricate a situation that would allow her to publish the inferior story.

Think about your own experiences. Are there instances where your integrity was ever sacrificed because you were honest? If so, were you really exhibiting integrity? If a professional is truly committed to integrity, he or she is committed to honesty. Although it would often make our lives materially easier if we were to be dishonest, there are rarely strong *moral* reasons that we could give for such behavior.

As we have come up with two aspects of integrity, honesty and loyalty, let us consider the rule that follows from the latter.

Rule of Loyalty

Follow through on the commitments that you have made, assuming that you have made them knowingly and in good faith.

We have said that a commitment to integrity requires one to be loyal. This is not an unreflective loyalty, like a bully's minions have on the playground or like the flying monkeys have to the Wicked Witch of the West. Instead, this is a loyalty perceived through our dependability and consistency. This authentic loyalty follows from a sincere commitment to integrity, and it is of the sort that requires that we make our commitments with self-awareness, not only to our values but to their consequences.

Consider Yolanda. She has decided to work for a prestigious literary magazine. In doing so, she accepts their high standards and is committed to upholding them in order to maintain the integrity of the organization. What about her commitment to her friend? Has she made an explicit commitment to aid him in whatever projects he decides to pursue? Clearly not. In virtue of asking Yolanda to publish his son's substandard work, Yolanda's friend is requiring her to become committed to a project without allowing her to reflect upon whether or not this is a project she really wants to be a part of. Thus, in this instance, Yolanda would probably have a greater loyalty to the commitment she made knowingly and self-reflectively, a commitment to the magazine for which she works.

Conflicts Involving Integrity

We just considered a case that included an apparent conflict of integrity. That is, if integrity is a commitment to our commitments, what happens when two or more of the things to which we are committed conflict? In this section, we will consider several potential situations in which integrity not only seemingly conflicts with another value but also those where it actually does compete with some other moral value or commitment. Our first situation centers on Yolanda and concentrates on a value conflict, between compassion and integrity. In our second conflict, we again address Yolanda's situation and the conflicts that arise from how to interpret integrity. Our last conflicts concentrate on the differing ways we can understand how to fulfill the loyalty aspects of a commitment to integrity. That is, how do we determine what our interpretation of integrity requires of us. These sorts of conflicts are difficult to appropriately adjudicate, since their context is often equally as important as the values that they seek to express. In considering these conflicts, we will review some safeguards for preventing actual conflict as well as guidelines for the resolution of conflicts.

In the case of Yolanda, we saw what happened when there appeared to be an apparent conflict between her value commitments. If Yolanda were to stay exclusively committed to the value of integrity, she could not publish the essay of her friend's son. However, if she were to stay exclusively committed to the value of compassion, she would have to publish the essay of her friend's son. This is a difficult situation, since it appears that two values are conflicting with one another. As with other conflicts, perhaps there is a middle way to proceed that would alleviate the all-or-nothing sensibility that seems to pervade in a situation where we are honoring only integrity or only compassion. We have seen that the CRM encourages us to look for middle ways to proceed, or creative compromises that can arise, not all of which have yet occurred to Yolanda, or ourselves in considering this case. Basically, the CRM requires us to recognize that although our value commitments may seem to compete, what actually is competing is the consequences of honoring one or another value exclusively. In interpreting our values, we are well served to deal with situations such as these by working creatively to find and utilize alternative value interpretations that are not at odds.

Yet there certainly would be a way to interpret integrity relative to Yolanda, which shows the conflict in this instance is a false one. With further analysis, it could become clear that only one of the commitments, to one's job and to one's personal relationships, seemingly competing, had actually been made by Yolanda herself. It was quite unreasonable for her friend to require her to support his actions when she herself had no voice in committing to them. Thus, when faced with an apparent conflict involving integrity, be sure it is an actual conflict. Are the two commitments which are in conflict both actual commitments for you? Are the values at stake values that you would choose to be committed to if they were not in conflict? That is, consider each value commitment in turn. Without the conflict, are both commitments those to which you would want to be committed if you were choosing freely and self-reflectively? The odds are that both commitments will not claim you equally. The odds also are that most conflicts between our personal and professional lives are not true conflicts upon further reflection. However, if there actually does seem to be a persisting conflict in commitments, consider the following.

In the movie *The Paper*, Marisa Tomei's character asks Michael Keaton's character to choose. Basically she wants to know, when things get to the absolutely fever-pitched, crisis level, when the options of family and work are diametrically opposed, which of the two Michael Keaton would choose. In this instance, Michael Keaton's character seems to be in a real bind. That is, if the two commitments were not in conflict, if his work were not requiring him to sacrifice his family and vice versa, he would want to be passionately committed to both. Here, Michael Keaton's character has freely chosen both of his commitments, and they conflict.

But as the bit of dialogue following this hypothetical situation indicates, "It is never just one big choice." We make decisions about our value commitments constantly throughout our day-to-day lives. Rarely do our commitments face off in one or the other situations. Often we must compromise. One way of doing so in a way that maintains our integrity is through appeal to the other values of our system. Hence, what is really in conflict here is not actually our value commitments, but the way in which they are to be interpreted relative to our finite and limited capacities. Since integrity includes a commitment to value commitments, use those commitments to your advantage. When value commitments face off, do not get stuck in choosing between two seemingly competing systems. Instead, allow your commitments to point you toward your greater commitments to other values and allow an appreciation of all of these commitments to guide your interpretation of the values at stake and thereby arrive at a compromise.

Another instance where our interpretation of integrity is diffi-cult to make concrete is in situations that seem to require whistle-blowing. Whistle-blowing is typically understood as "the attempt by an employee or a former employee of an organization to disclose what he or she believes to be wrongdoing in or by the organiza-tion."[10] In instances like that, an employee of an organization is often pulled between what he or she feels is the right thing to do and his or her loyalty to that commitment and between what he or she feels is their loyalty to the organization that employs them. Most of the time, loyalty to an employer or institution is not prob-lematic. However, in instances where an employer, institution, or their agents act in such a manner that the concrete way in which you are then asked to enact your loyalty requires you to sac-rifice your integrity, problems will arise. Such situations are not easily resolved.

Much of what needs to be considered in interpreting integrity in these difficult situations is summed up in the Rule of Honesty and Rule of Loyalty. However, interpreting integrity is not all that is to be considered when determining whether or not it is appro-priate to blow the whistle, that is, honesty and loyalty should be maintained unless there are important moral reasons not to do so. This is to say that it is alright, for nonmoral reasons to figure into one's interpretation of making integrity actual, but they are not to be the exclusive grounds for adjudicating the demands of loyalty when considering the decision of whether to blow the whistle on wrongdoing. Whistle-blowing requires us to explore all of the op-tions that could deal with a troubling situation. For example, is it necessary to go outside of the organization to blow the whistle? Could the problem be addressed by going to a superior? Further-more, once a decision to blow the whistle has been reached, how is the whistle best blown? Should whistle-blowing take place anony-mously or publicly, or somewhere in between the two options? In addition, we must consider the context of the situation that re-quires the whistle to be blown. Is great harm to unknowing inno-cent bystanders at stake? What is the level of risk assumed when blowing the whistle on wrongdoing? Although not exclusively moral or nonmoral, these contextual questions are important to consider when determining whether whistle-blowing is required by a com-mitment to integrity.

Clearly, not all of the issues relative to whistle-blowing are addressed here. Instead of exhausting the discussion of whistle-blowing, we have discussed it in terms of the conflicts of integrity that are a part of this topic. Whistle-blowing can involve conflicts with other values, and when we treat these values we will address this difficult issue again there. In approaching whistle-blowing in this manner, we are not letting this problem, whether to blow the whistle, drive our discussion. Instead, we are allowing our values and the requirements that a commitment to them entails center us in discussing the ways in which we behave morally in our professional lives.

Unfortunately, conflicts in integrity, seeming or true, cannot be solved by formula. Instead, only guidelines for their potential solution can be offered. Reflect on the situation and determine if there actually is a conflict. More often than not it is not a moral conflict. Rarely are there two moral commitments of equal standing pulling a professional, or for that matter, any person, in opposite directions. If the conflict at stake does seem actual do not despair. No value need be completely sacrificed for another. Compromise and allow the compromise to be guided by what integrity requires. Thus, let a commitment to our greater group of values aid your interpretation as you clarify, harmonize, and rank the values at stake.

Conclusion

In this chapter, we begin to see how our values approach to professional morality is going to work. We considered the value of integrity, what it means, and what it concretely requires. We saw that this value includes a commitment to our overarching value system. Thus, a commitment to integrity requires us to be honest as we keep our promises and to be loyal as we display dependability. Nonetheless, we still meet with difficult cases that will test our ability to interpret integrity and even our commitment to integrity. We saw this in the instance of Yolanda Biltmore, in the character played by Michael Keaton, and in the way in which it arises in whistle-blowing as well. How are we to deal with integrity issues? We can rely on the CRM as a procedure for thinking through a situation, and we can buttress this with rules that maintain our honesty and loyalty. When we are still left with conflicts involving integrity, we must examine them to see if the commitments that are pulling us into conflict are both moral. If so, we must compromise by maintaining sensitivity to the rest of the values in our system.

EXERCISES

1. Take the code of ethics for your proposed occupation. If you are uncertain about your career, pick any code. Consider the following.

    1. Is there an explicit or implicit appeal to integrity contained in the code?
    2. Define integrity relative to the way it is used in the code of ethics for your proposed occupation.
    3. In this code, what specific requirements must the professional meet because of the value of integrity? Are these requirements too extensive, or not extensive enough? Does this code include the specific requirements of integrity, such as honesty and promise keeping and loyalty and dependability, articulated in this chapter?
    4. For the professionals covered by this code, do you foresee any potential problems or conflicts they might face in acting out the value of integrity? Give three examples and explain each.

2. Consider these cases in the following manner. Each of these cases has integrity as its primary value.

    1. Apply the framework for moral analysis or the CRM, contingent upon whether a decision has already been made or whether the outcome of the case has yet to be determined.
    2. If the guides for interpreting integrity are helpful here, indicate which rule has been most helpful.
    3. Indicate how you would resolve this case. Be sure to explain your answers fully.

CASE 1: PROFESSIONAL INTEGRITY AND ACADEMIC TENURE

You are an assistant professor in your third year at a college of education at a large state university. Your principal research interest concerns the ways in which children develop tastes and preferences and how classroom instruction in music and art might be improved. For two years you have been involved in a study of these matters in local schools. As a result of your work, you have constructed a novel hypothesis about aesthetic development, and if the results of your observations confirm that theory, you believe that you will be able to make a major contribution to the theory of art education.

The regulations of your university require a decision to be made regarding your tenure within the next three years. When that decision is made, you must either be given tenure or fired. The principal criterion for tenure these days is publication. Because of the long-term nature of your research, it is very unlikely that your main research activity will yield publishable results before the decision regarding your tenure must be made.

You know that research grants are available for bureaucratic projects that would lead to quick publications, but you regard most of these studies as a waste of time, effort, and money, producing trivial or useless results that benefit no one. Furthermore, if you undertake such projects, you will have to abandon your time-consuming work with your present subjects, thereby giving up a study to which you are deeply committed, and which promises to benefit many. Yet, if you have no tangible results to present at the time of your tenure decision, you are likely to lose your job. What should you do?[11]

CASE 2: LYING FOR BUSINESS REASONS

Carl Montero was near the end of his first month on the job and was beginning to feel like he made the right decision about his career. When he signed up for the Ritz Furniture Company sales program, he was not sure that was what he wanted to do. He passed over several other opportunities, like the Army and technical school, to pursue this one. Carl was attracted to Ritz because of its sales training program, which was innovative and challenging. The old program hired established sales personnel and gave them Ritz routes; the new program took young people and showed them how things worked from the ground up.

On his first day at Ritz, Carl was assigned to Sam Kincaid, who was of the old school. At first, Carl was intimidated by Sam and the way he did things. Carl felt that Sam's approach differed greatly from what he had learned in training school. Although Sam scoffed at Carl's "fancy training," he was nice enough and they got along—at least until the last day of Carl's month on probation.

Carl and Sam were in Ivory's Department Store, and Carl was completing his first large sale. He was proud and excited. As Ivory's manager was signing the contract, she asked, "The usual shipping arrangement?" Sam cut in and said, "Of course!"

Carl was confused and later in the car asked Sam about the exchange. Sam responded, "Oh that, it was nothing. You see, what we do for important customers like Ivory's is to compute triple shipping charges. That way, when the order goes through, they end up with a hefty discount. We just pass the main expense off on the shipping department, which is then responsible for a big part of the bill, and then the purchasing guys are off the hook for most of the expense of the furniture."

"But that's lying!" Carl objected. "How can we do that?"

Sam chuckled and replied, "Look kid, it's either that or no business. You choose."[12]

CASE 3: PROMOTION AND PREGNANCY

Madeline Shepp was in charge of investor relations at a newly established and booming gourmet cookie company. The company, publicly traded on the NASDAQ exchange, was a hot commodity. At the same time the company's stock rose in the market, Madeline's stock rose in the company. With extensive business experience, an excellent command of the field, and great enthusiasm, Madeline's future with the company was bright. It had been indicated to her that if she kept up the good work, she was in line to become the company's first woman officer. In her early thirties, Madeline and her husband had an eighteen-month-old baby and had been trying to have another child for the past few months.

Recently, Madeline and her husband were delighted to realize that Madeline was pregnant with their second child. In the midst of an investor relation marketing blitz, and with plans for the same to occur the next year, Madeline's supervisors would not be nearly as delighted with the prospects of losing her for three months to maternity leave. Even though her position was protected under law, when she took her first maternity leave, Madeline found that upon her return, she had to work doubly hard to prove that she was still committed to her demanding work. Although a progressive company, with maternity and paternity leave, day care, and nursing rooms, Madeline's firm had to be concerned with the bottom line, and they were not at their strongest when Madeline was away from her desk. Furthermore, Madeline's good news coincided with her being considered for a promotion and bonus.

If Madeline had informed her supervisors immediately of her pregnancy, her firm could easily have adapted to her three-month long absence. With a healthy pregnancy, Madeline could work right up until her due date. Yet Madeline decided to conceal her pregnancy for several months, or at least until her promotion and year-end bonus were secured. Having made this decision, Madeline felt uneasy about withholding this information from her colleagues and supervisors. She also felt unsure about how to reconcile her commitments to her work with those to her family.

NOTES

1. Values have even become a kind of commodity. See Greg Burns and Nancy Millman, "Integrity for Hire" *Chicago Tribune*, September 21, 1997, Perspective Section, 1. This story reports how companies who are allegedly in trouble for violations of integrity are increasingly engaging in "a controversial corporate practice: hiring public figures with reputations for integrity to investigate high-profile company crises."

2. See the definition of integrity in Webster's *Ninth New Collegiate Dictionary* (Springfield, Mass.: Webster's Publishing, 1988), 628.

3. This brings us back to chapter 3 and our discussion of a holistic approach to moral action. There we stated that disparate moral commitments lead to disparate moral lives. Integrity becomes the antidote to such disparity.

4. Canon 1, Bylaw 19, "ACM Code of Professional Conduct," *The Constitution of the Association for Computing Machinery, Inc.*

5. See Ethical Considerations EC1.1-3 and Disciplinary Rules DR1.1.1.-1.3.3., "ACM Code of Professional Conduct."

6. Section III, specifically parts a, b, d, and f, "National Society of Professional Engineers' Code of Ethics for Engineers and Statement NSPE Executive Committee," *NSPE Publication No. 1102*, revised January 1987.

7. See Immanuel Kant, the famous duty theorist, who pointed out that were we to make promises with no intent of keeping them and then accept that this become a universal law, the notion of promises would become nonsensical. Thus, to make a promise is only meaningful when we recognize that we need to see our promises through. See Kant's second illustration of the duties which follow from the formula of the Law of Nature. Immanuel Kant, *Groundwork of the Metaphysic of Morals*, translated by H. J. Paton (New York: Harper and Row, 1964), 89–90.

8. For both quotes, see Rule 9, "D. Freedom and Integrity of Research by Academic Political Scientists: Principles for Funding Agencies," from American Political Science Association, the Committee on Professional Standards and Responsibilities, *Rules of Conduct* (1968).

9. Case adapted from Vincent Barry, *Personal and Social Ethics* (Belmont, Calif.: Wadsworth, 1978), 365.

10. Gene G. James, "In Defense of Whistle-blowing," in *Ethical Issues in Professional Life*, edited by Joan C. Callahan (Oxford: Oxford University Press, 1988), 315.

11. Adapted from "Case 3.2 Professional Integrity and Qualification for Academic Tenure," in Peter Windt, Peter Appleby, et al., *Ethical Issues in the Professions* (Englewood Cliffs, N.J.: Prentice Hall, 1989), 347.

12. Case adapted from "Decision Scenario 5, Lying for Business Reasons," in David Appelbaum and Sarah Lawton, *Ethics and the Professions* (Englewood Cliffs, N.J.: Prentice Hall, 1990), 247.

8

Respect for Persons

Respect means many things to many people. The classic song tells us, "R. E. S. P. E. C. T. Find out what it means to me." With respect, we will have to find out what it means, specifically in the context of our professional life. This can be quite complicated, since respect relates us to all sorts of things. One clue to discovering what respect means is that when respect is involved, there is a relationship. That is, if respect or a lack of respect is present, at one time or another, you have to have been involved with another party in some way. We either do or do not feel respect for people, including ourselves, institutions, organizations, and even ideas. In addition, we can show someone respect without feeling respect for them, and likewise, with some people, we both feel respect for them and show them respect. Thus this anthem for respect gives us insight into one of the main components of respect, because when respect is involved, there certainly is a lot to discover. A relationship of respect can take many forms and vary in many degrees. In general, respect is shown us when we earn it and sometimes even when we do not. But what does it mean to show someone respect, and particularly, what does it mean to show someone, or even oneself, respect within the context of one's professional life?

In this chapter we will take a close look at what it is to respect someone, both when they do and do not deserve it, and what sort of respect is at stake to be earned or denied. That is, we will consider whether we are still required to respect someone who is behaving in a manner that is not in any way professional, and if so to what degree. Or, even if someone is treating us in a way that has little to do with valuing us as a professional, is there any sort of minimal respect that we are entitled to demand?

As we consider this value, we begin our appreciation of it by understanding what respect for persons is. After doing so, we will go on to consider what respecting persons involves, as defined by some of the ethical codes of professionals. With these steps in implementing the value in place, we will look at a case that asks us to consider the best way to respect persons, when the well-being and dignity of many different persons is at stake. After discussing our case, we will formulate some guidelines for respecting persons that will help us as we discern some of the typical conflicts that arise in respecting persons.[1]

What It Is to Respect Persons

Consider this situation. It is a cold, rainy day, the kind of day that even once you go inside you cannot seem to shake its greyness. You are outdoors, and while outdoors, you are walking. You are absorbed in your own thoughts and tasks, which have as their primary goal, to get out of the bad weather. Meanwhile, someone is walking toward you on the sidewalk. As this walker and you are passing by one another, you sense, rather than consciously notice, that her feet have given out from under her. If you took the time to think about it, you would realize that she has slipped on the wet sidewalk. This stranger, next to you on the sidewalk, is falling. What do you do?

This situation calls for an immediate response. There is no time to apply the CRM, or any other criterion for that matter. If someone next to you on a path is falling, what do you do? Hopefully your response is to reach out and catch the person in their fall. If not catch her, maybe you instinctively reach your hand out to offer this passing stranger some balance that will slow down the fall. Maybe all of this has happened too fast, and after the stranger has slipped, landing in a muddy puddle, you offer her a hand or ask if she is alright.

Even if none of the preceding responses rings true for you, hopefully what you do not do is hold the falling person face down in the puddle, while throwing your head back in maniacal laughter. This would be troublesome, to say the least. The bothersome aspect of this response, and the origin of the other, more appropriate responses all spring from the same source. Basically, just because someone is a person, they have a certain status and are entitled to certain things. People are due a basic respect and have a dignity which must be respected.

In virtue of valuing respect for persons, professionals recognize that people are to be treated in a certain way. One of these ways can be understood as a negative, minimal account of how we are to respect persons. Minimally, respecting persons means not doing certain things, like harming others or holding them face down in a mud puddle. This face down in the mud puddle is of course physical harm, but you can imagine all sorts of other harms of emotional, psychological, or spiritual sorts.

In addition to this minimal, negative account of respecting persons, there also is a positive or proactive account of how we are to respect persons. Respecting persons in a proactive manner means doing certain things, like preventing someone from falling, extending someone a hand, or catching someone who is slipping. Again, this is a very literal interpretation of the physical preservation of the respect and dignity of others. Less literal examples that are more relevant for our professional life could include creating an environment that makes it difficult for respect for persons to be violated and likewise rewards those that do respect others. Hopefully you can imagine the way in which respect could be preserved or even furthered in a variety of manners in a variety of places, from educational and work settings to those of war-torn countries.

Thus respecting persons is about both not taking and taking certain actions. But the main point is, in virtue of being human, we have a minimum claim to be treated in a manner that is respectful. People need not be nice to us, but they must treat us with the regard due us as human beings, that is, with respect for our dignity.

All human beings are deserving of respect. But like many things we deserve, we often forget that others also deserve the very same things. That is, we are all entitled to be shown respect. If everyone is being shown respect, who is to do all of this showing of respect? The answer of course is everyone. So, not only is everyone entitled to be shown respect, but we also must show respect to everyone. Both of these are binding, regardless of whether they are carried out. But we all know it does not always work out this way. Often people do not get the respect they deserve and, more often, some people get more respect than they deserve. Even though things in the world may not seem just, since those who enact values may not be respected, while those who do not enact values sometimes are respected, values are no less binding. Even if respect is sometimes not enacted or is misplaced, some respect is owed to persons, regardless of how they have acted.

Another unifying thing to appreciate about respect is what it generally implies. We can respect our elders, respect someone's privacy, respect someone's feelings, respect the law, pay our respects, be right in every respect, and relate to something with respect to its origin. Notions of respect entail a relationship, but not each of them relate to persons. The aspects of respect, from these few examples, which relate to persons are those that respect a person, in the form of "our elders," or an important part of a person, in the form of someone's "privacy or feelings." When we respect a person or an important part of them, we are holding that part in high regard at best and with careful consideration at least.[2]

Thus, to respect persons is to hold them in some regard and relate to them with some regard. This regard can be measured on a continuum, from careful consideration to high regard or esteem. By careful consideration, we understand that we are to consider how other people would like to be treated. That is, when we relate to people, we are at least required to treat them in a manner which reflects some consideration. This consideration takes a concrete shape and form as we recognize that it includes a requirement to treat others as we would want to be treated.

Furthermore, we also might relate to someone in such a manner that we would want to honor or esteem them. That is, when we relate to some people, we want to show them more than careful consideration; we want to demonstrate that we hold them in high regard and esteem them. How much respect people deserve and how this is to be shown is never easy to determine but it certainly can be aided by what we know from our other values. For example, justice, in the form of distributive justice, addresses what people are entitled to relative to their situation, and compassion addresses what people are entitled to insofar as we are able to identify and relate to their particular situation. Determining how much respect each individual is entitled to, beyond the basic respect due to all, is not typically a conscious process. However, we would be well served to make it a conscious, thoughtful, and reflective one.

Think back to our rainy day example. As the stranger is slipping and falling into the muddy puddle, our responses vary. This various response rate to the stranger probably depends greatly on our physical reaction time. That is, since we have no relationship with the unlucky person, we just react to her situation. If our reflexes are good, our response will be quick. However, what if the person coming toward you is someone you know and hold in great esteem? Your response to this person being at risk is liable to be much more proactive than your response to the stranger. Why is this? In virtue of holding this individual in high regard, you relate to his or her peril in a manner which reflects that. Thus, if someone you hold in high esteem is falling, you are apt to do much to help him or her avoid the muddy puddle. In holding the person coming toward you in high regard, you are more attentive to his or her approach and thus better able to physically respond to his or her loss of balance. Likewise, you are liable to be more willing to adapt to what happens to the person if a fall does occur.

Staying with our rainy day example, what if the person coming toward you is someone you know and do not hold in high regard? How are you to react as this person goes down in the mud? Perhaps there is a part of you that is secretly glad about the accident, particularly if no more harm comes to this person than muddy clothing, but a secret gladness does not make for a moral professional. No one ever said that being a moral professional would be easy. Regardless of our personal feelings toward someone, the person still has dignity and is owed basic respect. In the instance that someone for whom you have little esteem is slipping, you need to be oriented toward thinking about how you would like to be treated if you were in the same situation. We would not like a passerby to be secretly glad that we were wallowing in the mud, leaving us to our mess, no matter what the passerby's relation to us. This sort of careful consideration that puts us in the place of one for whom we may have little esteem is at the very least required if we are to be valuing respect for persons. In addition, often an appreciation of another's position—wet, dirty clothes on a cold day—can help us cultivate respect for another that might not necessarily be clearly present.

This last instance, watching someone for whom you have little respect fall, demonstrates another significant aspect of respect. There is a difference between actually respecting someone and showing them respect. Feeling respect for someone is one thing; showing respect for someone is another. In short, we ought to feel respect for everyone, just because they are human, and especially for those who merit being held in high esteem. But realistically, in our concern with professional ethics, we are less concerned with feelings and more concerned with actions. What this means for us is that we are required to show everyone basic respect, even if it is not felt. You can *show* respect for someone, even though you *feel* little respect for the person.

Although this might seem hypocritical, this minimal amount of showing respect is that which we are all obligated to demonstrate. It is without hypocrisy, since we appreciate that even if someone is a terrible person, they are still a person and entitled to the respect that all people are basically entitled. This minimal, negative notion of respect returns us to not violating someone's dignity and requires us to not do certain things, through a careful consideration of the other person's circumstances. However, life would be quite dreary and without inspiration if obligatory respect were the primary way in which we related to one another. That is, everyone is entitled to be shown this minimum amount of respect *and* the opportunity to relate to others in such a manner as to earn their respect. This positive notion of respect requires us to do certain things for this other person whom we hold in high regard or esteem. This latter aspect of respect is what can make respecting others and being respected truly worthwhile and satisfying. When we respond to people who value us as human beings, whether in our personal or professional lives, we are inspired to be a valued human being. In being such a person, we thereby earn the respect we are given, as an environment is present that makes it possible for us to be a person worthy of respect.

An example of the difference between showing respect and feeling respect is easily imagined in our professional life. Think of the work situations you have been in where you have felt like your work was valued and you were thus valued as the one who provided those services or goods. In that sort of positive work environment, your opinions were valued and perhaps even sought out. Likewise, you desired to contribute to the overall environment in such a way as to appreciate and value the work and viewpoints of those around you. Together, everyone was positively respecting persons insofar as they furthered the ability of their colleagues to not only respect each other but themselves. In this situation, you both felt and showed respect. Now think of those work situations where you have not felt as though your work was valued. There you were present to provide a service or good and had no real presence in your workplace, apart from the existence of your labor. Granted, you were not harmed, nor did you harm anyone else, at least overtly, in this work environment, thus a negative preservation of your respect was safeguarded. But in this minimal amount of respect shown, none was actually felt, neither for yourself nor your colleagues. These two instances demonstrate the richness that is present when respect is felt and shown, and the lack when the minimal requirement of respect is present without the commensurate feeling.

Hence, we now know several things about respect for persons. First, respect for persons involves relationships. Next, respecting persons includes being shown respect and showing respect to others as something to which we are entitled or obligated, without need of elaborate explanations or defense. Showing respect can be done minimally, by not violating someone's dignity, or proactively, by holding someone in high regard. Finally, we have differentiated feeling respect for someone from showing respect for someone. This differentiation is significant, since what often actually counts when we relate to people is the respect we show them, not what we feel for them. This is the case because what we point to as indicating a show of respect is what is actually required of us in respecting people in our professional life. That is, although we may not respect people in that we do not hold them in high esteem, we will or at least should always show them a minimal amount of respect. This showing of respect need not mean we necessarily respect someone, rather it merely indicates that we have respect for them in virtue of their participation in humanity. Because of this participation in humanity, an individual is afforded particular things, like being shown respect. With these ground rules for respecting persons established, what do all of these aspects of respect share? What, in general, is involved when we show respect for someone?

What Respect for Persons Involves

Now that we know what respect for persons is, how are we to actually go about respecting persons? One way in which we can begin to determine what is involved in showing someone respect is through appealing to the ways in which respect is made manifest in our professional codes. Some of our most esteemed, established professions include those that provide care for people. Occupational therapists, nurses, speech pathologists, and physician's assistants all care for people. In a hospital setting, when giving care to patients, many professions and occupations are involved. Appreciating this, the American Hospital Association has come up with a *Statement on a Patient's Bill of Rights*. While primarily aimed at the relationship between physicians and patients, and expected to be binding when care is delivered in a hospital, this code points to the way in which a very important relationship, that between a health care provider and patient, is to preserve respect for persons. The statement begins by highlighting some of the things we have already discussed, as it tells us that it recognizes "that a personal relationship between the physician and the patient is essential for the provision of proper medical care."[3] As a consequence of this relationship, and the way in which it takes place within the institution of the hospital, the statement goes on to assert that there is a responsibility of the hospital and physician to maintain that certain rights are upheld. In listing these rights, the first one states, "The patient has the right to considerate and respectful care."[4]

Appreciating that the patient is entitled to respectful care, what does that then require of physicians in their actions and hospitals as institutions that allow physicians to do their work? The details of these questions are answered as the code goes on to articulate that respecting a patient requires one to value the patient's confidentiality, privacy, and autonomy. For example, it is claimed that "all communications and records pertaining to his care should be treated as confidential."[5] Furthermore, the privacy of a patient is upheld as all "case discussion, consultation, examination, and treatment . . . should be conducted discretely."[6] Finally, patient autonomy as a part of respecting persons is upheld as a patient "has the right to obtain from his physician complete, current information concerning his diagnosis, treatment, and prognosis. . . ." Furthermore, a patient "has the right to refuse treatment. . . ."[7] From the above we can see that respecting a patient includes a respect for confidentiality, privacy, and autonomy. Circumstances or actions that prevent the enactment of these are thus impediments to appropriately respecting persons.

Another field which has a great deal to do with relating to people and thus with respecting persons is that of human resources. In the *Code of Ethics* for the International Personnel Management Association, there is a pledge to "respect and protect the dignity of individuals."[8] Just like the code of the American Hospital Association, this statement alone does not provide us with much guidance for our behavior in respecting persons. Fortunately, the statement continues, and indicates that a human resources professional "will treat as privileged, information accepted in trust."[9] This statement indicates a recognition of the relationship between a human resources professional and an employee, in that information is accepted, somewhat like a gift, from someone else. In being "accepted" and not merely taken, a human resources professional recognizes the human dignity of a person and thus treats the information as privileged as a consequence of respecting that person. In doing so, a human resources professional protects those persons with whom he or she relates by upholding their confidentiality and privacy.

Furthermore, a human resources professional works to empower employees in such a manner as to "motivate employees to develop their full capability as competent, productive members of their organization."[10] This recognition of human development as a part of respecting persons goes far toward creating an atmosphere of not only autonomy but also one where respect must be proactively furthered, not just negatively not violated. That is, when individuals are fully able to use their capacities, like being fully informed by a physician, or allowed to be fully capable as an employee, their dignity is not only not violated but it is also promoted.

Together, these codes provide some concrete ways in which respect for persons can be enacted. Even though respect for persons is actualized in a very different manner by a physician than a personnel director, both occupations indicate that certain things occur as a consequence of respecting persons. In respecting persons, we should maintain their confidentiality and privacy and create an environment that allows them to be autonomous.

A Case Involving Respect for Persons

With this basic understanding of what respect for persons is and what it involves, we can look to a case in order to begin to explore how respect for persons is actually carried out. In the case that follows, keep in mind that we are owed respect, as is everyone else involved here. In this instance, how these two things are to be made commensurate is the primary issue.

> *A residential center in midcoastal Maine houses youths with behavioral problems, ages eight to eighteen. The assistant administrator, Judith Moore, has noticed a change in the behavior of one of the female residents. The change has taken place over a period of about five to six weeks. This resident has become overly friendly with one of the male counselors, who is twenty-three years old. Because of these sorts of potential problems, this counselor is assigned to males only.*
>
> *Noticing the behavioral change, Judith spoke first to the male counselor. In doing so, she explained that she noticed behavior that would make her believe that the fifteen-year-old girl was beginning to develop a crush on him. Judith, as assistant administrator, suggested*

*to the counselor that he be careful around her and keep the relation-
ship on a professional level.*

*Even after talking to the counselor, Judith continued to notice the
behavior in the fifteen-year-old girl, so she started doing some investigating. She checked her room for notes and journals. At first she found
notes to other friends saying that the teen liked the counselor, but nothing concrete appeared as far as being able to prove that anything was
going on between the girl and the counselor. Judith continued to watch
the teen's behavior and asked the other staff to pay attention to her behavior. She also continued to check her room for evidence of impropri-
eties. After a few weeks, she finally found notes from the male
counselor to the girl, saying how much he enjoyed kissing her, hugging
her, and how much he wants to be with her.*

*Judith immediately informed her supervisor and showed him the
notes from the male counselor, since everyone who worked or lived at
the center knew that under the rules of the residential center, the con-
tents of the teen's room were subject to search and seizure at any time.
After reviewing the notes, the supervisor of the center called in the counselor and confronted him with the evidence. The counselor admitted
everything, and because of the personal relationship between the supervisor and counselor, he was subsequently allowed to resign, with no explanation or reason for resignation to be given by the supervisor. At this
point, Judith was then called in and informed of this decision. She was
very upset. Upon being informed about the situation, Judith replied that
if the counselor was allowed to resign and was not reported to the
proper agency, he could find another job working with kids. Judith also
realized that if she were found to have knowledge of this situation, her
license could possibly be revoked. When Judith raised all of this with
her supervisor, she was informed that if she pursued this matter further,
her job would be in jeopardy and she would be summarily dismissed.
Judith was confounded by this situation and did not know what to do.*[11]

Stage I.

   1.   (*P*)resent the problem.

After realizing that a counselor who is a licensed professional
has entered into a physical relationship with a teen client, the counselor's supervisor allows him to resign. Judith, aware of the situation, knows that her professional code requires her to turn in this
counselor to the licensing board. She has been informed by her superior that if she does so, her job is in jeopardy.

   2.   (*C*)ollect the information.

Judith is an assistant administrator at a residential center for
youth with behavioral problems. She is aware of a twenty-three-year-

old male counselor who is involved in a physical relationship with a fifteen-year-old female resident. The male counselor is a personal friend of the supervisor of the facility. The supervisor is aware that the relationship has taken place. The male counselor is being allowed to resign from the facility without having this incident noted on his work history. The male counselor is likely to get another job in another residential facility, which will not know of his past relationship with a client. Judith's licensing board requires her to report such incidents to the authorities. Judith has been told that if she reports the incident, she will be fired.

Stage II.

3. (L)ist the relevant value(s).

Respect for persons is certainly a primary value in this case. Judith is trying to negotiate how to maintain her self-respect as a professional while at the same time respecting her supervisor and the employee she supervises. In addition to these people who have a claim to be respected, there is the issue of respecting the girl who is now involved with a counselor in her residential facility. In addition to these persons whom Judith must respect, Judith must also address the way in which she is charged with respecting the possible persons the male counselor may come into contact with in the future. That is, part of Judith's professional code recognizes that she is to respect her clients and uphold the reputation of her profession. By allowing the male counselor to continue working with children, she is potentially jeopardizing her duty to respect these future clients and the reputation of her profession.

Of course, other values are involved in this case, such as integrity and responsibility, as well as beneficence and nonmaleficence, but our concentration has been on how best to interpret respect for persons. Try to figure out the ways in which these other values are relevant. Can you think of any values that are also relevant that have not been mentioned?

4. (E)xplore the options and the ways theories apply.

Acting as a consequentialist, Judith must consider what action, on her part, would bring about the greater good. If she were to stay at her job, she would be able to help see the teen through the ramifications of having had a physical relationship with a staff member of the residential center. Yet, if while staying at her job, she helped perpetuate the falsehood that the male counselor left the center on good terms, the consequences brought about by that might be very damaging for another youth facility. Furthermore, if it were to be found that Judith participated in the cover-up, she could lose her ability to work in a field she truly enjoys. If Judith were to go against her supervisor and report the counselor's behavior and the supervisor's attempt to cover it up to the licensing board, it would be hard to tell what the consequences would be. As her supervisor threatened, Judith could lose her job. Potentially, Judith's conscientious behavior could end up being rewarded. However, there also is the possibility that Judith herself would be tainted by the scandal that involved her place of employment. The consequences in this situation would be hard to determine.

The rights theory is particularly relevant in this case, since Judith needs to consider who has a right to what in this situation. Clearly, one of the primary people who needs to be respected, and thus has rights, is the client of the residential facility, the fifteen-year-old girl who has been exploited by an authority figure. Judith is certainly working to uphold respect for this teen by getting the male counselor removed from the residential center. But what about respect for the male counselor? How much respect is actually owed those who have violated certain rules of professional practice? Judith needs to consider if confidentiality, as part of respect for persons, holds in this instance. Certainly, the confidentiality of the girl needs to be upheld, as does her privacy, because they are part of respect for persons. But does the counselor deserve these as well? What about the supervisor? What are his rights, and what are Judith's responsibilities in upholding them? Finally, what about the rights of Judith herself? How is she to be responsible to her conception of self-respect within her profession? That is, if Judith is to do what her supervisor has asked of her, will she be able to maintain her self-respect?

According to a duty-based theory, Judith would have to determine where the greater duty lay. Does she have a greater obligation to uphold the policies of her profession and the rules governing the organization of youth residential homes, or to follow the orders her supervisor has given her? Remember that an important part of any duty-based interpretation of respect for persons includes a consideration of the intentions at stake. In carrying out her duty, Judith needs to examine why she feels a certain course of action is required of her. Does a duty to follow her supervisor's orders seem more compelling because employment is superior to unemployment, according to Judith? Does a duty to report the actions of the male counselor seem more compelling because Judith never really liked him anyway? Finally, are there any ways of resolving these seemingly conflicting duties? That is, maybe there is another interpretation of her duty that Judith has overlooked that would allow her to fulfill all of her responsibilities to the best of her ability.

As a virtue theorist, Judith needs to determine how to act in such a manner that she would best express good character. In this instance, her situation may be more complicated, since her supervisor and the male counselor probably have a different idea of what a good character is. In being a person of good character and one who respects persons, Judith would need to consider all of these ideas of what a good character includes. This, of course, does not mean that she will necessarily determine that her and her colleagues' conception of good character concur, but she will consider the various conceptions of good character that are at stake. One thing a person of good character would do in this instance would be to protect future clients of residential homes. But a person of good character also would try to be a good professional and good employee, and help the male counselor learn from the situation so it would not happen again. By considering all of these actions, Judith herself needs to determine how best to express good character as a professional who values respect for persons.

Care theory certainly figures prominently in this case. As Judith is faced with caring for the clients of the residential facility, she must determine how to best care for those adolescents for whom she is immediately responsible. Likewise, in allowing the male counselor to continue to work with children, Judith must question whether she is really expressing care for those children that this counselor will potentially come into contact with. What about caring for this wayward counselor that has perpetuated this wrongdoing? Is there a way in which Judith can care for him, so that he might come to see that his behavior was harmful to this girl, not to mention that it may also have been punishable by law? Judith additionally must consider the best way to express care for the ongoing success of the residential facility where she works. The negative publicity that comes about as a consequence of this counselor's action could seriously threaten the center's ability to do the work to which it is committed. The determination of how best to enact care in this situation is a difficult one.

Finally, how would a narrative analysis deal with this moral problem? That is, within the context of all that is narratively relevant,

what should Judith do? How important to Judith are the guidelines
of her profession? Throughout her career, have sanctioning boards
and the consequences they bring about figured prominently? Also,
how committed is Judith to the well-being of the children who enter
the residential facilities in her state? In her past relationship to this
male counselor, how serious a threat does she think he poses to the
children he will come into contact with in the future? Within her
narrative history, it could be that Judith takes her role as protector
very seriously. As a consequence of her history or personal narrative,
Judith could react to this situation in many ways. Is it significant
for Judith's history that if she reports the male counselor she would
be going against her supervisor and potentially jeopardizing her job?
What is Judith's employment history, and how committed is she to
this particular job? Many things would need to be considered in a
well-developed application of the narrative theory. Think of some of
them and their consequences for Judith's action.

This case is complex, and there is a great deal to be considered.
What do you think has been left out in the preceding application of
theories to this case? How would you further develop the options to
be explored through each of the theories applied?

5. (A)ssess the rightness and wrongness of various outcomes.

Judith could follow the directions her supervisor has given her,
not mention the incident to anyone, and thereby keep her job. This
decision would demonstrate a respect (perhaps misplaced) for her
supervisor and the male counselor.

Judith could report the actions of the male counselor as well as
the attempts to cover them up to the local licensing committee that
oversees the administration of youth residential centers. This decision would demonstrate a respect for the clients in her care, as well
as for her profession.

Judith could talk to both the male counselor and their supervisor, explaining to them that she is planning to report the entire
situation to the local licensing board and that she would prefer that
this course of action be pursued by all three of them. This decision
would demonstrate a respect for her colleagues, for the clients in her
care, and for her profession.

6. (D)ecide.

In the previous section, we have only indicated a few of the
options that could actually be pursued by Judith. Try to think of

several more, or even the specific ways in which the options articulated earlier could be brought about. In doing so, come up with your own decision for the case, working to bring about the best possible way to respect all of the persons involved.

Hopefully, as a consequence of thinking about the potential options, you will agree that Judith should not follow the directions her supervisor has given her. Of the options remaining, arguably, it would be best for Judith to speak with the male counselor and her supervisor, explaining to them her plan to report the situation. This decision, of the three expressed, best preserves the value of respect for persons.

Stage III.

   7.   (*D*)efend.

In defending the decision articulated above, we can assess why it is that this way of proceeding best preserves the value of respecting persons. By speaking with her colleagues and informing them of her plan to report the incident to the licensing board, Judith is respecting the most people in the best way possible. Judith respects the male counselor and her supervisor by allowing them to take responsibility for their actions and to do the right thing. Possibly by knowing that Judith will report the event, regardless of the possibility of losing her job, her colleagues will be persuaded to come forward with the information they have about this incident. Even if they choose not to, she will be letting them know what she plans to do, and not sneaking off to report the incident, thereby preserving her colleagues' entitlement to know information that affects them. Obviously, by reporting the incident, Judith will be preserving a respect for the teen who has been exploited. Likewise, she also will be respecting those who might later come into contact with the male counselor. By meeting with her colleagues and being straightforward in her actions, Judith is best able to express her respect for persons.

   8.   (*R*)eflect.

Now that we have made this decision and defended it, all that is left to consider is that which allowed this situation to happen in the first place. Perhaps there could be more safeguards in place to prevent clients of the residential facility from becoming potentially involved with counselors. Additionally, more of an attempt could be made to keep track of the level of involvement of counselors with clients. Background checks or another means of determining whether the counselors who have been hired are actually fit to work with children could also be employed.

What about the policies that are in place at the residential facility? Can you come up with some means of ensuring that these policies are actually followed? In dealing with the difficult situation that Judith was in, perhaps there are ways of ensuring that employees are going to be protected when they attempt to do the right thing. Try to come up with some of these ways on your own.

Considering all of these questions for reflection, devise several more ways in which this situation could have been avoided. As a consequence of your reflection, try to not only avoid this situation having taken place, but also anticipate similar situations that could be avoided in the future.

Interpreting Respect for Persons: Guides to Help

Now that we have looked at a case that centered on respect for persons, we can consider some guidelines that would be helpful in resolving such a case. We begin by reflecting on what it is that respect for persons requires of us, at a minimum. In doing so, we come up with the following rule.

Negative Rule of Respect

In general, do not perform actions that violate a person's basic dignity as understood legally, socially, or morally.

In understanding respect for persons, we have recognized that everyone is entitled to be shown respect. In acting within our occupations, we must not engage in actions that diminish the dignity and humanity of others as it is spelled out by laws, social institutions, and professional codes. At the very least, we should not act in such a manner that we undermine someone's basic dignity as a person. Keep in mind that each person, regardless of his or her character, has dignity. This dignity is not, however, the only relevant aspect of a person. Thus, while obnoxious persons or criminals do not make us feel respect for them, and in fact may even lose some of the privileges accorded to those who are shown respect, they can expect that others will not take actions toward them that compromise their basic dignity.

In the case of Judith, think about what the counselor did by becoming physically involved with his client. He broke the rules that governed the administration of residential facilities. In doing so, his actions were required to be reported to the group that oversaw these facilities. Thus, in virtue of his actions, the counselor lost his right to confidentiality and privacy. He also lost some of the basic privileges granted by respect for persons. However, he did not lose all claims to have his dignity respected. That is, Judith could not take the situation into her own hands and ensure that the counselor never had any more dealings with children by following him around for the rest of his life. In dealing with this situation, Judith needs to uphold a minimal notion of respect for persons, relative to her colleague. She is obligated to do so in a qualified way, since her colleague, by becoming involved with a client of the facility, acted unprofessionally and thus compromised his status as a person deserving of respect.

Granted, we must at the very least not violate someone's basic dignity. But is that all that we are committed to when it comes to respect? In addition to not violating dignity, we can further dignity, as expressed in the following rule.

Positive Rule of Respect

Take actions that promote and foster the dignity of persons, by working to create an environment that enables people to respect themselves and one another.

This rule of respect concentrates on doing something proactive, relative to respecting persons and not merely minimally avoiding a violation of human dignity. In virtue of recognizing respect for persons as a value, we are committed to creating an environment that allows this value to be practiced. This is the goal of the Positive Rule of Respect, and it can be made manifest in a variety of ways. An environment of respect can be encouraged in as simple a manner as being courteous to your colleagues and not taking your frustrations out on them. Likewise, an environment of respect can be encouraged through more involved means, such as diversity education and sensitivity training, increased dialogue between management and staff, and many other programs. Basically it is not enough not to violate human dignity. Respecting persons requires us to encourage human flourishing.

The way values eventually are applied in the world is a lot like a science experiment. You apply absolutes, that is, values, into a context. This context is a situation that is constantly changing, the world. Sometimes the results are not really what you expected, so rather than throw out what you have committed yourself to as an absolute, you adjust the mixture that the absolute is being applied to. In short, when you respect certain people, your respect is not always returned or valued. Like an unreliable component of a science experiment, change the variable, so those you do respect will respect you in return. Of course, we do not always choose who we work with or those for whom we work, but we do choose our attitudes toward them. When dealing with difficult individuals and work situations, try to create an environment that allows for the most possible respect for persons to be expressed.

Relating this to the Judith situation, she has been given an ultimatum by her supervisor: "Go along with my plans, or you will be fired." This statement does not do much for Judith's potential ability to be autonomous. She is not being respected, even in a minimal manner, according to the Negative Rule of Respect. She can deal with this in several ways. She could first respond to her boss in a like manner, violating her own recognition of the importance of respecting others, or she could try to create an environment that would allow the most respect under these conditions to be expressed. Judith could allow the situation to cool down a bit and then approach her supervisor, explaining her perspective and why she thought it was in the best interest of all those involved. This would allow her to maintain her autonomy and self-respect, while still expressing respect for her supervisor.

Keep in mind that there are sometimes situations that do not allow for the creation of a respectful environment. In those cases, we fall back on our Negative Rule rather than our Positive Rule. Ideally, we will always be in work situations that will allow us to appeal to the Positive Rule of Respect. However, our ideals do not always inform our work situations. Consequently, when we are determining how best to respect others, we use, minimally, the Negative Rule and, ideally, the Positive Rule.

Conflicts Involving Respect for Persons

With all of our discussion of respecting persons, and what this includes, as well as rules to guide us in enacting respect, we might be lulled into thinking that respecting people and being respected are sure things. Of course, and unfortunately, life proves otherwise. In what follows, we will consider three typical conflicts that arise as we attempt to respect persons, including ourselves. These three conflicts, like all of those we will discuss, are not exhaustive or exclusive. It is quite possible that a conflict you face may be totally unlike these. However, by appreciating the issues involved in these conflicts, you can begin to frame your own perspective on what respecting persons means to you, as you determine how you want to be respected.

All three of the conflicts that follow involve interpreting the value of respect for persons. That is, respecting someone, including yourself, never actually conflicts with another value. Instead, interpreting respect for persons in one way may preclude interpreting respect for persons in another way. Thus our first conflict involves a difficulty in showing respect at the same time to two particular individuals. The second conflict addresses the problem when interpreting respect for persons comes into conflict with interpreting justice. Finally, we will consider what happens when respecting another person comes into conflict with respecting yourself.

In the first conflict, it is difficult to interpret the value of respecting persons in such a manner that we are able to respect two people at once. This is hard to conceptualize in the abstract, so we will make it concrete by returning to our case of Judith. It would be very difficult for Judith to demonstrate respect for the teenager for whom her residential facility is responsible and for her supervisor, who has asked her to be involved in covering up her colleague's wrongdoing. In situations where it is difficult to show respect for two people at the same time, we are well served to pull back from the situation and assess what our connection is to the two people in question. Like loyalty, an aspect of integrity, respect for persons requires different things of us, depending on the particular relationship we have to the persons we are respecting. That is, we show our respect for different people in different ways.

For Judith, respecting her supervisor would require her to do what he asked of her, while respecting her client would require her to ensure that her goal of dealing with the behavioral problems that brought her to the residential center were dealt with professionally. Both of these ways of respecting persons cannot be met in this circumstance. Thus, what is Judith's relationship to each of these individuals? She has freely taken on her job, thus has freely entered into a relationship of respect with her client. However, she did not choose her supervisor, and she did not choose to have to resolve the problem with the male counselor by allowing him to resign without noting his history of intimacy with a resident of the facility where they all work. Judith has not entered into this situation freely. Also, Judith is being told what to do, which demonstrates a lack of respect for her on the part of her supervisor. So, her supervisor is not acting respectfully toward Judith in requiring her to ignore the ethical standards of her profession, thus Judith is likely to be more compelled to act on the respect she feels for her client rather than that she would show to her supervisor.

Generally, in situations where our interpretation of respect for persons leads us to a conflict, in that both parties cannot be respected, we must analyze our relationship to each party and assess to which of them we have a greater bond. In doing so, it is often helpful to determine the amount of respect each party has for us, since when faced with a conflict, we are more inclined to respect those who respect us than those who show little or no respect for us.

In this second conflict, consider how interpreting respect for persons comes into conflict with interpreting justice. Like our previous example, this is hard to conceptualize in the abstract, so once again we return to Judith. Justice requires us to treat equals equally. Thus those who are on the same footing deserve to be equally respected. But what about when someone removes himself or herself from this state of similar footing? That is, when the male counselor at Judith's facility gets physically involved with a teen client, he is no longer equal to all of the other counselors at the facility. That is, he no longer has the same rights he had prior to this action, thus respect for persons is now sacrificed to justice. In determining the best way to handle this situation, certain things that are a part of respect for persons are not relevant, such as confidentiality, privacy, and autonomy.

In having respect for persons take a back seat to justice, we must be careful in our interpretation of justice. When we decide that someone no longer deserves the respect due a professional, as a consequence of his or her action, this is a determination that must be done in a careful manner. Fortunately, we do not make these sort of decisions in a vacuum. Typically, such determinations are not handled singularly. Justice is a public value, and there are often all sorts of safeguards to see that it is handled appropriately.

In short, there are times when we are no longer required to grant someone the respect due others in the profession. These situations are rare, but present. Usually this respect is lost as a consequence of a failure to fulfill the responsibilities of the profession. In determining that someone no longer need be respected, be certain you do not violate the Negative Rule of Respect.

In our third and final conflict we consider when respecting another person comes into conflict with respecting yourself. That is, in dealing with others respectfully, you can end up dealing with a situation that makes you feel as though you are not able to deal with yourself respectfully.

Occupationally, we are at the very least required to enact the Negative Rule of Respect. This rule, which tells us to not violate basic human dignity, holds for everyone, including ourselves. But we also are committed to the Positive Rule of Respect, which requires more. It requires that we promote the dignity of others, including ourselves, and this demands that we work to create an environment that fosters respect for persons. In Judith's case, it is not conceivable that she could still work for her supervisor, allowing the male counselor to move on to another job dealing with adolescents, and still maintain her self-respect. Thus, when put into situations in our work that require us to do things or be exposed to things that constitute a hostile work environment, it would be quite difficult to maintain self-respect without appealing to our Positive Rule of Respect. In attempting to remedy a situation that is not conducive to respect, the Positive Rule is relevant, as it requires us to work toward an environment that furthers our ability to respect ourselves as well as others.

Sometimes drastic measures are necessary. In cases of sexual harassment or discriminatory labor practices, creating a better work environment includes leaving the situation and working somewhere else. For those in supervisory positions, bettering the environment could include addressing the situation, educating the workforce, and other such strategies for improving the occupational atmosphere.

Work is not intended to be martyrdom. No one is paid enough for that. When your self-respect is so sacrificed by your work life, seek to change that work life, or seek to change that work. In doing so, appeal first to the Negative Rule of Respect, as it applies to yourself and others, then to the Positive Rule of Respect, as you attempt to better the situation.

Conclusion

Respecting persons is a complicated value. In its interpretation, we often are required to deal with other people and our relationships with them. In doing so, our professional lives are bound to become complicated. In this chapter, we have considered the complexity involved in what respecting persons means and what it requires of us. We saw that respecting persons means upholding the dignity of persons. Overall, as the case involving Judith and her colleague demonstrates, we must always accord to others basic respect, although beyond that, respect must be earned. Valuing respect means that we do not violate the dignity of others and that we seek to create an environment that enables us and those around us to show respect for persons. In doing so, we further not only the ability of others to be respected but also our own ability to have self-respect.

EXERCISES

1. Take the code of ethics for your proposed occupation. If you are uncertain about your career, pick any code. Consider the following:

   1. Is there an explicit or implicit appeal to respect for persons contained in the code? Explain, using specific examples.
   2. Define respect for persons relative to the way it is used in the code of ethics for your proposed occupation. Is the more prevalent definition of respect for persons a negative one, insofar as you are not to violate someone's dignity, or is the prevalent definition of respect for persons a positive one, insofar as you are to work toward creating a work environment that furthers the ability of your colleagues, supervisors, and employees to respect themselves and others?
   3. In this code, what specific requirements must the professional meet because of the value of respect for persons? For instance, does your code see upholding confidentiality and privacy as ways of respecting persons? Does it identify autonomy as a way of respecting persons?
   4. In general, are the requirements to respect persons in your code too extensive or not extensive enough? Does this code include any more specific requirements of respect for persons which have not been mentioned in this chapter, or any sanctions for when the requirements of respecting persons are not met?
   5. For the professionals covered by this code, do you foresee any potential problems or conflicts they might face in acting out the value of respect for persons? Give three examples and explain each.

2. Use the CRM to reach a decision in each of these cases, or if a decision has already been reached, use the framework for moral analysis to analyze the case. In doing so, consider all of the relevant values, but be especially alert to considerations of respect for persons and its requirements. In making your decision about how to resolve the case, articulate which guide for interpreting respect for persons is most helpful. Be sure to explain your answers fully.

Case 1: How Far Is Too Far?

In an upscale hotel in Miami, there were increasing problems between the hotel management and staff. To begin with, thefts were occurring in the rooms of those staying in the hotel. Loose change, jewelry, clothes, and other items were disappearing from rooms. After consulting with hotel security, management determined that the cleaning staff was the only group that could possibly be perpetrating the thefts. At the same time, it was noted that employees were taking longer and longer breaks, without noting this on their time cards. In addition, mysterious long distance phone charges were appearing on office telephones after business hours. After some thought, it was decided that cameras would be installed on the premises of the hotel. These cameras would be installed in hotel hallways, offices, elevators, break rooms, and employee locker rooms, where employees changed before going on and off their shifts.

Employees recognized that management needed to protect the assets of its guests as well as the hotel's assets in terms of lost work time and long distance phone bills. However, they were very upset about the installation of cameras in their changing rooms. Enough is enough, they thought, can't we even change our clothes without our boss watching?

Case 2: Hostile Work Environment or Office Humor?

The main office at an employee-owned shipping facility recently went online. All employees are networked. They have access to the Internet, and are now capable of communicating easily through e-mail. Upper management personnel have memos and updates routinely sent to them. It is up to them to pass these memos and updates on to the employees they supervise. Occasionally employees pass on jokes that they have received from friends or downloaded from the Internet. You have recently received several jokes in various postings. These jokes all have as their punch line a caricature of a particular ethnic group. You identify yourself as part of this ethnic group, and you find the jokes insulting. The first time, it did not bother you much, because you felt like one person had not exercised good judgment in passing on a joke. But now that these types of jokes are found humorous by several of those in your company, you are beginning to take offense. What do you do?

CASE 3: IMPLICATIONS OF TIGHTENING THE BELT

You are part of the group that oversees waste disposal for a major medical facility in New Mexico. Often the materials you deal with are harmless, but occasionally, they are a biohazard and pose a potential threat if not dealt with appropriately. You usually send materials to a local processing facility. This facility is expensive, but you are confident that they treat all of the materials they receive with great care. Recently you were informed that your department would have its budget cut by 10 percent. It is up to the discretion of each department to determine how to adjust to its smaller budgets. With this budget cut, it seems that you are going to have to let a valued employee go in a market that has few available jobs. Or you realize that you could choose to have your facility's waste treated by a processing group that ships its medical waste to Mexico. The rules south of the border are less strict with regard to waste disposal and you are concerned about exposing people to these materials. You are torn between retaining a valued employee and exposing strangers to a biohazard. How do you best express respect for persons here?

NOTES

1. It should be noted that although this chapter concentrates on respect for persons, persons are not the only entities which we have an obligation to respect. Yet respecting persons is such a complicated phenomenon that it is enough to consider this as our primary concentration at this point. Much of what is said here could apply to other entities entitled to respect, with a bit more justification and explanation, such as respect for animals, respect for the environment, and so on.
2. The discussion of respect in this paragraph is indebted to the definition of respect presented in *Webster's New World Dictionary of the American Language,* Second College Edition (New York: Simon and Schuster, 1984), 1211.
3. *Statement on a Patient's Bill of Rights,* from *Hospitals* 47:4 (February 16, 1973), 41.
4. Ibid.
5. Ibid., Right 6.
6. Ibid., Right 5.
7. Ibid., Rights 2 and 4, respectively.
8. Pledge 1, *Code of Ethics for the International Personnel Management Association,* Jay M. Shafritz, *The Facts on File Dictionary of Personnel Management and Labor Relations,* 2d ed. (New York: Facts on File, Inc., 1985), 129.
9. Ibid., Pledge 6.
10. Ibid., Pledge 2.
11. This case was presented by the following students of Youngstown State University. I use it with their permission and with gratitude: Jeff Scacchetti, Joe Warino, Bill Slosser, Kim Harberson, Suzanne Taylor, Vickie Yoder, Ernie Zolka, and Allison Mallow.

GROUP 1: READINGS ON INTEGRITY AND RESPECT FOR PERSONS

Introduction

In the following group of readings, we are challenged for the first time to make our newly introduced understanding of values commensurate with the understandings others have of morality in their professional lives. In doing so, we will especially concentrate on the ways in which the values of integrity and respect for persons, as discussed in chapters 7 and 8, are experienced. However, as we have come to appreciate, even though particular values may be highlighted, many are involved.

We begin with a selection by turn-of-the-century writer Paul Laurence Dunbar, *The Lynching of Jube Benson*. Here we are forced to deal with the brutality that we can visit upon one another when we go against our values of integrity and respect for persons. We see the violence of which we are capable, in spite of a commitment to such values. Here we see how Dr. Melville has gone on living his life after being a party to the unjust lynching of his friend, Jube Benson. In retelling his story to acquaintances who are far too eager for details, we hear how Dr. Melville violated his own integrity and was forced to question the beliefs and values he held throughout his life, prior to this horrendous event. In addition to the obvious concern with the value of integrity, through honesty and loyalty, and respect for persons, and through the egregious loss of Jube's life, we see the way in which other values also are of paramount concern. This story brings us to consider questions of justice, as we evaluate how punishment should be determined, and beneficence and nonmaleficence, insofar as Dr. Melville never did anything to stop the tide of events that led to Jube's death. In this powerful story, there is much to consider for our morality, professional and otherwise.

In the next selection by Ronald Duska, *Whistleblowing and Employee Loyalty*, we are pushed to question the relationship we have with our employers. That is, under what circumstances are we required to be loyal, and what does it mean to be loyal to our employers? Here Duska argues that loyalty, for a variety of reasons, is not properly a part of employee–employer relations. In not having a relationship of loyalty and in not experiencing ourselves as part of a team we are unable to go against, we are freed from a major barrier to blowing the whistle on wrongdoing. With this barrier removed, Duska does not argue for rampant whistle-blowing. Instead, he finishes this article with some carefully constructed points to consider when we feel challenged to blow the whistle. This reading brings to light many of the issues relevant to integrity, as well as to the values of beneficence and nonmaleficence and responsibility. As we define the value of integrity for ourselves, relative to our particular context, we are well served by considering the aspects and requirements of loyalty Duska brings to light.

We continue with a selection by Kenneth Kipnis, centered around the legal profession. In *Lying and the Law*, we see the various ways in which integrity, as exemplified by honesty, and respect for persons, as exemplified by providing fair and competent legal defense, is understood. However, as is the case with all of the values, sometimes the fields of our occupational practice do not make it easy for us to adhere to our commitments to values. Consequently we are required to search for creative solutions that will both satisfy our commitments to values and the constraints of practicing our occupation. Here Kipnis presents several scenarios a lawyer is likely to face in his or her practice, all of which require an examination of how far we should go to do our job, while at the same time maintaining a commitment to values. Kipnis leaves us with no hard and fast conclusions, but he goes far in presenting the problem and leaves us with the responsibility of working it out in our own professional lives.

In our last reading, *On Duties of Virtue toward Other Men Arising from the Respect Due Them*, we turn to a classic philosophical writer, the eighteenth-century German philosopher Immanuel Kant. Kant often is caricatured as a stuffy and an unyielding thinker, too concerned with rules and theories to have any true understanding of what it is to be human. But, as this selection indicates, he not only understands what it is to be human, as exemplified in his comments on how we relate to and tease our friends, but he also understands what it is to be humane, as he articulates that we are required to recognize the dignity of humanity and therefore respect our fellow human beings. Bracketing Kant's dated, gender-exclusive language, the presentation of our human dignity and the respect which follows from it is most clear as Kant tells us we must treat our fellows as ends and not merely as means. This requires us to recognize that people are not present merely for our needs and desires, but that they have value in themselves, which requires that we respect them and treat them accordingly. Appreciating Kant's perspective certainly enriches our understanding of what it is to have respect for persons and how we might apply it in our professional lives.

In all of these readings, varied as they are, we are brought face to face with some of the concrete consequences that follow from a commitment to integrity and respect for persons. By considering some of these situations now, and with careful reflection, you will be well prepared to interpret these values in your own professional experience.

The Lynching of Jube Benson

PAUL LAURENCE DUNBAR

Gordon Fairfax's library held but three men, but the air was dense with clouds of smoke. The talk had drifted from one topic to another much as the smoke wreaths had puffed, floated, and thinned away. Then Handon Gay, who was an ambitious young reporter, spoke of a lynching story in a recent magazine, and the matter of punishment without trial put new life into the conversation.

"I should like to see a real lynching," said Gay rather callously.

"Well, I should hardly express it that way," said Fairfax, "but if a real, live lynching were to come my way, I should not avoid it."

"I should," spoke the other from the depths of his chair, where he had been puffing in moody silence. Judged by his hair, which was freely sprinkled with gray, the speaker might have been a man of forty-five or fifty, but his face, though lined and serious, was youthful, the face of a man hardly past thirty.

"What, you, Dr. Melville? Why, I thought that you physicians wouldn't weaken at anything."

"I have seen one such affair," said the doctor gravely, "in fact, I took a prominent part in it."

"Tell us about it," said the reporter, feeling for his pencil and notebook, which he was, nevertheless, careful to hide from the speaker.

The men drew their chairs eagerly up to the doctor's, but for a minute he did not seem to see them, but sat gazing abstractedly into the fire, then he took a long draw upon his cigar and began:

"I can see it all very vividly now. It was in the summer time and about seven years ago. I was practicing at the time down in the little town of Bradford. It was a small and primitive place, just the location for an impecunious medical man, recently out of college."

"In lieu of a regular office, I attended to business in the first of two rooms which I rented from Hiram Daly, one of the more prosperous of the townsmen. Here I boarded and here also came my patients— white and black—whites from every section, and blacks from 'nigger town,' as the west portion of the place was called."

"The people about me were most of them coarse and rough, but they were simple and generous, and as time passed on I had about abandoned my intention of seeking distinction in wider fields and determined to settle into the place of a modest country doctor. This was rather a strange conclusion for a young man to arrive at, and I will not deny that the presence in the house of my host's beautiful young daughter, Annie, had something to do with my decision. She was a beautiful young girl of seventeen or eighteen, and very far superior to her surroundings. She had a native grace and a pleasing way about her that made everybody that came under her spell her abject slave. White and black who knew her loved her, and none, I thought, more deeply and respectfully than Jube Benson, the black man of all work about the place."

"He was a fellow whom everybody trusted, an apparently steady going, grinning sort, as we used to call him. Well, he was completely under Miss Annie's thumb, and would fetch and carry for her like a faithful dog. As soon as he saw that I began to care for Annie, and anybody could see that, he transferred some of his allegiance to me and became my faithful servitor also. Never did a man have a more devoted adherent in his wooing than did I, and many a one of Annie's tasks which he volunteered to do gave her an extra hour with me. You can imagine that I liked the boy and you need not wonder any more than as both wooing and my practice waxed apace, I was content to give up my great ambitions and stay just where I was."

"It wasn't a very pleasant thing, then, to have an epidemic of typhoid break out in the town that kept me going so that I hardly had time for the courting that a fellow wants to carry on with his sweetheart while he is still young enough to call her his girl. I fumed, but duty was duty, and I kept to my work night and day. It was now that Jube proved how invaluable he was as a coadjutor. He not only took messages to Annie, but brought sometimes little ones from her to me, and he would tell me little secret things that he had overheard her say that made me throb with joy and swear at him for repeating his mistress' conversation. But best of all, Jube was a perfect Cerberus, and no one on earth could have been more effective in keeping away or deluding the other young fellows who visited the Dalys. He would tell me of it afterward, chuckling softly to himself. 'An,' Doctah, I say to Mistah Hemp Stevens, 'Scuse us, Mistah Stevens, but Miss Annie, she des gone out,' an' den he go outer do gate lookin' moughty lonesome. When

Sam Elkins come, I say, 'Sh, Mistah Elkins, Miss Annie, she done tuk down,' an' he say, 'What, Jube, you don' reckon hit de—' Den he stop an' look skeert, an' I say, 'I feared hit is, Mistah Elkins,'—an' sheks my haid ez solemn. He goes outer de gate lookin' lak his bes' frien' done daid, an' all de time Miss Annie behine de cu'tain ovah de po'ch des' a laffin' fit to kill.' "

"Jube was a most admirable liar, but what could I do? He knew that I was a young fool of a hypocrite, and when I would rebuke him for these deceptions, he would give way and roll on the floor in an excess of delighted laughter until from very contagion I had to join him— and, well, there was no need of my preaching when there had been no beginning to his repentance and when there must ensue a continuance of his wrongdoing."

"This thing went on for over three months, and then, pouf! I was down like a shot. My patients were nearly all up, but the reaction from overwork made me an easy victim of the lurking germs. Then Jube loomed up as a nurse. He put everyone else aside, and with the doctor, a friend of mine from a neighboring town, took entire charge of me. Even Annie herself was put aside, and I was cared for as tenderly as a baby. Tom, that was my physician and friend, told me all about it afterward with tears in his eyes. Only he was a big, blunt man and his expressions did not convey all that he meant. He told me how my nigger had nursed me as if I were a sick kitten and he my mother. Of how fiercely he guarded his right to be the sole one to 'do' for me, as he called it, and how, when the crisis came, he hovered, weeping, but hopeful, at my bedside, until it was safely passed, when they drove him, weak and exhausted, from the room. As for me, I knew little about it at the time, and cared less. I was too busy in my fight with death. To my chimerical vision there was only a black but gentle demon that came and went, alternating with a white fairy, who would insist on coming in on her head, growing larger and larger and then dissolving. But the pathos and devotion in the story lost nothing in my blunt friend's telling."

"It was during the period of a long convalescence, however, that I came to know my humble ally as he really was, devoted to the point of abjectness. There were times when for very shame at his goodness to me, I would beg him to go away, to do something else. He would go, but before I had time to realize that I was not being ministered to, he would be back at my side, grinning and pottering just the same. He manufactured duties for the joy of performing them. He pretended to see desires in me that I never had, because he liked to pander to them, and when I became entirely exasperated, and ripped out a good round oath, he chuckled with the remark, 'Dah, now, you sholy is gittin' well. Nevah did hyeah a man anywhaih nigh Jo'dan's sho' cuss lak dat.' "

"Why, I grew to love him, love him, oh, yes, I loved him as well—oh, what am I saying? All human love and gratitude are damned poor things; excuse me, gentlemen, this isn't a pleasant story. The truth is usually a nasty thing to stand."

"It was not six months after that that my friendship to Jube, which he had been at such great pains to win, was put to too severe a test."

"It was in the summer again, and as business was slack, I had ridden over to see my friend, Dr. Tom. I had spent a good part of the day there, and it was past four o'clock when I rode leisurely into Bradford. I was in a particularly joyous mood and no premonition of the impending catastrophe oppressed me. No sense of sorrow, present or to come forced itself upon me, even when I saw men hurrying through the almost deserted streets. When I got within sight of my home and saw a crowd surrounding it, I was only interested sufficiently to spur my horse into a jog trot, which brought me up to the throng, when something in the sullen, settled horror in the men's faces gave me a sudden, sick thrill. They whispered a word to me, and without a thought, save for Annie, the girl who had been so surely growing into my heart, I leaped from the saddle and tore my way through the people to the house."

"It was Annie, poor girl, bruised and bleeding, her face and dress torn from struggling. They were gathered round her with white faces, and, oh, with what terrible patience they were trying to gain from her fluttering lips the name of her murderer. They made way for me and I knelt at her side. She was beyond my skill, and my will merged with theirs. One thought was in our minds."

"Who?" I asked.

"Her eyes half opened, 'That black—' She fell back into my arms dead."

"We turned and looked at each other. The mother had broken down and was weeping, but the face of the father was like iron."

" 'It is enough,' he said; 'Jube has disappeared.' He went to the door and said to the expectant crowd, 'She is dead.' "

"I heard the angry roar without swelling up like the noise of a flood, and then I heard the sudden movement of many feet as the men separated into searching parties, and laying the dead girl back upon her couch, I took my rifle and went out to join them."

"As if by intuition the knowledge had passed among the men that Jube Benson had disappeared, and he, by common consent, was to be the object of our search. Fully a dozen of the citizens had seen him hastening toward the woods and noted his skulking air, but as he had grinned in his old good-natured way, they had, at the time, thought nothing of it. Now, however, the diabolical reason of his slyness was apparent. He had been shrewd enough to disarm suspicion, and by now was far away. Even Mrs. Daly, who was visiting with a neighbor, had seen him stepping out a back way, and had said with a laugh, 'I reckon that black rascal's a-running off somewhere.' Oh, if she had only known."

" 'To the woods! To the woods!' that was the cry, and away we went, each with the determination not to shoot, but to bring the culprit alive into town, and then to deal with him as his crime deserved."

"I cannot describe the feelings I experienced as I went out that night to beat the woods for this human tiger. My heart smoldered within me like a coal, and I went forward under the impulse of a will that was half my own, half some more malignant power's. My throat throbbed dryly, but water nor whiskey would not have quenched my thirst. The thought has come to me since that now I could interpret the panther's desire for blood and sympathize with it, but then I thought nothing. I simply went forward, and watched, watched with burning eyes for a familiar form that I had looked for as often before with such different emotions."

"Luck or ill-luck, which you will, was with our party, and just as dawn was graying the sky, we came upon our quarry crouched in the corner of a fence. It was only half light, and we might have passed, but my eyes had caught sight of him, and I raised the cry. We leveled our guns and he rose and came toward us."

" 'I t'ought you wa'n't gwine see me,' he said sullenly, 'I didn't mean no harm.' "

" 'Harm!' "

"Some of the men took the word up with oaths, others were ominously silent."

"We gathered around him like hungry beasts, and I began to see terror dawning in his eyes. He turned to me, 'I's moughty glad you's hyeah, doc,' he said, 'you ain't gwine let 'em whup me.' "

" 'Whip you, you hound,' I said, 'I'm going to see you hanged,' and in the excess of my passion I struck him full on the mouth. He made a motion as if to resent the blow against even such great odds, but controlled himself."

" 'W'y, doctah,' he exclaimed in the saddest voice I have ever heard, 'w'y, doctor! I ain't stole nuffin' o' yo'n, an' I was comin' back. I only run off to see my gal, Lucy, ovah to de Centah.' "

" 'You lie!' I said, and my hands were busy helping the others bind him upon a horse. Why did I do it? I don't know. A false education, I reckon, one false from the beginning. I saw his black face glooming there in the half light, and I could only think of him as a monster. It's tradition. At first I was told that the black man would catch me, and when I got over that, they taught me that the devil was black, and when I had recovered from the sickness of that belief, here were Jube and his fellows with faces of menacing blackness. There was only one conclusion: This black man stood for all the powers of evil, the result of whose machinations had been gathering in my mind from childhood up. But this has nothing to do with what happened."

"After firing a few shots to announce our capture, we rode back into town with Jube. The ingathering parties from all directions met us as we made our way up to the house. All was very quiet and orderly. There was no doubt that it was as the papers would have said, a gathering of the best citizens. It was a gathering of stern, determined men, bent on a terrible vengeance."

"We took Jube into the house, into the room where the corpse lay. At sight of it, he gave a scream like an animal's and his face went the color of storm-blown water. This was enough to condemn him. We divined, rather than heard, his cry of 'Miss Ann, Miss Ann, oh, my God, doc, you don't t'ink I done it?'"

"Hungry hands were ready. We hurried him out into the yard. A rope was ready. A tree was at hand. Well, that part was the least of it, save that Hiram Daly stepped aside to let me be the first to pull upon the rope. It was lax at first. Then it tightened, and I felt the quivering soft weight resist my muscles. Other hands joined, and Jube swung off his feet."

"No one was masked. We knew each other. Not even the culprit's face was covered, and the last I remember of him as he went into the air was a look of sad reproach that will remain with me until I meet him face to face again."

"We were tying the end of the rope to a tree, where the dead man might hang as a warning to his fellows, when a terrible cry chilled us to the marrow."

"'Cut 'im down, cut 'im down, he ain't guilty. We got de one. Cut him down, fu' Gawd's sake. Here's de man, we foun' him hidin' in de barn!'"

"Jube's brother, Ben, and another Negro came rushing toward us, half dragging, half carrying a miserable-looking wretch between them. Someone cut the rope, and Jube dropped lifeless to the ground."

"'Oh, my Gawd, he's daid, he's daid!' wailed the brother, but with blazing eyes he brought his captive into the center of the group, and we saw in the full light the scratched face of Tom Skinner—the worst white ruffian in the town—but the face we saw was not as we were accustomed to see it, merely smeared with dirt. It was blackened to imitate a Negro's."

"God forgive me; I could not wait to try to resuscitate Jube. I knew he was already past help, so I rushed into the house and to the dead girl's side. In the excitement they had not yet washed or laid her out. Carefully, carefully, I searched underneath her broken finger nails. There was skin there. I took it out, the little curled pieces, and went with it to my office."

"There, determinedly, I examined it under a powerful glass, and read my own doom. It was the skin of a white man, and in it were embedded strands of short, brown hair or beard."

"How I went out to tell the waiting crowd I do not know, for something kept crying in my ears, 'Blood guilty! Blood guilty!' "

"The men went away stricken into silence and awe. The new prisoner attempted neither denial nor plea. When they were gone I would have helped Ben carry his brother in, but he waved me away fiercely, 'You he'ped murder my brothah, you dat was *his* frien', go 'way, go 'way! I'll tek him home myse'f.' I could only respect his wish, and he and his comrade took up the dead man and between them bore him up the street on which the sun was now shining full."

"I saw the few men who had not skulked indoors uncover as they passed, and I—I—stood there between the two murdered ones, while all the while something in my ears kept crying, 'Blood guilty! Blood guilty!' "

The doctor's head dropped into his hands and he sat for some time in silence, which was broken by neither of the men, then he rose, saying, "Gentlemen, that was my last lynching."

Whistleblowing and Employee Loyalty

Ronald Duska

The releasing of evidence of the rushed cleanup at Three Mile Island is an example of whistleblowing. Norman Bowie defines whistleblowing as "the act by an employee of informing the public on the immoral or illegal behavior of an employer or supervisor."[1] Is it right to report the shady or suspect practices of the organization one works for? Is one a stool pigeon or a dedicated citizen? Does a person have an obligation to the public which overrides his obligation to his employer or does he simply betray a loyalty and become a traitor if he reports his company?

Discussions of whistleblowing generally revolve around four topics: (1) attempts to define whistleblowing more precisely; (2) debates about whether and when whistleblowing is permissible; (3) debates about whether and when one has an obligation to blow the whistle; and (4) appropriate mechanisms for institutionalizing whistleblowing.

In this [selection] I want to focus on the second problem, because I find it somewhat disconcerting that there is a problem at all. When I first looked into the ethics of whistleblowing it seemed to me that whistleblowing was a good thing, and yet I found in the literature claim after claim that it was in need of defense, that there was something wrong with it, namely that it was an act of disloyalty.

If whistleblowing was a disloyal act, it deserved disapproval, and ultimately any action of whistleblowing needed justification. This disturbed me. It was as if the act of a good Samaritan was being condemned as an act of interference, as if the prevention of a suicide needed to be justified. My moral position in favor of whistleblowing was being challenged. The tables were turned and the burden of proof had shifted. My position was the one in question. Suddenly instead of the company being the bad guy and the whistleblower the good guy, which is what I thought, the whistleblower was the bad guy. Why? Because he was disloyal. What I discovered was that in most of the literature it was taken as axiomatic that whistleblowing was an act of disloyalty. My moral intuitions told me that axiom was mistaken. Nevertheless, since it is accepted by a large segment of the ethical community it deserves investigation.

In his book *Business Ethics*, Norman Bowie, who presents what I think is one of the finest presentations of the ethics of whistleblowing, claims that "whistleblowing . . . violate[s] a *prima facie* duty of loyalty to one's employer." According to Bowie, there is a duty of loyalty which prohibits one from reporting his employer or company. Bowie, of course, recognizes that this is only a *prima facie* duty, i.e., one that can be overridden by a higher duty to the public good. Nevertheless, the axiom that whistleblowing is disloyal is Bowie's starting point.

Bowie is not alone. Sissela Bok, another fine ethicist, sees whistleblowing as an instance of disloyalty.

> The whistleblower hopes to stop the game; but since he is neither referee nor coach, and since he blows the whistle on his own team, his act is seen as a violation of loyalty [italics mine]. In holding his position, he has assumed certain obligations to his colleagues and clients. He may even have subscribed to a loyalty oath or a promise of confidentiality. . . . Loyalty to colleagues and to clients comes to be pitted against loyalty to the public interest, to those who may be injured unless the revelation is made.[2]

Bowie and Bok end up defending whistleblowing in certain contexts, so I don't necessarily disagree with their conclusions. However, I fail to see how one has an obligation of loyalty to one's company, so I disagree with their perception of the problem, and their starting point. The difference in perception is important because those who think employees have an obligation of loyalty to a company fail to take into account a relevant moral difference between persons and corporations and between corporations and other kinds of groups where loyalty is appropriate. I want to argue that one does not have an obligation of loyalty to a company, even a *prima facie* one, because companies are not the kind of things which are proper objects of loyalty. I then want to show that to make them objects of loyalty gives them a moral status they do not deserve and in raising their status, one lowers the status of the individuals who work for the companies.

But why aren't corporations the kind of things which can be objects of loyalty?

Loyalty is ordinarily construed as a state of being constant and faithful in a relation implying trust or confidence, as a wife to husband, friend to friend, parent to child, lord to vassal, etc. According to John Ladd "it is not founded on just *any* casual relationship, but on a specific kind of relationship or tie. The ties that bind the persons together provide the basis of loyalty."[3] But all sorts of ties bind people together to make groups. I am a member of a group of fans if I go to a ball game. I am a member of a group if I merely walk down the street. I am in a sense tied to them, but don't owe them loyalty. I don't owe loyalty to just anyone I encounter. Rather I owe loyalty to persons with whom I have special relationships. I owe it to my children, my spouse, my parents, my friends and certain groups, those groups which are formed for the mutual enrichment of the members. It is important to recognize that in any relationship which demands loyalty the relationship works both ways and involves mutual enrichment. Loyalty is incompatible with self-interest, because it is something that necessarily requires we go beyond self-interest. My loyalty to my friend, for example, requires I put aside my interests some of the time. It is because of this reciprocal requirement which demands surrendering self-interest that a corporation is not a proper object of loyalty.

A business or corporation does two things in the free enterprise system. It produces a good or service and makes a profit. The making of a profit, however, is the primary function of a business as a business. For if the production of the good or service was not profitable the business would be out of business. Since non-profitable goods or services are discontinued, the providing of a service or the making of a product is not done for its own sake, but from a business perspective as a means to an end, the making of profit. People bound together in a business are not bound together for mutual fulfillment and support, but to divide labor so the business makes a profit. Since profit is paramount if you do not produce in a company or if there are cheaper laborers around, a company feels justified in firing you for the sake of better production. Throughout history companies in a pinch feel no obligation of loyalty. Compare that to a family. While we can jokingly refer to a family as "somewhere they have to take you in no matter what," you cannot refer to a company in that way. "You can't buy loyalty" is true. Loyalty depends on ties that demand self-sacrifice with no expectation of reward, e.g., the ties of loyalty that bind a family together. Business functions on the basis of enlightened self-interest. I am devoted to a company not because it is like a parent to me. It is not, and attempts of some companies to create "one big happy family" ought to be looked on with suspicion. I am not "devoted" to it at all, or should not be. I *work* for it because it pays me. I am not in a family to get paid, but I am in a company to get paid.

Since loyalty is a kind of devotion, one can confuse devotion to one's job (or the ends of one's work) with devotion to a company.

I may have a job I find fulfilling, but that is accidental to my relation to the company. For example, I might go to work for a company as a carpenter and love the job and get satisfaction out of doing good work. But if the company can increase profit by cutting back to an adequate but inferior type of material or procedure, it can make it impossible for me to take pride in my work as a carpenter while making it possible for me to make more money. The company does not exist to subsidize my quality work as a carpenter. As a carpenter my goal may be good houses, but as an employee my goal is to contribute to making a profit. "That's just business!"

This fact that profit determines the quality of work allowed leads to a phenomenon called the commercialization of work. The primary end of an act of building is to make something, and to build well is to make it well. A carpenter is defined by the end of his work, but if the quality interferes with profit, the business side of the venture supersedes the artisan side. Thus profit forces a craftsman to suspend his devotion to his work and commercializes his venture. The more professions subject themselves to the forces of the marketplace, the more they get commercialized; e.g., research for the sake of a more profitable product rather than for the sake of knowledge jeopardizes the integrity of academic research facilities.

The cold hard truth is that the goal of profit is what gives birth to a company and forms that particular group. Money is what ties the group together. But in such a commercialized venture, with such a goal there is no loyalty, or at least none need be expected. An employer will release an employee and an employee will walk away from an employer when it is profitable to do so. That's business. It is perfectly permissible. Contrast that with the ties between a lord and his vassal. A lord could not in good conscience wash his hands of his vassal, nor could a vassal in good conscience abandon his lord. What bound them was mutual enrichment, not profit.

Loyalty to a corporation, then, is not required. But even more it is probably misguided. There is nothing as pathetic as the story of the loyal employee who, having given above and beyond the call of duty, is let go in the restructuring of the company. He feels betrayed because he mistakenly viewed the company as an object of his loyalty. To get rid of such foolish romanticism and to come to grips with this hard but accurate assessment should ultimately benefit everyone.

One need hardly be an enemy of business to be suspicious of a demand of loyalty to something whose primary reason for existence is the making of profit. It is simply the case that I have no duty of loyalty to the business or organization. Rather I have a duty to return responsible work for fair wages. The commercialization of work dissolves the type of relationship that requires loyalty. It sets up merely contractual relationships. One sells one's labor but not one's self to a company or an institution.

To think we owe a company or corporation loyalty requires us to think of that company as a person or as a group with a goal of human enrichment. If we think of it in this way we can be loyal. But this is just the wrong way to think. A company is not a person. A company is an instrument, and an instrument with a specific purpose, the making of profit. To treat an instrument as an end in itself, like a person, may not be as bad as treating an end as an instrument, but it does give the instrument a moral status it does not deserve, and by elevating the instrument we lower the end. All things, instruments and ends, become alike.

To treat a company as a person is analogous to treating a machine as a person or treating a system as a person. The system, company, or instrument get as much respect and care as the persons for whom they were invented. If we remember that the primary purpose of business is to make profit, it can be seen clearly as merely an instrument. If so, it needs to be used and regulated accordingly, and I owe it no more loyalty than I owe a word processor.

Of course if everyone would view business as a commercial instrument, things might become more difficult for the smooth functioning of the organization, since businesses could not count on the "loyalty" of their employees. Business itself is well served, at least in the short run, if it can keep the notion of a duty to loyalty alive. It does this by comparing itself to a paradigm case of an organization one shows loyalty to, the team.

What is perceived as bad about whistleblowing in business from this perspective is that one blows the whistle on one's own team, thereby violating team loyalty. If the company can get its employees to view it as a team they belong to, it is easier to demand loyalty. The rules governing teamwork and team loyalty will apply. One reason the appeal to a team and team loyalty works so well in business is that businesses are in competition with one another. If an executive could get his employees to be loyal, a loyalty without thought to himself or his fellow man, but to the will of the company, the manager would have the ideal kind of corporation from an organizational standpoint.

But businesses differ from teams in very important respects, which makes the analogy between business and a team dangerous. Loyalty to a team is loyalty within the context of sport, a competition. Teamwork and team loyalty require that in the circumscribed activity of the game I cooperate with my fellow players, so that pulling all together, we can win. The object of (most) sports is victory. But the winning in sports is a social convention, divorced from the usual goings on of society. Such a winning is most times a harmless, morally neutral diversion.

But the fact that this victory in sports, within the rules enforced by a referee (whistleblower), is a socially developed convention taking place within a larger social context makes it quite different from competition in business, which, rather than being defined by a context, permeates the whole of society in its influence. Competition leads not only to winners but to losers. One can lose at sport with precious few serious consequences. The consequences of losing at business are much more serious. Further, the losers in sport are there voluntarily, while the losers in business can be those who are not in the game voluntarily (we are all forced to participate) but are still affected by business decisions. People cannot choose to participate in business, since it permeates everyone's life.

The team model fits very well with the model of the free-market system because there competition is said to be the name of the game. Rival companies compete and their object is to win. To call a foul on one's own teammate is to jeopardize one's chances of winning and is viewed as disloyalty.

But isn't it time to stop viewing the corporate machinations as games? These games are not controlled and are not over after a specific time. The activities of business affect the lives of everyone, not just the game players. The analogy of the corporation to a team and the consequent appeal to team loyalty, although understandable, is seriously misleading at least in the moral sphere, where competition is not the prevailing virtue.

If my analysis is correct, the issue of the permissibility of whistleblowing is not a real issue, since there is no obligation of loyalty to a company. Whistleblowing is not only permissible but expected when a company is harming society. The issue is not one of disloyalty to the company, but the question of whether the whistleblower has an obligation to society if blowing the whistle will bring him retaliation. I will not argue that issue, but merely suggest the lines I would pursue.

I tend to be a minimalist in ethics, and depend heavily on a distinction between obligations and acts of supererogation. We have, it seems to me, an obligation to avoid harming anyone, but not an obligation to do good. Doing good is above the call of duty. In between we may, under certain conditions have an obligation to prevent harm.

If whistleblowing can prevent harm, then it is required under certain conditions.

Simon, Powers and Gunnemann set forth four conditions:[4] need, proximity, capability, and last resort. Applying these, we get the following:

1. There must be a clear harm to society that can be avoided by whistleblowing. We don't blow the whistle over everything.
2. It is the "proximity" to the whistleblower that puts him in the position to report his company in the first place.
3. "Capability" means that he needs to have some chance of success. No one has an obligation to jeopardize himself to perform futile gestures. The whistleblower needs to have access to the press, be believable, etc.
4. "Last resort" means just that. If there are others more capable of reporting and more proximate, and if they will report, then one does not have the responsibility.

My position could be challenged in the case of organizations who are employers in non-profit areas, such as the government, educational institutions, etc. In this case my commercialization argument is irrelevant. However, I would maintain that any activity which merits the blowing of the whistle in the case of non-profit and service organizations is probably counter to the purpose of the institution in the first place. Thus, if there were loyalty required, in that case, whoever justifiably blew the whistle would be blowing it on a colleague who perverted the end or purpose of the organization. The loyalty to the group would remain intact.

NOTES

1. Norman Bowie, *Business Ethics* (Englewood Cliffs, N.J.: Prentice Hall, 1982), 140. For Bowie, this is just a preliminary definition. His fuller definition reads, "A whistleblower is an employee or officer of any institution, profit or non-profit, private or public, who believes either that he/she has been ordered to perform some act or he/she has obtained knowledge that the institution is engaged in activities which a) are believed to cause unnecessary harm to third parties, b) are in violation of human rights or c) run counter to the defined purpose of the institution and who inform the public of this fact." Bowie then lists six conditions under which the act is justified (pp. 142–43).
2. Sissela Bok, "Whistleblowing and Professional Responsibilities," *New York University Education Quarterly*, Vol. II, 4 (1980), p. 3.
3. John Ladd, "Loyalty," *The Encyclopedia of Philosophy*, Vol. 5, p. 97.
4. John G. Simon, Charles W. Powers, and Jon P. Gunnemann, *The Ethical Investor: Universities and Corporate Responsibility* (New Haven: Yale University Press, 1972).

Lying and the Law

KENNETH KIPNIS

In the criminal law, ethical problems can begin with the decision to represent. For every accused rapist, murderer, kidnapper, and extortionist; for every felon who is apprehended and brought to trial, there is an attorney endeavoring to clear the client of the charge. No matter how diabolically corrupt the defendant, no matter how fiendishly loathsome the offense, the attorney's professional responsibility will likely be to try to soften the judgement and mitigate the sentence as much as possible. It is possible broadly to distinguish between two different types of moral reservation about rendering assistance to the guilty (or, in civil cases, to those whose cause is not just). In the first place, the concern may be that, in discharging professional responsibilities, there is a risk that the attorney's moral character may be "tainted" by his or her systematic association with wrongdoers. The second reservation is that, in defending and assisting wrongdoers, the attorney is, ethically, something like an "accessory after the fact"; an accomplice, so to speak, in the wrongdoing itself.

For most of us most of the time, the interests of others ought to and do play a role in our deliberations about what we should do. But once an attorney has agreed to represent a client, there may be an overriding professional obligation to set aside concern for others and champion the interests of that one person. Being an attorney makes a big moral difference. Thus, for most of us, it may make a decisive difference if it is pointed out to us that what we propose to do will mean, say, that a rapist will once again endanger others. But the rapist's attorney, within the framework of her role, is not supposed to take that consequence into account. The professional's concern must be for the client and not for the client's future victims. The interests of others don't directly figure into the equation. In a sense, this is the essential posture of the advocate.

The False Plea

Our concern now is not with the slow process by which character is corrupted, but rather with the immediate conditions for moral complicity in wrongdoing. Some might compare the attorney to the driver of the getaway car at a bank robbery. In removing the robbers from the scene of their crime, the driver does what he can to see to it that the criminals do not pay for their wrongdoing. How, one might wonder, is the attorney's "professional responsibility" any different? Though the suspects have been apprehended, the lawyer seems equally to assist wrongdoers in evading the just consequences of their actions. While the lawyer and the driver may be different in the eyes of the law, are they ethically distinguishable?

Let us look at questions of complicity as they might emerge in the course of a criminal case. Rodney Soames, the potential client, tells his attorney that he has committed the rape with which he has been charged. Following the crime, the victim, a Miss Margaret Gregor, called the police and gave them a rough description of her assailant. Among other things, he was said to be wearing a red and white striped sweater. Within forty-five minutes of the attack, Soames, wearing such a sweater, was spotted in the neighborhood and taken into custody. The following day Miss Gregor, a high-strung, emotionally distraught young woman, picked him out of a lineup. Except for saying that he was on his way to a friend's house and that he wanted to talk to a lawyer, Soames has told the police nothing. He is twenty-five, single, and steadily employed as a stock clerk.

Clearly one question that may arise is whether the attorney can properly take this client's case, undertaking to represent him as his advocate in the anticipated criminal proceedings. It is true that the attorney, if she accepts the case, will be "helping a rapist." But it is important here to distinguish between two senses in which one can help a wrongdoer. If what one does is to help a wrongdoer commit a wrongdoing, then one is clearly complicitous. But there are lots of ways in which one can "help a wrongdoer" that do not involve complicity in wrongdoing. If a convicted axe-murderer asks me for the time of day, I do not come to share in any guilt if I show him my watch. The same axe-murderer has a right to send a postcard and, accordingly, to have the assistance of officers of the postal service. Not only is it permissible for an officer of the postal service to give effect to the criminal's decision to mail the card; it would be manifestly improper for the official to refuse to do so. What needs to be shown is not that the attorney assists a rapist, but rather that she assists the rapist in doing something that is wrong. What is it, exactly, that the attorney will be doing for the rapist as the proceedings get under way? Only as we assess what is involved in legal advocacy on behalf of the guilty can we address the question of whether the attorney has overstepped the bounds of the ethical.

As the proceedings commence, the attorney's responsibility will be to see to it that her client, even if he is guilty, gets that to which the law entitles him. The Constitution guarantees to criminal defendants, regardless of their culpability, such important protections as the right to counsel, the right to due process, the right to present evidence on their own behalf, the right to cross-examine witnesses, the right to a public trial by jury, the right to appeal to the state for that which is guaranteed as a matter of law. In complex legal systems such as ours, this respect for the dignity of the defendant cannot be secured without skilled legal assistance. There are rules that the community sets for itself before it can properly punish one of its members, rules that secure for all of us a right to a fair hearing before the verdict is spoken. The defense attorney's job is, in the first place, to see to it that the community honors its own rules and, in the second place, to see to it that the court gets a chance to hear what can be said on the defendant's behalf.

It should be remembered that, in criminal proceedings, lawyers are virtually never in a position to do anything directly for their clients. Rather they request that certain things be done, they advance arguments, they petition. The ultimate disposition is always in the hands of another: the judge, the prosecutor, the jury, the appeals court, the warden, the governor. This is not to say that lawyers bear no responsibility for what these others do. Some responsibility is there. But it does serve to remind us that the petitions of legal representatives are but a part of a much larger decision-making apparatus involving judges, juries, prosecutorial adversaries, and a huge and complex body of law. The defense attorney's job is to see to it that that machine does not dishonor the community's own standards of fairness.

At the moment the chief problem is the arraignment. The client will appear before the judge to enter a plea of "guilty" or "not guilty." (No one is "innocent" in the American legal system.) Procedurally, the entry of the plea is the first formal step a defendant takes in the criminal process. If he pleads "guilty" to the facts, trial is essentially waived and all that remains is the sentencing. On the other hand, if he pleads "not guilty," then, unless the plea is later changed, the state will be "put to its proof" in the forum of a criminal trial. The prosecutor may be obliged to prove beyond a reasonable doubt that the defendant committed the crime for which he is charged. But now, since neither has looked at the state's evidence, it is not clear to the client or the attorney whether the prosecutor can meet the burden of proof. A crossroads has been reached and the attorney must make her first ethical decision: Should she assist the client in entering a plea of "not guilty"?

Perhaps the first answer that comes to mind begins with the observation that, since in this case to plead "not guilty" is to lie, and since it is wrong to lie, the defendant is prohibited from entering a plea of "not guilty." The rapist ought to plead "guilty" to the charge; after all, he committed the crime. Because it is wrong to lie—wrong knowingly to deny what is true—he should "'fess up" and tell the truth. Accordingly, if what the lawyer and the client jointly undertake to do is to lie, it would seem that they are partners in wrongdoing at the very outset of the criminal process.

But is the rapist ethically culpable for a lie told in entering his plea of "not guilty"? Some would protest that a plea of guilty is not really an assertion at all. Rather it is more like what the starter does at a footrace in calling "Ready, set, go!" What the starter says, it can be argued, is not something that can be true or false. Rather, it is a signal that certain things that it would be pointless or improper to do prior to the signal—running toward the finish line, for example—have now become appropriate. In a similar way the doctor's pronunciation of death is a signal that that which used to be the body of a person can now be treated as a corpse. Likewise a plea of "not guilty" signals that the charges will be contested and that a date for a formal trial must be set. The plea is therefore a move in a game, a mere legal formality, carrying none of the weight of a dishonest protestation of innocence.

But this rejoinder won't do. While it is true that the plea signals the applicability of certain procedures, it is equally true that the procedures have their applicability specifically because the defendant has denied committing the crime. The trial can occur precisely because there is disagreement (contradictory assertions) on the issue of whether or not the defendant committed the crime. As a society, we are committed to the principle that only the guilty should be punished. The defendant's guilt is the very reason for punishment. Since there are only two ways in which guilt can be adjudicated—either a guilty plea is accepted, usually before trial, or there is a verdict of "guilty" at trial—the terms "guilty" and "not guilty" do carry weight as assertions. To enter a plea of "not guilty" is to declare publicly "I didn't do it." If the declaration is false, we must regard the defendant as having lied. That a plea also serves as a key move in the criminal process does not entail that it cannot count as an assertion.

Some might protest that the plea cannot be counted as a culpable lie because it is not entered under oath. But while it is true that perjury, to be a crime, requires that the false assertion be one which is made under oath, it is not the case that non-perjurious dishonesty is innocent. The perjuror, it seems, lies twice: once in promising to tell the truth and a second time in the lie itself. The solemnity of the oath may also contribute to the culpability of the offense. But while we may have more reason to condemn the perjuror (who lies twice), we surely have some reason to be critical of those who lie, but less often.

Perhaps it can be argued that the plea of "not guilty" should not be condemned because, while the assertion is false (and known by the asserter to be false), it is not likely to produce false beliefs among those who hear it. An actor in a play may deliver the line "It is raining outside," but no one in the audience forms beliefs about the weather on that basis. While what he says may be false and, indeed, known to be false, the actor avoids culpability simply because no members of the audience can be expected to form false beliefs on the basis of what he says. Likewise, with the false plea of "not guilty," it may be equally unlikely that minds will be changed. The prosecutor, one supposes, has assembled evidence in support of the charge and has formed a responsible judgment that the defendant did indeed commit rape. When the defendant says "not guilty," it is not as if the prosecutor will sheepishly apologize for his mistake and drop charges. What we have when a plea of "not guilty" is entered is not so much a reason to form a judgment as a reason to withhold judgment until all the evidence has been weighed. Perhaps the false plea of "not guilty" is excusable just as the actor's false assertion is.

Still, it may be that the reason few take such protestations of innocence seriously is that we have come to expect defendants to enter pleas of "not guilty" in spite of guilt. Since we "know" that guilty defendants will often lie about their involvement in crime—to avoid punishment if for no other reason—they will not be credited when they declare their innocence. We do not exculpate known or suspected liars on the grounds that they cannot get away with their deception. If the reason why we don't believe defendants' assertions that they are not guilty is that we almost always have reason to believe they are lying, then the fact that we are not misled by their lies is not a reason for excusing the lies. It would thus appear that, even though no one is misled, a lie is told; and, insofar as lying is wrong, the defendant commits just such a wrong in his lie whether or not he succeeds in misleading others.

But is it clear that lying is always wrong? Cases readily come to mind in which, if we are not certain that a lie is justifiable, we are at least less than certain that it is wrong. Other important values can sometimes compete with honesty. An aunt asks us what we think of her hat. Must we speak our minds freely regardless of the effect on her sensibilities? Isn't it permissible, under the circumstances, to pretend? Absolutist positions on this issue are not uniformly persuasive. The standard philosophers' example involves a murderer who asks you if his erstwhile victim is at home. You saw your neighbor enter his house only moments earlier. It would appear that you should have both a right not to contribute to the enterprise of the killer and another right not to be threatened for refusing assistance. If, under the circumstances, the only way to secure these two rights is to lie, then perhaps the lie can be excused. Perhaps you can ethically lie to the murderer without incurring moral blame.

The correlative issue that emerges in the case of the criminal defendant's plea involves the obligation to assist officials in bringing oneself to justice. While the rapist cannot be excused from his crime, is he culpable as well for not cooperating with the officers of the criminal justice system in their effort to deprive him of his liberty? I think this is a difficult question. In part, the Fifth Amendment restriction on being compelled to testify against oneself is evidence of some sensitivity to the complexity of the moral issues here. At a minimum, if the defendant has other obligations that will be compromised by prolonged imprisonments—a condition that will likely be satisfied if he has any positive obligations at all—those obligations must be placed in the balance before we can judge whether the accused is culpable for not publicly acknowledging his guilt. If we suspect that the punishment meted out for the crime will be excessive or that the act, though criminal, was not a wrongdoing, then these considerations should also give us pause before we condemn anyone for hesitating before submitting to punishment. Moreover, loss of liberty is such a serious consequence that it may be necessary generally to excuse those who are not eager to embrace it. The point is that it can be a difficult moral question whether or not lying is permissible to avoid punishment. While we may revere the virtuous George Washington for confessing that he cut down the cherry tree, there may not always be an overriding duty to declare publicly one's wrongdoings when asked to do so. It may not be reasonable to expect everyone to measure up to George Washington's standard, especially when the punishment meted out is so much greater than the one he faced. Because of the consequences he faces if he confesses, it does not seem certain that the rapist is morally prohibited from falsely denying guilt. And if we cannot say confidently that, all things considered, the rapist is morally obligated to confess his crime, then we cannot say confidently that the lawyer is unethical in assisting the rapist in entering a plea of "not guilty." Of course the lawyer does not herself lie in entering the plea on her client's behalf: "Your Honor, my client enters a plea of 'not guilty.' " It is worth observing that some legal systems—the system in the Federal Republic of Germany, for example—function without allowing for a "guilty" plea. There, the defense attorney's job is always to present the defense.

Concerting a False Defense

Let us suppose then that Rodney Soames will now stand trial for the crime of rape. The prosecution's chief witness is the victim, who claims to have gotten a good look at her assailant. She has told the police that the rapist wore a red and white striped sweater. Your client was picked up wearing such a sweater and was still wearing it when the victim identified him in the lineup. Such sweaters are currently popular attire; hundreds have been sold in the city. The young woman's identification may have been influenced by the fact that the distinctive sweater was not worn by any of the others in the lineup. Your client has shared with you the details of the rape and has told you that he was convicted on an assault charge eighteen months earlier in another state. The prosecution's case seems weak. There is the matter of the sweater, and, because of darkness in the woman's apartment where the rape took place and problems with the young woman's eyesight, the victim may not be a credible witness. There are no other witnesses.

In discussions with your client, you tell him that because the punishment for rape has recently been set quite high, juries have been reluctant to convict. However, they do seem to take a dim view of defendants who are unwilling to take the stand to give their version of what happened. Your client decides to try to lie his way to an acquittal, taking the stand and claiming that he has been incorrectly identified as the rapist; he was just innocently walking from his home to a friend's house when he was arrested by the police. Thinking that he stands a good chance of being believed by the jury, he wants to take the stand and lie under oath, thus committing the crime of perjury. Because of an air of innocence and believability about him, it seems to you that he is quite likely to get away with it. (Do you tell him this?) Though you have neither suggested nor encouraged perjury, he has come to his decision on the basis of the facts, opinions, judgments, and observations that his lawyer shared with him. He has been apprised of the punishment for perjury but elects to take his chances. How ought the defense attorney to deal with a client who intends to commit perjury?

If one looks back on what has happened, it may seem that the problem is rooted in the attorney's knowing too much. It is a widespread view that a criminal lawyer can better serve the client if he or she *doesn't* know what happened. Problems of complicity can be avoided if attorneys artfully arrange their relationship with the client to "preserve deniability" of knowledge concerning the offense. The classic statement of this approach is in Robert Traver's novel *Anatomy of a Murder*.[1] The lawyer is interviewing a client who is accused of first-degree murder.

> *I paused and lit a cigar. I took my time. I had reached a point where a few wrong answers to a few right questions would leave me with a client—if I took his case—whose cause was legally defenseless. Either I stopped now and begged off and let some other lawyer worry over it or I asked him the few fatal questions and let him hang himself. Or else, like any smart lawyer, I went into the Lecture. I studied my man. . . . He apparently did not realize how close I had him to admitting that he was guilty of first degree murder. . . . The man was a sitting duck. . . .*
>   *And what is the Lecture?*
>   *The Lecture is an ancient device that lawyers use to coach their clients so that the client won't quite know he has been coached, and his*

*lawyer can still preserve the face-saving illusion that he hasn't done
any coaching. For coaching clients, like robbing them, is not only
frowned upon, it is downright unethical and bad, very bad. Hence the
Lecture, an artful device as old as the law itself, and one used constantly by some of the nicest and most ethical lawyers in the land.*

The lawyer in the novel informs his client that if the facts are as
he has stated them, there is no legal defense and he will probably be
electrocuted. But, he goes on, if the client acted in a blind rage, there
is a possibility of saving his life. He suggests that his client think it
over. Not surprisingly, the client soon "recollects" the rage.

*"Who, me? I didn't tell him what to say." the lawyer can later comfort
himself. "I merely explained the law, see," It is a good practice to scowl
and shrug here and add virtuously: "That's my duty, isn't it?"*

But the cultivation and protection of the lawyer's ignorance are
not consistent with the obligation of a counselor to get the facts. In its
Standards Relating to the Defense Function, the American Bar Association condemns "the tactic, occasionally advocated by unscrupulous
lawyers . . . of advising the client at the outset not to admit anything
to the lawyer which might handicap the lawyer's freedom in calling witnesses or in otherwise making a defense." It is not just a question of
what the attorney knows but, equally important, what the attorney
should know. If, as was argued in the last chapter, counseling requires
that attorneys try to find out what happened, they fail in their obligations as counselors if, preserving deniability, they ask the client not to
tell them anything. Excessive concern for clean hands may therefore do
more damage to professional integrity than excessive concern for the
client. This is because lay clients cannot be expected to make judgments
about which facts will help them and which ones will not.

In any event, Rodney Soames has already told his lawyer that he
did it. What is the attorney's obligation now?

One option is to abandon the client. To put your client on the
stand and build on his perjured testimony is to carry zealous advocacy
too far. How would abandonment work? In criminal procedures, the
bond between the attorney and the client can often be similar to that
of a marriage: The court's permission must be obtained before the
lawyer-client relationship can be dissolved. And, as with divorce, there
may have to be good grounds for severing the tie. The attorney can go
to the judge and ask to be removed from the case. Since getting a new
attorney will take the court's time—justice delayed is justice denied—
the judge will want to know the reasons. It is here that the attorney
may face an insuperable difficulty. For she cannot explain her request

by saying "My client wants to perjure himself on the witness stand" without letting the judge know that Rodney Soames is guilty. Apart from the violation of confidentiality, Soames cannot be expected to receive a fair trial in a courtroom dominated by a judge who has been told by the defendant's own attorney that the defendant intends to lie under oath about what he did.[2]

Maybe she can hint at the reason without disclosure. "Your Honor, I have an ethical problem with my client." But in practice this ends up being just as bad, for the words themselves are a clanging bell to experienced judges who will then be alert to what is going on. They will know what the lawyer is saying just because they know what the lawyer is unable to say.

In fact, even if we suppose that the attorney is able to withdraw from representation without compromising the judicial proceedings, that won't solve the problem either. For, knowing now how the game is played, the "innocent" and believable Mr. Soames will not make the mistake of telling the next attorney the truth.[3] The second attorney will rise in court to build on perjured testimony. However, he will not realize that that is what he is doing. And even if we were to require attorneys with "ethical problems" to resign and disclose the defendant's perjurious intentions to all subsequent lawyers, there would still be an ineliminable dilemma. For either some (unethical?) attorney will go forward to defend the perjurious Soames, thus perpetrating a fraud upon the court, or, if the bar is sufficiently "upright," no attorney will. If the former, we are back where we started; with his lawyer's assistance, Soames will get to present his perjurious case. But now suppose no lawyer will represent him. Let us suppose that all the lawyers who would have represented him have been disbarred. In that case, Soames cannot receive a fair trial, because the proceedings will not be fair in the absence of such legal representation. Because legal representation is required for a trial to be fair, and because no lawyer will represent Soames, the state cannot offer Soames a fair trial. Moreover, since, by its own rules, the state cannot properly punish people unless it offers them a fair trial; and since, because of a legal profession that refuses to defend Soames, the state cannot offer Soames the fair trial to which he is entitled, *the state cannot properly punish this rapist.* The ethics of the legal profession should not make it impossible for the state to punish the guilty. This is an equally unacceptable result.

Building on Perjured Testimony

So what is it like to build on perjured testimony? In the first place, the attorney should work to discourage her client from committing the crime of perjury. She should tell him of the possibility that he will be found out and, if so, what the punishment is likely to be. She should advise him not to proceed with his plan. If she is unsuccessful in dissuading him, she may not then assist in the fabrication of his story. She may not suggest how the lie should be told. It would seem, however, to be acceptable to warn the client that some particular aspect of his story may permit the prosecutor to undermine his credibility upon cross-examination. But the lie itself must be the client's handiwork. At this stage, all the attorney owes to the client is the advice not to commit perjury and the assessment of what may happen if the defendant goes ahead anyway and lies under oath.[4]

The attorney will have to put Soames on the witness stand and let him speak. Obviously the questions that she asks her client must not signal in any way that the testimony is perjured. She may not sit back, for example, and ask him merely to tell his story if that is not how she would treat a truthful witness. Nor should she question her client in a way that might expose the perjury: That is the responsibility of the prosecutor. As Monroe Freedman has put it:

> . . . the criminal defense attorney, however unwillingly in terms of personal morality, has a professional responsibility as an advocate in an adversary system to examine the perjurious client in the ordinary way and to argue to the jury, as evidence in the case, the testimony presented by the defendant.[5]

This posture has attracted critics. For example, Sissela Bok takes issue with Freedman in her book *Lying*:

> If, that is, a lawyer has a client who lies to the court and thus commits perjury, Professor Freedman holds that his defense lawyer has the professional responsibility to ask questions which do not contest this testimony and even to use the false testimony in making the best case for the client to the court officers and the jury. That this can involve lying is beyond doubt. Nor is there serious doubt that such instances are not rare in actual practice. Yet perjury has traditionally been more abhorred than other lying. How is it, then, that it has come to be thus defended, albeit by a minority of commentators? Defended, moreover, not just as a regrettable practice at times excusable, but actually as a professional responsibility.[6]

In the first place, it should be plain that while perjury—lying under oath—would be committed by the client, it cannot be committed by the client's attorney, since, unless counsel takes the stand as a witness, what the lawyer says to the court is not spoken under oath. So Freedman cannot be said to advocate that lawyers commit perjury. Still,

Bok suggests that, in endeavoring to make the best case for a perjurious client, a lawyer guided by commentators such as Freedman will
lie in adverting to the testimony of the lying witness. Lies told to the
court seem to be culpable, and Bok takes attorneys like Freedman to
task for advocating such mendacity on the part of defense attorneys.
But is mendacity a necessary part of responsible advocacy in cases such
as this one?

In the Code of Professional Responsibility (Ethical Consideration
7-24) is contained the following admonition:

> In order to bring about just and informed decisions, evidentiary and
> procedural rules have been established by tribunals to permit the in-
> clusion of relevant evidence and argument and the exclusion of all
> other considerations. The expression by a lawyer of his personal opin-
> ion as to the justness of a cause, as to the credibility of a witness, as
> to the culpability of a civil litigant, or as to the guilt or innocence of
> an accused is not a proper subject for argument to the trier of fact.
> It is improper as to factual matters because admissible evidence
> possessed by a lawyer should be presented only as sworn testimony.
> It is improper as to all other matters because, were the rule otherwise,
> the silence of a lawyer on a given occasion could be construed unfa-
> vorably to his client. However, a lawyer may argue, on his analysis of
> the evidence, for any position or conclusion with respect to any of the
> foregoing matters.

In the related Disciplinary Rules lawyers are warned that, in rep-
resenting a client, a lawyer shall not "knowingly make a false statement of law or fact" (DR 7-102 [A] [5]); and, even more strongly, in
appearing in a professional capacity before a tribunal, neither shall an
attorney assert "personal knowledge of the facts in issue, except when
testifying as a witness" (DR 7-106 [C] [3]). What this means is that if
there is some matter of fact that is to be determined by the court,
lawyers involved in the case are prohibited from expressing as their
own beliefs or as things known to them any personal statements concerning that matter. Not only are lawyers prohibited from lying on behalf of their clients. They have been traditionally *prohibited as well
from asserting what they know to be true*.

In these passages the code is making an important and easily
overlooked distinction between, on the one hand, advancing, on the
basis of evidence presented to the court, an argument for conclusions
that the attorney knows to be false, and, on the other hand, asserting
the truth of those conclusions. If one studies the "assertions" of skilled
attorneys, one will readily note the prevalence of such expressions as "I
ask the jury to consider that . . ." or "I submit that   " or "The con
clusion that must be drawn from this evidence is that . . ." and so on.

In criminal defense work, the task of the advocate is not, as Bok seems to suppose, convincingly to assert that the defendant is innocent: It is rather to present arguments for acquittal on the basis of the evidence presented to the court. Thus, in her summation, the argument presented by Soames's defense attorney could go as follows:

"As the jury in this case it is your solemn responsibility to reach a verdict. You have heard Rodney Soames tell his story, a story that the prosecution has been unable to refute. You must now ask yourselves whether you believe the defendant's clear explanation of what took place on that fateful afternoon, or whether you will accept the judgment of an emotionally distraught rape victim, rightly angered by the sexual assault committed upon her person, enraged at the man in the red and white striped sweater whom she dimly saw, without her glasses, in the shadows of her darkened apartment. You must ask yourselves whether, when she identified Rodney Soames in the police lineup only hours after her assault, she saw her assailant or saw merely an innocent bystander whose only mistake was to go to his job on that day dressed in the wrong clothes."

"Rape is a terrible offense, and the punishment for it is properly very severe. For that reason great care must be taken before tarring this young man with that broad brush. While it is true that the man who raped Margaret Gregor deserves to be punished, I submit that it is equally true that the prosecution has not proved that Rodney Soames is that man. I ask that, in issuing your verdict in this case, you tell the prosecutor and the police that, before they put anyone through the ordeal of a criminal trial, they make sure they can support their accusations with hard evidence. I ask that you find the defendant not guilty."

A careful reading of the lawyer's summation to the jury will not disclose any lies told by her to the court. Still, what Soames's lawyer says to the jury is, in a sense, wholly misleading. Soames has raped Margaret Gregor and his defense attorney knows it. She is arguing that the jury should form the judgment that Soames is not guilty when in fact she knows he is. In *ordinary discourse* when someone presents powerful arguments for the conclusion P (where P is some proposition), listeners are typically entitled to assume that the speaker believes P. At the least, listeners are entitled to feel wronged if they find out later on that the speaker knew all along that P was false. They are entitled to feel wronged even if line-by-line scrutiny of what was said fails to disclose a single materially false statement. It is not that lawyers lie; it is that, in this special way, they are dishonest.

But the problem with this criticism of defense attorneys is that it fails to take into account the degree to which language in a criminal trial differs from ordinary discourse. The jury in a criminal trial is not supposed to be taking what the defense attorney says as an assertion that the client is innocent. As has been noted earlier, what the attorney believes is irrelevant. Rather, the issue is whether or not the evidence adduced at trial supports, beyond a reasonable doubt, the proposition that the defendant committed the crime with which he has been charged. If juries and others are misled, it is not because defense attorneys are dishonest. It is rather because the required conventions of criminal defense work are insufficiently understood. Bok suggests (pp. 171–73) that judges should warn juries about this. Perhaps it is advisable that judges generally instruct those in the court that, if defense attorneys are unable to dissuade clients from lying under oath, they may be required knowingly to build upon perjured testimony. Judges should make it clear that in undertaking to represent their clients, defense attorneys are not guaranteeing the truthfulness of what defendants say in court. And neither are defense attorneys supposed to let their personal beliefs about the client's guilt or innocence affect the manner in which they discharge their obligations of advocacy. Instructions such as these would seem ample to blunt criticisms of dishonesty.

Lying to the Judge

Having heard the arguments and the evidence, the jury finds Soames guilty of the crime of rape. In the interests of expediting sentencing, the judge asks Soames's attorney whether her client has any prior convictions. If Soames has no prior convictions, then it would seem appropriate for defense counsel to disclose this. To delay the proceedings might be to antagonize the judge. You don't want the judge to be deciding your client's punishment when he is angry at the defense. But, as we noted earlier, Rodney Soames was convicted eighteen months earlier on an assault charge in another state. And more to the point, the judge's question is completely improper. Other officers of the judicial system should have provided that information to the court in the form of a presentence report. The judge should not be relying on the defense attorney for information that may damage her client's cause.

At this stage four responses are possible. The attorney can answer the question truthfully: "Yes, your honor, my client was convicted on an assault charge." But here there is a betrayal of the client. Damaging confidential information is revealed to the court. The lawyer is no longer working for the client but for the court against the client. In the light of the arguments reviewed earlier on confidentiality in the criminal process, this answer seems unacceptable.

The attorney can refuse to answer the question. "Your honor, that is an improper question." Unfortunately, this answer may be equivalent to the first. If attorneys generally answer such improper questions when truthful answers will further the interests of their clients and refuse to answer them when the truth will damage those interests, then the judge will know (or at least have good reason to believe) that the client has a criminal record. The betrayal occurs as surely as if the attorney had spoken up directly.

A third response is to finesse the question. When asked, "Does your client have any prior convictions?" the quick-witted defense attorney can answer, "None that I can say, your honor." While judges may conceivably be misled once or twice by this dodge (and even this is unlikely), almost certainly the only one fooled will be the client. Experienced judges will be familiar with the gambit. The criticisms of the first two responses apply equally to this third.

The final response is to lie. "Your honor, my client has no criminal record." The justification for such deception is premised on the propositions that (1) the judge has no right that defense counsel provide him with this information; that (2) the information the judge is requesting is information that the attorney is obligated not to disclose; and that (3) all nondeceptive responses will have the practical effect under the circumstances of disclosing to the judge the very information that the judge is not entitled to receive from the attorney and that the attorney is obligated not to disclose. Under the circumstances it would appear to be obligatory for the attorney to lie to the judge.

But it may be unwise to hasten to this conclusion. For lying can be justified only if attorneys in general freely answer improper questions *when truthful answers are in the interests of their clients.* While it may not be open to Soames's defense attorney to see to it that all lawyers abide by a nondisclosure rule here, whether it serves their clients' interests or not, it is open to the legal profession to make such a determination. Suppose that the standard answer to such questions were something like this: "Notwithstanding whether or not my client has a criminal record, as a member of the legal profession I will face disciplinary proceedings if I proffer an answer to your inquiry. I respectfully ask that you withdraw the question without prejudice to my client." If attorneys routinely respond in this way, the case for deception cannot be made. The rule here is that if it is improper for attorneys truthfully to answer questions when the truth will hurt a client, it is equally improper to answer when the truth will help. This principle sets an important limit to zealous advocacy.

NOTES

1. Robert Traver, *Anatomy of a Murder* (New York: St. Martin's Press, Inc., 1958), 32–35.
2. See *Lowery v. Cardwell* 575 F.2d 727 (1978).
3. The second attorney would know if, as a condition of representation, he or she secures from Soames a waiver of confidentiality as regards communications from the first attorney. The first attorney could thus be required *by Soames,* her former client, to disclose all she knew to subsequent attorneys working on the same matter. The first attorney could also have a professional obligation to prevent former clients from defrauding and/or otherwise implicating in wrongdoing other subsequent attorneys who would not be aware of client deception. Such disclosure to a fellow officer of the court, solely to prevent a colleague from being unknowingly implicated in wrongdoing, is not a breach of professional ethics. Of course the disclosure should not go beyond the attorney(s).
4. Though lawyers are legally prohibited from "suborning perjury," and though the Code of Professional Responsibility provides that lawyers shall not participate in the creation of false evidence, there is a thin line separating the giving of legal advice and complicity in the fabrication of the lie. There is a question, for example, about whether the attorney can recount the stories of defendants who have succeeded in persuading the court. I once spent a good part of a day listening to uncontested divorce proceedings, each lasting less than ten minutes. In every case—there were dozens—the complaining wife reported being struck on repeated occasions by her husband and, afterwards *in each instance,* rushing to show her bruises to a friend. The friend was then put on the stand to testify that she or he indeed did observe the bruises on each of the aforementioned occasions. The overall effect was a bit like an audition, with different actors attempting common lines. It was the standard way unhappy couples got divorced in that particular jurisdiction.

    Would it have been unethical for an attorney to discuss this script with a client couple who were no longer able to endure the legal bonds of matrimony? It is important that permissive principles not be extended too broadly. For the main argument here for coaching witnesses would be drawn from personal morality rather that professional ethics and would appear to be predicated on the existence of an oppressive legal system. As Chapter 2 should have made clear, the present work assumes that the system is defensible. Professional responsibility would militate in favor of collective action on the part of the legal profession to change the law. Indeed, in many jurisdictions, "no-fault divorce" laws have been passed that obviate the pathetic charades of earlier years.
5. Monroe H. Freedman, *Lawyers' Ethics in an Adversary System* (Indianapolis: The Bobbs-Merrill Company, Inc., 1975), 40–41. In both this chapter and the

preceding one, I am deeply indebted to the work of Freedman, whose arguments are echoed in much of my discussion.

6. Sissela Bok, *Lying: Moral Choice in Private and Public Life* (New York: Pantheon Books, 1978), 167–68.

On Duties of Virtue toward Other Men Arising from the Respect Due Them

IMMANUEL KANT

§37.

Moderation in one's demands generally, that is, willing restriction of one man's self-love in view of the self-love of others, is called *modesty*. Lack of *such moderation* (lack of modesty) as regards one's worthiness to be *loved* by others is called *egotism*. But lack of modesty in one's claims to be **respected** by others is *self-conceit*. The *respect* that I have for others or that another can require from me is therefore recognition of a *dignity* in other men, that is, of a worth that has no price, no equivalent for which the object evaluated could be exchanged. Judging something to be worthless is contempt.

§38.

Every man has a legitimate claim to respect from his fellow men and is *in turn* bound to respect every other.

　　Humanity itself is a dignity; for a man cannot be used merely as a means by any man (either by others or even by himself) but must always be used at the same time as an end. It is just in this that his dignity (personality) consists, by which he raises himself above all other beings in the world that are not men and yet can be used, and so over all *things*. But just as he cannot give himself away for any price (this would conflict with his duty of self-esteem), so neither can he act contrary to the equally necessary self-esteem of others, as men, that is, he is under obligation to acknowledge, in a practical way, the dignity of humanity in every other man. Hence there rests on him a duty regarding the respect that must be shown to every other man.

§39.

To be *contemptuous* of others, that is, to deny them the respect owed to men in general, is in every case contrary to duty; for they are men. At times one cannot, it is true, help inwardly *looking down* on some in comparison with others; but the outward manifestation of this is, nevertheless, an offense. What is *dangerous* is no object of contempt, and so neither is a vicious man; and if my superiority to his attacks justifies my saying that I despise him, this means only that I am in no danger from him, even though I have prepared no defense against him, because he shows himself in all his depravity. Nonetheless I cannot deny all respect to even a vicious man as a man; I cannot withdraw at least the respect that belongs to him in his quality as a man, even though by his deeds he makes himself unworthy of it. So there can be disgraceful punishments that dishonor humanity itself (such as quartering a man, having him torn by dogs, cutting off his nose and ears). Not only are such punishments more painful than loss of possessions and life to one who loves honor (who claims the respect of others, as everyone must); they also make a spectator blush with shame at belonging to a species that can be treated that way.

Remark

On this is based a duty to respect a man even in the logical use of his reason, a duty not to censure his errors by calling them absurdities, poor judgment and so forth, but rather to suppose that his judgment must yet contain some truth and to seek this out, uncovering, at the same time, the deceptive illusion (the subjective ground that determined his judgment that, by an oversight, he took for objective), and so, by explaining to him the possibility of his having erred, to preserve his respect for his own understanding. For if, by using such expressions, one denies any understanding to a man who opposes one in a certain judgment, how does one want to bring him to understand that he has erred? The same thing applies to the censure of vice, which must never break out into complete contempt and denial of any moral worth to a vicious man; for on this supposition he could never be improved, and this is not consistent with the Idea of a *man*, who as such (as a moral being) can never lose entirely his predisposition to the good.

§40.

Respect for the law, which in its subjective aspect is called moral feeling, is identical with consciousness of one's duty. This is why showing respect for man as a moral being (holding his duty in highest esteem) is also a duty that others have toward him and a right to which he cannot renounce his claim. This claim is called *love of honor*, and its manifestation in external conduct, *respectability*. An offense against respectability is called *scandal*, an example of disregarding respectability that might lead others to follow it. To *give* scandal is quite contrary to duty. But to *take* scandal at what is merely unconventional but otherwise in itself good is a delusion (since one holds what is unusual to be impermissible as well), an error dangerous and destructive to virtue. For a man cannot carry his giving an example of the respect due others so far as to degenerate into blind imitation (in which custom is raised to the dignity of a law), since such a tyranny of popular mores would be contrary to a man's duty to himself.

§41.

Failure to fulfill mere duties of love is *lack of virtue*. But failure to fulfill the duty arising from the *respect* owed to every man as such is a *vice*. For no one is wronged if duties of love are neglected; but a failure in the duty of respect infringes upon a man's lawful claim. The first violation is opposed to duty as its *contrary*. But what not only adds nothing moral but even abolishes the worth of what would otherwise be to the subject's good is *vice*.

For this reason, too, duties to one's fellow men arising from the respect due them are expressed only negatively, that is, this duty of virtue will be expressed *only indirectly* (through the prohibition of its opposite).

On Vices that Violate the Duties of Respect for Other Men

These vices are A) *arrogance*, B) *defamation*, and C) *ridicule*.

A. Arrogance

§42.

Arrogance (... the inclination to be always *on top*) is a kind of *ambition* in which we demand that others think little of themselves in comparison with us. It is, therefore, a vice opposed to the respect that every man can lawfully claim.

It differs from **pride proper**, which is *love of honor*, that is, a concern to yield nothing of one's human dignity in comparison with others (so that the adjective *"noble"* is usually added to "pride" in this sense); for arrogance demands from others a respect it denies them. But *pride* itself becomes a fault and an offense when it, too, is merely a demand upon others to concern themselves with one's importance.

Arrogance is, as it were, a solicitation on the part of one seeking honor for followers, whom he thinks he is entitled to treat with contempt. It is obvious that this is *unjust* and opposed to the respect owed to men as such; that it is *folly*, that is, frivolity in using means to something so related to them as not to be worth being taken as an end; that an arrogant man is even a *conceited ass*,[1] that is, that he shows an offensive lack of understanding in using such means as must bring about, on the part of other men, the exact opposite of his end (for the more an arrogant man shows that he is trying to obtain respect, the more everyone denies it to him). But it might not be so readily noticed that an arrogant man is always *mean* in the depths of his soul. For he would not demand that others think little of themselves in comparison with him unless he knew that, were his fortune suddenly to change, he himself would not find it hard to grovel and to waive any claim to respect from others.

B. Defamation

§43.

By defamation or backbiting I do not mean *slander*, a *false* defamation to be taken before a court; I mean only the immediate inclination, with no particular aim in view, to bring into the open something prejudicial to respect for others. This is contrary to the respect owed to humanity as such; for every scandal given weakens that respect, on which the impulse to the morally good rests, and as far as possible makes people skeptical about it.

The intentional *spreading* of something that detracts from another's honor—even if it is not a matter of public justice, and if what is said is true—diminishes respect for humanity as such, so as finally to cast a shadow of worthlessness over our race itself, making misanthropy (shying away from men) or contempt the prevalent cast of mind, or to dull one's moral feeling by repeatedly exposing one to the sight of such things and accustoming one to it. It is, therefore, a duty of virtue not to take malicious pleasure in exposing the faults of others so that one will be thought as good as, or at least not worse than, other men, but rather to throw the veil of love of man over their faults, not merely by softening our judgments but also by keeping these judgments to ourselves; for examples of respect that we give others can arouse their striving to deserve it. For this reason, a mania for spying on the morals of others is by itself already an offensive inquisitiveness on the part of anthropology, which everyone can resist with right as a violation of the respect due him.

C. Ridicule

§44.

Wanton faultfinding and *mockery*, the propensity to expose others to laughter, to make their faults the immediate object of one's amusement, is a kind of malice. It is altogether different from *banter*, from the familiarity among friends in which one makes fun of their peculiarities that only seem to be faults but are really marks of their pluck in sometimes departing from the rule of fashion (for this is not derision). But holding up to ridicule a person's real faults, or supposed faults as if they were real, in order to deprive him of the respect he deserves, and the propensity to do this, a mania for *caustic* mockery, has something of fiendish joy in it; and this makes it an even more serious violation of one's duty of respect for other men.

This must be distinguished from a jocular, even if derisive, brushing aside with contempt an insulting attack of an adversary, by which the mocker (or, in general, a malicious but ineffectual adversary) is himself made the laughing stock. This is a legitimate defense of the respect one can require from him. But when the object of his mockery is really no object for wit but one in which reason necessarily takes a moral interest, then no matter how much ridicule the adversary may have uttered and thereby left himself open to laughter, it is more befitting the dignity of the object and respect for humanity either to put up no defense against the attack or to conduct it with dignity and seriousness.

Remark

It will be noticed that under the above heading virtues were not so much commended as rather the vices opposed to them censured.

But this is already implicit in the concept of the respect we are bound to show other men, which is only a *negative* duty. I am not bound to *revere* others (regarded merely as men) that is, to show them *positive* high esteem. The only reverence to which I am bound by nature is reverence for law as such; and to revere the law, but not to revere other men in general or to perform some act of reverence for them, is man's universal and unconditional duty toward others, which each of them can require as the respect originally owed others.

NOTE

1. The distinction between being "foolish" and being "a conceited ass" is, as in *Anthropology from a Pragmatic Point of View*, Ak. VII, 210, that between *Torheit* and *Narrheit*. "A fool is one who sacrifices things of value to ends that have no value, for example, domestic happiness to public glamour. A man whose folly is offensive is called a conceited ass."

Group 1: Readings on Integrity and Respect for Persons

EXERCISES

Dunbar:

1. How do you understand Gordon Fairfax's present attitude about the lynching of Jube Benson? What do you think this attitude is supposed to demonstrate?
2. What values do Gordon's actions throughout this story violate? Show how his actions violate them.
3. Explain several interpretations of the value of integrity as presented in this story. Also explain how the values of respect for persons and responsibility are interpreted by Gordon or other characters in the story.
4. Do you think that acting in the heat of the moment, that is, responding to the death of his beloved, allows Gordon to be held less or more responsible for his actions? For example, are there ever any conditions that you can imagine where you are not bound by your commitment to values?
5. Consider the beginning and the end of the story. What lessons about integrity and respect for persons do you think Dunbar was trying to convey to the listeners in Gordon's study? Do you think Dunbar was successful?

Duska:

1. What kind of loyalty, according to Duska, do we have to our places of employment? In answering this question, explain why this is the only loyalty we have to our places of employment.
2. What, according to Duska, are the appropriate conditions for loyalty and the appropriate parties to whom we should be loyal?
3. Give an example of the kind of argument employers use to engender loyalty in their employees. Do you find this perspective persuasive, that is, would you be tempted to be loyal to an employer using this sort of rhetoric? Why or why not?
4. Present the conditions under which Duska argues that it is allowable for someone to blow the whistle on wrongdoing. Compare this to the sorts of conditions under which it is required for someone to blow the whistle on wrongdoing. What do you see as the primary difference between these two sets of circumstances?
5. Do you see yourself as a whistle blower in any situation, no situation, or in some very special circumstances? Explain your answer in as detailed a manner as possible.

Kipnis:

1. Explain what Kipnis means by the "two senses in which one can help a wrongdoer." Do you think that this is an accurate distinction?
2. Explain the conflicts in interpreting values that arise in the scenario Kipnis titles "The False Plea." Do you think that one of the solutions Kipnis suggests preserves values more than any other? Can you think of a creative solution that would both preserve professional integrity (honesty) and best serve a client's interests?
3. Explain the conflicts in interpreting values that arise in the scenario Kipnis titles "Lying to the Judge." Do you think a lawyer's professional obligations and value commitments should change, contingent upon who he or she is relating to? That is, does the lawyer's obligation to integrity change relative to dealing with the judge or his or her client?
4. Discuss the different ways in which the legal profession could both uphold values and be true to its mission of providing a credible defense for those accused of wrongdoing. Focus your answer by considering the specific scenarios Kipnis presents.
5. Do you think that there are any professions, perhaps like the legal profession, that are, by their very nature, particularly at risk in trying to both preserve values and fulfill their professional obligations?

Kant:

1. What are Kant's conclusions, and how does he argue for them? What values does he employ, and what sort of theory does he use? Do you agree with his conclusions? Why or why not?

2. How do you think Kant's discussion relates to the way in which respect for persons is to be enacted specifically by a professional? Give examples.

3. How are the Negative Rule of Respect and the Positive Rule of Respect relevant to Kant's argument? Explain. In your answer, be sure to address the issue of self-esteem.

4. Discuss how a Kantian understanding of respect for persons would have changed the outcome of the Dunbar story. Be sure to not only consider the lynching, but also the various other ways in which respect for persons was violated and how a Kantian approach could have remedied that violation.

5. Discuss one of Kant's three vices that violate our duties of respect. That is, indicate how arrogance, defamation, or ridicule is present in professional life by giving a concrete example from a specific profession. Likewise, indicate how these vices could be overcome through an appreciation of respect for persons.

9

Justice

For most of us, claims of justice and injustice are familiar. We often hear people complain that life is not fair, whether or not it actually is. Many groups of people, including minorities, gays and lesbians, handicapped people, women, and white men, have insisted that they are not getting a fair shake. Those who have less or who are treated as second-class citizens may seem to be the most concerned about justice, but, in fact, justice is of concern to everyone. We all want to be treated fairly and to get what is rightfully ours.

Sometimes we recognize justice in the activities of professionals we meet in our everyday lives. Suppose your insurance agent sends you a letter informing you that your clean driving record qualifies you for a good driver's discount on your car insurance, even though others who lack clean driving records must pay more. You feel pride, perhaps, but most importantly you believe that justice is served. All is right with the world. You earned the discount that others could have earned but did not, thus you are rightly rewarded for your accomplishment. You judge that your insurance agent acted justly in assigning you a lower rate for your car insurance.

At other times, we recognize injustice in the way a professional acts. Suppose a store clerk waits first on someone behind you in line. How do you feel then? Probably you feel angry. You have been mistreated. Something that rightfully should have been yours first, namely, the clerk's help, was given instead to someone else. You deserved the clerk's attention before this other person, and since you did not get it, the clerk acted unjustly.

Sometimes issues of justice and injustice are this crystal clear to us. We get what we have earned; there is justice. We do not get what we deserve; there is injustice. But in many instances it is not clear how justice ought to be enacted, because it is not clear what we have earned or what we deserve. Is it just that American workers overall received an average pay raise of 3.3 percent in 1997, while the CEOs at 365 of the nation's largest companies received, on average, a 35 percent pay increase?[1] Would it be just if all professional workers received the same pay, or if there were salary caps? Is it fair that in 1997 after California voters passed Proposition 209, which eliminated using race-based preferences for admissions, the University of California–Berkeley Law School admitted only one black student, while in 1996 it admitted seventy-five black students and enrolled twenty?[2] Are admission programs that use race-or sex-based preferences just?

To answer questions like these, we need to consider more carefully what justice is, what it involves, and how to translate it into concrete action. In what follows, we consider all of these issues, namely, definitions, implications, and interpretations of justice. Along the way, we discuss a case in which justice is the central value at stake. We point out difficulties faced in deciding how to enact justice and rules that provide help in enacting it. Finally, we consider several types of conflicts that involve justice. As always, at the end of the chapter, there are review questions and cases for analysis and resolution.

Definitions

To practice justice at work, we need to first understand what justice means. The dictionary offers three definitions of the word, aside from its legal and idiomatic meanings.[3] First, justice is fairness or the quality of being just. Second, justice is equity or the principle of moral rightness. And third, justice is the upholding of what is just, especially fair treatment and due reward in accordance with honor, standards, or law. In summary, all three definitions take "just" to be synonymous with fair and "unjust" to mean the same as unfair.

In one sense, these definitions should not surprise us. When we previously considered the insurance agent and the shop clerk, we used the words "fair" and "reward" in aiming to describe justice and injustice. These definitions tell us that in valuing justice, we are committed to the fair and equitable treatment of persons. Justice entails rewarding persons in accordance with their desert, honor, or some other standard. With delivering the reward comes the possibility of withholding the reward. Since justice is fairness, it includes both rewarding those persons who deserve it, withholding reward from those who deserve it, and punishing those who deserve it. Fairness means rewarding those who deserve to be rewarded and not those who do not deserve to be rewarded. Justice thus entails both rewarding and punishing; both can be fair. Much depends on the situation.

Now, this rewarding and punishing, which is part of carrying out justice, can be accomplished only by those who have power. Bosses can reward and punish, as can governments, parents, and professionals in their treatment of their clients and the public. We must keep in mind that even when those in power are acting justly and rewarding and punishing fairly, questions still may be asked about how in the first place they got the power to enact justice. For instance, were they elected or appointed, were they chosen due to their superior abilities, family name, and so on? We should not automatically assume that because an employer treats her employees fairly that she acquired her position of authority fairly. Questions of fairness can be asked about future decisions (about who should get what) and about past actions (who got what).

In another sense, there may be a way in which the three definitions of justice surprise us. Although many of us equate justice with equality, note that nowhere in the definitions of justice is anything said about equality. Equality means sameness, but justice, which is about equity, means fairness. And fairness is sometimes about inequality and other times about equality. Fairness is treating people as they are owed or as they deserve. Sometimes they are owed equal treatment, and sometimes they are owed unequal treatment. As our first example suggests, to the insurance agent, not all clients deserve the same insurance rates. Not all have proven themselves to be equally careful drivers. Some clients deserve special rewards, in the form of reduced rates, that others do not deserve. This is equitable; it is a fair, but unequal, treatment of persons. In the second example, to the shop clerk, every client should be on a par with every other client. No reason is given for waiting on clients out of turn and, lacking this reason, clients are right to assume that each is equally deserving of the clerk's attention, thus each should be waited on in order and not according to some other standard. The shop clerk is wrong to have waited on clients out of order, he acted unjustly. In this case, the unequal treatment of persons was unfair. There ought to have been a fair, equal treatment of persons. This would have been equitable.

To some, justice may seem to be about social issues and policies, and not about individual persons and professionals making decisions in their lives. It is true that we ask about the justice of social policies like capital punishment, censorship, affirmative action, and the welfare program. Many of the public aspects of our lives are governed by the way in which federal and state laws as well as the courts have interpreted justice. However, justice is not only an issue for social policies; it is pertinent to our individual professional and personal lives. We need not simply accept the social interpretations of justice offered by the laws. We are free to judge these interpretations of justice as being wrong or incomplete, and to argue for reinterpretations of justice. In doing so, we are interpreting justice ourselves. The United States has a long history of civil disobedience wherein some legal interpretations of justice are challenged. Investigative reporters have refused to name their sources, though ordered to do so by grand juries.[4] Nurses have refused to call for resuscitation teams when patients have asked to be let die, even though the nurses may be legally liable.[5] Thus justice is not exclusively or infallibly defined by the laws or the courts. Legal decisions provide interpretations of justice insofar as justice is understood at that time by those making the decisions. Our lives take place in the context of these socially driven and temporally limited interpretations of justice, whether right or wrong, but we are not limited to these interpretations.

Apart from judging these legal interpretations of justice, we also decide how to enact justice in our professional and personal lives in areas where the laws and the courts do not give concrete guidance. Some occupations have specific directives about how to be a just professional. We will examine several of these in the next section. For now it is important to note that many decisions about justice are often made by ordinary people, when the legal interpretations of justice are not relevant or are too vague. Teachers and parents decide what punishment is appropriate for wayward students and children. Friends often decide how much to censor the truth about a bad haircut from an ill-shorn friend. Employers decide how much employees will be paid and who will get raises and how much and who will not get raises. Ordinary persons and especially ordinary professionals inevitably must decide who should get what and/or who deserves what. In making these decisions, they are interpreting the value of justice in much the same way as the laws and courts do, although their decisions may not be subject to the same public scrutiny. All decisions about who deserves what have an effect on the lives of others, thus all should be carefully made, whether or not they have to be publicly justified.

Now that we have seen that justice means fairness, we know that putting justice into practice in our professional lives will involve careful consideration of what persons deserve. Figuring out what is equitable means making decisions about who deserves what. Sometimes these decisions about how to enact justice may make use of legal interpretations of justice, but no *moral* decision about how to act justly can depend solely on a legal interpretation of what is just. Next we look at some ways in which particular professions have recognized and described a professional's commitment to justice.

Common Ways of Expressing Justice

The professional codes of ethics speak directly of justice and fairness. The *Code of Professional Responsibility* of the American Bar Association states that lawyers are guardians of the law, and that law grounded in respect for the dignity of the individual makes justice possible.[6] The *Standards of Practice* of the American Association of Advertising Agencies decries unfair competitive practices such as circulating rumors about competitors.[7] The *Code of Ethics* of the Society of Professional Journalists claims that journalists have a duty to act with fairness and to seek the truth, since informing the public is the forerunner of justice.[8] But in addition to these general claims about a professional's commitment to justice, ethicists and professionals have developed more concrete ways of thinking about the value of justice. Enacting justice can take various forms, depending on what type of action or behavior is to be accomplished fairly. As a consequence, we can distinguish between different ways of expressing justice, even though in all cases we are aiming to give people what they deserve. The three most common forms of justice are retributive, compensatory, and distributive.[9] Let us look at each in turn.

Retributive Justice

Justice understood as retribution concerns fair punishment practices. Sometimes it is on grounds of retribution that state legislators argue for capital punishment. Judges and juries dole out retributive justice in passing sentences on convicted criminals. Teachers also enact retributive justice in setting penalties for late work and in grading exams and papers. Supervisors and human resource personnel are concerned with retributive justice when they decide whether and/or how to punish an employee for lewd or threatening behavior. Justice thus includes the idea that it is fair and necessary to punish people for their wrong or unsatisfactory actions.

Retributive justice is guided by laws and other formalized social interpretations of justice. Judges and juries work within the confines of the law in assigning appropriate punishments. There are general social agreements on the scale of crimes deserving of punishment, such that some crimes are more serious and deserve more punishment than others. Teachers and employees also work in the context of laws and general social agreements. For instance, state law may determine whether it is legal for a teacher to punish a student by using corporeal punishment. But general social agreement, and not law, supports the view that teachers may lower a student's grade if work is not turned in on time. Employees are not allowed to slander colleagues, but there are laws and policies that protect them from abusive colleagues too. Hence, laws and social agreements about what is fair punishment help guide our thinking about retributive justice, but they are not the final word.

Professionals must, in addition, look at what professional codes of ethics say about retributive justice in order to have a fuller sense of what is available to assist them in applying justice retributively. To this end, many of the professional codes of ethics refer at least implicity to retributive justice. The codes speak about accountability and the need to punish professionals who violate professional standards. One part of accountability is exposing those who are not acting professionally. Implicit in this exposure is the idea that the punishment of those not living up to professional standards is right and fair. So, for instance, when pharmacists are told to expose "illegal or unethical conduct in the profession"[10] and architects are expected to report wrongdoing,[11] the reason for reporting the wrongdoing of others is at least in part to punish them, that is, for retributive justice to be carried out. Some professions also have developed elaborate procedures for bringing to justice those colleagues deserving of punishment. The American Psychological Association, for instance, distinguishes among three types of sanctions that reflect three different levels of seriousness in infringements of the code. The least serious infractions deserve advisories or warnings; more serious violations of the code deserve reprimands or censures; and finally, the most serious infringements of the code call for resignation or expulsion from the profession.[12] Hence, justice as retribution, as fair punishment practices, is recognized by professions in their concern for accountability.

Compensatory Justice

Justice understood as compensation concerns fair reward practices. Compensatory justice is what we do when we settle on an equitable way of rewarding individuals or groups for their achievements or benefitting individuals or groups because of their disadvantages. It is compensatory justice when businesses have bonus plans in place that allow those individuals who have done the most business for the company to earn the largest bonuses. It would be unjust in such a situation for every member of the business to expect to receive an equal bonus. It also is compensatory justice when we compensate groups of people or individuals for past harms done to them or for disadvantages they may have. The bus company may offer cash payments to those injured by a negligent bus driver. An employer may decide to give preferential treatment in hiring to women and minority candidates who have for many years suffered from marketplace and educational discrimination. If a school administrator recommends that more bilingual teachers be hired to ease the transition for non-English speaking children, the administrator is aiming to compensate the children for what is lacking in their educational environment.

Like retributory justice, compensatory justice is meted out within the limits of legal and social interpretations of justice. Laws determine certain fair and unfair ways for workers to be compensated. For example, in 1998, workers in the United States must be paid at least the minimum wage of $5.15 per hour. Also, it is illegal for stockbrokers to trade stocks, and thus make money based on insider trading. On the other hand, laws and social agreements frequently are not very specific about what is fair compensation. They do not tell us how much a corporate officer should be compensated or how much school administrators should do to compensate non-

English speaking students. Questions like these have to be answered in specific situations, and we cannot address them here. But we can at least look at what some of the professional codes of ethics have to say about compensatory justice.

The codes themselves focus on the compensation of the professional, not on the professional's role in bringing about fair compensation for others. The codes insist that professionals be fairly rewarded for their services. For instance, physical therapists receive payment for their services that is "deserved and reasonable."[13] For social workers, the code provides even more guidance in the matter of appropriate recompense. Their code claims that a social worker's fee must be "fair, reasonable, considerate, and commensurate with the service performed and with due regard for the client's ability to pay."[14] It is interesting to note that in 1971, the American Medical Association, in its *Principles of Medical Ethics*, said that the physician's fee should be commensurate with the patient's ability to pay, but in the 1980 *Principles*, this statement was omitted.[15] Thus, compensatory justice is treated by the codes insofar as they specify how professionals ought to be rewarded for their work.

Not all codes dictate how a professional is to be compensated. Also, the codes do not speak to all of the issues of compensatory justice since, as a group, the codes say little about how professionals should compensate others. Perhaps the idea of compensating others is covered by statements in the codes that speak of competency, integrity, and allocation of services. No doubt the major way in which professionals reward others is by providing their technical expertise to others in a responsible way that respects persons. Thus, when the codes refer to the values of integrity, respect for persons, beneficence and nonmaleficence, and responsibility, they are in fact specifying how professionals carry out compensatory justice toward others. So compensatory justice can be enacted by means of the other values. In any case, we know that the codes by themselves cannot do all of the work of informing a professional about how to enact compensatory justice.

Distributive Justice

Justice understood as distribution has to do with fair allocation practices. It concerns how the benefits and burdens that come with living in a society are passed out. The following are all questions of allocation: Who gets the scarce medical resource and who does not?

Which student gets more of the teacher's time and attention and which gets less? Who should pay more federal income tax and who should pay less? In asking all of these questions, we are seeking to discover a fair way of distributing benefits and burdens.

The resources or the benefits and burdens to be passed out by means of distributive justice are money, goods, and services. Government officials decide how to spend federal tax money, insurance carriers and health care providers and patients decide how much time, effort, and money to spend on addressing a patient's symptoms, and teachers consider how much time should be spent on each task or subject and which students warrant more of their time. We carry out distributive justice as individuals when we decide how to spend our time and money. Sometimes questions about how to allocate resources fairly are answered by societies, public officials, or laws, but other times they are answered by individuals. Distributive justice also presupposes a limited supply of resources. Only a certain number of transplant organs are available. Only a limited amount of gasoline is available in the world. If there were unlimited resources, then everyone could receive the needed medical resources. Similarly, all students could have as much of their teacher's time and attention as they desired. But fair distribution becomes important when equal distribution is either impossible (not everyone in need can receive the scarce medical resource) or wrong (not everyone should pay the same income tax).

By looking at what various codes say about distributive justice, we can see the importance of fairness and nondiscrimination. The codes speak especially of how to distribute the professional's service. They claim that there must be equal or at least fair access to the professional's service, and that the professional should not unfairly discriminate among clients. Dentists are told that they "shall not refuse to accept patients because of the patient's race, creed, color, sex, or national origin."[16] Educators are reminded that they shall not unfairly deny benefits or grant advantage to any student "on the basis of race, color, creed, sex, national origin, marital status, political or religious beliefs, family, social or cultural background, or sexual orientation."[17] It is more complicated for public administrators. They are required to express equality (and thereby treat clients identically) and equity (and thereby treat clients unequally or preferentially where there has been long-term discrimination).[18] The code for public administrators sees that in allocating services to clients, justice requires both equal and unequal treatment of clients. This is consistent with our earlier definitions of justice as fairness.

Thus, while the professional codes of ethics do not tell professionals how to allocate their time and services, they do insist that the allocation process be fair and nondiscriminatory.

One additional point must be noted after these explanations of justice as retribution, compensation, and distribution. The point is, it is not always easy to isolate one form of justice from another. When a bus company compensates an injured passenger, it also is being punished for having contributed to injuring the passenger. There is retribution as well as compensation. When the school administrator compensates non-English speaking children by hiring more bilingual teachers, he also is allocating resources. Compensatory justice is at work, but there also is distributive justice in his action. Thus the same action often can be seen as involving more than one form of justice.

In summary, then, justice can be expressed in these three forms: retribution, compensation, and distribution. The professional codes of ethics offer guidelines on how to fairly punish, compensate, and allocate goods and services. The codes are concerned with realizing justice when they speak of fairness, deserved and reasonable payment, discrimination, and treating others equally and equitably. After this brief look at the way in which the codes help specify the professional's commitment to justice, let us next consider a case in which justice is a central value.

A Case Involving Justice

The following case describes the actions of a South African employer. In explaining his actions and reasons, the employer interprets and enacts the value of justice. Possibly not all of us would have chosen to enact justice in the way he did, but his action is one possible expression of an employer's commitment to justice. In addition to showing us one way of acting justly, the case also reminds us that justice, like all of the other values, can be interpreted and put into action in different ways by different people. Consider the actions of this employer.

Alan Nelson, a white South African lawyer, bought 110 acres of run-down vineyards in 1989. He decided that in order to make the vineyard a success, he would need the support of his workers. He gathered them together and promised that if they would work hard, he would reward them appropriately. Suspecting empty promises, six of *the eleven workers left, and Nelson hired eleven more workers. These sixteen laborers planted new vines and learned to prune and pick only ripe grapes. They were paid the equivalent of $40 a week and given lodging in sparse bungalows.*

In 1995, the wines began to win prizes at South African wine shows. In 1997, Nelson decided that he would give twenty-five acres, worth $500,000, to his workers in reward for their seven years of hard work.

Nelson said: "I am stretched to my financial limit as it is with the land I already have under cultivation. I wouldn't have been able to develop that parcel for at least twenty years. . . . For my purposes, what I have is a workforce that is more loyal and dedicated than ever before."
He continued: "I have told the workers that if we repeat our success this year, they will get land on which they can build houses. I don't want to make it look like a donation. I want people to feel like they have achieved something, which, of course, they have." He concluded: "It is my desire that in ten years . . . we will be one of the model wine farms in South Africa and one of the country's best wine estates. The workers should have their own homes and cars and be the best paid in the business. That's what I want. That's how we will test our success."

One of the workers on Nelson's farm, a Mr. Skippers, laughs at talk that Nelson's action is just a publicity stunt. Skippers says: "In the past, I saw whites as a different breed. . . . Now I see them as people, white people who can treat us as their equals. Alan did that for me."[19]

You might wonder first how this case is relevant to aspiring professionals. Not many of us will ever find ourselves in a situation like this, where we are employers and landowners in a country long governed by racial apartheid. On the other hand, if we take the case more generally, many of us will find ourselves in situations like this one. Many of us will be employers or supervisors faced with questions of how to motivate workers and how to reward good work. You might also be wondering whether this case is more about generosity than justice. It was certainly generous and kind of Alan Nelson to give away part of his land, but maybe he overreacted and did too much. After all, it seems more extravagant than fair to reward workers who together earn $640 a week with a piece of land worth $500,000. On the other hand, Alan Nelson is the one who decided to act and who judged that because of the workers' achievement, the land was an appropriate reward. He uses the language of reward and achievement, and in so doing he shows us that in his eyes his actions reflect justice, not generosity. We must remember that justice, like all of the moral values, can be interpreted in different ways. Perhaps another person would have rewarded the vineyard workers with higher wages or better living conditions, but Alan Nelson chose to give them land.

This is a provocative case but it is also a complex one. It is complicated by several factors. One is that we have both Alan Nelson's actions and his words to consider in making any judgment about what he did. Do we judge Nelson on the basis of his actions or words? His action is certainly generous, beneficent, and just, but are his reasons for giving away his land moral ones? He gives reasons based on self-interest as well as moral reasons, thus, the morality of his action depends on sorting out these reasons. Although self-interest can be part of a moral explanation, it cannot be the only part. A second factor is that even if Nelson's reasons are moral, they need not all be aimed at expressing justice. His action may express integrity, in the form of loyalty and promise keeping, or beneficence and nonmaleficence and the rule of proportionality, or possibly other values. However, in Nelson's claim that his action is not a donation but a recognition of his workers' achievements, the notion of justice is present. A third factor is we have the words of others, both pro and con, and their reflection on Nelson's action. Should we count the views of the workers who benefitted from Nelson's action, or the views of those who are suspicious of Nelson's motives? Neither group of people offers complete objectivity. Both have goods at stake as a result of Nelson's action. While some see only justice motivating Nelson's action, others see only self-interest. For our purposes, we will ignore their claims and consider only how Nelson views his action and the decision-making process that led up to it.

Nelson made a decision to give away part of his land. Keeping in mind all that we have said so far, we can use the framework for moral analysis to consider how he made his decision. Since his decision is already made, we begin with it and work back to uncover his rules, theories, and values.

Decision:

Give the vineyard workers twenty-five acres of land for their hard work.

Rule:

Workers should be rewarded appropriately for their achievements.
Employers should keep promises.
Employers should take actions that encourage workers to be loyal and dedicated.

Theory:

Nelson does not tell us what his moral perspective is, however, it seems that he is acting on the basis of a doing theory rather than a being theory. His action is a product of his concern for doing the right thing, not a result of his reflection on who he is or what kind of person he wants to be. So, if we eliminate virtue, care, and narrative theories as not evident in Nelson's rules, then his theory has to focus on either consequentialism, rights, or duties.

First, consequentialism could easily be Nelson's theory. On this account, Nelson keeps promises, motivates workers, and gives appropriate rewards, because doing so brings about more good consequences than bad. Nelson follows those rules that maximize the greatest amount of good. His rules of keeping promises and encouraging and rewarding workers achieve good ends for both Nelson and the workers and their families. Everyone benefits from the hard work of the employees, and if their hard work is furthered when their employer keeps promises and encourages and rewards them, then there is good reason to perform such actions. Thus, consequentialism provides a good context for explaining Nelson's rules and actions.

Second, Nelson's theory could just as easily be a duty theory. He may be considering what duties or obligations employers have. He may have chosen the rules he did because they reflect the way in which employers are obligated to act, regardless of the consequences of following the rules. On this account, Nelson is acting on the basis of his understanding of how he, as an employer, is obligated to act. He is concerned with doing what is right in itself, without regard for whether it has good results. Hence, duty theory works well as a perspective out of which Nelson could have formulated his rules and chosen how to act.

Third, rights theory, the last type of doing theory, does not, however, seem to be evidenced in Nelson's remarks, thus it need not be considered in any depth. It is, of course, possible that Nelson thought about his relationship to his workers in terms of rights. In this case, he might have acted as he did in order to respond to their right to be treated with dignity, or their right to be rewarded fairly for their work. But there is nothing in the case to suggest that Nelson thought of his action in the context of rights, hence we are left with consequential and duty theories as the more likely perspectives out of which Nelson formulated his rules and made his decision.

Value:

Justice, Integrity, Beneficence and Nonmaleficence

Justice is especially evident in this case. Nelson appeals to justice when he decides to reward his workers in appropriate ways. Justice also is expressed in his statement that the land is not a donation, because the workers have achieved and earned this reward. Finally, Skippers views Nelson's decision as reflecting justice, since Nelson treated his black workers fairly and did not discriminate. As we have seen, justice is about fair rewarding, giving to people what they deserve, and treating people equitably, which often means treating them equally. Consider for a moment the three forms of justice we discussed earlier.

Retributive justice is not explicitly present in the case, since there is no punishment to be handed out. At the same time, the threat of retributive justice is present. If Nelson's promise of a suitable reward is contingent upon hard work, then the threat is that in the absence of hard work, there will be no reward. Implicitly, it is understood that there is punishment in the form of no reward, which will follow upon the workers' decision not to work hard. Also, in deciding to uphold his promise, Nelson may have considered the possibility of retributive justice enacted by his workers. How might they decide to punish him if he were to fail to keep his promise? So retributive justice is alluded to in Nelson's promise to the workers, and in his decision to fulfill his promise.

Compensatory justice is the most obvious form of justice evident in the case. Nelson is an employer and, as such, he has the power and authority to decide how to recompense his employees. Part of his task is to assign appropriate rewards and recognize achievements by giving to his employees what they deserve. Nelson's action speaks directly to the value of fair compensation.

Distributive justice becomes a factor in this case due to Nelson's decision to fairly compensate his employees. Once he decided to reward them, he had to settle on how and with what to reward them. As his comments indicate, he had more land than he could cultivate. Perhaps he had more land than he had money. So in thinking about how to reward, he decided to reallocate his goods. By giving land, which he could not use, he could compensate his workers. In this case, carrying out compensatory justice entailed distributory justice. In fact, both reward (compensatory justice) and punishment (retributive justice) can be enacted by the way goods and services are allocated (distributive justice).

In addition, both integrity and beneficence and nonmaleficence are expressed in Nelson's rules. Integrity is revealed when Nelson is honest with his workers about their chances for reward and when he keeps the promise he made to his workers. He is acting on the Rules of Honesty and Loyalty, discussed in chapter 7. Acting with integrity involves dealing honestly with people and being loyal to those to whom you have commitments, whether personal or professional. Nelson is truthful with the workers about the work they will do and the benefit they may gain, and he upholds his promise, thus is loyal to his workers. Because he is honest and loyal, he acts with integrity.

Beneficence and nonmaleficence can be seen in Nelson's decision to take actions and make promises. He needs the workers' hard work to have a successful vineyard. To ensure that having a successful vineyard also is important to his workers, he tied their good to the good of the vineyard. If it did well, they would do well. All would benefit by hard work, hence the workers could not separate their good from their employer's good. Beneficence and nonmaleficence for everyone is achieved by the hard work of the employees. If promising rewards help them work hard, then that is a way of expressing beneficence and nonmaleficence.

Thus we have seen in this case how the value of justice and other values as well pertain to the most typical of situations, namely, employer–employee relations. Justice can take on various forms, depending on whether the situation involves punishment, reward, or allocation. It also can be translated into concrete action in diverse ways. You might think of other ways for Nelson to have enacted justice. For instance, why not give the workers shares in the company instead of land? Nevertheless, fairness, however it may be translated into rules and actions, is a value that is central to the life of a professional. In the next section, we will look at two rules that can help us translate justice into action.

Interpreting Justice: Guides to Help

We have seen that justice is defined as fairness and that justice takes on several forms, depending on the sort of situation we are facing. We now need to make clear what it means to be fair. In other words, how is justice enacted? What guides us in assessing what is fair? Two rules can help us determine what is fair. They do not answer every question concerning how a professional should interpret justice, but they offer guidelines. However, before looking at the rules, two points must be made.

The first is that when we translate justice into action, we usually are going to have to make a comparison. Justice is comparative. It involves comparing the actions or needs or merits of one person to those of another. In order to assess what is fair, we need to consider what a person deserves or is owed, and our assessment of this is not made in a vacuum but through comparison to others. What is fair to one can only be determined by assessing what is fair to others. Thus the practice of justice forces us to view persons by how they compare to others. To put it another way, there is no absolute justice. Instead, there is justice relative to the persons, resources, and situation at hand. For instance, no computer programmer can complain that her employer treats her unjustly, since she "deserves" a million dollar salary, if, when she is compared to others who are similarly skilled and doing similar work, it is discovered that her $40,000 salary is similar to theirs. There is fairness, thus justice in the $40,000 salary within the context of present resources and employment practices. She is treated as others who are similar to her in relevant ways are treated, and this is fair.

The second is that although the definition of justice speaks of equity and not of equality, the enacting of justice often, but not always, entails equal treatment. From the beginning of our discussion of justice, we have seen that it is carried out in different ways in different circumstances. For the shoppers waiting in line for the clerk's attention, justice requires taking each customer in the order in the queue. For insured motorists, justice would not be served by assigning cheaper rates to those first in line and higher rates to those at the end of the line. Fairness here has nothing to do with first come, first served and equality. Insured motorists must be compared one against the other in terms of characteristics relevant to the assignment of insurance rates. If there are differences relevant to insurance costs, then it is fair to treat those who differ in different ways. In short, sometimes it is fair to treat people in similar ways, that is, equally, and other times it is fair to treat them in dissimilar ways, that is, unequally. We need the rules to help us determine whether a particular situation is one in which justice means equal or unequal treatment.

With these two points in mind, we now turn to the two rules of justice that provide guidelines for how to interpret this value. Unlike the rules we have discussed for other values, these rules are not distinct or free standing. They have to be used together, and they must be used in order because the first rule specifies what fairness is and the second rule gives information helpful in carrying out the first rule. The second rule is necessary in order to practice the first rule, but by itself the second rule does not tell us how to act, and it does not explain fairness. Together, these rules give us a procedure for enacting justice.

First Rule of Fairness

Treat equally those persons who are equals and treat unequally those persons who are unequals.

The first rule tells us what it means to act justly. When justice prevails, those persons who are equal in relevant ways are treated similarly, while those who differ in relevant ways are treated dissimilarly. Sometimes justice is equality, sometimes inequality, but justice always entails equity.

Second Rule of Sameness

Persons are equals, unless there is some inequality or difference between them that is morally relevant to the situation at hand.

The second rule tells us how to apply the first rule. To know whether justice is enacted by treating certain persons similarly or dissimilarly we must determine whether in the case at hand they are similar in relevant respects. We assume persons are equals. They may be unequals if upon reflection differences are found between them that are morally relevant. But the assumption is equality. The burden of proof is on those who see inequality. For justice as fairness to involve unequal treatment, the inequality of persons must be demonstrated. In the absence of any such demonstration, justice operates by positing that persons are equals, and thus they require equal treatment.

Let us illustrate the use of these rules. Suppose you are a bank loan officer. On one of the mortgages your bank finances, four payments have been missed. You have written letters to the person holding the mortgage, to no avail. Now you are wondering what to do. Justice may not be your only moral concern in this situation, but it is one of your concerns. Justice, we know, requires having to make comparisons. So you begin with the Rule of Fairness. Insofar as you have a commitment to act justly, your professionalism demands that you treat equal persons equally and unequal persons unequally.

Next, you wonder whether this person whose loan is delinquent is equal to other persons whose loans have been delinquent. In simple terms, is this person the same as all other persons whose loans are past due? This applies the Rule of Sameness. If equality is present, then this person deserves to be treated as all persons with past due loans have been treated. But before assuming the equality of those with delinquent mortgages, you should investigate to see if there is some inequality relevant to the situation that would warrant unequal treatment of this person. The following possible inequalities might surface: the person holding the mortgage was critically injured and is recuperating, but no one has managed the person's financial affairs for months; or while his payments are four months' overdue, they are not six months' overdue; or he defaulted on his last mortgage and is presently being sued for payment by his last mortgage holder. If any or all of these points turn up upon investigation, then there are relevant differences between this and other delinquent mortgage holders. This defaulting mortgage holder is unequal to others in a morally relevant way, and due to this difference, justice means you must treat him in unequal ways. Perhaps you simply wait for the person to recover and resume his payments. Perhaps you send another letter, more demanding than if the customer was one month overdue but not threatening legal action, as you would if a customer were six months' overdue. Perhaps you immediately call a lawyer and initiate a suit to recover your money or take possession of the house. The point is, if relevant differences turn up, then people must be treated in ways that take into account those differences, or there will be no justice.

But of course we must remember that some differences and inequalities are not morally relevant. This means that they have nothing to do with the particular situation. They are differences that are morally insignificant or are not morally relevant to the case. For instance, in this case, the nationality or sex of the person holding the mortgage is morally irrelevant. Applying the second Rule of Sameness necessitates proving that a difference is morally relevant. If a difference cannot be shown to be morally relevant, then the difference is inconsequential, thus the persons must be treated as equals.

Conflicts Involving Justice

In the example of the loan officer just discussed, it is clear that the biggest problem when translating justice into action occurs as a result of trying to apply the Rules of Fairness and Sameness. It will not always be evident whether a difference between persons is morally significant. To determine whether to treat persons as unequals or equals, we have to decide whether a particular difference between them is morally relevant in the given situation. This is not easy.

We have said earlier that our assumption is that people are equals. We take it for granted that persons are equals, and we must be convinced that persons are unequals before justice translates into unequal treatment. What does it take to demonstrate that persons are in fact different in morally relevant ways? It takes looking at the situation and judging what traits or skills are relevant to performing the specific task. It takes proving that a trait or skill is necessary, or is crucial or part of the task to be done and not just an accidental, unrelated, or irrelevant fact. For instance, a program that is testing candidates who are applying to become firefighters can prove that the skill of being able to carry 200 pounds is relevant to the candidate's performance as a firefighter. Thus, it is just to treat unequally candidates who can carry 200 pounds and those who cannot. However, the skill of speaking French is an accidental, irrelevant fact about some candidates. Speaking French is not relevant to succeeding as a firefighter, and so it is not just to treat differently those candidates who speak French.

It is in cases like this that we must decide whether persons are equals or unequals by proving whether there are morally relevant differences between them. Even when we agree that justice should be practiced, well-meaning people still sometimes disagree about whether a particular trait or skill is morally relevant. We must simply do our best to offer convincing evidence when we believe that a trait or skill is morally relevant, and thus calls for unequal treatment.

But in addition to these conflicts inherent to enacting justice, there seem to be occasions in which justice comes into conflict with other values. In the example of the overdue mortgage, we noted that justice may not be the loan officer's only concern. Let us consider two other values the loan officer may also be aiming to put into practice that might create problems for his realization of justice. Perhaps there are value conflicts here, but at least there are difficulties when acting justly seems to get in the way of acting for the sake of other values.

Suppose for a moment that the loan officer, in the process of applying the Rules of Fairness and Sameness, reflects on his commitment to the value of compassion. He may find that he has empathy and sympathy for the person who has missed mortgage payments, especially if the loan officer himself has experienced financial difficulties. He may decide to express compassion and fellow feeling for the customer by not holding him strictly to the rules of justice. This might involve not bothering to assess whether the customer is equal or unequal to other customers, or it might entail choosing to treat him as being unequal to others because the officer feels compassion for him. In either case, the decision of how to treat the customer is made on the basis of compassion and not justice, since justice would call for a demonstration of the customer's inequality. The loan officer may believe that he has to choose between acting justly and acting compassionately.

A second possible conflict might occur if the loan officer focuses on his commitment to beneficence and nonmaleficence. Suppose he judges that, while justice is relevant to the case, the most crucial concern is beneficence and nonmaleficence. Given this, the loan officer would want to ensure the bank's best interests (safeguard its money, avoid litigation), the customer's best interest (avoid losing his home), and his own best interest (to be a successful loan officer). To achieve these ends, the loan officer might decide by means of the Rule of Proportionality that, overall, more good comes from ignoring justice. Instead of spending time calling the customer or checking his recent credit or medical history, the loan officer simply adopts a hard line. To achieve the most good for the most people, the money must be paid as soon as possible. In this scenario, no attention is paid to possible differences between this customer and others. No attempt is made to determine how the Rule of Fairness and Rule of Sameness apply. Instead, all concerns about fairness are dropped for the sake of recouping the money as soon as possible. So to act for beneficence and nonmaleficence might mean that the loan officer cajoles, begs, and threatens to get the customer to pay. To act out of justice might take more time and effort. From the point of view of beneficence and nonmaleficence, all efforts at justice, which entail figuring out if the customer is equal or unequal to other delinquent customers, slow down and perhaps get in the way of a quick recovery of the overdue money. Thus beneficence and nonmaleficence might be interpreted in such a way that the loan officer recognizes a conflict between justice and beneficence and nonmaleficence, since the same action does not realize both values.

But are these really value conflicts? Is justice in conflict with compassion or beneficence and nonmaleficence? No, the values themselves do not conflict. A commitment to justice does not require us to be uncommitted to compassion and beneficence and nonmaleficence. Instead, what happens is that in some situations the action that serves justice does not further compassion or beneficence and nonmaleficence. When we enact justice, we sometimes arrive at actions that do not express compassion or beneficence and nonmaleficence. The actions by which we practice justice may conflict with other possible actions that would enact compassion or some other value. What can we do about these conflicts?

The answer lies in first remembering that acting ethically and professionally are complex endeavors. Acting as a moral professional means translating values into action, and in the process of this translation there will be uncertainties and tensions. There are questions about how to enact a single value, like justice, and there are questions about how to be faithful to all of the values. Sometimes one value is more central to a situation than others, and then the act can rightfully focus on enacting that value. At other times, a decision might have to be made about which value is more fundamental in order to know which action to take. As we have said before, the best procedure to follow when values lead to conflicting actions is to clarify, harmonize, and rank. Clarify the situation, the possible actions to be taken, and the values at issue. Harmonize the values that seem to be at odds by looking for a compromise or searching out an action that realizes several values. Finally, rank the values at stake by deciding which value is of primary concern in this situation, and choose the action that expresses that value. Conflicts are inevitable, but resolving them is not impossible if we follow this strategy.

Conclusion

This chapter has considered what justice is and how to realize it in concrete actions. We have seen that justice means fairness and that it can be enacted in three main ways: retributive, compensatory, and distributive. To exemplify justice, we used the moral framework to analyze the case of Alan Nelson, a vineyard owner, to see how he reached his decision to give away part of his land. We discussed the first Rule of Fairness and the second Rule of Sameness as concrete guides for translating justice into action. Finally, we recognized that there are times in which acting for the sake of justice may conflict with acting for the sake of compassion, beneficence and nonmaleficence, or some other value. From all of this, we learned that the moral professional works to enact justice, but must do so in the context of a commitment to many values. It is this commitment to values, reflected in the theories of ethics and in the professional codes of ethics, which both enlivens and complicates the moral life.

EXERCISES

1. Take one of the codes of ethics, either one assigned to you or one of your choice. Describe the ways in which it expresses the three forms of justice and/or the two rules that apply justice. Be specific. Also note several ways in which the code omits referring to certain forms of justice or ways of applying justice. For instance, does the code speak only of retributive justice and not of compensatory justice? Or how does the code reflect the Rules of Fairness and Sameness? Finally, discuss a problem you think might arise in a professional's attempt to use the code to decide how to enact justice.
2. Use the CRM to reach a decision in each of these cases. In doing so, consider all of the relevant values, but be especially alert to considerations of justice. Identify whether the case is concerned with justice in the form of retribution, compensation, or distribution.

CASE 1: INFORMING EMPLOYEES OF A CORPORATE MOVE

You are a member of the Human Resources (HR) Department of a major corporation. You and several other members of the HR staff serve on a committee, along with members of senior management. The purpose of the committee is to plan for the corporation's move from a suburban location (forty-five minutes from New York City) to a downtown location (New York City). The move will happen in six to eight months. The issue your committee is facing is when to notify the employees of the impending move. It is possible that some employees will be unhappy about the move into the city and will choose to find other jobs rather than commute from their suburban homes. The corporation hopes to avoid losing too many employees. Senior management is suggesting that employees be told only two months before the move, which effectively limits their chances to find other jobs.

CASE 2: THE ARMED PHARMACIST

Mr. Gray is a pharmacist who works in a small neighborhood pharmacy. He became a pharmacist in part because his mother advised him to and in part because he liked to help people. He has worked for more than twenty years at the neighborhood pharmacy.

In 1990, he was conned by two men in the store, and he came out from behind the counter. He and a co-worker were then ordered at gunpoint to lie on the floor while the two men robbed him and the store of $900. Gray recalls feeling "absolute, complete helplessness—you're not sure if they are going to eliminate the witnesses." The robbers were never caught.

The pharmacy added a buzzer system to control entry to its front door after 3 P.M., it installed a panic button wired to a burglar alarm, and it imposed a rule that no one could work alone. The pharmacy also allowed Gray to arm himself. He brought to work his .32-caliber Beretta automatic and wore it loaded, in a holster behind his back.

On January 18, 1997, Gray was working with an assistant. A man came into the store, ordered the assistant to hand over the money, and flashed a gun. The assistant began taking small bills out of the cash register and dropping them on the floor. The man rushed at the cash register. Gray, who was talking on the telephone with a customer, noticed the commotion. He dropped the phone and drew his pistol as the robber turned and began to raise his gun. Gray fired, and the robber fell down dead with a single gunshot wound to the head.

The assistant called 911, and the police arrived in a few minutes. Both Gray and his assistant were questioned at the local police station. Gray worried: "Will anyone understand that I didn't intend to kill, but to stop a crime?" He said: "I can't say I'm glad I did it—killed somebody. But I'm glad it didn't turn out the way it could have." Gray's assistant believed he saved her life, and perhaps his own. She said: "I thought my life was going to be over—flash, right in front of my eyes."

The county prosecutor's office called Gray two days later to tell him it had ruled the shooting a justifiable homicide.

The pharmacy has now installed a bullet-deflecting Plexiglass window above its counter, a Plexiglass door, and armored plates on the lower shelves.[20]

1. Did Gray act justly in shooting the robber?
2. Was Gray's action morally right?
3. What type of justice is involved in Gray's action?
4. Should Gray's employer have let him carry a weapon?
5. Is Gray's employer doing enough to ensure the safety of its employees?

CASE 3: THE ATTORNEY WHOSE CLIENT NEEDS AN ADVANCE

An attorney is handling the case of a client who was injured in a motorcycle accident. The client has serious back injuries. An orthopedic surgeon has recommended back surgery. Unfortunately the client has no health insurance, and the hospital will not allow the client to be admitted without a $3,000 deposit. The client asks the attorney to advance him the $3,000 from the amount he expects to earn in the settlement of his case. What should the attorney do?

NOTES

1. Reported in *The Chicago Tribune* (April 10, 1998), and *Business Week* (April 20, 1998), p. 65.
2. The description of Proposition 209 comes from Beth Anne Turner, "Campus Affirmative Action Office Fears Ripple Effect," *The Jambar* 76:52 (November 22, 1996), p. 1. The number of students in the University of California–Berkeley Law School comes from a speech by President Bill Clinton as reported by Colleen De Baise, "Affirmative Action: Clinton Cautions Against Resegregating Colleges," *College News* 8:1 (September 1997), p. 1.
3. From *The American Heritage Dictionary of the English Language*, 3rd ed. (Boston, Mass.: Houghton Mifflin, 1992), 979, 1955.
4. See *U.S. v. Caldwell*, 408 U.S. 714.
5. See Barbara Huttmann, "A Crime of Compassion," *Newsweek* (August 8, 1983), p. 15.
6. See the preamble to *The Code of Professional Responsibility* of the American Bar Association.
7. See the preamble and statement 4 in the *Standards of Practice*, the American Association of Advertising Agencies.
8. See the preamble to the *Code of Ethics*, the Society of Professional Journalists.
9. Peter A. Facione, Donald Scherer, and Thomas Attig, *Ethics and Society*, 2d ed. (Englewood Cliffs, N.J.: Prentice Hall, 1991), 187–190, speak of distributive, compensatory, and retributive justice as does Jacques P. Thiroux, *Ethics: Theory and Practice*, 5th ed. (Englewood Cliffs, N.J.: Prentice Hall, 1995), 135–36. Gregory R. Beabout and Daryl J. Wennemann, *Applied Professional Ethics* (Lanham, Md.: University Press of America, 1994), 54–56, identify five aspects to justice: substantive, distributive, commutative, procedural, and retributive.
10. *Code of Ethics*, American Pharmaceutical Association, Statement 4.
11. *Code of Ethics and Professional Conduct*, American Institute of Architects, Statement R.4. 104.
12. Summarized on page 46 in Patricia Keith-Spiegel and Gerald P. Koocher, *Ethics in Psychology: Professional Standards and Cases* (New York: Random House, 1985). They refer to an unpublished report of the APA Task Force on

Ethics System Procedures (1981), authored by G.P. Koocher, P. Keith-Spiegel, and L. Klebanoff.

13. *Code of Ethics*, American Physical Therapy Association, Principle 5.

14. *Code of Ethics*, National Association of Social Workers, Principle I.

15. See the American Medical Association, *Judicial Council—Opinions and Reports* (Chicago, Ill.: AMA, 1971), vi-viii, and *American Medical News* (August 1/8, 1980), p. 9.

16. *Principles of Ethics and Code of Professional Conduct*, American Dental Association, Statement I-A.

17. *Code of Ethics of the Education Profession*, National Education Association, Principle I.

18. *Workbook and Study Guide for Public Administrators*, American Society for Public Administration, Key Principles 1 and 2.

19. Robert Block, "In South Africa's Cape, A Winemaker Shares the Fruit of Labor," *The Wall Street Journal* (January 20, 1998), pp. A1 and A6.

20. This case is summarized from the article by Angelo B. Henderson, "Beyond the Statistics: A Druggist Confronts the Reality of Robbery," *The Wall Street Journal* (January 20, 1998), pp. A1 and A8.

10

Compassion

It may seem unusual for an entire chapter in a professional ethics book to be dedicated to compassion. When pushed to define this important value, we often are at a loss. We know, at the very least, that compassion is something we feel, but what do feelings have to do with our professional lives? It is true that feelings are not a necessary part of executing our work. We could even imagine doing what our work requires of us like automatons, having no real harm come about as a consequence of our lack of feeling. But, by being automatons, we are merely doing our job, like a machine would do it, without demonstrating any compassion, whether or not we have the corresponding feeling. In doing so, we are not being professional. This is the case, returning to the language of chapter 1, because there is no relational sensitivity being exhibited. Without this sensitivity, which certainly owes a great deal to the value of compassion, there is no professional life.

Remember that the other aspect of being a professional, technical acumen, or doing one's job well, can be traced to a commitment to following through on obligations. To do one's job technically well can be understood as doing one's job in a responsible manner. In chapter 12, we will consider that which makes us obligated—responsibility. But for now, as we consider compassion, which is not an obligation, but an actual emotion, we highlight the fact that compassion is a feeling. Having compassion means to have concern for

- - -

something or someone, thus to be emotionally involved with others in a particular way. This involvement, in not being an obligation but a feeling, is the significant difference between compassion and responsibility. We mention this difference here, not to get ahead of ourselves, but to focus on a key aspect of compassion. Even though it is impossible to be obligated or made to feel compassion, as a value professionals recognize as being central to their practice, we can be obligated to act compassionately. That is, compassion is a feeling to be prized and cultivated. It is also a way of acting. Even if a person does not feel compassion, he or she can still show compassion or act in a compassionate way. It is primarily this showing of compassion that we recognize as being central to relational sensitivity, thus central to our professional lives.

Thinking of our professional life as exhibiting compassion is really not all that radical. It need not require that we go about drastically changing the world and making it a better place. However, it does require us to recognize that we are in the world, and because of that, we recognize that our actions in the world have effects. This realization is based on the underlying recognition that, through compassion, we are connected to others in virtue of our shared humanity. At root, compassion is a feeling we have in response to the feelings and experiences of another person. This ability to reflect on our thoughts and feelings, insofar as we feel things about our feelings and think things about our thoughts, is uniquely human. It is that which we share as a species with everyone else in the world.

Keeping this implicit connectedness in mind, in what follows we will explore the implications of this feeling and how it is that compassion adds something significant to the experiences of our professional life, as a central way of showing relational sensitivity. As usual, we begin with examining what compassion means as a value and the complications involved in that definition. We continue by considering the way in which compassion is utilized by us and by the professional code of the National Association of Social Workers. In addition, we will assess how it is that particular professions interpret compassion in their codes, and the wider lessons we can draw from that. As we continue, we will consider the ways in which compassion gets played out in the professional world. Through an analysis of a decision made by Duke University, we will see the ways in which an institution that recognizes the value of compassion behaves. All of this will leave us with some guidelines to help us interpret the value of compassion. Finally, we will consider the conflicts that can arise and the pitfalls to avoid when we are committed to compassion and its related issues.

What Is Compassion?

Compassion is the value that leads us to be concerned with others in such a manner that our concern is translated into professional action. The concern that compassion includes is a concern for others with whom we are involved, in that we know their situation, insofar as we know the obstacles they face. In being related to others and their obstacles, we involve our commitment to all of our other values. This is what is meant by relational sensitivity, namely, acting in a professional manner with reference to those around us. Compassion is that value which keeps us honest, not honest in the truth telling sort of way, but honest in terms of being authentic. In virtue of authentically having a concern for those around us in our professional life, we are anchored to all else, including our work and the way in which our work involves others. In short, compassion is that value which expresses concern or care for the suffering of others. Through compassion, we recognize that we are concerned or care about one another, about our work, or about anything at all.

Considering the etymology of compassion, this concept of concern is not too difficult to appreciate. Compassion comes from the Latin root "com," meaning together, and "pati," to suffer.[1] Through compassion, we suffer together. In suffering together, the focus is not so much on the misery but on the community engendered when that suffering is shared. Of course, that shared feeling is not all that compassion is, for if that were true, everyone would be wallowing in suffering, making no attempt to do anything about it. What compassion adds to the situation, over and above a feeling of shared suffering, is a willingness to do something about it.[2]

As professionals, this shared feeling and a willingness to do something about it is primarily articulated in three sorts of relationships. Compassion is present between employees and employers, among colleagues, and between employees and the clients they serve. Within these relationships it is the same value being enacted, but the context differs, thus the expression of the value differs. The key aspect of compassion in each of these relationships is a concern for the best interest of the one for whom we feel compassion. As a result of feeling compassion for someone, you try to bring about action or act yourself or with others in such a manner as to perform some action in the best interest of the person suffering. When asked why we are doing what we do, the answer often will be, "Because I feel compassion."

We can look at each of the three relationships just mentioned and see how compassion is made manifest. If your employer feels compassion for you, he or she is concerned with your best interest. For example, in chapter 1, when Bart showed up at work intoxicated, his supervisor felt compassion for him and acted in Bart's best interest by getting him home. If we recall chapter 5, we remember the example of colleagues attempting to act in each other's best interest, when a colleague was responding to the insensitive comments that Bob Fritz made to his female employees. As a result of sharing the suffering his colleagues were experiencing, another employee was trying to determine how to act in their best interest. Finally, in chapter 4, we see how Rev. Giannini, as a professional, was attempting to act in his client's best interest. In this instance, Rev. Giannini was also balancing how he could maintain the best interest of both of his clients, a mother and her teenaged son.[3] Within each of these very different relationships and situations, compassion was acted on and viewed as the central value at stake, contingent upon the context.

Now that we have appreciated that compassion begins with a shared feeling of suffering and ends with acting in the best interest of the person suffering, something still seems to be missing. There must be some sort of mechanism for determining what is the best interest of the person for whom we feel compassion. How is this best interest to be determined? The easiest way in which to determine someone's best interest is typically to ask them. For example, if you are a teacher and one of your students (your client) is having difficulty with the material you are teaching, hopefully you feel compassion for them. Being confused about your course work is certainly suffering, and it probably is a feeling that we can all understand and a suffering we can all share. To address the suffering, the student's teacher can act in his best interest by asking the student what it is he specifically does not understand. His answer informs the teacher about how she can act in the best interest of her confused student. Thus the first step in determining how to act in someone's best interest consists of simply asking them, "How can I help?"

Unfortunately, sometimes suffering is so great that answering this simple request can seem overwhelming. Or sometimes we are not in direct contact with those who are suffering. In these instances, we must use a different method. We will use a standard of substitution. This standard allows us to act in someone's best interest when they are unable to tell us what their best interest is, because we substitute what it is we would want if we were in the same circumstances. Let us return to our confused student. We have already determined that the compassionate teacher will attempt to aid the student in his understanding. But what should the teacher do when the student is so confused that he is completely unable to articulate what it is he needs help with? In these cases, since the teacher is unable to ask the student how she can help, she would apply the standard of substitution and thereby treat the student the way she herself would like to be treated.

Now the crucial aspect of the standard of substitution is the imaginative aspect. That is, when the teacher is trying to determine how she would like to be treated, she is not thinking about how she would like to be treated as a teacher. Instead she is imagining that if she was in the same situation as this student, how would she like the teacher to treat her? Thus not only must we determine how we would like to be treated, but we must also determine the conditions of desired treatment relative to the perspective of the person who is suffering. In using her imagination, the teacher appreciates the perspective of her suffering student and is able to act in his best interest, understanding this best interest as the way in which she would like to be treated.

In using the standard of substitution for determining someone's best interest, it is important to keep in mind all of the relevant aspects of the situation. If you do not do so, you are not actually attempting to act in the suffering person's best interest, but in your own. That is, if the teacher were to aid the student in the manner that suited her, she would have little concern for what the student's best interest was. Instead, she would be acting in what she thinks should be the student's best interest, assuming that, as a teacher, she knows better. This "knowing better" is paternalism. Through paternalism, we act like a parent, in a manner that "knows best." When we act paternalistically, we are no longer acting in the best interest of the one who is suffering, but in the best interest we think the sufferer should have. These sorts of actions are not compassionate, but condescending.[4]

Thus it is through compassion that we appreciate the way in which we are connected to others in such a way that we share their suffering. This shared feeling pushes us to improve the situation that is the source of the suffering, as a way of expressing our concern for those who are suffering. In being so concerned, we attempt to act in the best interest of those who are suffering, to alleviate that suffering. Finally, this desire to act in or for the best interest of those for whom we feel compassion is aided by asking the suffering person how we can help, or by putting ourselves in the position of the other person. Without this imaginative effort, the action that comes about from compassion cannot be in someone else's best interest. When we act in what we determine to be a person's best interest, rather than in his or her actual best interest, we are no longer acting compassionately, but paternalistically.

What Compassion Involves

With this preliminary understanding of compassion, we turn to our professional codes in order to begin to see how compassion is actually to be enacted in our professional lives. We begin with the *Code of Ethics* for the National Association of Social Workers (NASW). Although this code does not mention the term *compassion* explicitly, it is very much about acting in the best interest of others from a sense of concern for their situation. Acting thus, a social worker is thereby acting professionally, a professionalism that would be incomplete without compassion.

The NASW *Code of Ethics* begins by establishing the parameters of its code. This is accomplished through listing the professional relationships the code governs. The code states that "it represents standards of ethical behavior for social workers in professional relationships with those served, with colleagues [and], with employers."[5] These three types of relationships are typically those shared by all professionals and delineate the parameters in which compassion is relevant. The code then goes on to determine the various requirements needed in those relationships.

In looking at the first relationship, between professionals and clients, we see that social workers must seek "advice and counsel of colleagues" in instances where "such consultation is in the best interest of clients."[6] Furthermore, when having to end a professional relationship, social workers should take "care to minimize possible adverse effects"[7] and attempt to continue service elsewhere "in relation to the clients' needs and preferences."[8] From these statements, we see the general way in which professionals are to demonstrate compassion. It has been determined that acting in the best interest of those being served is required of professional social workers. When treating their clients professionally, social workers are not required to make sure that all of the needs of their clients are met. This would be impossible and would prevent them from doing the work they are actually supposed to be doing. Instead, they are to act in the best interest of their clients relative to the specific context delineated by their professional relationship, including such things as consultations with colleagues and termination of service.

Just as this is the case for social workers, so it is for all professionals. We cannot treat all people with compassion all of the time. This is beyond human capacity. However, as professionals, we can at least treat those with whom we have relationships with compassion. This compassion is to be shown within the parameters of the professional relationship. In another example, that of dealing with relationships with colleagues, social workers are told to "create and maintain conditions of practice that facilitate ethical and competent professional performance by colleagues."[9] In doing so, social workers are upholding the best interest, as defined professionally, of their colleagues insofar as they support their professional performance.

Likewise, in their dealings with employers and employees, social workers have to work to further their employees' and employers' best interests within their professional capabilities. In evaluating employees, the evaluation is to be done in "a fair, considerate, and equitable manner."[10] In their dealings with the organizations that employ them, social workers "should adhere to the commitments made to the employing organization" and, in doing so, they "should act to prevent and eliminate discrimination in the employing organization's . . . policies and practices."[11] That is, in being professionally involved with an organization, social workers should act to prevent suffering in the form of discrimination, thereby acting in the best interest of the organization (employer) and those who would suffer (employees) from these unethical practices.

While many of the professional codes require actions directed toward the best interests of others, most do not explicitly mention compassion. One exception is the American Medical Association's *Principles of Medical Ethics*, which states that physicians shall "be dedicated to providing competent medical service with compassion and respect for human dignity."[12]

Yet even though most codes appeal to acting compassionately, they do not appeal to feeling compassion. The distinction made in the codes follows the distinction recognized at the beginning of the chapter. There is a difference between requiring a professional to act compassionately and requiring a professional to feel compassion. As has been stated, we cannot be required to feel certain emotions, but we can be required to act in a certain manner. Since compassion, like most emotions, is complex, our codes have ignored the emotional state behind the actions. Instead of dealing with an emotional state, we deal with the actions that stem from it as we are required to act compassionately. In doing so, we bypass any chance of losing a commitment to compassion.

Requiring compassionate action, even if the feeling of compassion is absent, we are claiming that professionals must exhibit relational sensitivity. Professionals are required to act in the best interests of those who fall within the three primary relationships in which they practice: employees and employers, colleagues, and the clients being served. Even though those with whom we are in professional relationships do not always uphold our best interests, we now know that those who fail to act in the best interests of those with whom they are in professional relationships do not express relational sensitivity, thus they are thereby neither professional nor upholding the standards of the codes of their professional organizations.

A Case Involving Compassion

With this understanding of what compassion is and what it involves, we look to Duke University for an example of how it is enacted. Since what follows is not a case to be solved but a situation in which a decision has already been made, we can use our framework for moral analysis to understand how compassion is and can be a part of our professional lives.

> With the Duke basketball team riding high and consumers snapping up apparel bearing the university's name, Duke plans to announce a far-reaching code of conduct tomorrow to insure that products bearing its name are not made in sweatshops.
> ... Duke has one of the most popular names on sports gear and has 700 licensees that make apparel at hundreds of plants in the United States and in more than 10 other countries. Duke's code bars licensees from using forced or child labor and requires them to maintain a safe workplace, pay at least the minimum wage, and recognize the right to form unions. Then, in a move that makes it the first university to adopt a tough enforcement mechanism, Duke's code requires licensees to identify all factories making products with Duke's name and to allow unimpeded visits by independent monitors.

"We're doing it because it's the right thing to do," said . . . Duke's director of trademark licensing. "We cannot tolerate having the sweat and tears of abused and exploited workers mixed with the fabric of the products which bear our marks."

. . . About $20 million worth of goods carrying the Duke name are sold every year.[13]

Initially one might think that this case is not especially relevant to professionals seeking to enact compassion. Many people will never find themselves in a similar situation, being in a position to develop policy for a major apparel label, but they might possibly be employees of a major apparel label. Part of being an employee of any organization and being committed to the value of compassion is bringing to the attention of those who do develop policy the consequences of that policy for those it affects. Of course, this has to be done in a sophisticated manner, or one is not apt to be an employee of a major apparel label for long.

Many of us will be employees of organizations that bring about actions with which we are not completely comfortable, or which even cause suffering to those around us. A commitment to compassion allows us to work to alleviate those conditions of suffering through the appropriate means, hence to act in the best interest of those being harmed. Understood in this more inclusive sense, the actions of Duke University are relevant for all of us when interpreting compassion.

You might be wondering whether the case is more about promotion and good public relations rather than compassion. That is, Duke could be adopting this code because it fosters good media relations and free publicity, and not because it is committed to the value of compassion. Needless to say, this move by Duke University will certainly bring about good publicity, as stories and discussions about Duke's new code are covered by the media.[14] However, we do not have unimpeded access to the motives and intentions of those at Duke who made this decision. Consequently, our discussions of the situation must rely on the information we are given, while at the same time we must be cognizant of other motives that might be operating. It should be noted that not all apparel labels with as wide a circulation as Duke University have taken the same steps to ensure that their clothing not be made in sweatshops. Thus, given what was said, it is at least likely that the action of Duke University stemmed from the value of compassion.

With a sensitivity to all of these concerns, it is still a fact that Duke made a decision to not have its apparel made in sweatshops.

Consequently. we can use the moral framework to analyze the reasoning of this institution Since a decision is already made, we begin with that and work backward to uncover the rules, theories, and values in operation.

Decision:

Adopt a code of conduct to ensure that Duke apparel is not made in sweatshops.

Rule:

Workers should not have to work in sweatshop conditions.
It is wrong to have exploited workers making your products.
Employers should take actions that encourage good working conditions.

Theory:

From this case, it is not completely clear what the moral perspective of Duke University is. However, it does seem that its actions were based more on being theories than doing theories. Overall, Duke seemed concerned with what a university is and the kind of institution it would like to be. Even so, in making the decision it made, it is certainly possible to interpret the actions of Duke as being concerned with consequences, duties, and rights. In what follows, we will briefly attempt to fill in the way in which Duke might have utilized moral theories from both the perspective of being and doing theories. We begin with doing theories.

Consequentialism could certainly be one of Duke's theories. Adopting a code of conduct that ensures Duke's apparel is not made in sweatshops would certainly bring about the good consequences of the workers not being exploited. Furthermore, with the additional aspect of allowing for inspections of working conditions, Duke has gone even further to bring about the good consequences implied by its rule as well as good consequences to Duke. Likewise, a duty theory also could be operative. Perhaps Duke sees that ensuring that workers have decent conditions under which to work is simply "the right thing" for a university to do. Regardless of the consequences of potentially increasing labor costs, Duke is committed to a safe workplace for those that make their apparel. On the other hand, rights theory, the last of our doing theories, also could be used.

Duke has determined that workers have certain rights, such as they should not have to work in sweatshops. In order to best uphold these rights, Duke has adopted a code that prevents these rights from being violated. All three of the doing theories provide good contexts for explaining Duke's rules and actions. Either one works well as a perspective out of which Duke could have formulated its rules and chosen how to act. However, the quoted statements sound most like a duty theory.

Next, consider how being theories could have provided the perspective out of which Duke translated values into rules and actions. Clearly, virtue theory is relevant in this instance. Duke, in adopting its code of conduct, is concerned with acting as an institution with good character. Keep in mind that an institution with good character is typically made up of people of good character. In this instance, people attempting to determine a course of action that would reflect good character determined that their institution should take action to encourage good working conditions for those that make its products. Such action would also best care for those that make Duke apparel. In encouraging good working conditions, Duke is caring well for those that make its products. Thus, the care theory could certainly be one of the ways in which Duke has come to adopt the rules that led to its actions. Finally, the narrative theory might be applicable in this case as well. As such, we might find that as a part of its history, Duke has attempted to protect those who have been exploited. In not being able to tolerate the "sweat and tears" of those who manufacture its apparel, we could see that this action by Duke is consistent with its history as an institution. Just as with the doing theories, being theories are all relevant for interpreting Duke's rules and actions, but virtue theory is especially evident in the spokesperson's statement that the institution cannot tolerate its workers' laboring in severe and unsafe working conditions. In this we are shown that the institution desires to live up to its own sense of what a good institution is.

Value:

Compassion, Respect for Persons, Beneficence and Nonmaleficence.

With an understanding of how the moral theories might have been used, we turn to the values to see what the theories are interpreting. The first value, compassion, is especially evident in this case. Duke appeals to compassion when it recognizes the suffering of workers who must labor in sweatshops. It has empathy for those workers, so much so that this shared feeling of suffering leads it to take action that alleviates the workers' poor conditions. Compassion is the underlying value that allows Duke to adopt a code that keeps products bearing the Duke name from being made in sweatshops. Thereby, Duke is acting in the best interest of its employees, namely, of those who make its apparel.

Another relevant value is respect for persons. When we determine that people should not be exploited, we are recognizing that everyone should be respected in such a manner that they need not bear excruciatingly difficult and dangerous working conditions. If Duke were to allow workers to remain in such conditions, it would be violating the Negative Rule of Respect, which requires us to not violate a person's dignity as a consequence of valuing respect for persons. Finally, the values of beneficence and nonmaleficence are relevant insofar as Duke is attempting to bring about good and prevent harm to those who make products which bear the university's name.

From this discussion, we can see the way in which a decision that demonstrates compassion is enacted by an institution. Also evident is the way in which all of our theories are relevant for interpreting compassion. Finally, in this case, compassion is closely tied to the values of respect for persons and beneficence and nonmaleficence. Rarely will we encounter a situation where one value is solely relevant to the rules and actions of moral professionals. When many values are relevant to a professional's action, sometimes there is confusion and conflict, but at other times the values together support taking a certain course of action—then we can be confident that the action we undertake is morally right.

Interpreting Compassion: Guides to Help

Now that we have seen how compassion is present in professional life, we can consider some guides that will help us interpret compassion in our own professional lives. Understandably, it is not always clear to professionals how they should act to realize this value. For example, although we all probably agree that it was a good thing for Duke University to adopt a code that prevents those that make its apparel from having to work in sweatshop conditions, we all might not agree that this is the best way for Duke to have acted on the value of compassion. What we need now is further clarity about how to act out a commitment to the value of compassion. Keep in mind that no rule can determine exactly how any value is to be acted upon, but rules can help guide our interpretation of values.

Rule of Alleviating Suffering

When confronted with the suffering of those with whom you are professionally related, work to alleviate that suffering, particularly when doing so causes you no undue moral burden.

Of course, the world would be a much better place if we all worked to alleviate suffering at all times. However, in doing so, little else would get done. We can imagine a future world, such as Star Trek, where the blights of poverty, hunger, and disease have been eliminated from earth. Yet even in the Star Trek world, professionals still have a need to alleviate suffering, particularly in the form of saving the world from unforeseen threats. So suffering of all sorts is prevalent, in greater and lesser degrees, and we do not have the abilities or resources to alleviate all suffering. However, as professionals who are committed to the value of compassion, we should work toward alleviating that suffering when confronted with the suffering of those in our professional circle.

In recognizing the suffering of another, it is incumbent upon us to have concern for those who are suffering, or at the very least, as professionals, to act with concern for those who are suffering. This concern, like the suffering, can take a variety of forms. We can take precautions to ensure safe working environments for our employees, we can support fair labor practices that affect us and our colleagues, and we can implement educational and training programs that increase relational sensitivity in our employees, employers, and colleagues. In short, we can do our work with a sensitivity to those around us that reflects our concern for their well-being.

With this rule, we recognize as a guide that we should work to alleviate suffering when it is reasonably in our power to do so, and in doing so no undue moral burdens are created. The next rule attempts to direct this alleviation of suffering. Remember, compassion is about not only sharing in a feeling of suffering, but especially about acting in the best interest of the one who is suffering. In acting in someone's best interest, we must keep the following guide in mind.

Rule of Best Interest

When acting in someone's best interest, act in his or her actual best interest, not in what you think to be his or her best interest.

Throughout history, there have been many examples of individuals who, in attempting to act in the best interest of others and as a consequence of not really appreciating the subtleties of the situation, have caused more harm than good, even when their actions stemmed from the best intentions. The extent of harm caused can be as major as that brought about by relief organizations that arrive in impoverished countries and inadvertently set up whole economies dependent upon outside aid, and as minor as a relative helping you "fix" your plumbing and ending up causing more damage than was originally there. It is important to appreciate that those who act in someone's best interest have the power to change the other person's circumstances. Such power should be handled carefully and adjudicated with a sensitivity to the circumstances. To reiterate an earlier discussion in the chapter, when attempting to determine what is in a person's best interest, ask the person. When that is impossible or unduly difficult, apply the standard of substitution. In either instance, do not act as though you alone are capable of determining what course of action expresses the best interest of those whose interests are at stake.

Conflicts Involving Compassion

To act compassionately as a moral professional it is not enough to recognize when others are suffering. We also must take action to help relieve their suffering. And since compassion must thus be translated into action, it is not surprising that conflicts will arise in its interpretation. Here we will highlight a problem in enacting compassion, a type of conflict involving compassion, and a general pitfall that can arise in interpreting compassion.

One problem that arises in interpreting compassion has to do with a difficulty we face as we attempt to respond to the suffering of others. In some instances, several persons are suffering, and the best interests of the parties compete. What is in the best interest of one person may conflict with what is in the best interest of another. What alleviates one person's suffering may contribute to the suffering of another. Returning to the circumstances faced by Rev. Giannini, we can consider his case. As you remember, in order to show compassion to his client, the teenager who spoke with him, Rev. Giannini did not feel that he could tell the teen's mother about the specifics of the discussion. Talking to the mother, in detail, would have caused the boy suffering insofar as his trust would have been betrayed. However, in not speaking to the teen's mother at all, Rev. Giannini would not have shown much compassion toward the mother, since he would have done nothing to alleviate her worries about her son, and in fact he may have contributed to those worries by staying silent.

As stated, it seems that in acting out of compassion, Rev. Giannini is facing a conflict in trying to meet the best interests of both of the parties for whom he feels compassion. Acting in the mother's best interest would violate the teen's, and vice versa. This is a potential conflict in interpreting compassion. Sometimes in meeting the best interest of those for whom we feel compassion, we are limited because of the interests of others to whom we must also act compassionately. Usually these limitations come about from our professional context. It is Rev. Giannini's job to serve his congregation, and in doing so, he exhibits compassion to both of his clients. This sometimes requires him to modify his compassionate response to one person in order to be able to respond compassionately to another. Rev. Giannini did this, as you recall, by letting the mother know that he talked with her son, while not disclosing any of the details of the discussion.

From the conflict faced by Rev. Giannini, we can further understand one of the primary conflicts in interpreting compassion. Often we will not be able to accomplish as much action in the best interest of others as we would like, or as the situation may require. It is important to note that when we act in the best interest of those who are suffering, there are typically many demands placed upon us as well, that is, there are other values to which we are committed. In the face of this difficulty, it is important that we not stop acting compassionately but remain steadfast in our commitment to compassion, even if the results that our commitment elicits are less than we would hope for. In short, acting in someone's best interest is typically not accomplished with one action; suffering is not usually eliminated in one isolated moment.

Another problem that can arise when interpreting compassion is not an actual conflict but instead a pitfall. Sometimes compassion can be confused with pity or sympathy. That is, you can feel badly for someone and sympathize with them or feel pity for them, though you do not do anything about their suffering. Without the attempt to alleviate suffering, we are no longer dealing with the value of compassion. Think of the way in which we are all guilty of walking by those who suffer on the busy streets of our cities, or the way in which we just change channels as the suffering of the world is presented to us in our living rooms. This could have been the response of those in charge of apparel at Duke University. These individuals could have been horrified by the conditions that workers were forced to endure, without attempting to change those conditions. But they were not. When faced with the knowledge of the difficult and dangerous conditions faced by those who made its apparel, Duke attempted to change the situation. It enacted compassion; it did not just sympathize or pity others.

In considering these problems and conflicts involving compassion, we should be both encouraged and somewhat daunted. We should be encouraged to remain committed, not only to recognizing suffering but to alleviating it. We should be daunted as we recognize the difficulties in responding to all of those who suffer in our professional circles, and in reconciling compassion to other values, such as justice and responsibility. These daunting conditions should not paralyze us, however, since the realization of any moral value takes thoughtful reflection and careful consideration.

Conclusion

In this chapter, we defined and interpreted the value of compassion. Compassion is a value that is expressed through the relationships we encounter in our professional lives. We exhibit it as we deal with our employers and employees, our colleagues, and the clients we serve. In exhibiting compassion, we not only feel the suffering of others, but attempt to do something about it through acting to further the best interest of those in need. Compassion is realized by using the Rule of Alleviating Suffering and the Rule of Best Interest. Interpreting the best interest of those in need is complicated, and when it cannot be discovered through asking someone "How can I help?" we are to apply the standard of substitution. This standard requires that we use our imaginations to put ourselves in the situation of the one who is suffering and determine how we would like to be treated in similar circumstances. Overall, compassion requires us to maintain an absolute commitment to this value, while at the same time maintain an acute sensitivity to the circumstances affecting the way in which it is actualized.

EXERCISES

1. Take the code of ethics for your proposed occupation. If you are uncertain about your career, pick any code. Consider the following:

   1. Is there an explicit or implicit appeal to compassion contained in the code? Explain, using specific examples.
   2. Define "best interest" relative to the way it is used in the code of ethics for your proposed occupation. In doing so, demonstrate the way in which it is relevant for relationships between employers and employees, colleagues, and between employees and the clients they serve.
   3. In this code, what specific requirements must the professional meet because of the value of compassion? Does this code include any more specific requirements of compassion that have not been mentioned in this chapter, or any other relationships in which the professional must exhibit compassion?
   4. For the professionals covered by this code, do you foresee any potential problems or conflicts they might face in acting on the value of compassion? Give three examples and explain each.

2. Use the CRM to reach a decision in each of these cases, or if a decision has already been reached, use the framework for moral analysis to analyze the case. In doing so, consider all of the relevant values but be especially alert to considerations of compassion and its requirements. Be sure to explain your answers fully.

CASE 1: WELFARE TO WORK

As a consequence of the new welfare policy, a national grocery store chain has started to hire individuals whose welfare benefits will soon run out. The chain has targeted women who are single mothers. The job program they have developed provides basic life skills training, for example, how to create a budget, as well as normal on-the-job training. The program has received funding from the city, which covers the losses incurred from the extra time spent training these employees. This funding will run out in approximately three months.

You are in charge of the program and have been amazed at the quality of work accomplished by these individuals. After their training, which is expensive and extensive, 80 percent of the employees remain with your company and are as good as, if not better than, the employees who are hired and trained by traditional methods. The employees hired under this program have a loyalty to their work that the traditional employees lack. When the funding runs out, it is up to you to determine whether the training program will continue or if it will cease and women who are losing their welfare benefits will not be hired. What will you do and why?

CASE 2: TO GRADE OR NOT TO GRADE?

You are a teacher at a medium-sized, moderately competitive university. In one of your classes, a student has received an "F" on the midterm. This student runs track and has had to miss several classes because of a successful season. Each of these absences has been excused. Upon returning the grade to the student, you receive a phone call from her athletic advisor, who asks you about the student's performance in class. You explain that the student is of average ability and would be doing fine in the class if she attended regularly, but since she has had to miss so many classes because of a successful season, her grade has been compromised.

The advisor explains to you that this student would not be able to attend college if she were not on athletic scholarship. She must remain eligible for competition if she is to remain on scholarship. This requires grades of at least a "D" at midterm and a "C" in the course. At the student's request, the advisor asks if you would schedule a make-up exam for the student. What do you do?

CASE 3: BUILDING PROFITS AND BUILDING COMMUNITY

A specialty bicycle manufacturer has set up operations in the low-rent district of a major metropolitan area. In the vicinity of its organization are several public housing developments. Poverty and crime are a major concern in the area, particularly for families with children. Due to its low overhead and the boom in the bicycle business, this company has increased profits by 200 percent over the last two years. Now that it is in a more secure financial position, it has decided to give something back to the community in which it operates. Once a week, on Friday afternoons, it opens up its testing track to the children of the community. For several hours a week, it pulls out all of its old prototypes and lets the children ride them around the track. Employees take turns volunteering, since many of the children have never ridden a bicycle and must be taught how. The employees enjoy horsing around with the kids, the parents are happy to have their children in a safe environment, and the kids think the whole experience is great. As an unexpected benefit, vandalism and graffiti occurring on the company's premises has dropped dramatically since the program began.

NOTES

1. References on the etymology of compassion are from *Webster's New World Dictionary of the American Language*, Second College Edition (New York: Simon and Schuster, 1984), 289.

2.   Ibid.

3.   We will return to this sort of a conflict in interpreting compassion at the end of the chapter.

4.   A more detailed discussion of paternalism takes place in chapter 11. There, through our discussion of the values of beneficence and nonmaleficence, we see how paternalism can be particularly insidious.

5.   Preamble, *NASW Code of Ethics*, National Association of Social Workers, Inc., copyright © 1980.

6.   Section II, The Social Worker's Ethical Responsibility to Clients, F-8, *NASW Code of Ethics*.

7.   Section II, The Social Worker's Ethical Responsibility to Clients, F-10, *NASW Code of Ethics*.

8.   Section II, The Social Worker's Ethical Responsibility to Clients, F-11, *NASW Code of Ethics*.

9.   Section III, The Social Worker's Ethical Responsibility to Colleagues, J-3, *NASW Code of Ethics*.

10.   Section III, The Social Worker's Ethical Responsibility to Colleagues, J-10, *NASW Code of Ethics*.

11.   Section III, The Social Worker's Ethical Responsibility to Employers and Employing Organizations, L and L-3, (respectively), *NASW Code of Ethics*.

12.   Principle 1, *Principles of Medical Ethics*, American Medical Association.

13.   Steven Greenhouse, "Duke to Adopt a Code to Prevent Apparel From Being Made in Sweatshops," *New York Times*, March 8, 1998, Section 1, 13.

14.   The irony of the fact that a discussion of this situation in the present text is generating still more good publicity for Duke University is not lost on the authors.

Introduction

This group of readings focuses especially on how a moral professional translates the values of justice and compassion into action. The first selection, *Harrison Bergeron*, a short story by Kurt Vonnegut, set in 2081, concerns a couple and their wayward son. As the story develops, it comes to include not just a family but news announcers, ballerinas, and musicians. In this way, the ethical questions raised are especially pertinent to professionals practicing their occupations. The story raises questions about what is fair and what is meant by equality, while also considering the issues of competition among professionals and the role of the government in regulating professionals. Vonnegut's depiction of the future may cause you to question how justice ought to be interpreted, or it may lead you to wonder whether values such as compassion and respect for persons are more important than justice.

The second reading by Lisa H. Newton is the essay, "Reverse Discrimination As Unjustified," which raises the practical question of the morality of reverse discrimination. The question is: Should we use reverse discrimination to make up for the wrongs of previous discrimination? In reverse discrimination, those who were formerly discriminated against are now given special opportunities and benefits, with the result that others are then denied these opportunities and benefits. Reverse discrimination, however, is not the only way of addressing the claims of those who were treated unjustly. We also could consider preferential treatment, affirmative action, and quota hiring. Not all of these responses necessarily deny opportunities to others in the process of redressing past injustices. Newton focuses on reverse discrimination and looks to Aristotle and to the meanings of the terms *justice* and *equality* for an answer to the question. In doing so, she reaches a conclusion about the morality of society's and even an individual's decision to practice reverse discrimination.

The third selection, *Justifying Reverse Discrimination in Employment*, by George Sher, also addresses reverse discrimination, especially in employment practices. He offers a way of understanding compensatory justice, which he believes avoids the problems associated with previous attempts to justify reverse discrimination. He defines justice and works to understand how it is to be applied in a world where people do not have equal access to social goods and opportunities, such as education and food. Even though Newton and Sher reach different conclusions about the morality of reverse discrimination, both adopt the same strategy. They attempt to clarify justice and to consider the consequences of acting on a commitment to this value.

Finally, the fourth reading, *Compassion*, by Lawrence Blum, considers what compassion is, what it implies, and how it operates. In brief, compassion involves imaginatively dwelling on the negative condition of another person and having an active regard for the good of that other person. Blum goes on to explain that compassion is related to other values, such as justice and beneficence. This helps remind us that our enacting of any one value is always done in the context of our commitment to all of the values. Just as Vonnegut's story raises questions about the limits of justice, so Blum's article looks at the limits of compassion. As professionals, we need to consider when compassion is appropriate and how far we should go in showing compassion.

These readings will aid you as you establish your own views of how to enact justice and compassion. You may never be called on to develop a policy on preferential hiring, or to attach the handicap radios to those with advantages, but you will need to act justly and compassionately toward others in your professional life. Although the interpretations of justice and compassion may be various and occasionally may even seem to compete, practicing these values at work is a crucial part of being a moral professional.

Harrison Bergeron

Kurt Vonnegut

The year was 2081, and everybody was finally equal. They weren't only equal before God and the law. They were equal every which way. Nobody was smarter than anybody else. Nobody was better looking than anybody else. Nobody was stronger or quicker than anybody else. All this equality was due to the 211th, 212th, and 213th Amendments to the Constitution, and to the unceasing vigilance of agents of the United States Handicapper General.

Some things about living still weren't quite right, though. April, for instance, still drove people crazy by not being springtime. And it was in that clammy month that the H-G men took George and Hazel Bergeron's fourteen-year-old son, Harrison, away.

It was tragic, all right, but George and Hazel couldn't think about it very hard. Hazel had a perfectly average intelligence, which meant she couldn't think about anything except in short bursts. And George, while his intelligence was way above normal, had a little mental handicap radio in his ear. He was required by law to wear it at all times. It was tuned to a government transmitter. Every twenty seconds or so, the transmitter would send out some sharp noise to keep people like George from taking unfair advantage of their brains.

George and Hazel were watching television. There were tears on Hazel's cheeks, but she'd forgotten for the moment what they were about.

On the television screen were ballerinas.

A buzzer sounded in George's head. His thoughts fled in panic, like bandits from a burglar alarm.

"That was a real pretty dance, that dance they just did," said Hazel.

"Huh?" said George.

"That dance—it was nice," said Hazel.

"Yup," said George. He tried to think a little about the ballerinas. They weren't really very good—no better than anybody else would have been, anyway. They were burdened with sashweights and bags of birdshot, and their faces were masked, so that no one, seeing a free and graceful gesture or a pretty face, would feel like something the cat drug in. George was toying with the vague notion that maybe dancers shouldn't be handicapped. But he didn't get very far with it before another noise in his ear radio scattered his thoughts.

George winced. So did two out of the eight ballerinas.

Hazel saw him wince. Having no mental handicap herself, she had to ask George what the latest sound had been.

"Sounded like somebody hitting a milk bottle with a ball peen hammer," said George.

"I'd think it would be real interesting, hearing all the different sounds," said Hazel, a little envious. "All the things they think up."

"Um," said George.

"Only, if I was Handicapper General, you know what I would do?" said Hazel. Hazel, as a matter of fact, bore a strong resemblance to the Handicapper General, a woman named Diana Moon Glampers. "If I was Diana Moon Glampers," said Hazel, "I'd have chimes on Sunday—just chimes. Kind of in honor of religion."

"I could think, if it was just chimes," said George.

"Well—maybe make 'em real loud," said Hazel. "I think I'd make a good Handicapper General."

"Good as anybody else," said George.

"Who knows better'n I do what normal is?" said Hazel.

"Right," said George. He began to think glimmeringly about his abnormal son who was now in jail, about Harrison, but a twenty-one-gun salute in his head stopped that.

"Boy!" said Hazel, "that was a doozy, wasn't it?"

It was such a doozy that George was white and trembling, and tears stood on the rims of his red eyes. Two of the eight ballerinas had collapsed to the studio floor [and] were holding their temples.

"All of a sudden you look so tired," said Hazel. "Why don't you stretch out on the sofa, so's you can rest your handicap bag on the pillows, honeybunch." She was referring to the forty-seven pounds of birdshot in a canvas bag, which was padlocked around George's neck. "Go on and rest the bag for a little while," she said. "I don't care if you're not equal to me for a while."

George weighed the bag with his hands. "I don't mind it," he said. "I don't notice it any more. It's just a part of me."

"You been so tired lately—kind of wore out," said Hazel. "If there was just some way we could make a little hole in the bottom of the bag, and just take out a few of them lead balls. Just a few."

"Two years in prison and two thousand dollars fine for every ball I took out," said George. "I don't call that a bargain."

"If you could just take a few out when you came home from work," said Hazel. "I mean—you don't compete with anybody around here. You just set around."

"If I tried to get away with it," said George, "then other people'd get away with it—and pretty soon we'd be right back to the dark ages again, with everybody competing against everybody else. You wouldn't like that, would you?"

"I'd hate it," said Hazel.

"There you are," said George. "The minute people start cheating on laws, what do you think happens to society?"

If Hazel hadn't been able to come up with an answer to this question, George couldn't have supplied one. A siren was going off in his head.

"Reckon it'd fall all apart," said Hazel.

"What would?" said George blankly.

"Society," said Hazel uncertainly. "Wasn't that what you just said?"

"Who knows?" said George.

The television program was suddenly interrupted for a news bulletin. It wasn't clear at first as to what the bulletin was about, since the announcer, like all announcers, had a serious speech impediment. For about half a minute, and in a state of high excitement, the announcer tried to say, "Ladies and gentlemen—"

He finally gave up [and] handed the bulletin to a ballerina to read.

"That's all right—" Hazel said of the announcer, "he tried. That's the big thing. He tried to do the best he could with what God gave him. He should get a nice raise for trying so hard."

"Ladies and gentlemen—" said the ballerina, reading the bulletin. She must have been extraordinarily beautiful, because the mask she wore was hideous. And it was easy to see that she was the strongest and most graceful of all the dancers, for her handicap bags were as big as those worn by two-hundred-pound men.

And she had to apologize at once for her voice, which was a very unfair voice for a woman to use. Her voice was a warm, luminous, time-less melody. "Excuse me—" she said, and she began again, making her voice absolutely uncompetitive.

"Harrison Bergeron, age fourteen," she said in a grackle squawk, "has just escaped from jail, where he was held on suspicion of plotting to overthrow the government. He is a genius and an athlete, is under-handicapped, and should be regarded as extremely dangerous."

A police photograph of Harrison Bergeron was flashed on the screen—upside down, then sideways, upside down again, then right side up. The picture showed the full length of Harrison against a back-ground calibrated in feet and inches. He was exactly seven feet tall.

The rest of Harrison's appearance was Halloween and hardware. Nobody had ever born heavier handicaps. He had outgrown hindrances faster than the H-G men could think them up. Instead of a little ear radio for a mental handicap, he wore a tremendous pair of earphones, and spectacles with thick wavy lenses. The spectacles were intended to make him not only half blind, but to give him whanging headaches besides.

Scrap metal was hung all over him. Ordinarily, there was a cer-tain symmetry, a military neatness to the handicaps issued to strong people, but Harrison looked like a walking junkyard. In the race of life, Harrison carried three hundred pounds.

And to offset his good looks, the H-G men required that he wear at all times a red rubber ball for a nose, keep his eyebrows shaved off, and cover his even white teeth with black caps at snaggle-tooth random.

"If you see this boy," said the ballerina, "do not—I repeat, do not—try to reason with him."

There was the shriek of a door being torn from its hinges.

Screams and barking cries of consternation came from the televi-sion set. The photograph of Harrison Bergeron on the screen jumped again and again, as though dancing to the tune of an earthquake.

George Bergeron correctly identified the earthquake, and well he might have—for many was the time his own home had danced to the same crashing tune. "My God—" said George, "that must be Harrison!"

The realization was blasted from his mind instantly by the sound of an automobile collision in his head.

When George could open his eyes again, the photograph of Harri-son was gone. A living, breathing Harrison filled the screen.

Clanking, clownish, and huge, Harrison stood in the center of the studio. The knob of the uprooted studio door was still in his hand. Bal-lerinas, technicians, musicians, and announcers cowered on their knees before him, expecting to die.

"I am the Emperor!" cried Harrison. "Do you hear? I am the Emperor! Everybody must do what I say at once!" He stamped his foot and the studio shook.

"Even as I stand here—" he bellowed, "crippled, hobbled, sickened—I am a greater ruler than any man who ever lived! Now watch me become what I *can* become!"

Harrison tore the straps of his handicap harness like wet tissue paper, tore straps guaranteed to support five thousand pounds.

Harrison's scrap-iron handicaps crashed to the floor.

Harrison thrust his thumbs under the bar of the padlock that secured his head harness. The bar snapped like celery. Harrison smashed his headphones and spectacles against the wall.

He flung away his rubber-ball nose, revealed a man that would have awed Thor, the god of thunder.

"I shall now select my Empress!" he said, looking down on the cowering people. "Let the first woman who dares rise to her feet claim her mate and her throne!"

A moment passed, and then a ballerina arose, swaying like a willow.

Harrison plucked the mental handicap from her ear, snapped off her physical handicaps with marvelous delicacy. Last of all, he removed her mask.

She was blindingly beautiful.

"Now—" said Harrison, taking her hand, "shall we show the people the meaning of the word dance? Music!" he commanded.

The musicians scrambled back into their chairs, and Harrison stripped them of their handicaps, too. "Play your best," he told them, "and I'll make you barons and dukes and earls."

The music began. It was normal at first—cheap, silly, false. But Harrison snatched two musicians from their chairs, waved them like batons as he sang the music as he wanted it played. He slammed them back into their chairs.

The music began again and was much improved.

Harrison and his Empress merely listened to the music for a while—listened gravely, as though synchronizing their heartbeats with it.

They shifted their weights to their toes.

Harrison placed his big hands on the girl's tiny waist, letting her sense the weightlessness that would soon be hers.

And then, in an explosion of joy and grace, into the air they sprang!

Not only were the laws of the land abandoned, but the law of gravity and the laws of motion as well.

They reeled, whirled, swiveled, flounced, capered, gamboled, and spun.

They leaped like deer on the moon.

The studio ceiling was thirty feet high, but each leap brought the dancers nearer to it.

It became their obvious intention to kiss the ceiling.

They kissed it.

And then, neutralizing gravity with love and pure will, they remained suspended in air inches below the ceiling, and they kissed each other for a long, long time.

It was then that Diana Moon Glampers, the Handicapper General, came into the studio with a double-barreled ten-gauge shotgun. She fired twice, and the Emperor and the Empress were dead before they hit the floor.

Diana Moon Glampers loaded the gun again. She aimed it at the musicians and told them they had ten seconds to get their handicaps back on.

It was then that the Bergerons' television tube burned out.

Hazel turned to comment about the blackout to George. But George had gone out into the kitchen for a can of beer.

George came back in with the beer, paused while a handicap signal shook him up. And then he sat down again. "You been crying?" he said to Hazel.

"Yup," she said.

"What about?" he said.

"I forget," she said. "Something real sad on television."

"What was it?" he said.

"It's all kind of mixed up in my mind," said Hazel.

"Forget sad things," said George.

"I always do," said Hazel.

"That's my girl," said George. He winced. There was the sound of a riveting gun in his head.

"Gee—I could tell that one was a doozy," said Hazel.

"You can say that again," said George.

"Gee—" said Hazel, "I could tell that one was a doozy."

Reverse Discrimination As Unjustified

LISA H. NEWTON

I have heard it argued that "simple justice" requires that we favor women and blacks in employment and educational opportunities, since women and blacks were "unjustly" excluded from such opportunities for so many years in the not so distant past. It is a strange argument, an example of a possible implication of a true proposition advanced to dispute the proposition itself, like an octopus absentmindedly slicing off his head with a stray tentacle. A fatal confusion underlies this argument, a confusion fundamentally relevant to our understanding of the notion of the rule of law.

Two senses of justice and equality are involved in this confusion. The root notion of justice, progenitor of the other, is the one that Aristotle (*Nichomachean Ethics* 5.6; *Politics* 1.2; 3.1) assumes to be the foundation and proper virtue of the political association. It is the condition which free men establish among themselves when they "share a common life in order that their association bring them self-sufficiency"—the regulation of their relationship by law, and the establishment, by law, of equality before the law. Rule of law is the name and pattern of this justice; its equality stands against the inequalities—of wealth, talent, etc.—otherwise obtaining among its participants, who by virtue of that equality are called "citizens." It is an achievement—complete, or, more, frequently, partial—of certain people in certain concrete situations. It is fragile and easily disrupted by powerful individuals who discover that the blind equality of rule of law is inconvenient for their interests. Despite its obvious instability, Aristotle assumed that the establishment of justice in this sense, the creation of citizenship, was a permanent possibility for men and that the resultant association of citizens was the natural home of the species. At levels below the political association, this rule-governed equality is easily found; it is exemplified by any group of children agreeing together to play a game. At the level of the political association, the attainment of this justice is more difficult, simply because the stakes are so much higher for each participant. The equality of citizenship is not something that happens of its own accord, and without the expenditure of a fair amount of effort it will collapse into the rule of a powerful few over an apathetic many. But at least it has been achieved, at some times in some places; it is always worth trying to achieve, and eminently worth trying to maintain, wherever and to whatever degree it has been brought into being.

Aristotle's parochialism is notorious, he really did not imagine that persons other than Greeks could associate freely in justice, and the only form of association he had in mind was the Greek *polis*. With the decline of the *polis* and the shift in the center of political thought, his notion of justice underwent a sea change. To be exact, it ceased to represent a political type and became a moral ideal: the ideal of equality as we know it. This ideal demands that all men be included in citizenship—that one Law govern all equally, that all men regard all other men as fellow citizens, with the same guarantees, rights, and protections. Briefly, it demands that the circle of citizenship achieved by any group be extended to include the entire human race. Properly understood, its effect on our associations can be excellent: it congratulates us on our achievement of rule of law as a process of government but refuses to let us remain complacent until we have expanded the associations to include others within the ambit of the rules, as often and as far as possible. While one man is a slave, none of us may feel truly free.

We are constantly prodded by this ideal to look for possible unjustifiable discrimination, for inequalities not absolutely required for the functioning of the society and advantageous to all. And after twenty centuries of pressure, not at all constant, from this ideal, it might be said that some progress has been made. To take the cases in point for this problem, we are now prepared to assert, as Aristotle would never have been, the equality of sexes and of persons of different colors. The ambit of American citizenship, once restricted to white males of property, has been extended to include all adult free men, then all adult males including ex-slaves, then all women. The process of acquisition of full citizenship was for these groups a sporadic trail of half-measures, even now not complete: the steps on the road to full equality are marked by legislation and judicial decisions which are only recently concluded and still often not enforced. But the fact that we can now discuss the possibility of favoring such groups in hiring shows that over the area that concerns us, at least, full equality is presupposed as a basis for discussion. To that extent, they are full citizens, fully protected by the law of the land.

It is important for my argument that the moral ideal of equality be recognized as logically distinct from the condition (or virtue) of justice in the political sense. Justice in this sense exists *among* a citizenry, irrespective of the number of the populace included in that citizenry. Further, the moral ideal is parasitic upon the political virtue, for "equality" is unspecified—it means nothing until we are told in what respect that equality is to be realized. In a political context, "equality" is specified as "equal rights"—equal access to the public realm, public goods and offices, equal treatment under the law—in brief, the equality of citizenship. If citizenship is not a possibility, political equality is unintelligible. The ideal emerges as a generalization of the real condition and refers back to that condition for its content.

Now, if justice (Aristotle's justice in the political sense) is equal treatment under law for all citizens, what is injustice? Clearly, injustice is the violation of that equality, discriminating for or against a group of citizens, favoring them with special immunities and privileges or depriving them of those guaranteed to the others. When the southern employer refuses to hire blacks in white-collar jobs, when Wall Street will only hire women as secretaries with new titles, when Mississippi high schools routinely flunk all black boys above ninth grade, we have examples of injustice, and we work to restore the equality of the public realm by ensuring that equal opportunity will be provided in such cases in the future. But of course, when the employers and the schools *favor* women and blacks, the same injustice is done. Just as the previous discrimination did, this reverse discrimination violates the public equality which defines citizenship and destroys the rule of law for the areas in which these favors are granted. To the extent that we adopt a program of discrimination, reverse or otherwise, justice in the political sense is destroyed, and none of us, specifically affected or not, is a citizen, a bearer of rights—we are all petitioners for favors. And to the same extent, the ideal of equality is undermined, for it has content only where justice obtains, and by destroying justice we render the ideal meaningless. It is, then, an ironic paradox, if not a contradiction in terms, to assert that the ideal of equality justifies the violation of justice; it is as if one should argue, with William Buckley, that an ideal of humanity can justify the destruction of the human race.

Logically, the conclusion is simple enough: all discrimination is wrong prima facie because it violates justice, and that goes for reverse discrimination too. No violation of justice among the citizens may be justified (may overcome the prima facie objection) by appeal to the ideal of equality, for that ideal is logically dependent upon the notion of justice. Reverse discrimination, then, which attempts no other justification than an appeal to equality, is wrong. But let us try to make the conclusion more plausible by suggesting some of the implications of the suggested practice of reverse discrimination in employment and education. My argument will be that the problems raised there are insoluble, not only in practice but in principle.

We may argue, if we like, about what "discrimination" consists of. Do I discriminate against blacks if I admit none to my school when none of the black applicants are qualified by the tests I always give? How far must I go to root out cultural bias from my application forms and tests before I can say that I have not discriminated against those of different cultures? Can I assume that women are not strong enough to be roughnecks on my oil rigs, or must I test them individually? But this controversy, the most popular and well-argued aspect of the issue, is not as fatal as two others which cannot be avoided: if we are regarding the blacks as a "minority" victimized by discrimination, what is a "minority"? And for any group—blacks, women, whatever—that has been discriminated against, what amount of reverse discrimination wipes out the initial discrimination? Let us grant as true that women and blacks were discriminated against, even where laws forbade such discrimination, and grant for the sake of argument that a history of discrimination must be wiped out by reverse discrimination. What follows?

First, are there other groups which have been discriminated against? For they should have the same right of restitution. What about American Indians, Chicanos, Appalachian Mountain whites, Puerto Ricans, Jews, Cajuns, and Orientals? And if these are to be included, the principle according to which we specify a "minority" is simply the criterion of "ethnic (sub) group," and we're stuck with every hyphenated American in the lower-middle class clamoring for special privileges for *his* group—and with equal justification. For be it noted, when we run down the Harvard roster, we find not only a scarcity of blacks (in comparison with the proportion in the population) but an even more striking scarcity of those second-, third-, and fourth-generation ethnics who make up the loudest voice of Middle America. Shouldn't they demand *their* share? And eventually, the WASPs will have to form their own lobby, for they too are a minority. The point is simply this: there is no "majority" in America who will not mind giving up just a bit of their rights to make room for a favored minority. There are only other minorities, each of which is discriminated against by the favoring. The initial injustice is then repeated dozens of times, and if each minority is granted the same right of restitution as the others, an entire area of rule governance is dissolved into a pushing and shoving match between self-interested groups. Each works to catch the public eye and political popularity by whatever means of advertising and power politics lend themselves to the effort, to capitalize as much as possible on temporary popularity until the restless mob picks another group to feel sorry for. Hardly an edifying spectacle, and in the long run no one can benefit: the pie is no larger—it's just that instead of setting up and enforcing rules for getting a piece, we've turned the contest into a free-for-all, requiring much more effort for no larger a reward. It would be in the interests of all the participants to reestablish an objective rule to govern the process, carefully enforced and the same for all.

Second, supposing that we do manage to agree in general that women and blacks (and all the others) have some right of restitution, some right to a privileged place in the structure of opportunities for a while, how will we know when that while is up? How much privilege is enough? When will the guilt be gone, the price paid, the balance restored? What recompense is right for centuries of exclusion? What criterion tells us when we are done? Our experience with the Civil Rights movement shows us that agreement on these terms cannot be presupposed: a process that appears to some to be going at a mad gallop into a black takeover appears to the rest of us to be at a standstill. Should a practice of reverse discrimination be adopted, we may safely predict that just as some of us begin to see "a satisfactory start toward righting the balance," others of us will see that we "have already gone too far in the other direction" and will suggest that the discrimination ought to be reversed again. And such disagreement is inevitable, for the point is that we could not *possibly* have any criteria for evaluating the kind of recompense we have in mind. The context presumed by any discussion of restitution is the context of rule of law: law sets the rights of men and simultaneously sets the method for remedying the violation of those rights. You may exact suffering from others and/or damage payments for yourself if and only if the others have violated your rights; the suffering you have endured is not sufficient reason for them to suffer. And remedial rights exist only where there is law: primary human rights are useful guides to legislation but cannot stand as reasons for awarding remedies for injuries sustained. But then, the context presupposed by any discussion of restitution is the context of preexistent full citizenship. No remedial rights could exist for the excluded; neither in law nor in logic does there exist a right to *sue* for a standing to sue.

From these two considerations, then, the difficulties with reverse discrimination become evident. Restitution for a disadvantaged group whose rights under the law have been violated is possible by legal means, but restitution for a disadvantaged group whose grievance is that there was no law to protect them simply is not. First, outside of the area of justice defined by the law, no sense can be made of "the group's rights," for no law recognizes that group or the individuals in it, qua members, as bearers of rights (hence *any* group can constitute itself as a disadvantaged minority in some sense and demand similar restitution). Second, outside of the area of protection of law, no sense can be made of the violation of rights (hence the amount of the recompense cannot be decided by any objective criterion). For both reasons, the practice of reverse discrimination undermines the foundation of the very ideal in whose name it is advocated; it destroys justice, law, equality, and citizenship itself, and replaces them with power struggles and popularity contests.

Justifying Reverse Discrimination in Employment

GEORGE SHER

A currently favored way of compensating for past discrimination is to afford preferential treatment to the members of those groups which have been discriminated against in the past. I propose to examine the rationale behind this practice when it is applied in the area of employment. I want to ask whether, and if so under what conditions, past acts of discrimination against members of a particular group justify the current hiring of a member of that group who is less than the best qualified applicant for a given job. Since I am mainly concerned about exploring the relations between past discrimination and present claims to employment, I shall make the assumption that each applicant is at least minimally competent to perform the job he seeks; this will eliminate the need to consider the claims of those who are to receive the services in question. Whether it is ever justifiable to discriminate in favor of an incompetent applicant, or a less than best qualified applicant for a job such as teaching, in which almost any increase in employee competence brings a real increase in services rendered, will be left to be decided elsewhere. Such questions, which turn on balancing the claim of the less than best qualified applicant against the competing claims of those who are to receive his services, are not as basic as the question of whether the less than best qualified applicant ever *has* a claim to employment.[1]

I

It is sometimes argued, when members of a particular group have been barred from employment of a certain kind, that since this group has in the past received less than its fair share of the employment in question, it now deserves to receive more by way of compensation.[2] This argument, if sound, has the virtue of showing clearly why preferential treatment should be extended even to those current group members who have not themselves been denied employment: if the point of reverse discrimination is to compensate a wronged *group*, it will presumably hardly matter if those who are preferentially hired were not among the original victims of discrimination. However, the argument's basic presupposition, that groups as opposed to their individual members are the sorts of entities that can be wronged and deserve redress, is itself problematic.[3] Thus the defense of reverse discrimination would only be convincing if it were backed by a further argument showing that groups can indeed be wronged and have deserts of the relevant sort. No one, as far as I know, has yet produced a powerful argument to this effect, and I am not hopeful about the possibilities. Therefore I shall not try to develop a defense of reverse discrimination along these lines.

Another possible way of connecting past acts of discrimination in hiring with the claims of current group members is to argue that even if these current group members have not (yet) been denied *employment*, their membership in the group makes it very likely that they have been discriminatorily deprived of *other* sorts of goods. It is a commonplace, after all, that people who are forced to do menial and low-paying jobs must often endure corresponding privations in housing, diet, and other areas. These privations are apt to be distributed among young and old alike, and so to afflict even those group members who are still too young to have had their qualifications for employment bypassed. It is, moreover, generally acknowledged by both common sense and law that a person who has been deprived of a certain amount of one sort of good may sometimes reasonably be compensated by an equivalent amount of a good of another sort. (It is this principle, surely, that underlies the legal practice of awarding sums of money to compensate for pain incurred in accidents, damaged reputations, etc.) Given these facts and this principle, it appears that the preferential hiring of current members of discriminated-against groups may be justified as compensation for the *other* sorts of discrimination these individuals are apt to have suffered.[4]

But, although this argument seems more promising than one presupposing group deserts, it surely cannot be accepted as it stands. For one thing, insofar as the point is simply to compensate individuals for the various sorts of privations they have suffered, there is no special reason to use reverse discrimination rather than some other mechanism to effect compensation. There are, moreover, certain other mechanisms of redress which seem prima facie preferable. It seems, for instance, that it would be most appropriate to compensate for past privations simply by making preferentially available to the discriminated-against individuals equivalent amounts of the very same sorts of goods of which they have been deprived; simple cash settlements would allow a far greater precision in the adjustment of compensation to privation than reverse discriminatory hiring ever could. Insofar as it does not provide any reason to adopt reverse discrimination rather than these prima facie preferable mechanisms of redress, the suggested defense of reverse discrimination is at least incomplete.

Moreover, and even more important, if reverse discrimination is viewed simply as a form of compensation for past privations, there are serious questions about its fairness. Certainly the privations to be compensated for are not the sole responsibility of those individuals whose superior qualifications will have to be bypassed in the reverse discriminatory process. These individuals, if responsible for those privations at all, will at least be no more responsible than others with relevantly similar histories. Yet reverse discrimination will compensate for the privations in question at the expense of these individuals alone. It will have no effect at all upon those other, equally responsible persons whose qualifications are inferior to begin with, who are already entrenched in their jobs, or whose vocations are noncompetitive in nature. Surely it is unfair to distribute the burden of compensation so unequally.[5]

These considerations show, I think, that reverse discriminatory hiring of members of groups that have been denied jobs in the past cannot be justified simply by the fact that each group member has been discriminated against in other areas. If this fact is to enter into the justification of reverse discrimination at all, it must be in some more complicated way.

II

Consider again the sorts of privations that are apt to be distributed among the members of those groups restricted in large part to menial and low-paying jobs. These individuals, we said, are apt to live in substandard homes, to subsist on improper and imbalanced diets, and to receive inadequate educations. Now, it is certainly true that adequate housing, food, and education are goods in and of themselves; a life without them is certainly less pleasant and less full than one with them. But, and crucially, they are also goods in a different sense entirely. It is an obvious and well-documented fact that (at least) the sorts of nourishment and education a person receives as a child will causally affect the sorts of skills and capacities he will have as an adult—including, of course, the very skills which are needed if he is to compete on equal terms for jobs and other goods. Since this is so, a child who is deprived of adequate food and education may lose not only the immediate enjoyments which a comfortable and stimulating environment bring but also the subsequent ability to compete equally for other things of intrinsic value. But to lose this ability to compete is, in essence, to lose one's access to the goods that are being competed for; and this, surely, is itself a privation to be compensated for if possible. It is, I think, the key to an adequate justification of reverse discrimination to see that practice, not as the redressing of *past* privations, but rather as a way of neutralizing the *present* competitive disadvantage *caused* by those past privations and thus as a way of restoring equal access to those goods which society distributes competitively.[6] When reverse discrimination is justified in this way, many of the difficulties besetting the simpler justification of it disappear.

For whenever someone has been irrevocably deprived of a certain good and there are several alternative ways of providing him with an equivalent amount of another good, it will *ceteris paribus* be preferable to choose whichever substitute comes closest to actually replacing the lost good. It is this principle that makes preferential access to decent housing, food, and education especially desirable as a way of compensating for the experiential impoverishment of a deprived childhood. If, however, we are concerned to compensate not for the experiential poverty, but for the effects of childhood deprivations, then this principle tells just as heavily for reverse discrimination as the proper form of compensation. If the lost good is just the *ability* to compete on equal terms for first-level goods like desirable jobs, then surely the most appropriate (and so preferable) way of substituting for what has been lost is just to remove the *necessity* of competing on equal terms for these goods—which, of course, is precisely what reverse discrimination does.

When reverse discrimination is viewed as compensation for lost ability to compete on equal terms, a reasonable case can also be made for its fairness. Our doubts about its fairness arose because it seemed to place the entire burden of redress upon those individuals whose superior qualifications are bypassed in the reverse discriminatory process. This seemed wrong because these individuals are, of course, not apt to be any more responsible for past discrimination than others with relevantly similar histories. But, as we are now in a position to see, this objection misses the point. The crucial fact about these individuals is not that they are more *responsible* for past discrimination than others with relevantly similar histories (in fact, the dirty work may well have been done before any of their generation attained the age of responsibility), but rather that unless reverse discrimination is practiced, they will *benefit* more than the others from its effects on their competitors. They will benefit more because unless they are restrained, they, but not the others, will use their competitive edge to claim jobs which their competitors would otherwise have gotten. Thus, it is only because they stand to *gain* the most from the relevant effects of the *original* discrimination that the bypassed individuals stand to *lose* the most from *reverse* discrimination.[7] This is surely a valid reply to the charge that reverse discrimination does not distribute the burden of compensation equally.

NOTES

1. In what follows I will have nothing to say about utilitarian justifications of reverse discrimination. There are two reasons for this. First, the winds of utilitarian argumentation blow in too many directions. It is certainly socially beneficial to avoid the desperate actions to which festering resentments may lead—but so too is it socially useful to confirm the validity of qualifications of the traditional sort, to assure those who have amassed such qualifications that "the rules of the game have not been changed in the middle," that accomplishment has not been downgraded in society's eyes. How could these conflicting utilities possibly be measured against one another?

    Second and even more important, to rest a defense of reverse discrimination upon utilitarian considerations would be to ignore what is surely the guiding intuition of its proponents, that this treatment is *deserved* where discrimination has been practiced in the past. It is the intuition that reverse discrimination is a matter not (only) of social good but of right which I want to try to elucidate.
2. This argument, as well as the others I shall consider, presupposes that jobs are (among other things) *goods*, and so ought to be distributed as fairly as possible. This presupposition seems to be amply supported by the sheer economic necessity of earning a living, as well as by the fact that some jobs carry more prestige and are more interesting and pay better than others.
3. As Robert Simon has pointed out in "Preferential Hiring: A Reply to Judith Jarvis Thomson," *Philosophy & Public Affairs* 3:3 (1974): 312–20, it is also far from clear that the preferential hiring of its individual members could be a proper form of compensation for any wronged group that *did* exist.
4. A version of this argument is advanced by Judith Jarvis Thomson in "Preferential Hiring," *Philosophy & Public Affairs* 2:4 (1973): 364–84.
5. Cf. Simon, "Preferential Hiring," sec. III.

6. A similar justification of reverse discrimination is suggested, but not ultimately endorsed, by Thomas Nagel in "Equal Treatment and Compensatory Discrimination," *Philosophy & Public Affairs* 2:4 (1973): 348–63. Nagel rejects this justification on the grounds that a system distributing goods solely on the basis of performance determined by native ability would itself be unjust, even if not *as* unjust as one distributing goods on a racial or sexual basis. I shall not comment on this, except to remark that our moral intuitions surely run the other way: the average person would certainly find the latter system of distribution *far* more unjust than the former, if indeed, he found the former unjust at all. Because of this, the burden is on Nagel to show exactly why a purely meritocratic system of distribution would be unjust.

7. It is tempting, but I think largely irrelevant, to object here that many who are now entrenched in their jobs (tenured professors, for example) have already benefited from the effects of past discrimination at least as much as the currently best qualified applicant will if reverse discrimination is not practiced. While many such individuals have undoubtedly benefited from the effects of discrimination upon *their original* competitors, few if any are likely to have benefited from a reduction in the abilities of the *currently best qualified applicant's* competitor. As long as none of them have so benefited, the best qualified applicant in question will still stand to gain the most from that *particular* effect of past discrimination, and so reverse discrimination against him will remain fair. Of course, there will also be cases in which an entrenched person *has* previously benefited from the reduced abilities of the currently best qualified applicant's competitor. In these cases, the best qualified applicant will *not* be the single main beneficiary of his rival's handicap, and so reverse discrimination against him will *not* be entirely fair. I am inclined to think there may be a case for reverse discrimination even here, however; for if it is truly impossible to dislodge the entrenched previous beneficiary of his rival's handicap, reverse discrimination against the best qualified applicant may at least be the fairest (or least unfair) of the practical alternatives.

Compassion

Lawrence Blum

This paper offers an account of compassion as a moral phenomenon. I regard compassion as a kind of emotion or emotional attitude; though it differs from paradigmatic emotions such as fear, anger, distress, love, it has, I will argue, an irreducible affective dimension.

Compassion is one among a number of attitudes, emotions, or virtues which can be called "altruistic" in that they involve a regard for the good of other persons. Some others are pity, helpfulness, well-wishing. Such phenomena and the distinctions between them have been given insufficient attention in current moral philosophy. By distinguishing compassion from some of these other altruistic phenomena I want to bring out compassion's particular moral value, as well as some of its limitations.[1]

The Objects of Compassion

How must a compassionate person view someone in order to have compassion for him?[2] Compassion seems restricted to beings capable of feeling or being harmed. Bypassing the question of compassion for plants, animals, institutions, I will focus on persons as objects of compassion. A person in a negative condition, suffering some harm, difficulty, danger (past, present, or future) is the appropriate object of compassion. But there are many negative conditions and not all are possible objects of compassion. The inconvenience and irritation of a short detour for a driver on his way to a casual visit are not compassion-grounding conditions.[3] The negative condition must be relatively central to a person's life and well-being, describable as pain, misery, hardship, suffering, affliction, and the like. Although it is the person and not merely the negative condition which is the object of compassion, the focus of compassion is the condition.

Compassion can be part of a complex attitude toward its object; it is possible to have compassion for someone in a difficult or miserable situation without judging his overall condition to be difficult or miserable. It is therefore necessary to distinguish the conditions for someone being an appropriate object of compassion from the conditions for compassion being the appropriate dominant response to the person. One might predominantly admire and take pleasure in the happiness of a blind person who has gotten through college, found a rewarding job, made close friends—someone whose life is generally happy and who does not dwell on what he misses by being blind. Nevertheless one can also feel compassion for him because his life is deficient and damaged by his blindness.

It is not necessary that the object of compassion be aware of his condition; he might be deceiving himself with regard to it. Nor, as in the case of the happy blind man, need he think of it as a substantial affliction, even if he is aware of it as a deficiency.

That compassion is limited to grave or serious negative conditions does not exclude other altruistic emotions from being entirely appropriate to less serious states. One can feel sorry for, commiserate with, or feel sympathy for a person's irritation, discomfort, inconvenience, displeasure. Nor are all altruistic attitudes primarily directed to particular persons: they can be directed to classes of persons (the blind) or to general conditions (poverty). In addition, there are altruistic virtues not so clearly involving emotions, which come into play in regard to less serious negative conditions: considerateness, thoughtfulness, helpfulness. It would be considerate or thoughtful to warn an acquaintance of an unexpected detour so that he could avoid needless inconvenience and irritation. Such virtues as these, while not necessarily involving emotion or feeling, do involve attention to another's situation and a genuine regard for the other's good, even when more self-regarding attitudes are conjointly brought into play.

Not all altruistic emotions are focused on negative states. Someone might take delight in giving pleasure to others. Though this altruistic attitude shares with compassion a regard for the good of others, compassion focuses on pain, suffering, and damage, whereas this other attitude focuses on pleasure. The capacity for one altruistic attitude is no assurance of the capacity for others. It is quite possible for a compassionate person to be insensitive to the pleasures of others. A focus on misery and suffering in the absence of regard for others' joys and pleasures constitutes a limitation in the moral consciousness of the merely compassionate person.[4]

The Emotional Attitude of Compassion

The compassionate person does not merely believe that the object suffers some serious harm or injury; such a belief is compatible with indifference, malicious delight in his suffering, or intense intellectual interest, for example of a novelist or psychologist for whom the suffering is primarily material for contemplation or investigation. Even a genuine interest in relieving someone's suffering can stem from meeting an intellectual or professional challenge rather than from compassion.

Compassion is not a simple feeling-state but a complex emotional attitude toward another, characteristically involving imaginative dwelling on the condition of the other person, an active regard for his good, a view of him as a fellow human being, and emotional responses of a certain degree of intensity.

Imaginatively reconstructing someone's condition is distinct from several sorts of "identification" with the other person. For instance, it does not involve an identity confusion in which the compassionate person fails to distinguish his feelings and situation from the other person's.[5] Such a pathological condition actually precludes genuine compassion because it blurs the distinction between subject and object.

In a second type of identification the subject "identifies" with the object because of having had an experience similar to his, the memory of which his experience evokes. ("I can identify with what you are going through, since I've suffered from the same problem myself.") Here no identity confusion is involved. While such identification can promote compassion and imaginative understanding it is not required for it. For compassion does not require even that its subject have experienced the sort of suffering that occasions it. We can commiserate with someone who has lost a child in a fire, even if we do not have a child or have never lost someone we love. The reason for this is that the imaginative reconstruction involved in compassion consists in imagining what the other person, given his character, beliefs, and values is undergoing, rather than what we ourselves would feel in his situation. For example I might regard my son's decision to work for the CIA with distress, while someone with different beliefs and values might regard such a decision with pride; yet this other person may well be able to understand my reaction and to feel compassion for me in regard to it.

The degree of imaginative reconstruction need not be great. The friend in the previous example might find it difficult to reconstruct for herself the outlook and set of values within which my son's decision is viewed with distress. But to have compassion she must at least dwell in her imagination on the fact that I am distressed. So some imaginative representation is a necessary condition for compassion, though the degree can be minimal. Certainly a detailed and rich understanding of another person's outlook and consciousness, of the sort available only to persons of exceptional powers of imagination, is not required for compassion.

Nevertheless, as a matter of empirical fact, we often do come to understand someone's condition by imagining what our own reactions would be. So expanding our powers of imagination expands our capacity for compassion. And conversely the limits of a person's capacities for imaginative reconstruction set limits on her capacity for compassion. Finding another person's experience opaque may well get in the way of compassion. Persons who are in general quite poor at imagining the experiences of others who are different from themselves, may well be less likely to have compassion for them. Yet this failure of imagination is typically not a purely intellectual or cognitive failure; for it can itself be part of a more general failure to regard the other as fully human, or to take that humanity sufficiently seriously. That a white colonialist in Africa does not imagine to himself the cares and sufferings of the blacks whom he rules cannot be separated from the fact that he does not see them as fully human.

A second constituent of compassion is concern for or regard for the object's good. It is not enough that we imaginatively reconstruct someone's suffering; for, like belief, such imagining is compatible with malice and mere intellectual curiosity. (In fact it is likely to be a component of them.) In addition we must care about that suffering and desire its alleviation. Suppose a neighbor's house burns down, though no one is hurt. Compassion would involve not only imagining what it is like for the neighbor to be homeless but also concerned responses such as the following: being upset, distressed, regretting the different aspects of his plight (his homelessness, his loss of prized possessions, his terror when inside the burning house, etc.); wishing the tragedy had not happened;

giving thought to what might be done to alleviate the neighbor's situation; worrying whether he will be able to find another place to live; hoping that he will obtain a decent settlement from the insurance company; hoping and desiring that, in general, his suffering will be no greater than necessary.

The relation between concern for another person's good and these thoughts, feelings, hopes, desires is a necessary or conceptual one; compassionate concern would not be attributed to someone who lacked them (or at least most of them). This concern is not merely tacked on to the imaginative reconstruction as a totally independent component of compassion. Rather the manner in which we dwell on the other's plight expresses the concern for his good.

These concerned reactions must be directed toward the other's plight and not merely caused by it. The distress that is part of compassion cannot take as its focus the vivid realization that I might be afflicted with a like misfortune; for it would then be self-regarding rather than altruistic.

Compassion also involves viewing the other person and his suffering in a certain way. I can put this by saying that compassion involves a sense of shared humanity, of regarding the other as a fellow human being. This means that the other person's suffering (though not necessarily their particular afflicting condition) is seen as the kind of thing that could happen to anyone, including oneself insofar as one is a human being.[6]

This way of viewing the other person contrasts with the attitude characteristic of pity, in which one holds oneself apart from the afflicted person and from their suffering thinking of it as something that defines that person as fundamentally different from oneself. In this way the other person's condition is taken as given whereas in compassion the person's affliction is seen as deviating from the general conditions of human flourishing. That is why pity (unlike compassion) involves a kind of condescension, and why compassion is morally superior to pity.

Because compassion involves a sense of shared humanity, it promotes the *experience* of equality, even when accompanied by an acknowledgment of actual social inequality. Compassion forbids regarding social inequality as establishing human inequality. This is part of the moral force of compassion: by transcending the recognition of social inequality, it promotes the sensed experience of equality in common humanity.

Sometimes the reason we feel pity rather than compassion is that we feel that the object has in some way brought the suffering on himself or deserved it, or in any case that he has allowed himself to be humiliated or degraded by it. But such ways of regarding the object do not necessarily undermine compassion, and they are not incompatible with it. It would be a mistake to see the essential difference between pity and compassion in such differing beliefs about the object's condition. No matter how pitiful or self-degraded one regards another human being, it is possible (and not necessarily unwarranted) to feel compassion and concern for him, simply because he is suffering.

A fourth aspect of compassion is its strength and duration. If the distress, sorrow, hopes, and desires of an altruistic attitude were merely passing reactions or twinges of feeling, they would be insufficient for the level of concern, the imaginative reconstruction, and the disposition to beneficent action required for compassion. Though there are degrees of compassion, the threshold of emotional strength required from compassion (in contrast with other altruistic attitudes) is relatively high and enduring. Because well-wishing and pity can be more episodic and less action-guiding, they are morally inferior to compassion. As the etymology of the word suggests, compassion involves "feeling with" the other person, sharing his feelings. In one sense this means that the subject and the object have the same feeling-type: distress, sorrow, desire for relief. But in a more important sense the feelings are not the same, for the relation between their subjects and their objects are different. The focus of my neighbor's distress is *his own* homelessness; the focus of my distress in having compassion for him is *my neighbor's* homelessness (or his distress at his homelessness). This can partly be expressed as a matter of degree. My neighbor suffers; in "suffering with" him there is a sense in which I suffer too, but my suffering is much less than his.

Compassion and Beneficent Action

When it is possible for her to relieve another person's suffering without undue demands on her time, energy, and priorities, the compassionate person is disposed to attempt to help. We would hardly attribute compassion to X if she were to saunter by on a spring day and, seeing an elderly man fall on the sidewalk, walk right by, perhaps with a sad shudder of dismay, leaving the old man lying alone.

Characteristically, then, compassion requires the disposition to perform beneficent actions, and to perform them because the agent has had a certain sort of imaginative reconstruction of someone's condition and has a concern for his good. The steps that the person takes to ameliorate the condition are guided by and prompted by that imaginative reconstruction and concern. So the beneficent action of a compassionate person has a specific sort of causal history, which distinguishes it from an equally beneficent action that might be prompted by other sorts of attitudes and emotions.

Compassionate action may extinguish or diminish compassion itself, most obviously when its object is relieved of the negative condition by the action. But even merely *engaging* in action may involve a shift in the subject's consciousness from the imaginative reconstruction of the object's condition to a focus on the expected relief of that condition, thereby diminishing the compassion (though not the regard for the other's good and hence not the moral value of the attitude or state of mind).

Compassion, however, is not always linked so directly to the prompting of beneficent actions. For in many situations it is impossible (without extraordinary disruption of one's life and priorities) for the compassionate person herself to improve the sufferer's condition (for instance, when one is concerned for the welfare of distant flood victims). In other situations the beneficence might be inappropriate, as when intervention might jeopardize the sufferer's autonomy. Compassionate concern, in such cases, involves hope and desire for the relief of the condition by those in a position to provide it. It does not involve an active setting oneself in readiness to perform beneficent acts, once one firmly believes such acts to be impossible or inappropriate.

In the cases so far discussed a link exists between compassion and beneficent action, through the desire that action be taken by someone to relieve the sufferer's condition. But compassion is also appropriate in situations in which nothing whatever can be done to alleviate the affliction, as for instance when someone is suffering from incurable blindness or painful terminal cancer. In such situations compassionate concern involves sorrowing for the person, hoping that the condition might—all expectations to the contrary—be mitigated or compensated, being pleased or grateful if this occurs, and similar responses.

Because being compassionate involves actively giving thought to the relief of the sufferer's condition, a compassionate person may discover the possibility of beneficent action when it seemed unclear whether any existed. Compassion often involves resisting regarding situations as absolutely irremediable. On the other hand the compassionate person may for this reason fail to see and hence to face up to the hopelessness of the sufferer's situation.

That compassion is often appropriate when there is little or no scope for the subject's disposition to beneficence indicates that compassion's sole significance does not lie in its role as motive to beneficence. Even when nothing can be done by the compassionate person to improve the sufferer's condition, simply being aware that one is an object or recipient of compassion can be an important human good. The compassionate person's expression of concern and shared sorrow can be valuable to the sufferer for its own sake, independently of its instrumental value in improving his condition. Nor does the good of recognizing oneself to be an object of compassion depend on the compassionate person wanting to convey his attitude, though the recipient can in addition value the intention to communicate.

The compassionate attitude is a good to the recipient, not only because it signifies that the subject would help if she could but because we are glad to receive the concern of others, glad of the sense of equality that it promotes. Yet it is morally good to be compassionate even when—as often happens—the object of compassion is unaware of it. For any concern for the welfare of others, especially when it promotes the sense of equality, is (*ceteris paribus*) morally good. In this, compassion contrasts with attitudes and feelings such as infatuation or admiration which may convey goods to their recipients but which are without moral value because they do not essentially involve a regard for their recipient's good. The moral significance of compassion is not exhausted by the various types of goods it confers on its recipients.

Compassion can hurt its recipients. It may, for instance, cause him to concentrate too much on his plight, or to think that people around him see him primarily in terms of that plight. But these dangers and burdens of compassion can be mitigated to the extent that a person recognizes that compassion is not the sole or the dominant attitude with which one is regarded.

Compassion can also be misguided, grounded in superficial understanding of a situation. Compassion is not necessarily wise or appropriate. The compassionate person may even end up doing more harm than good. True compassion must be allied with knowledge and understanding if it is to serve adequately as a guide to action: there is nothing inherent in the character of compassion that would prevent—and much that would encourage—its alliance with rational calculation. Because compassion involves an active and objective interest in another person's welfare, it is characteristically a spur to a deeper understanding of a situation than rationality alone could ensure. A person who is compassionate by character is in principle committed to as rational and as intelligent a course of action as possible.

NOTES

1. Compassion has a particular cultural history: its sources are Christian, [and] it was further developed by Romanticism, especially by the German Romantics. Though I do not focus on this history explicitly, my emphasis on compassion as a particular moral emotion among others should leave room for the results of such a historical account.

2. In general I will use feminine pronouns to refer to the person having compassion (the "subject") and masculine pronouns to refer to the person for whom she has compassion (the "object").

3. I am taking a conceptual rather than a moral point. The compassionate person cannot regard the object of her compassion as merely irritated or discomforted; but of course a genuinely compassionate person might mistakenly

take an inconvenience to be a serious harm. To say that compassion is "appropriate" in this context is, then, simply to say that the object actually possesses the compassion-grounding feature which the subject takes him to possess. I do not discuss the further issue of when compassion is *morally* appropriate or inappropriate.

4. Nietzsche saw this focus on misery and suffering as a kind of morbidity in the compassionate consciousness; this view formed part of his critique of compassion.
5. Philip Mercer, *Sympathy and Ethics* (Oxford: Clarendon Press, 1972), and Max Scheler, *The Nature of Sympathy*, translated by Werner Stark (London: Routledge & Kegan Paul, 1965).
6. This way of viewing the other's plight differs from fundamentally self-regarding sentiment in which the person's plight is regarded as a symbol of what could happen to oneself. It is not actually necessary that one believe that the afflicting condition *could* happen to oneself: one might have compassion for someone suffering napalm burns without believing that there is any possibility of oneself being in that condition.

EXERCISES

Vonnegut:

1. In this future world, would the terms *profession* and *professional* have any meaning? Why or why not?
2. What should the government's role be in ensuring equality and fairness? What should its role be in preparing people for professions and in monitoring the way people practice their professions?
3. How do you understand competition among professionals? Is competition among professionals ever fair? Why or why not?
4. Is Vonnegut suggesting that equality is bad? Does this mean that justice is not or should not be a value? Explain.
5. Is there any place for compassion in this future world? Discuss whether or not there is any indication that the persons in 2081 value compassion. Do you see a way for compassion to be enacted in 2081? Explain your answer.

Newton:

1. What are the two senses of justice that Newton discusses? How are they related to each other? Are they related to the Rule of Fairness and the Rule of Sameness? Explain why or why not.
2. What is Newton's conclusion regarding reverse discrimination? How do the two senses of justice she points out play a role in reaching this conclusion?
3. Aside from the question of justice, what are some difficulties that confront reverse discrimination, either in practice or in principle? Do you agree that these are insoluble difficulties? Why or why not?
4. Do you see a distinction between preferential treatment and reverse discrimination? Does Newton? Are there various types of reverse dis-

crimination? Would distinguishing between types of reverse discrimination affect Newton's conclusion? Why or why not? In Vonnegut's story, the talented and the intelligent wear handicaps to make them equal to others. Is this an example of the reverse discrimination that Newton is opposed to? Why or why not?

5. It has been argued that the term *reverse discrimination* is an oxymoron, since those in positions of power cannot be discriminated against, but instead can only give others a chance by stepping aside. What would Newton say to this? What do you think?

Sher:

1. Why does Sher think that reverse discrimination is a plausible interpretation of justice? Do you agree with him? Why or why not?
2. Sher limits his discussion to reverse discrimination in employment. Why does he limit it to this? Do his reasons apply just as well to reverse discrimination in promotion or other areas? Why or why not?
3. What are some possible attempts at justifying reverse discrimination that Sher rejects and why does he reject them?
4. How does responsibility play a part in the discussion of reverse discrimination? Is the question of responsibility used to argue for or against reverse discrimination? Explain.
5. Sher talks about compensation and Newton speaks of restitution. Are they talking about the same thing? Explain why or why not. What do they say about these issues? Do you agree or disagree? Why?

Blum:

1. Blum calls compassion an "altruistic emotion." What does this mean? Do you agree that compassion is an emotion of this type?
2. According to Blum, how is compassion related to justice, especially to the Rule of Sameness?
3. Blum claims that compassion is related to beneficence, or at least to beneficent actions. How exactly are they related?
4. Can showing compassion ever be wrong? How does Blum answer this question? How would Vonnegut answer it? How would you answer it? Explain.
5. Does compassion have a role to play in interpreting justice? How might compassion contribute to the discussion of justice in the workplace?

11

Beneficence and Nonmaleficence

Remember the space shuttle, Challenger, that blew up with the seven astronauts aboard in January 1986? Engineers had warned that the O-ring seals did not function properly in extremely cold weather. Was a warning enough? What should a professional do to protect others from harm? Recall that charges were filed against the paparazzi who followed Princess Diana's car in August 1997. Did their determined efforts to snap photos contribute to the accident that led to her death? After the accident, did they fail to come to the aid of the victims because they were still taking pictures? What are a professional's obligations to do good for another? Consider Mother Theresa, who worked her whole life among the poor in India, bringing comfort and care. Are professionals required to make the sacrifices she did? And what about the thirty-nine doctors who agreed to be human guinea pigs and test the first AIDS vaccine on themselves?[1] Should professionals risk harm to themselves for the sake of helping someone else?

Instances such as these show that there are many issues that concern us when we consider how professionals should put into practice the values of beneficence and nonmaleficence. These examples and many more show that persons in professions and occupations can relate to other people and their environment, either in ways that cause harm to others or help others. Indeed, this is true for all of us. In our relationships with others, we can do good, prevent harm, fail to prevent harm, or not do good. Doing good and pre-venting harm are ways we enact the values of beneficence (to do good) and nonmaleficence (to do no harm).

In this chapter, we will come to understand how a professional should express beneficence and nonmaleficence. We will focus on the specific ways in which professional behavior recognizes the values of beneficence and nonmaleficence and makes this recognition practi-cally applicable. We will look at several professional codes of ethics in order to see how particular professions have interpreted the val-ues of beneficence and nonmaleficence. We also will consider two cases in which the actions of professionals were grounded on the val-ues of beneficence and nonmaleficence, and we will use the frame-work for moral analysis from chapter 6 to help us understand the reasons for their actions. Based on these codes and our analysis of the cases, we will discuss three rules that help us enact beneficence and nonmaleficence, namely, the Rule of Reasonable Care, the Rule of Proportionality, and the Rule Against Paternalism. Finally, we will describe some typical conflicts or moral dilemmas that arise when professionals try to put into practice their commitment to beneficence and nonmaleficence. Considering these types of conflicts now may help us avoid or resolve such conflicts in the future.

Relating Beneficence and Nonmaleficence

Let us first consider the nature of beneficence and nonmaleficence as we attempt to clarify how professionals should put these values into practice. We are treating beneficence and nonmaleficence to-gether in this chapter, although they are in fact separate values. They are distinguishable, yet closely related. Sometimes they are in-terpreted in ways that lead to incompatible actions. Basically, benef-icence and nonmaleficence express the same thing. They are both expressions of a commitment to bringing about good outcomes. There is no exact point at which one begins and the other ends. Beneficence and nonmaleficence are like the opposite ends of a con-tinuum or line. At some point in the middle of the line, beneficence and nonmaleficence overlap. For instance, sometimes we do so little good that all we are doing is preventing harm. Doing good is not fundamentally different from preventing harm. Both values express that good or benefit is to be done and bad or harm is to be avoided. For example, promoting the good serves already to prevent some po-tential harm, and avoiding harm is already a good.

In some accounts of professional ethics, beneficence and non-maleficence are treated separately, and there are several good reasons to do so.[2] A good reason for separating beneficence and nonmalefi-cence is that sometimes one is relevant to a case, while the other is not. Sometimes in a case, it is more fitting or exact to speak of one way of bringing about good outcomes and not the other. For in-stance, in the Challenger disaster, the value at stake in the engi-neer's action was more precisely nonmaleficence than beneficence. It strikes us that preventing harm is more pertinent to the case than doing good. In Mother Theresa's situation the opposite is true. We see her life and her actions as expressing primarily the value of benefi-cence and not nonmaleficence. It was not enough for Mother Theresa not to harm others, she had to make the lives of others better.

But there is more. Not only do we separate beneficence and nonmaleficence when we apply them in specific cases, but we also recognize that in some cases there are conflicts between actions that follow from beneficence and nonmaleficence. A conflict between an action grounded on beneficence and one grounded on nonmaleficence can be seen in a quite ordinary case. For example, when an ortho-dontist tightens the braces on a patient's teeth, he does so to bene-fit the patient, although it causes harm in the form of pain to the patient. If he acts beneficently, he tightens the braces, but then he hurts the patient. If he acts nonmaleficently, aiming to prevent harm, he does not tighten the braces, but then he fails to benefit the patient. Granted, this is a pretty simple conflict, and it is easily resolved by realizing that the harm is small and short term, while the benefit is great and long lasting. Further, this shows that doing good and preventing harm cannot always be realized by the same act, and that beneficence and nonmaleficence can give rise to con-flicting courses of action. This fact gives us another good reason for treating beneficence and nonmaleficence separately.

Even though there are some good reasons for treating benefi-cence and nonmaleficence separately, an account that does so fails to recognize that both are about doing good, to a greater or lesser degree. The reasons in favor of treating beneficence and nonmalefi-cence together are even more compelling. Any attempt to separate beneficence from nonmaleficence depends on a precision that lan-guage does not have. Does the orthodontist's work do good, since it keeps the patient healthy? Or does his work prevent harm, in that it serves to avoid future harm to the patient that results from poorly placed teeth? It is arbitrary whether fundamentally the case is about beneficence or nonmaleficence. It does not make sense to quibble about the name of the value at stake, since we are naming the same thing—doing good—merely to a greater or lesser degree, in both instances. What is clearly relevant is the whole scope of benefiting and avoiding harm. The question of which value—beneficence or nonmaleficence—is at stake will usually be easy to answer. But in cases where it is not, we will not waste time trying to answer this question, which is only of theoretical interest and adds little to the concrete enactment of the value. Because beneficence and nonmaleficence are two different ways of expressing the same thing, we will try to find ways to both do good and prevent harm, recognizing that frequently both are at issue in specific cases.

Recognizing Beneficence and Nonmaleficence

Now that we have seen the reasons in favor of treating beneficence and nonmaleficence together, let us move on and consider what we know about the way in which these values are enacted in the world. Beneficence and nonmaleficence are values for a professional, but what are we supposed to do with them? What helps a professional express the values of beneficence and nonmaleficence? These questions will not be completely answered in this section, but we will begin to answer them here as we consider what follows from recognizing the values of doing good and preventing harm. To do so, we will start by looking at the way in which some professionals have acted and at the way codes have required them to act. Mother Theresa was committed to doing good, the thirty-nine doctors who volunteered to test an AIDS vaccine on themselves were committed to doing good and preventing harm, and Challenger engineers were committed to avoiding harm. A professional's morality is rightly questioned when no attention seems to be paid to doing good or avoiding harm, as in the case of the paparazzi, who apparently failed to help after Princess Diana's car crash.

Professional codes validate our commitments to beneficence and nonmaleficence and give us some ways of beginning to consider how they are to be interpreted. The medical profession, as governed by the Hippocratic Oath, promises to "keep them [the sick] from harm."[3] The physician's duty is frequently described as, "Above all, do no harm."[4] Both nurses and physical therapists are required to protect the public from harm in the form of incompetent, unethical, or illegal practices.[5] Pastoral counselors are said to "protect the public" and to act "for the benefit of the people they serve."[6] Social workers are directed to "promote the general welfare of society."[7] Certified public accountants have a "public interest responsibility," which is to further "the collective well-being of the community of people and institutions the profession serves."[8] Architects have obligations to the public,[9] engineers have as their primary obligation "to protect the safety, health, property, and welfare of the public,"[10] and journalists are reminded that "the purpose of distributing news and enlightened opinion is to serve the general welfare."[11] We cannot look at all of the codes of ethics here, nor would we want to, nor do all occupations even have codes; nevertheless, the above examples establish a strong connection between professionals and a commitment to beneficence and nonmaleficence.

Clearly, beneficence and nonmaleficence are central to morality in general and to professionals in particular. Moral persons and moral professionals of all kinds share a commitment to doing good and preventing harm. With this established, we are left to consider the next question, which is a "so what?" question. So ... what are we supposed to make of beneficence and nonmaleficence? Beneficence and nonmaleficence are central, so what? What are professionals who are committed to beneficence and nonmaleficence supposed to do? The short answer is that professionals are supposed to enact beneficence and nonmaleficence. However, the long answer recognizes that there are many ways of enacting beneficence and nonmaleficence, hence there are difficulties of interpretation that bedevil any attempt to act beneficently and nonmaleficently. Of course, there will be uncertainties and disagreements about how beneficence and nonmaleficence ought to be practiced. There will be questions regarding to whom beneficence and nonmaleficence should be directed, as well as questions about which actions are beneficent or nonmaleficent. Let us look at the points involved in these questions in more detail so that we fully recognize and are prepared for the issues that are involved in enacting these values.

Beneficent and nonmaleficent actions can be directed toward individuals, a group, an institution, or society at large. There may be times when a professional decides to act beneficently toward a client, even though doing so does not promote beneficence toward all persons. A mail carrier may stop to chat with a shut-in client who otherwise has no one to talk to the whole day, or may aid in opening the mail for a disabled client who asks for help. Clearly the value of beneficence is served by taking time for these clients. But suppose there are other clients or businesses waiting to receive their mail? Are their rights to be treated beneficently being sacrificed unfairly? To whom should we practice beneficence and nonmaleficence, and when?

The example of the friendly mail carrier shows that beneficence and nonmaleficence can be directed to different persons or groups, and consequently, that these values can be interpreted in different ways. Many professional codes recognize that the professional's commitment to beneficence and nonmaleficence includes responsibilities to diverse groups, such as clients, colleagues, society, the profession, and more. In acknowledging a commitment to beneficence and nonmaleficence, we must be aware of whose benefit we are aiming at and whose harm we are avoiding. We also will be faced with having to compare and weigh the amount of good that comes from acting beneficently and nonmaleficently toward a particular person, like the shut-in client, against the amount of good that comes from acting beneficently and nonmaleficently toward a group of persons, like the other customers waiting for their mail. Because there are many persons and groups with whom a professional interacts, there are many potential persons toward whom beneficence and nonmaleficence can be practiced. And it may be hard to find an action that benefits all of those to whom the professional could express beneficence and nonmaleficence.

There also may be times when a professional could choose to act in one of several ways but is not sure which action does a better job of exhibiting the values of beneficence and nonmaleficence. That is, it may not be clear which action is more grounded in beneficence or nonmaleficence than another. Suppose one music teacher believes that she benefits her students by insisting that they play a piece perfectly before moving on to a new piece. A second music teacher believes she benefits her students by allowing them to move on to a new piece after a few weeks of work, whether or not the piece is played perfectly. Who is right? Which approach is more beneficent? That is, how do you bring about the most good as a professional music teacher? The first teacher benefits the pupils by teaching them discipline and the sense of accomplishment that comes from meeting high standards. The second teacher benefits the pupils by teaching them that music is fun and that it is enough to do their best work, whether or not they do their work perfectly.

If you are a new music teacher deciding which approach to adopt, or if you are selecting a music teacher, you will quite likely be puzzled by these two interpretations of beneficence. There will be many situations like this one in which beneficence and nonmaleficence can be acted on in different ways. We may be unsure of which action best realizes beneficence and nonmaleficence. We will have to make choices among these various interpretations of beneficence and nonmaleficence. Recognizing and using beneficence and nonmaleficence requires us to carefully consider both *who* is benefitted and protected by our actions and *what* benefit or protection is achieved by our actions.

Two Cases Involving Beneficence and Nonmaleficence

We next discuss two cases, one dealing with beneficence and the other with nonmaleficence. Our aim is to use what we have learned in the last section to inform our discussion of these cases. Specifically, we will see some examples of how professionals have acted for the sake of beneficence and nonmaleficence, and how they have dealt with the questions of who is to be helped and which action helps. We want to be able to recognize beneficence and nonmaleficence as it is practiced in the cases, and we want to see the way in which questions arise concerning the interpretation of beneficence and nonmaleficence in action.

Beneficence

The Hanna Andersson Case

Hanna Andersson is a Swedish-style clothing company in Oregon. Most of its business is mail order, and most of the clothing it sells is children's clothing. Each catalog has an explanation of a special program sponsored by the company called "Cash for Kids." In this program, once a year every school-age child of a Hanna employee receives a $100 check made out to the child's school. The children present the checks to their schools and can make suggestions on how to use the money. Every $100 helps tight school budgets. The catalog concludes, "Yet, even more importantly, it gives kids the signal that their education is valued by the community. What nicer way for business to support schools than to begin with our own children?"

The catalog asks, "Why not start a program at your company?" It offers a toll-free number that other companies might use to get information on how to set up a "Cash for Kids" program.[12]

Let us first analyze this case using the framework for moral analysis that we developed in chapter 6 to see how beneficence is at work. Since decisions have already been made in the case, the framework is more useful to us than the Case Resolution Model.

Decision:

Enact company programs that benefit children.

Rule:

It is right for business to support children's education.

It is right for companies to advertise their programs that benefit children.

It is right for companies to offer help to other companies that want to start programs that benefit children.

Theory:

The company's reasoning may be seen to reflect a number of different theories. A consequential theory is likely, since the company's program brings about more good consequences than bad and overall more good than harm. For example, children are getting money for their schools, employees are getting the benefit of being able to help their children's schools, and the company is getting good public relations. But it may also be that the company recognizes that businesses and those that run them have duties to the communities that support them or to the employees who work for them but live in the community or the employees have the right to have good benefits. Hence, a duty or rights theory also is possible. Or, perhaps Hanna Andersson enacted these programs in order to reflect virtue and live up to the standard or the ideals set by the company's founder. The company's action could then be seen to follow from a virtue theory. Likewise, there may be a care theory at work, since the company may be motivated by a desire to care for others, and the program clearly accomplishes this. Or there may be a narrative theory at work, since the company might be acting out of the context of the life story and goals of the company and its founders, which include a felt responsibility to give back to the community.

Value:

Beneficence, primarily; Responsibility and Compassion, secondarily.

The Andersson case is one in which professionals at a company have acknowledged and acted on the values of beneficence, responsibility, and compassion. Actions were taken to put values into practice. Hanna Andersson is acting to benefit the lives of others, and enacting this value is commendable, although, as we have said, there are usually questions that can be asked about any particular decision in which beneficence and nonmaleficence are made concrete. There are uncertainties and disagreements about almost every particular decision to enact beneficence. For instance, some people may believe that the company is being intrusive by donating money to schools and encouraging children to suggest how the schools should spend the money. Perhaps more harm than good results from this involvement. Others may claim that it is unfair of the company to give money to some schools and not others because it potentially improves the educational offerings for some children and not others; it benefits schools based not on need but on how many children of employees attend the school. These are some of the concerns that might be raised about Hanna Andersson's decision to enact a specific company program to benefit children.

Now what have we learned by looking at this case? We have seen a particular way in which beneficence was put into practice. We know that the value of beneficence can be enacted in concrete cases, because it was enacted by Hanna Andersson in this case. We have also seen that it is possible to question any particular decision about how to enact beneficence. There will always be debate regarding what action best expresses beneficence. We discovered that in Hanna Andersson's interpretation of beneficence, the company probably considered both goods and harms. Professionals in the company made a decision about how to benefit others, and in doing so, they had to decide how much to benefit them, that is, at what cost to the company to benefit them. Interpreting beneficence, in this case and in many cases, involves considering both benefits and harms. With these points noted, let us look at a case where nonmaleficence has been put into practice.

Nonmaleficence

The Tarasoff Case

In August 1969, Prosenjit Poddar was a voluntary outpatient receiving psychotherapy under the care of Dr. Lawrence Moore, a psychologist employed at Cowell Memorial Hospital at the University of California at Berkeley. Prosenjit confided to Dr. Moore that he intended to kill Tatiana Tarasoff when she returned from Brazil. After conferring with another psychologist at the hospital and with the assistant to the director of the department of psychiatry, Dr. Moore decided that Prosenjit should be committed to a mental hospital for observation. He then told campus police officers that he was requesting Prosenjit's commitment, and he sent a letter to the police chief asking for the police's help in carrying out Prosenjit's confinement. Campus police briefly detained Prosenjit but released him when he appeared rational and agreed to stay away from Tatiana. Dr. Moore's superior, the director of the department of psychiatry at the hospital, then asked the police to return Dr. Moore's letter, directed that all letters and notes that Dr. Moore had taken as a therapist be destroyed, and ordered that no further action be taken to commit Prosenjit to the mental hospital for observation. Neither Tatiana nor her parents were informed of Prosenjit's threat. In October 1969, shortly after her return from Brazil, Prosenjit killed Tatiana.[13]

Let us first look at how nonmaleficence was enacted by the therapist in this case. Again, decisions have already been made, so we will use the framework for moral analysis. Dr. Moore seems to have reasoned in the following way:

Decision:

Get Prosenjit committed to a mental hospital for observation.

Rule:

It is right for therapists to take seriously their clients' threats.

Theory:

The therapist's reasoning could reflect consequentialism. Dr. Moore may have assessed future consequences and decided that overall more good would come from isolating Prosenjit and further evaluating him. Dr. Moore may have used a rights theory and focused

on his rights as a therapist to do what was in the best interests
of his client. Or he may have decided that he had a duty to his
client to do everything possible to protect and benefit the client.
That is, maybe the decision reflects a care theory in that the therapist was aiming to care for his client by doing what was necessary to protect him and keep him out of harm's way. Perhaps Dr.
Moore used a virtue theory and acted on his vision of what
a virtuous therapist would do. Maybe he employed a narrative
theory and acted on the basis of his past experience in dealing
with the verbal threats of clients or his knowledge of this client
in particular.

Value:

Nonmaleficence, Beneficence.

Nonmaleficence is evident in this case in many different ways.
Decisions were made that had an impact on how nonmaleficence
was expressed or not expressed. If we look just at Dr. Moore's decision to commit Prosenjit, we see that by his action he attempted to
prevent harm. Other decisions, like Dr. Moore's decision not to inform Tatiana of the threat against her life, may not have taken nonmaleficence into account but instead were based on other moral or
nonmoral reasons. These decisions did however raise the issue of
nonmaleficence, since they allowed possible future harm to take
place. The decisions of Dr. Moore's superior to destroy records and
give up commitment attempts may have been made out of respect
for persons in the form of confidentiality, but the decisions failed to
prevent possible future harm, and thus failed to fulfill a commitment to nonmaleficence.

The real problem in this case centers on how best to enact nonmaleficence. Again, this is a problem of interpretation. It involves
deciding to whom harm ought to be prevented, which harm ought to
be prevented, and what action does the best job of avoiding harm.
There was potential harm to Tatiana, of course, but there also was
potential harm to Prosenjit and to the counseling relationship. Perhaps some of those who made decisions believed that nonmaleficence to a client ought to be enacted before nonmaleficence to a
third party. Perhaps some thought that having the campus police
check on Prosenjit to warn him to stay away from Tatiana was
a sufficient step to take to avoid harm. After Tatiana's death, a
lawsuit was filed by her parents, and the subsequent court ruling

determined that the therapists did not do enough to prevent harm. The ruling said:

> *The majority opinion [Justice Tobriner] affirmed that therapists have an obligation to warn third parties of their patients' threats of violence. He said: "When a therapist determines, or pursuant to the standards of his profession should determine, that his patient presents a serious danger of violence to another, he incurs an obligation to use reasonable care to protect the intended victim against such danger." The dissenting opinion [Justice Clark] argued that confidentiality is crucial to treating the mentally ill and that there are policy considerations against requiring therapists to warn potential victims against harm.*[14]

In this case, after it is too late to help Tatiana, we have a rule requiring therapists to practice nonmaleficence by warning third parties of their clients' threats. Dr. Moore acted for nonmaleficence toward Prosenjit and Tatiana in trying to have Prosenjit admitted to a hospital. But when he was overruled on this decision, he failed to continue to practice nonmaleficence. Because he didn't warn Tatiana or complain about his superior's action of not pursuing Prosenjit's hospital admission, Dr. Moore did not do all he should have in acting nonmaleficently. In agreeing to destroy records and thereby to remove himself from Prosenjit's case, he failed to adequately protect persons from harm. Dr. Moore's interpretation of nonmaleficence was inadequate because there were steps he could easily have taken to prevent harm but did not.

What have we learned by looking at the Tarasoff case? We have seen that although professionals are committed to the value of nonmaleficence, they may not always know how to enact it. Some professionals do a more thoughtful, complete job of interpreting nonmaleficence than others. We have learned that the courts sometimes get involved to dictate how professionals ought to act on the value of nonmaleficence. Also, while we have said that it is always possible to question any particular enactment of a value, including that of nonmaleficence, it is obvious from the Tarasoff case that more questions are raised when there is an apparent failure to enact nonmaleficence than when there is a clear enactment of it. In other words, we object more strenuously when nonmaleficence is not put into practice at all, and less strenuously when there is disagreement over how it is put into practice.

As we recognize beneficence and nonmaleficence in specific cases, we will be faced with questions like these. How should we enact beneficence and nonmaleficence? To whom should we practice it, and what action best expresses it?

Interpreting Beneficence and Nonmaleficence: Guides to Help

We have seen in the previous sections that while beneficence and nonmaleficence are values for professionals, it is not always clear to professionals how they should act to realize those values. Values get interpreted when they are put into practice, and we may not always agree on the particular interpretations others make. Some may find that Hanna Andersson should have benefitted others in a different way, by offering more money to the schools of employees' children or by providing a benefit to all schools in the community. Probably all of us agree with the court that Dr. Moore and his associates should have enacted nonmaleficence in a different way. Their interpretation of nonmaleficence was insufficient to fully express the value or save Tatiana's life. What we need now is more clarity on how to live out beneficence and nonmaleficence. No moral rule can provide an exact formula detailing how to interpret beneficence and nonmaleficence, but several rules provide useful guidelines for deciding how to act beneficently and nonmaleficently. The first rule that helps us interpret beneficence and nonmaleficence is the Rule of Reasonable Care, the second is the Rule of Proportionality, and the third is the Rule Against Paternalism. These rules provide guides for judging how to practice beneficence and nonmaleficence.

Reasonable care, often called due care, means sensible precautions or actions within reasonable limits. A professional's actions as a consequence of commitments to beneficence and nonmaleficence are to take reasonable care to prevent harm and do good. Taking reasonable care translates into doing what a typical, thoughtful professional would do. It means preventing harm and benefitting others by using sensible precautions and actions within reasonable limits. The absence of reasonable care is neglect or negligence. To neglect or to be negligent is to abandon the client or the public or whomever, thus to fail to take reasonable precautions to prevent the occurrence of harm. Professionals are always required to uphold their commitments to beneficence and nonmaleficence in their actions, unless doing so would require superhuman efforts.

Rule of Reasonable Care

Benefit others and avoid harming them by taking sensible precautions and by acting within reasonable limits.

In the Tarasoff case, Judge Tobriner used the Rule of Reasonable Care. He stated that a psychotherapist has the obligation to use reasonable care to protect intended victims from harm perpetrated by their clients. He did not say that therapists must protect all intended victims from all harm. This, after all, would be impossible, since the therapist cannot be with an intended victim at all times. Nor did he say that therapists must absolutely and at all costs protect intended victims from harm. Rather, they must use reasonable care to prevent harm from coming to the intended victims of their clients by warning those seemingly in harm's way. Reasonable care in this case means acting to prevent a client from harming another. Reasonable care requires acting in this way, both because the psychotherapists had a special relationship to their client and because they could foresee the possible consequences of their actions and their client's actions. Dr. Moore and his associates failed to use reasonable care, so harm occurred that they might have been able to prevent. Since they did not use the Rule of Reasonable Care, they ended up inadequately interpreting nonmaleficence. To give one more example, the *Code of Professional Conduct* of the American Institute of Certified Public Accountants makes use of this same rule when it speaks of the accountant's obligation to use "due professional care."[15] Accountants thus also must use reasonable care to benefit their clients and to protect them from harm.

So the Rule of Reasonable Care helps professionals understand how to express beneficence and nonmaleficence. It does not, however, provide all of the answers. A professional may still wonder what constitutes reasonable care. Reasonable care seems to vary from place to place and time to time. What counts today in New York as taking reasonable care is different than what taking reasonable care meant fifty years ago in New York, or what taking reasonable care means today in Idaho. The requirements of reasonable care vary. Thus, context is relevant to determining what it means to take reasonable care. Usually what counts as reasonable care is determined by individual professionals who use their knowledge of professional codes of ethics, accepted professional standards and standards of care, and laws to make concrete their underlying value commitments. These codes, standards, and laws together help us interpret the context within which we are applying beneficence and nonmaleficence.

The reasonable care standard works as a rule for interpreting beneficence and nonmaleficence. It tells us, "It is right to use reasonable care in protecting others from harm and in benefitting others." We must avoid harm and do good by taking reasonable care. But we cannot take infinite care or superhuman care, so we cannot do all possible good and avoid all possible harm. Some harm will follow, and some good will be left undone in spite of our efforts at reasonable care. However, our inability to do all good and avoid all harm should not discourage us. There still is plenty of good to be done and harm to be avoided by taking reasonable care. However, only reasonable care, not extraordinary care, can be expected of moral persons and moral professionals.

The second rule that helps us interpret beneficence and nonmaleficence is proportionality, which involves cost-benefit analysis or risk-benefit analysis. It involves assessing how much moral good and moral harm comes from taking a certain action. The benefits and costs are totalled, and if the benefits of acting outweigh the costs, then the action realizes beneficence and nonmaleficence. If, on the other hand, the costs outweigh the benefits, then overall the action does not express beneficence and nonmaleficence. Proportionality is a consequential procedure that compares the moral benefits of acting a certain way to the moral burdens of acting in order to decide whether the action should be done. The benefits and burdens that are compared and weighed are moral benefits and burdens, not just economic or legal benefits and burdens. To enact the values of beneficence and nonmaleficence, the Rule of Proportionality is helpful.

Rule of Proportionality

Benefit others and avoid harming them when the moral benefits of acting outweigh the moral burdens of acting.

There are many aspects to consider when assessing benefits and burdens. You will want to look at how much good an act would bring about and how significant the good would be, or, in other words, how much harm would be avoided and how significant the harm would be. These are called the magnitude of the good or harm and the severity of the good or harm. Further, in assessing proportionality, you will need to consider the level of risk to yourself in helping. You can assess whether and to what extent you will be put in danger or seriously compromised by your act of helping. You also can consider whether there are others available to help who might be better qualified than you to help, or who bear some greater responsibility for helping than you do. For instance, the Rule of Proportionality tells us that an action which prevents a great harm realizes beneficence and nonmaleficence to a greater degree than does an action which prevents a small harm. When there is only a small risk to ourselves in helping, the Rule of Proportionality more clearly obligates us to help than when there is a great risk to ourselves in helping. If a swimmer is struggling in the water and we are Red Cross certified in lifesaving then there is little risk to ourselves, and proportionality tells us to help. If we are nonswimmers then proportionality tells us to find another way to help besides jumping into the water, since the risk to ourselves is great and the chance we can benefit small. When there is someone else available and better able to help, for example, a lifeguard on duty, then we, the average swimmers, are less obligated to help save the struggling swimmer than when there is no one else available or better qualified to help.

We can see proportionality at work in the Hanna Andersson case. Hanna Andersson may have used the Rule of Proportionality to decide how to act beneficently. In order to benefit others, the company devised a program that did significant good. It focused on trying to improve the educational opportunities of employees' children. Doing good did not put the company at serious risk, since the amount of money given away to schools did not bankrupt or greatly compromise the company. Meeting the educational needs of children also served to benefit the company, since in reflecting the company's desire to do good to children, employees, and the community, it fostered good customer relations. Because there is good to children, employees, and the company that could be achieved by these acts of benefit with no harm to customers or employees and little cost to the company, the Rule of Proportionality shows that beneficence is furthered by this program.

Even with the Rule of Proportionality there is still room for individual judgments. The decision maker has to assess how great the level of benefit is and how serious the risk of harm. The decision maker must judge whether the benefits outweigh the burdens, or vice versa. Sometimes the commitment to beneficence and nonmaleficence seems to require more than doing just those actions whose moral benefits are brought about when there are minimal moral burdens. Sometimes we should do an action that benefits or avoids harm, even if the costs of doing so are great. Look at whistle blowers who make public their company's dangerous practices, even at the cost of losing their jobs and being sued. So there may be times when a commitment to beneficence or nonmaleficence means that professionals must do good or prevent harm, even though the costs are high. The Rule of Proportionality, like that of Reasonable Care, does not usurp the judgments of individual professionals. It does not provide all of the answers. What it does provide is a method for helping us determine what the commitment to beneficence and nonmaleficence requires.

The third rule, the Rule Against Paternalism, is a rule of a different sort. Unlike the first two rules, Reasonable Care and Proportionality, it is a negative rule, that is, a rule telling us how not to act in realizing beneficence and nonmaleficence. It is a warning rule which advises us that certain types of actions are not good ways of enacting beneficence and nonmaleficence. Let us consider what paternalism is and then see why, generally speaking, we should not act paternalistically in order to try to do good or avoid harm.

Paternalism is the act of treating another as a parent treats a child. There are two characteristics of a paternal act. First, it involves an action chosen for another person. This means that the other person did not decide for himself or herself. In fact, the wishes or preferences of the other person may have been ignored or overruled by the one deciding. Second, paternalism involves an action done in the best interests of the other person, as understood by the one deciding. The action is chosen by the paternal decision maker in order to bring about some good to the person decided for, or to avoid some harm to the person decided for. Paternalism, in other words, is decision making for another person out of beneficence and nonmaleficence toward that person.

Now why is paternalism generally not a good way to enact beneficence and nonmaleficence? Strictly speaking, paternalism applies only in caregiving relationships, typically those between parents and children. In these relationships, the acting parent, the one responsible for the dependent, must decide for the dependent, who is not capable of deciding for himself or herself. No one disputes the need for this kind of paternalism. But problems arise when decision makers use paternalism outside of cases involving parents and children. When professionals are tempted to act paternalistically toward clients or colleagues, generally there are two reasons such paternalism is bad. First, in most professional and personal relationships, paternalism is not an appropriate way of expressing beneficence and nonmaleficence, because the paternal decision maker forces on the other person his judgment of what he thinks does good or avoids harm to that other person. By acting paternally, the decision maker dictates that his view of what does good or avoids harm is the only view. But can we really do good and avoid harm to others by coercing them to accept our help and our view of what helps? This is not really helping. It is beneficence and nonmaleficence gone awry, since it allows for only one interpretation of beneficence and nonmaleficence, and this interpretation may be made quite apart from any consideration of reasonable care, proportionality, or the needs of those affected.

Second, paternalism is generally not a good way of acting, because it ignores the preferences and choices of the one for whom a decision is being made. Paternalism may finally result in self-centered actions, in that it allows the decision maker to act on his view of what is best for another rather than on the other person's view of what is best for herself. In doing so, a paternal act also does not acknowledge integrity and respect for persons. Paternalism, even though seemingly motivated by beneficence and nonmaleficence toward another, is not sensitive to commitments we have to other values. Since paternalism in most situations is neither a good way to express beneficence and nonmaleficence toward a person nor a good way of treating persons, it should be avoided.

Rule Against Paternalism

Do not benefit others and avoid harming them by making decisions for them in what you take to be their best interests.

It is nevertheless tempting for professionals to act paternalistically. A lawyer may want to agree to an out-of-court settlement, believing it is in the client's best interests, even though he cannot reach his client to obtain consent. A legislator may vote in favor of a law requiring motorcyclists to wear helmets because it is for the good of the motorcyclists. Professionals sometimes feel that they have more knowledge and authority than their clients, thus are better judges of what benefits them. Professionals may feel that they are like parents to their clients, who are like children. But this paternalism is to be avoided. Complicated cases will exist in which clients are children or are enfeebled and cannot act for themselves. But, in these cases, the client's childlike state needs to be substantiated, and the authority of the professional to act as a surrogate parent also needs to be established. There may be extreme cases in which a professional-client relationship is very similar to the parent–child relationship, and thus paternalism might be appropriate.

The Rule Against Paternalism, like our other rules, is not absolute. It does not provide all of the answers. But the paternalism that is acceptable between parents and children is not acceptable between professionals and clients or colleagues. Hence, the Rule Against Paternalism reminds us that we should not do good and avoid harm to others if in doing so we are treating them like children, that is, deciding for them, according to our view of their best interests.

We have described three guides to help in interpreting beneficence and nonmaleficence. These guides, the Rule of Reasonable Care, the Rule of Proportionality, and the Rule Against Paternalism, advise us in translating our commitments to beneficence and nonmaleficence into action. Together these rules point out that a commitment to beneficence and nonmaleficence does not mean that we are expected to do all good and avoid all harm under all circumstances. Rather our commitments to beneficence and nonmaleficence mean that we should take reasonable care to do good and avoid harm, and we should consider proportionality and avoid paternalism.

Conflicts Involving Beneficence and Nonmaleficence

The earlier sections have considered what beneficence and nonmaleficence are and what a commitment to making them real requires of professionals. There is much to reflect on in using the rules for putting beneficence and nonmaleficence into practice. But there is one more complication to face when discussing beneficence and nonmaleficence. Occasionally, beneficence and nonmaleficence compete with other values. Sometimes the choice to do an action aimed at realizing beneficence or nonmaleficence comes at the cost of not being able to do an action that realizes justice or integrity or some other value. We all remember times when we have felt as though we had to choose between being honest, which would hurt someone's feelings, and not being honest, which would avoid hurting someone's feelings. Should we act with integrity and thus fail to prevent harm, or should we act out of beneficence and so sacrifice integrity? This may be a moral dilemma in which we have to choose between incompatible actions. If so, in choosing between incompatible actions, we may have to choose between the values grounding those actions.

One common type of conflict occurs when beneficence and non-maleficence seem to be incompatible with integrity. There are times when in order to benefit others we may have to compromise our integrity, our principles, and our honesty. We have already considered the "benevolent lie"—an untruth spoken in order to be kind. Employers sometimes ask that reports not be filed or that they not be filed until after a certain date in order to spare the company from the harm of government or shareholder scrutiny. Students and parents ask teachers for special favors and special considerations on grounds that students would be harmed without them. Professionals find themselves in situations where beneficence can be enacted if integrity is compromised. Likewise, in situations where integrity is upheld, we can fail to enact nonmaleficence. Our earlier case of Georgine, the chemist, is a good example. She did not take the biological warfare job, and thereby, since she had no job and could not contribute to the support of her family, she failed to benefit her family. She did so because she was unwilling to give up her integrity. She resolved the conflict between an action grounded on integrity and an action grounded on beneficence by choosing the action that expressed her integrity.

Integrity is not the only value that can come into conflict with beneficence and nonmaleficence. Any of the other values can be interpreted in a situation in a way that competes with the interpretation of beneficence and nonmaleficence offered in that situation. Although it is just as possible for compassion or responsibility or any other value to compete with beneficence and nonmaleficence, it is more likely integrity that competes with them in specific cases. This is so because the other values are similar to beneficence and nonmaleficence in that they aim explicitly to meet the needs of others, while integrity is less like beneficence and nonmaleficence in that it pays more attention to being true to oneself and one's value commitments than to meeting the needs of others.

Another type of situation in which there seems to be a conflict involving beneficence and nonmaleficence occurs when the two values themselves compete. Sometimes the choice to act to realize one seems to fail to do that which would realize the other. Maybe there are two actions, both of which we cannot do, one of which avoids harm and the other of which does good. Suppose on your way into the office you find a wallet. You stop, open it up, and discover it belongs to the chief financial officer of the company where you work, who is well compensated for his work. It also contains $200. It occurs to you that you could return the whole wallet, including the money to the CFO, and that that action avoids harm to the CFO but benefits no one but you, who might be rewarded for this action. Meanwhile, it crosses your mind that you could return the wallet minus the money and put the $200 in the Salvation Army kettle to be used to feed and clothe the homeless. This action benefits others but harms the CFO. Is nonmaleficence in conflict with beneficence here? Should we avoid harming others, or should we benefit others?

We will let you decide this for yourself, but an important point must be noted here. A situation like this is not really a conflict situation where beneficence and nonmaleficence compete. It is not the case that to choose the beneficent act requires us to ignore the claims of nonmaleficence, or vice versa. We said earlier that beneficence and nonmaleficence coexist on a continuum, so to speak of one is already to speak of the other. In the lost wallet example, we are not really choosing between an action that expresses beneficence and one that expresses nonmaleficence. Rather we are debating between interpretations of beneficence and nonmaleficence. We are asking which action does more overall good and to whom should we do good and avoid harm. Each action, returning the money or donating the money, is a way of practicing beneficence and nonmaleficence in a certain way to certain people. Situations like this, where beneficence and nonmaleficence seem to be competing values, are in fact, when we look more closely, cases in which interpretations or applications of beneficence and nonmaleficence compete, and not conflicts between the values per se.

Now how are we to deal with these situations where beneficence and nonmaleficence come into conflict with other values or where there are competing interpretations of beneficence and nonmaleficence? There is no single answer. Each professional decides for himself or herself how to resolve situations where values compete or interpretations of values compete. Nevertheless, there are some guidelines about how to proceed in addressing situations where values or their interpretations compete. Most of these points have been made before, so we simply summarize them here.

First, as we discussed in chapter 6, where there are situations that involve competing values, a professional should clarify, harmonize, and rank. Look first for ways to avoid treating the competing values as though they were locked in a standoff. Determine whether more information helps, or if talking to a boss or colleague or a clarification of the task helps dissipate the value conflict. Make sure it really is a value conflict that confronts you. Maybe the values only seem to conflict. Or maybe one of the two actions is not really backed by a value. If it is a value conflict and there seems to be a moral dilemma, work to harmonize the values. Avoid having to make an either-or choice by looking for creative solutions. Perhaps you can act on one value first and act on the other value later. Or try to bring together those who will be affected by the decision, explain it to them, and ask them to help you decide how to realize the values. Finally, if you must, rank the values. Decide which value is more important in this case, and act on it. Be prepared to defend the action you have chosen and the value that you have designated as overriding.

Second, the Rule of Proportionality is helpful in situations where beneficence and nonmaleficence compete with other values or where interpretations of beneficence and nonmaleficence compete. Decide whether to act for beneficence or integrity or some other value by judging which action realizes more overall moral good. Or consider which interpretation of beneficence and non-maleficence to act on by determining which choice maximizes more overall moral good than harm. Reflect on who is benefitted and harmed, how many are benefitted and harmed, and the magnitude and severity of the benefit and harm. Georgine, the chemist, might have used the Rule of Proportionality to decide whether the minor temporary good to her family caused by her taking the job was less significant than the serious permanent good to her sense of integrity caused by refusing the job. Since the action that expresses benefi-cence produces less overall good than the action that expresses integrity, Georgine acts for the sake of integrity. Hence, the Rule of Proportionality can be used to decide cases when interpretations of beneficence and nonmaleficence compete and cases when these values compete with other values.

Finally, we may be able to resolve conflicts between values and conflicts between value interpretations by observing that the value of nonmaleficence seems to be especially fundamental. Avoiding harm seems to many to be a prerequisite for doing good. Avoiding harm is a more basic or necessary value than doing good. Before professionals can benefit, they must above all take care not to harm. There are of course exceptions. Sometimes a small harm ought to be done for the sake of a far-reaching good. Sometimes even a large harm to a few should be done for the sake of benefitting many. Thus, it is not always true that nonmaleficence supersedes beneficence, but there are many day-to-day situations in which we recognize that we have an especially strong commitment to nonmaleficence. If a stranger is waving from the side of the road because his car has broken down, an accountant on her way to work certainly must avoid hitting the stranger with her car. She must act nonmaleficently, but she may or may not feel that she must pull over to help, and she may or may not act beneficently. Oftentimes we find it is more basic and hence more important to avoid harm than it is to do good or to act to realize other values. Use the Rule of Proportionality—in cases where interpretations of beneficence and nonmaleficence compete and in cases where they conflict with other values. This will help you decide whether a particular case is one in which nonmaleficence is indeed the most important value to be considered or not.

Conclusion

In this chapter, we explored the values of beneficence and nonmaleficence and considered how professionals ought to put them into practice. We found that they are related yet separate values. Professionals have recognized the values of beneficence and nonmaleficence. Many professionals see their role mainly in terms of working to protect and to benefit. Nevertheless, there are complexities involved in coming to understand how to interpret beneficence and nonmaleficence and in learning how to deal with situations where they compete with other values and where their own interpretations compete. We developed several rules that help us determine what actions express our commitment to beneficence and nonmaleficence. Finally, we considered typical types of conflict situations involving beneficence and nonmaleficence and offered suggestions on how to resolve those conflicts.

EXERCISES

1. Take the code of ethics of the profession you are considering and look for the ways in which it expresses beneficence and nonmaleficence. If you are uncertain about your career, pick any code. Consider these questions:

    1. Does the code identify beneficence and nonmaleficence as values for the professional?
    2. In this code, what specific requirements must the professional meet because of the values of beneficence and nonmaleficence?
    3. In this code, with regard to beneficence and nonmaleficence, do you think that too little or too much is required of professionals? Explain.

4. For the professionals covered by this code, do you see any problems or conflicts they might face in acting out the values of beneficence and nonmaleficence? Explain.
5. For the professionals covered by this code, how do you think they should deal with these conflicts? Explain.

2. Here are some cases to consider. Apply the framework for moral analysis if decisions have already been made. Apply the Case Resolution Model (CRM) if decisions are yet to be made. For example, in Case 3, apply the framework for moral analysis to the nurse's decision and, in Case 2, use the CRM to make a decision. Also consider whether the Rule of Reasonable Care, the Rule of Proportionality, or the Rule Against Paternalism is helpful in analyzing or resolving each case. If there are conflicts involving beneficence and nonmaleficence, state them and explain how you would resolve them.

CASE 1: THE VETERINARIAN AND THE PET OWNER

You are a veterinarian specializing in small domestic animals. You have examined a terrier who was brought in by his owner because he was chewing on his paw. You discover a small lump on the dog's paw which does not seem painful to the dog but is at least an irritant and hence the dog is chewing it. You suspect it is just a cyst but it could be a sign of something more serious, and only a biopsy can diagnose it with certainty. You tell the dog's owner all of this and recommend the one-day surgery to check and remove the lump. The dog's owner is concerned but reports that he is out of work right now and that the family finances cannot handle any additional major bills. He tells you that the surgery will have to wait, and he asks you if there are any inexpensive pills or home remedies that would temporarily relax the dog, or ease the irritation so the dog would quit chewing his paw. What do you say or do?

CASE 2: THE CHEMICAL COMPANY'S NEW HIRE

You are a new hire at a large chemical company. You have a degree in chemical engineering. After several weeks of orientation at the main office, you are taken to look at some of the company's chemical plants.

At one plant you are shown a drying shed where a chemical product is being washed with benzine and then dried. In spite of the open windows and fans, it is obvious that much of the benzine evaporates into the air. You know benzine is a carcinogen.

On the way out, you mention to the plant supervisor who showed you around that the conditions in the shed are dangerous to the health of the people working there. The supervisor tells you not to worry about it since everyone working at the plant starts in the shed but eventually moves on to better positions. He tells you, "We've all been there and we're all okay."

You wonder what to do now.

CASE 3: NURSES AND THE PATIENT IN PAIN

Olga Kercik, age eighty, arrived at the emergency room after falling down some icy steps. She was found to have a broken pelvis and taken in for immediate surgery. After surgery, Olga was given a nonaddictive, nonnarcotic pain medication every few hours. But as she recovered from the anesthetic, she began to complain about the pain. The nurses tried to reassure her that some pain was normal and that she would receive another pain pill soon. But as the day wore on, Olga became more unhappy, gritting her teeth, moaning, and calling for the nurses repeatedly. The nurses knew that a stronger narcotic drug would probably do a better job of relieving Olga's pain, but some doctors are cautious about using such drugs because of their addictive nature. The nurses were not sure how the surgeon would feel about being called at home, or how he would feel if they instead summoned the resident on call. What should the nurses do?

NOTES

1. This was widely reported in the newspapers and on television news in September 1997. See, for example, Sue Ellen Christian, "50 Ready to Risk Own Lives to Test AIDS Vaccine," *The Chicago Tribune* (September 21, 1997), Section 1, pp. 1, 14.
2. Some separate the values of beneficence and nonmaleficence. See Ronald Munson, *Intervention and Reflection: Basic Issues in Medical Ethics*, 3rd ed. (Belmont, Calif.: Wadsworth, 1988), pp. 33–37; and Tom L. Beauchamp and James F. Childress, *Principles of Biomedical Ethics*, 4th ed. (New York: Oxford University Press, 1994), pp. 189–317. Others distinguish the principles of benevolence and nonmalevolence. See Gregory R. Beabout and Daryl J. Wennemann, *Applied Professional Ethics* (Lanham, Md.: University Press of America, 1994).
3. See *The Hippocratic Oath*, paragraph 2.
4. See, for example, Charles C. Lund, "The Doctor, the Patient, and the Truth," *Annals of Internal Medicine* 24: 6 (1946); pp. 955–59; and Bernard C. Meyer, "Truth and the Physician," in *Ethical Issues in Medicine: The Role of the Physician in Today's Society*, edited by E. Fuller Torrey (Boston, Mass.: Little, Brown and Company, 1968), pp. 161–77.
5. See the American Nurses' Association, *Code for Nurses*, Section 3, and the American Physical Therapy Association, *Code of Ethics*, Principle 7.

6. See the American Association of Pastoral Counselors, *Code of Ethics*, Principle II.
7. National Association of Social Workers, *Code of Ethics*, Statement P.
8. American Institute of Certified Public Accountants, *Code of Professional Conduct*, Article II.
9. American Institute of Architects, *Code of Ethics and Professional Conduct*, Canon II.
10. National Society of Professional Engineers, *Code of Ethics for Engineers*, Rules of Practice.
11. The Society of Professional Journalists, *Code of Ethics*, I.
12. Summarized from the Hanna Andersson Winter 1997 Catalog.
13. Taken from *Tarasoff v. Regents* of the University of California, 17 Cal. 3d 425 (1976).
14. Ibid.
15. American Institute of Certified Public Accountants, *Code of Professional Conduct*, Rule 201.

12

Responsibility

It is hard to think of anything more central to any moral approach, or any kind of endeavor at all, than responsibility. The centrality of responsibility is particularly the case with a values-based approach to professional ethics. Without the notion of responsibility, in this case to values, the whole structure we have worked so hard to erect is without meaning or purpose. It would be as though we had labored long and hard to build a house, and then, with the house completed and all of the furniture moved in, we decided that this was not the place we wanted to live after all.

Here is where we are. We have pretty much completed filling in the structure of our value-based approach to ethics. The details of the system, as we have seen, are best determined by each individual case. Yet for the details to be worked out, for our values to be made real or actualized in the world, we have to take our responsibilities seriously and be committed to carrying out the values of professional ethics. Not only do we have to admire the house we have built and furnished, but we have to move in and live there, a task that is impossible if we are not responsible. In a way, responsibility brings us back full circle to the first value we considered—integrity. Previously we stated that integrity was, for our purposes, a commitment to the values of professional ethics. What makes us committed to anything, including values, in the first place? In short, responsibility does. We recognize our responsibility, and in doing so, we also recognize that we need a way to interpret what that requires of us. Responsibility requires that we follow through on the values that we have recognized as a basic part of what it is to be human and, more specifically, what it is to be a practicing professional. Without this basic recognition of responsibility and a desire to follow through on it, there is little pertinence to the values of professional ethics, or to professional ethics at all.

Nothing is quite as liberating as to be without responsibilities. Being without responsibility is like having a day off—from everything. Such a possibility could include being freed from phones, people, and all of the other various and sundry demands of the outside world. In being freed from all of these demands, we also are freed from all of our connections. That is, in virtue of being connected to people, tasks and being connected to the world in any way, we have some responsibility to them and to it. Responsibility has varying degrees, from that of an airplane pilot, who is responsible for the lives of his or her passengers, to the minimal types of responsibility we experience as we fulfill the expectation of driving down the correct side of the road on a highway, or not pushing people out of the way while we wait our turn at the post office. Recognizing that responsibility is that which makes us care at all about being ethical, professional or otherwise, we bring this book and this approach to professional ethics to a close by considering this keystone value.

In the rest of this chapter, we will consider a working definition of responsibility, in a manner similar to that of integrity. Responsibility also is a two-tiered sort of value, but the more global tier in this instance is even more crucial to the rest of our values than any other value alone. Once we have considered what responsibility is and what it involves, we will look at a case that involves responsibility from many different perspectives. This case indicates in a very complicated way all the pervasive levels at which responsibility can be appreciated and how it is that in each one all of the other values of our approach are implicitly present. Finally, we will consider some guides to interpreting responsibility and some of the typical conflicts that arise when responsibility is at stake.

What Is Responsibility?

When considering responsibility, we have many things to think about. We have mentioned that responsibility is like integrity, in that it is a two-tiered value. On one level, responsibility is that which is the precondition for the possibility of our doing ethics, or being and thinking about things in an ethical way. On a more local level, remaining consistent with the language of chapter 7, responsibility can be understood as being the inventory of those specific things required of us when we are responsible to someone or something or for someone or something. The global level of responsibility makes it possible for us to recognize and take seriously that we are being responsible to or for someone or something.

We begin by looking at the global aspect of responsibility as that which justifies, or leads us to act on, our other values, including the local considerations of responsibility. In its more global aspect, responsibility is that which binds us to the world and our fellow beings. We have responsibilities to ourselves and to others, and recognizing this is the precondition for fulfilling these responsibilities, as well as one of the first signs of maturity. Think about a baby or a small child. There is not much that this little one cares about other than the satisfaction of needs and having those needs fulfilled in an immediate manner. Even staying away from a hot stove may not seem initially worthwhile when balanced with a need to satisfy curiosity. However, as we grow up, we see that our needs are really just a few among the many needs not only of ourselves but others, and we cannot always have everything we want. Granted, we may want what someone else has, but we recognize that it is theirs, so we do not take it without asking, whether it is a possession, person, or sovereignty. Likewise we may want to exclusively do those things that make us happy, but we recognize that doing them might require us to do other things first, whether eating dinner before having dessert or finishing a major project at work or school before going out with friends or reading a novel.

Truly, responsibility does pull on us, and in its presence we can have it drag us down or pull us forward. Although this sounds quite serious, laden with obligation and steeped in duty, it is only one side of responsibility. The other side of this value, in looking at it globally, comes from seeing the possibilities that come from recognizing its positive pull on us. When we see that we are responsible, we can feel bogged down and just stop there, or we can see how this responsibility is to be made manifest and thereby fulfilled. By now it should be no big surprise that the way in which responsibility is to be made manifest and fulfilled is through the enactment of our six values, including responsibility. In being made manifest or real, responsibility connects us to other people and the world, which is no small thing.

Being connected to the world is possible through appreciating responsibility in its global sense, which serves as a precondition for recognizing the obligation and eventual fulfillment of all of our responsibilities. This enables all of our values to be made actual, including responsibility in its local sense. This being connected to the world gives our life meaning, even if that meaning is a negative one. For example, you are responsible for paying your taxes, and this may fill you with resentment, especially around the middle of April every year. Even so, this responsibility of being a taxpayer connects you to the government, its offices, and the whole citizenry, most of whom are in a similar situation. Likewise, you are responsible to your supervisor at work. If you enjoy your job and are pleased about the way you do your work, this connection to an organization represented by an individual may make this responsibility a positive one. If you find your job demeaning or uninteresting, you will feel quite negative about your responsibilities there. In short, it is through responsibility, in this global sense, that we see our connections to others, recognizing and taking them seriously enough to fulfill them.

Clearly, the fulfillment of our responsibilities is accomplished through all of our values—integrity, compassion, justice, and the rest. While those have been discussed previously, we now look to the way in which the local sense of responsibility is played out as a consequence of recognizing our responsibilities.[1] That is, once we recognize we have responsibilities, we need to know more about them, particularly since we will go on to determine what they involve in their fulfillment. For the most part, responsibility comes in two forms—responsibility to and responsibility for. That is, we either have responsibility to someone or something, and are thereby morally accountable to an entity. Or we are responsible for someone or something and are thereby the moral agents or cause of something, directly or indirectly. Of course, real life is never as clean and simple as definitions. Often we are both responsible to and for the same someone or something, or the nature of our responsibility changes relative to the circumstances. With that stated, we will finish this section by examining how it is that these two types of responsibility are to be understood.

Who are you responsible to? Or, what kinds of things do you have a responsibility to? That is, to whom do you provide an accounting of yourself, professionally or otherwise? The answer to these similar questions can be quite varied. Are you responsible to your supervisor? Are you responsible to your parents, your spouse, yourself, your God? All of these things to which we are responsible have in common the idea of duty or obligation. Things we are responsible to involve a duty or an obligation that we accept from a relationship we have with another outside of ourselves. For example, if you are a mail carrier, your responsibility comes from your obligation and duty to deliver the mail, "in rain, sleet, or snow." You thus have a responsibility to the people on your mail route, as well as a responsibility to your supervisor, whose job it is to see that you follow through on this responsibility. This duty of delivering the mail is a part of the responsibilities you have in virtue of your job. They are put upon you. In that sense, they are not consciously chosen, but, they are accepted as a part of agreeing to do the job you have chosen to undertake. Arguably, the decision to take one job over any other is a free choice to a greater and lesser degree, however, once you choose your job, you do not often get to choose all of the responsibilities that go along with it. These responsibilities are those things and those people we are responsible to, sometimes, whether we like it or not. In short, responsibilities *to* things or people are those responsibilities that include duties, obligations, and connections put upon us, which we have not freely chosen, except derivatively, as we choose to accept the conditions under which these responsibilities are the case.

In addition to responsibilities to something or someone, we can understand our responsibilities as being for something or someone. That is, for whom or for what are you responsible? Are you responsible for seeing that the garbage is taken out on Monday nights, for the computer maintenance at work, for feeding your cat or educating your children, or bringing the yams to Thanksgiving dinner? Those things *for* which we are responsible are those actions and events we cause, or have some sort of causal relationship to, as we are the agent of bringing them about. Think again of the example of a mail carrier. The mail carrier has many responsibilities *to* various people and entities, however, deciding to be a mail carrier is a responsibility *for* doing something and having a particular occupation. When someone decides to be a mail carrier, he or she decides to assume responsibility for mail delivery. In doing so, a mail carrier takes on the responsibilities of this particular occupation. Thus the responsibilities for something are those we put on ourselves, which we have freely chosen, but included within them are often those responsibilities that are put upon us.

In sum, responsibility centers around the concept of duty and obligation. These duties and obligations bind us to individuals, communities, and institutions in a variety of positive and negative ways. Once bound, and recognizing that we need to fulfill our responsibilities, we see that they are of two primary types. We see that we are responsible *to* people and entities, and we are responsible *for* people and entities. The distinction between these two types of responsibility is not absolute. However, it can be understood generally as we appreciate that those things and people to which we are responsible are those responsibilities that we have not directly chosen freely, while those things and people for which we are responsible include those responsibilities that we have chosen to take on freely.

What Responsibility Involves

Now that we know what responsibility is, in its global and local sense, we are free to examine how it can be actualized in our professional lives. To do this, we will turn to some of the professional codes for a look at how responsibilities are to be followed through. Responsibility, just like the other values considered by the codes, is referred to generally, though interpretation is required to see exactly what it involves of us.

We begin to address what professional responsibility involves by looking at two professional codes, the American Bar Association's *Model Rules of Professional Conduct* and the *Code of Ethics and Standards of Practice for Environmental Professionals*. Here there are various articulations of what it is to be responsible. In the ABA code, the preamble appeals to "A Lawyer's Responsibilities," while Rule 3.8 appeals to the "Special Responsibilities of a Prosecutor," and still further, in Rule 5 and its subsections, we learn more about the responsibilities of a "Partner or Supervisory Lawyer" and those of a "Subordinate Lawyer" and "Nonlawyer Assistants." In each of these sections we learn more about the value of responsibility and what is expected of those in the legal profession in order to satisfy their responsibilities. Likewise, in the EP code and standards, various sections are presented which explain not only what is obligated of environmental professionals, but what is expected. By looking at each of these sections, we can begin to appreciate the way in which responsibility is pertinent in our professional life.

The preamble of the ABA code specifies the lawyer's responsibilities by listing certain duties and obligations, among them, "be competent, prompt, and diligent."[1] Under the creed of the EP code, we learn, "The objectives of an Environmental Professional are to recognize ... societal and individual human needs with responsibility for physical, natural, and cultural systems."[3]

In this initial analysis of responsibility, demonstrated through the American Bar Association and the National Association of Environmental Professionals, we see that being a member of these professions requires one to be responsible. Being responsible includes following through on the duties and obligations of the profession, not just in any way, but professionally, thus any commitment to responsibility requires that one execute their job well.

The preamble of the American Bar Association's *Model Rules of Professional Conduct* continues, "the lawyer's professional responsibilities are prescribed in the Rules of Professional Conduct."[4] Thus in choosing to assume the responsibility of being a lawyer, it is indicated that a lawyer takes on several different types of responsibilities, such as those articulated in the Rules of Professional Conduct. In applying these rules, lawyers are able to determine specifically what their professional responsibilities entail. That is, not only must lawyers perform their jobs well, they must perform their jobs well in specific as well as general ways. In the Rules of Professional Conduct, we learn more about what exactly lawyers are required to do, dependent on their professional context. For example, in Rule 3.8, it is stated that, among other things, a prosecutor shall "not seek to obtain from an unrepresented accused a waiver of important pretrial rights, such as the right to a preliminary hearing."[5] Thus prosecuting attorneys must be certain that specific duties and obligations which are relevant to their profession are fulfilled.

Other than these specific duties of each kind of legal practice, there is an additional general expectation of attorneys. Under Rule 5.1, the responsibilities of a supervisory lawyer are indicated. The kinds of responsibilities articulated here express what sort of obligations lawyers have for those to whom they are responsible, that is, those who report to them and whose work they oversee. A lawyer with supervisory authority "shall make reasonable efforts to ensure that the other lawyer conforms to the rules of professional conduct."[6] Thus in a supervisory capacity it is not enough that a lawyer fulfill his or her own responsibilities. He or she must make an effort to ensure that those for whom he or she is responsible fulfill the duties and obligations of their own responsibilities. As stated, this can seem very daunting, but remember, supervisors also get credit for the good work of those for whom they are responsible.

Looking at the *Code of Ethics and Standards of Practice for Environmental Professionals*, we see some of the same themes of responsibility in operation. An environmental professional is called upon to be "responsible and ethical in . . . professional activities."[7] This seems to call for environmental professionals to take seriously the duties and obligations of their jobs. Likewise, environmental professionals are required to be responsible for the ethical as well as technical aspects of their jobs. An environmental professional will conduct his or her "professional activities in a manner that ensures consideration of technically and economically feasible alternatives."[8] Thus being an environmental professional requires acting knowledgeably and communicating various alternatives, upholding technical duties, and fulfilling ethical duties, both of which are obligations. Once again we see some of the same themes of responsibility in operation. An environmental professional is called upon to be "personally responsible for the validity of all data collected, analyses performed, or plans developed by me or under my direction."

As we have seen in these codes, not only does responsibility involve following through on one's duties and obligations, it also requires appreciating the subtleties of the responsibilities relative to one's specific duty. For example, you are required to see that those for whom you are responsible, or those whom you supervise, follow through on their duties and obligations. In short, responsibility involves taking seriously your own duties and their completion, as well as the completion of the duties for which you are indirectly or peripherally responsible. This requirement of responsibility does not mean that a professional has to see that everyone, everywhere follows through on their responsibilities. However, it does suggest that a professional is required to see that those for whom he or she is responsible and with whom he or she is affiliated follow through on their responsibilities. Responsibility in this latter sense requires one to be obligated for the way in which others do their work. In short, responsibility requires that you not only do your job well, but see to it that others for whom you are responsible also are doing their jobs well.

A Case Involving Responsibility

Since the value of responsibility involves duties and obligations, context is important in determining which particular duties and obligations are at stake. Let us turn to a specific case that involves various responsibilities that obligate professionals, not all of which can be fulfilled.

> *Michael Stocks is a newly hired nurse in the emergency room of a Los Angeles hospital. He recently passed his state boards, after completing his nursing training at a local university. Michael was pleased to get this job, since nursing cutbacks have been the norm in this part of the country. He was particularly pleased to be working in his area of expertise, emergency medicine. The hospital where he works is situated in a middle-class neighborhood, which itself is situated close to a trauma center. Typically, violent injuries such as gunshot wounds are treated at this center. This evening, about two hours into his shift, Michael heard people shouting outside of the hospital doors. There were neighbors, teenagers, and police, all screaming, trying to get anyone from inside of the hospital to help. A fifteen-year-old boy had just been shot, a seeming victim of a drive-by shooting, while playing basketball at an adjacent playground. He was presently lying in an alley, bleeding profusely. Intuitively, Michael thought to help, but as he looked around at his colleagues, none of whom were going outside of the hospital, he was reminded of the policy to which he had just been introduced during his training and orientation session. Hospital staffers are not to leave their duties or the building facilities to treat people outside of the hospital. They are not permitted to go outside of the hospital and bring people into the ER for treatment. All patients must be delivered to the ER, by police, friends, family, ambulance, and so on. As Michael and his coworkers were standing around the emergency room, the friends, neighbors, and local police were pleading with the ER staff to come out and treat the young man. Michael had no idea what to do.[9]*

Since, as stated, there is no decision in this case, we begin with Stage I of the CRM to help us determine how Michael ought to follow through on his responsibilities.

Stage I.

   1.   *(P)*resent the problem.

Michael is being asked to treat a patient outside of the hospital, and hospital policy forbids employees to leave their duties or to bring patients into the facility.

   2.   *(C)*ollect the information.

Michael is a newly hired ER nurse. There is someone bleeding profusely, from a gunshot wound, in an alley outside of the hospital. The hospital has a policy that its staff members are not to leave their duties or the building to treat patients or bring patients into the hospital for treatment. Michael and his coworkers are standing around the ER.

Stage II.

   3. (*L*)ist the relevant value(s).

In this case, responsibility is the primary value at stake. Although other values are certainly important here, we will concentrate on an analysis that will allow Michael to satisfy his responsibilities and, in doing so, to maintain his integrity. Thus Michael's fellow employees', and the hospital's integrity all are at stake. In addition, compassion is certainly a relevant value for this case. In addition to these three, what other values are centrally relevant to our analysis?

   4. (*E*)xplore the options and the ways theories apply.

Acting as a consequentialist, Michael must consider whether a greater good would be attained by treating the young man in the alley and going against hospital policy or not treating the young man in the alley, thus upholding hospital policy. If Michael were to leave the ER and attempt to help the teen by bringing him into the hospital, he could be bringing about good consequences by saving a life. Furthermore, the boy's friends, neighbors, and the police certainly would be appreciative and would probably stop screaming outside of the doors of the hospital, bringing further good consequences in terms of peace and quiet to those in the vicinity. Yet what of the hospital's policy? If Michael were to obey this policy, he would be fulfilling a responsibility to his employer, thereby bringing about good consequences insofar as he did not abandon his other patients or put the hospital at risk for a potential lawsuit.

The rights theory is relevant in this case, since Michael must consider not only who has rights in this situation but whose rights deserve to be fulfilled if others need to be sacrificed. That is, in best fulfilling his responsibilities, whose rights will be honored and whose rights will be sacrificed? What rights does Michael's employer have? In what manner should Michael fulfill his employer's right to have Michael be responsible for doing his job in such a way that he follows hospital guidelines? What about Michael's rights? How can he be responsible to his conception of what a nurse does? In what way can he juggle his right to be a nurse, in the manner he sees fit, with his employer's right to have him follow policy? Last but not least, what about the rights of the teenager who is bleeding in an alley? All of these considerations of rights are relevant for Michael to determine how he can best, as a right theorist, fulfill his responsibility.

According to a duty-based theory, Michael would have to determine where the greater duty lay. Does he have a greater duty to follow his employer's policy or to attempt to save a life? Furthermore, if Michael determines that his greater duty is to save a life, he must consider the best means of fulfilling this duty. Also crucial to an interpretation of a duty-based theory is the intentions Michael might have. He should consider all of these things carefully as he determines what a duty-based theory would require of him. Finally, are there any ways of resolving these seemingly conflicting duties? That is, maybe there is another duty Michael has overlooked that would allow him to not only abide by hospital policy but also to help the teen in the alley.

As a virtue theorist, Michael has his work cut out for him. A virtue theorist would aim to act in such a manner that he would best express good character. In this instance, as with all, good character includes the good character of an employee and a regular person. Ideally, a good employee and good person are the same, but in expressing the virtue of a professional, these two demands would need to be balanced. On the one hand, a person of good character would help those in need, and obviously someone who is a victim of a gunshot wound is in need. On the other hand, a person of good character would fulfill his or her responsibilities to his or her employer by following policy. In short, Michael needs to determine how best to express good character as a helping professional.

Care theory figures prominently in this case. As Michael is faced with the challenge of caring for the teen in the alley, he must determine how to best care for those patients he is now caring for in the ER. How would Michael best care for all of his patients? Again, the teen is not a patient of Michael's, so Michael may have a greater responsibility to care for the patients he already has than to the injured teen. However, as a nurse, does Michael not have a responsibility to care for those who could benefit from his expertise? What would a caring nurse do in this situation, and who should the nurse be caring for?

Finally, how would a narrative analysis deal with this moral problem? That is, within the context of all that is narratively relevant, what should Michael do? How important are rules to Michael within the history of his career? When rules come into conflict with what Michael may or may not see as the focus of his career, namely, helping people, which has traditionally won out? Other things to be considered in a narrative analysis are the ways in which all of the other members of the ER staff are behaving in this situation. Is it significant for Michael's history that to help the teen would be "going against the crowd"? Many things would need to be considered in a well-developed application of the narrative theory. Think of some of them and their consequences for Michael's action.

This case is not a clear and simple one. Much more than this cursory treatment of theories would need to be considered in determining the best outcome for all of those involved. How would you further develop the options to be explored through each of the theories applied?

5. (A)ssess the rightness and wrongness of various outcomes.

Michael could leave the hospital premises and attempt to aid the injured teenager.

Michael could honor hospital policy and wait for an ambulance or someone else to bring the injured teen into the ER.

Michael could arrange for the teen to be immediately brought into the ER and to commence treatment as soon as the patient crossed the threshold of the hospital entrance. He could continue to care for the patients his superiors (to whom he is responsible) have told him to care for (those for whom he is responsible).

6. (D)ecide.

This is a very serious case, with much at stake. There is a life at stake, the future of the hospital's policy, and potentially Michael's employment, among the more relevant concerns. With that understood, rather than make a decision here, in a few sentences, consider the decision yourself. What has been left out of this application of the CRM? What decision should Michael make in order to honor all of his responsibilities? Or, if honoring all of his responsibilities is impossible, what is the best way for Michael to maintain his responsibilities as much as possible?

Stage III.

    7. (*D*)efend.

Since you had to make the decision in step 6, defend it now. Articulate the reasons that led you to your decision. What are some potential objections to your perspective, and why do you think these objections pose no real challenge to your decision?

    8. (*R*)eflect.

Reflect on the decision you just made. Is there any way this decision could be avoided in the future? What about the hospital's policy? Could it be amended or adapted to preserve the primary reasons for its existence, without requiring employees to leave injured people outside of the doors of the hospital? What about Michael? As a consequence of having faced this sort of difficult situation once, what will he do in the future if he feels torn between employer policy and what he feels is his responsibility to his profession? What kind of strategies can you come up with to avoid this sort of situation in the future?

From this case, we can see some of the myriad complications involved in interpreting the value of responsibility. Perhaps because it is so all encompassing, responsibility is at stake in the cases where the most is at stake. With that appreciated, we consider some rules that aid us in interpreting responsibility in its multiple manifestations.

Interpreting Responsibility: Guides to Help

As the case of Michael indicates, responsibility is a complicated value. Having a commitment to this value can seem overwhelming. However, it need not be, and in what follows, we appeal to some general guidelines to help us in interpreting this value.

Rule of Responsible Professionalism

Follow through on your responsibility to enact values.

Returning to chapter 1, a professional does his or her job well (with technological acumen) and treats people well (with relational sensitivity). Appreciating this, we have said that there is a global interpretation of responsibility that requires us to take seriously our commitment to values. It is a good rule of thumb to consistently keep this notion of responsibility in mind. Keeping it in mind will allow us to be the moral professionals each of us is capable of being. Often, this recognition does not require more of us than driving in the right direction down a one-way street. Yet other times, when faced with a moral conflict or situation that requires resolution, recognizing that we are responsible and thereby have responsibility forces us to see that we must consider and work to uphold all of the values.

What does this mean then for Michael Stocks? Realizing that he is committed to the values of professional ethics, Michael must resolve his commitments in such a way that he remains a professional. Remember, Michael's goal is to remain a professional, not merely to remain employed. In considering such a goal, Michael must not only consider the situation he is currently in but the situation in which he will remain after these events come to pass. Considering the values, Michael can make a decision relative to his understanding of himself and his professionalism.

The first rule is thus general, in that it requires us to be professionals. But what about our responsibilities as professionals? The next rule addresses this situation.

Rule of Responsibility Placement

Determine carefully where your responsibilities lie. Follow through on the responsibilities you have, assuming that you have taken them on or chosen them knowingly and that they do not explicitly undermine any of your other overriding responsibilities.

Taking responsibility for, or being responsible to, is a commitment that should not be taken lightly. Earlier in this chapter, we articulated the difference between the two types of responsibility by showing that one includes responsibility over which we have little control, while the other includes responsibility over which we have more control. Considering this, it would follow from the above rule that the responsibilities we have freely chosen in general override any responsibilities that have been put upon us. If the latter requires that we violate or come into an irreconcilable conflict with any of our other values, then we no longer need hold that original responsibility should we need to abandon it. In general, choose carefully to or for whom you are responsible. Try not to take on responsibilities that you cannot or will not carry out, or that explicitly undermine your other responsibilities.

With this second rule in mind, let us return to Michael. Michael has freely chosen to be a professional nurse, thus Michael has a responsibility for nursing. As part of this, he is working in a Los Angeles hospital that has asked him not to treat people outside of hospital grounds, so he has a responsibility to not treat certain people. This latter responsibility may conflict with Michael's responsibility as a nurse. Thus should Michael choose to violate this responsibility, by going against hospital policy, he could do so without regret and with complete regard for the responsibility he had chosen freely. That is, were Michael to have known that a commitment to his responsibilities to the hospital would require him to let someone die that his training could have helped, he would not have agreed ahead of time to such a responsibility. So this rule is supposed to help us avoid those sorts of situations.

Conflicts Involving Responsibility

By now, conflicts involving values should probably seem quite obvious, so you can no doubt discern the potential conflicts that relate to the value of responsibility. For the most part, the conflicts of responsibility are of three types—a conflict of responsibility discernment, that is, a problem with interpreting responsibility; a conflict when once your responsibilities have been determined, you find that you cannot fulfill all of your responsibilities; and a conflict when your responsibilities within your professional life clash with the responsibilities outside of your professional life.

Let us consider this first conflict involving responsibility. The problem here is not that responsibility comes up against something else, but rather that it is difficult to interpret responsibility. When Michael is faced with the problem of whether to treat the teenager in the alley, he must determine what his responsibility is. Like all of us, when faced with a difficult situation, he must determine what his obligations are, relative to the situation. The outcome of this assessment cannot be determined independently of the situation. Thus, in assessing the situation, we need to ask to whom or what we are responsible and for whom or what we are responsible. As is, this is not really a conflict but rather a problem, which left unresolved can lead to a conflict.

Once we have determined what our responsibilities are, what is to be done if not all of our responsibilities can be fulfilled? Returning to Michael, he cannot both remain in the building and provide treatment to the injured teen. Yet, in a way, he is obligated to do both. When more than one thing obligates you in such a manner that fulfilling one obligation precludes fulfilling another, you are in conflict. Responsibilities may come into conflict. We have seen that often middle-ground solutions can avoid the problem of having to choose between mutually exclusive actions. Ideally, Michael should try to creatively fulfill both obligations, but if he has to abdicate responsibility to or for one of his duties, he will need to justify this by an appeal to the other values. Sacrificing one responsibility for another should always be tempered by an appeal to other values. If Michael were to violate hospital policy, he would do so through appeal to beneficence and nonmaleficence, compassion, respect for persons, and integrity as a nursing professional. Yet, if he were to fail to treat the teen, he would uphold hospital policy but he would not be able to justify his actions through the values of compassion, respect for persons, or integrity. In short, we cannot ignore or walk away from any of the claims of values and remain moral.

The problem of multiple responsibilities in our personal and professional lives is one that will follow all moral professionals throughout their careers. Because we are obligated to so many different things at different times in our lives, it will always be difficult to determine which of these obligations should be binding at which time. For example, let us say that you have a pet. Clearly, owning a pet obligates you. You are responsible for caring for your pet in all of the ways a pet needs care. But let us say that in addition to having the pet, you also have a job, probably so you can buy food so the pet can eat. Are you responsible for your pet while you are at your job? Of course you are, but that does not mean you duck out of your workplace to go check on the animal. However, it does mean that you provide an adequate environment for your pet when you are not home to care for it. With a pet, this example is not very complicated. You walk dogs and let cats sit on your lap. The situation becomes more complex as those responsibilities that pull on us require more of our time. This is obviously the case with working parents, who must consistently balance, if not actually juggle, all of their many responsibilities, all of which bind them at all times.

With responsibilities that are always binding, it is important to keep in mind that all responsibilities are not all equally binding at all times. That is, your children are generally not always sick at the same time you need them to be healthy enough to go to day care so you can go to work, and you do not always have to work extended hours throughout your career, which would make it impossible for you to be a community volunteer. With that said, human beings are finite, and we often are not equally able to fulfill all of our responsibilities to a standard that may be satisfying. Thus, we typically choose the way in which we allocate our limited abilities to fulfill our responsibilities. When making these choices, we should acknowledge that these are moral choices. In making such an acknowledgment, we are able to appeal to the guidelines that we have developed. In doing so, we will be better able to make decisions that are not merely contingent upon the immediate situation, but also are commensurate with our overarching commitment to values. Decisions that mesh with our values, personal and professional, usually are the easiest ones with which to live.

Conclusion

When discussing responsibility, we have dealt with the value that makes all of our other ones prized and worthwhile. It is through responsibility that we appreciate not only our connectedness to others but our need for ways to make the moral obligations that come from that connection concrete. As professionals, this requires us to do our job professionally, while at the same time we see that those around us do their best to do their jobs professionally, a task aided by our appreciating to whom and what and for whom and what we are responsible. In doing so, we apply the Rule of Responsible Professionalism and the Rule of Responsibility Placement in order to interpret responsibility and enact the rest of our values. Consequently, in our work lives, we put our values to work in becoming moral professionals.

EXERCISES

1. Take the code of ethics for your proposed occupation. If you are uncertain about your career, pick any code. Consider the following:

   1. Is there an explicit or implicit appeal to responsibility contained in the code? Explain, using specific examples.
   2. Define responsibility relative to the way it is used in the code of ethics for your proposed occupation. Does it have a global sense?

Does it have a local sense? Is the more prevalent definition of responsibility a responsibility to someone or something, or a responsibility for someone or something?

3. In this code, what specific requirements must the professional meet because of the value of responsibility? Are these requirements too extensive or not extensive enough? Does this code include any specific requirements of responsibility or any sanctions for when the requirements of responsibility are not met?

4. For the professionals covered by this code, do you foresee any potential problems or conflicts they might face in acting out the value of responsibility? Give three examples and explain each.

2. Use the CRM to reach a decision in each of these cases. In doing so, consider all of the relevant values, but be especially alert to considerations of responsibility and its requirements. In making your decision about how to resolve the case, articulate which guide for interpreting responsibility is most helpful. Be sure to explain your answers fully.

CASE 1: RESPONSIBILITIES OF A REPO MAN

Your job is in the collections department of a rent-to-own company. A local family of seven, including five children, has a significant relationship with the store. They have in their possession from your store a computer, a living room suite, and a 56-inch color television, totaling over $5,500. The customer's account is now eighty-three days late and will be a complete loss to the company in seven days. The family has been fifteen to thirty days late in paying, and now you have learned that the husband is in the hospital, causing the unemployed wife and family to turn to welfare. Numerous phone calls have gone unanswered, certified letters have been returned, and through recent collection visits, you have encountered extremely confrontational individuals. Although many attempts have been made, you have not been in verbal contact with the customer for fifty days. You go to the customer's home to attempt repossession. The front door is open, but no one answers your calls or poundings on the door frame. You see some of the rented items directly from your vantage point at the door. You need to pick up this merchandise, but you see no one who is capable of giving authorization. What do you do?[10]

CASE 2: RESPONSIBILITY AND COMMUNITY

You are in charge of strategic planning for a local chain of grocery stores. This chain has had a presence in the community throughout your life and that of your parents. You remember walking to the store in your neighborhood and having the store manager greet you by name while the cashiers made sure you did not spend too much money on candy. You are proud of your association with this organization.

The community in which this chain was established has fallen on hard times for the last twenty years or so. The steel industry was its base, and when that industry pulled out of town, the community never fully recovered. As a consequence of this economic wound, there has been a mass exodus from the community proper to the surrounding suburbs. This drop in population has hurt all of the stores that are closer to the downtown area, while boosting all of the suburban, outlying locations. As you draw up the plans for next year, you and your colleagues must consider what to do about one store in particular. This store has been operating at a loss for some time, and it is located on the "border" between downtown and the beginning of the suburban area. Nearby the store is a retirement facility, most of whose residents do not drive and depend on this store for their groceries. In addition to concern for the residents, you are concerned about the problem of urban flight. That is, you know that one more empty building in the neighborhood will not help resuscitate the town. You are scheduled to meet tomorrow with the rest of the committee, and you need to come up with some options about what to do with this store.

CASE 3: JUNIOR DEPARTMENT MEMBER'S RESPONSIBILITY

Rita is a junior faculty member in one of the high-powered academic departments of her university. She has a tenure track position, which includes being on probation the first years of her appointment at the university. Thus far, Rita has proven to be a good colleague, with a solid track record in academic service and scholarship at her school. She enjoys her work and is appreciative of her contact with students, which to her makes her job worthwhile.

Because of a retirement, Rita is moved away from her office at the end of the hall, closer to a more trafficked part of the department. While there, she is acutely aware of the actions of one of her more senior, tenured colleagues. This individual rarely shows up for his office hours, is consistently insensitive to student appointments, and cancels class whenever it seems to suit his needs. Furthermore, she has heard him lie on more than one occasion about his whereabouts. Rita is troubled by this situation, particularly because this individual never seems to feel any remorse about his actions, and she doubts that he will acquire any scrutiny for his unprofessional behavior. Since she is committed to the well-being of students, Rita feels an obligation to take their side when she feels that their needs are not being considered. After all, she says,

"If it weren't for the students, why would we be here at all?" How should Rita resolve her responsibility to her students with her awareness of this colleague's unprofessionalism?

NOTES

1. Much of this discussion of the global and local senses of responsibility assumes what was discussed in chapter 7. If these terms are unclear to you, review this chapter, especially sections 7.1 and 7.2, and consider the following. We have six values—integrity, respect for persons, justice, compassion, beneficence and nonmaleficence, and responsibility. Each makes it possible for us to be moral professionals. But without regard for integrity and without a recognition of responsibility, we would not be committed to being moral professionals. The way in which integrity and responsibility lead us to enact values and thereby to become moral professionals is their global sense. But at the same time, integrity and responsibility also must be enacted as part of the six values that make up the practice of a moral professional. The way in which integrity and responsibility concretely give us the means to understand our connections to ourselves and others is their local sense.
2. See the "Preamble," American Bar Association's *Model Rules of Professional Conduct*, American Bar Association.
3. Introductory section, *Code of Ethics and Standards of Practice for Environmental Professionals*, National Association of Environmental Professionals.
4. See the "Preamble," *Model Rules of Professional Conduct*.
5. Ibid., Rule 3.8, "Special Responsibilities of a Prosecutor."
6. Ibid., section for Law Firms and Associations, Rule 5.1, "Responsibilities of a Partner or Supervisory Lawyer."
7. See the section, "Ethics, As an Environmental Professional I Will," #1, *Code of Ethics and Standards of Practice for Environmental Professionals*, National Association of Environmental Professionals.
8. See the section, "Guidance for Practice As an Environmental Professional, As an Environmental Professional I Will," #8, *Code of Ethics and Standards of Practice for Environmental Professionals*, National Association of Environmental Professionals.
9. This case is based on the death of Christopher Seryce, who at fifteen years of age died in the alley outside of Ravenswood Hospital in Chicago, Illinois, on May 16, 1998. Effective May 25, hospital officials revoked a hospital policy that discouraged its personnel from aiding those outside of the ER. See Lindsey Tanner's story of Tuesday, May 19, 1998, "Teen Dies As Hospital Workers Watch," from the Associated Press Wire Release. Thanks to Youngstown State University students from Introduction to Professional Ethics, Spring 1998, for bringing this case to the attention of the class.
10. Thanks to the students of Youngstown State University from Introduction to Professional Ethics, Spring 1998, for bringing up this case.

GROUP 3: READINGS ON BENEFICENCE AND NONMALEFICENCE AND RESPONSIBILITY

Introduction

This last group of readings raises many of the salient issues concerning how values are to be enacted by professionals, focusing especially on beneficence and nonmaleficence and responsibility. The first is a work of fiction, *Settled Score*, by Sara Paretsky, featuring the engaging lawyer turned private investigator, V.I. Warshawski. As V.I. works a case and deals with her relationships, the issues of holism and separatism are revisited. As the case is worked through, we get to see how a professional works through the negotiations required to maintain values in the face of multiple demands. At play in the background of this drama are the main characters of this mystery: a psychiatrist, a physician, and musicians, all of whom are involved in a discussion about the nature of responsibility. Ultimately, related questions of confidentiality, intention, beneficence and nonmaleficence, and compassion also arise.

In the next selection, *The Social Responsibility of Business Is to Increase Its Profits*, Milton Friedman articulates what he sees as the limits of corporate responsibility in a classic text. Originally a *New York Times* editorial in 1970, Friedman's piece is as topical now as it was then. For him, the question of responsibility is answered only by distinguishing between ends, agents of corporations, shareholders, and corporations. His viewpoint states that the efforts of corporations are misspent in attempts to do anything other than increase profits for their shareholders within the legal limits of the way in which we are to practice business, or as he describes it, within the "rules of the game." Friedman does not argue that it is a bad idea to do things for society, rather, individuals are not to do things, which in their opinion, are for society while acting as agents of a corporation, since corporations themselves have no moral responsibility.

From a different perspective, Richard DeGeorge, in *Corporations and Moral Responsibility*, presents an alternative notion of the responsibilities of a corporation and its representative members. Against Friedman's perspective, which he terms the *organizational view*, DeGeorge presents a detailed list of what the responsibilities of corporations are and are not. Not only does DeGeorge address the moral responsibilities of corporations, he also addresses those of management and workers. These responsibilities are multiple, and DeGeorge argues that when they are actualized, not only is there good management, but also corporate excellence, moral and otherwise.

The last reading, *The Duty to Treat Patients with AIDS and HIV Infection*, by Albert R. Jonsen, considers whether health care professionals, especially physicians, are required to treat those who are HIV positive or who have AIDS. In this piece, Jonsen treats the question of why certain professions and professionals are required to undertake difficult tasks, even those that may put them at risk. Beneficence and nonmaleficence are relevant values, as are justice and responsibility, as Jonsen looks at reasons that would or would not require treatment. By addressing this practical, concrete problem, Jonsen shows us how values can guide concrete moral decision making.

Through a careful consideration of all of these readings, perhaps you can begin to articulate your own view of what your social responsibilities are, both inside and outside a corporation or an institution. Likewise, you can consider how you will enact beneficence and nonmaleficence throughout your professional life. Although the readings suggest different interpretations of the values, they agree that the values are central to a moral professional's life. Thus the readings as a whole support the view that remaining true to beneficence and nonmaleficence and responsibility, in the various manners in which we interpret them, is crucial to maintaining a commitment to values in our lives, both professional and otherwise.

Settled Score

SARA PARETSKY

I

"It's such a difficult concept to deal with. I just don't like to use that word." Paul Servino turned to me, his mobile mouth pursed consideringly. "I put it to you, Victoria: you're a lawyer. Would you not agree?"

"I agree that the law defines responsibility differently than we do when we're talking about social or moral relations," I said carefully. "No state's attorney is going to try to get Mrs. Hampton arrested, but does that—"

"You see," Servino interrupted. "That's just my point."

"But it's not mine," Lotty said fiercely, her thick dark brows forming a forbidding line across her forehead. "And if you had seen Claudia with her guts torn out by lye, perhaps you would think a little differently."

The table was silenced for a moment: we were surprised by the violent edge to Lotty's anger. Penelope Herschel shook her head slightly at Servino.

He caught her eye and nodded. "Sorry, Lotty. I didn't mean to upset you so much."

Lotty forced herself to smile. "Paul, you think you develop a veneer after thirty years as a doctor. You think you see people in all their pain and that your professionalism protects you from too much feeling. But that girl was fifteen. She had her life in front of her. She didn't want to have a baby. And her mother wanted her to. Not for religious reasons, even—she's English with all their contempt for Catholicism. But because she hoped to continue to control her daughter's life. Claudia felt overwhelmed by her mother's pressure and swallowed a jar of oven cleaner. Now don't tell me the mother is not responsible. I do not give one damn if no court would try her: to me, she caused her daughter's death as surely as if she had poured the poison into her."

Servino ignored another slight headshake from Lotty's niece. "It is a tragedy. But a tragedy for the mother, too. You don't think she meant her daughter to kill herself, do you, Lotty?"

Lotty gave a tense smile. "What goes on in the unconscious is surely your department, Paul. But perhaps that was Mrs. Hampton's wish. Of course, if she didn't *intend* for Claudia to die, the courts would find her responsibility diminished. Am I not right, Vic?"

I moved uneasily in my chair. I didn't want to referee this argument: it had all the earmarks of the kind of domestic fight where both contestants attack the police. Besides, while the rest of the dinner party was interested in the case and sympathetic to Lotty's feelings, none of them cared about the question of legal versus moral responsibility.

The dinner was in honor of Lotty Herschel's niece, Penelope, making one of her periodic scouting forays into Chicago's fashion scene. Her father—Lotty's only brother—owned a chain of high-priced women's dress shops in Montreal, Quebec, and Toronto. He was thinking of making Chicago his U.S. beachhead, and Penelope was out looking at locations as well as previewing the Chicago designers' spring ideas.

Lotty usually gave a dinner for Penelope when she was in town. Servino was always invited. An analyst friend of Lotty's, he and Penelope had met on one of her first buying trips to Chicago. Since then, they'd seen as much of each other as two busy professionals half a continent apart could manage. Although their affair now had five years of history to it, Penelope continued to stay with Lotty when she was in town.

The rest of the small party included Max Loewenthal, the executive director of Beth Israel, where Lotty treated perinatal patients, and Chaim Lemke, a clarinetist with the Aeolus Woodwind Quintet. A slight, melancholy man, he had met Lotty and Max in London, where they'd all been refugees. Chaim's wife, Greta, who played harpsichord and piano for an early music group, didn't come along. Lotty said not to invite her because she was seeing Paul professionally, but anyway, since she was currently living with Aeolus oboist Rudolph Strayarn, she probably wouldn't have accepted.

We were eating at my apartment. Lotty had called earlier in the day, rattled by the young girl's death and needing help putting the evening together. She was so clearly beside herself that I'd felt compelled to offer my own place. With cheese and fruit after dinner Lotty had begun discussing the case with the whole group, chiefly expressing her outrage with a legal system that let Mrs. Hampton off without so much as a warning.

For some reason Servino continued to argue the point despite Penelope's warning frowns. Perhaps the fact that we were on our third bottle of Barolo explained the lapse from Paul's usual sensitive courtesy.

"Mrs. Hampton did not point a gun at the girl's head and force her to become pregnant," he said. "The daughter was responsible, too, if you want to use that word. And the boy—the father, whoever that was."

Lotty, normally abstemious, had drunk her share of the wine. Her black eyes glittered and her Viennese accent became pronounced.

"I know the argument, believe you me, Paul: it's the old 'who pulled the trigger?'—the person who fired the gun, the person who manufactured it, the person who created the situation, the parents who created the shooter. To me, that is Scholastic hairsplitting—you know, all that crap they used to teach us a thousand years ago in Europe. Who is the ultimate cause, the immediate cause, the sufficient cause, and on and on."

"It's dry theory, not life. It takes people off the hook for their own actions. You can quote Heinz Kohut and the rest of the self-psychologists to me all night, but you will never convince me that people are unable to make conscious choices for their actions or that parents are not responsible for how they treat their children. It's the same thing as saying the Nazis were not responsible for how they treated Europe."

Penelope gave a strained smile. She loved both Lotty and Servino and didn't want either of them to make fools of themselves. Max, on the other hand, watched Lotty affectionately—he liked to see her passionate. Chaim was staring into space, his lips moving. I assumed he was reading a score in his head.

"I would say that," Servino snapped, his own Italian accent strong "And don't look at me as though I were Joseph Goebbels. Chaim and I are ten years younger than you and Max, but we share your story in great extent. I do not condone or excuse the horrors our families suffered, or our own dispossession. But I can look at Himmler, or Mussolini, or even Hitler and say they behaved in such and such a way because of weaknesses accentuated in them by history, by their parents, by their culture. You could as easily say the French were responsible, the French because their need for—for—*rappresaglia*—what am I trying to say, Victoria?"

"Reprisal," I supplied.

"Now you see, Lotty, now I, too, am angry: I forget my English. . . . But if they and the English had not stretched Germany with reparations, the situation might have been different. So how can you claim responsibility—for one person, or one nation? You just have to do the best you can with what is going on around you."

Lotty's face was set. "Yes, Paul. I know what you are saying. Yes, the French created a situation. And the English wished to accommodate Hitler. And the Americans would not take in the Jews. All these things are true. But the Germans chose, nonetheless. They could have acted differently. I will not take them off the hook just because other people should have acted differently."

I took her hand and squeezed it. "At the risk of being the Neville Chamberlain in the case, could I suggest some appeasement? Chaim brought his clarinet and Max his violin. Paul, if you'll play the piano, Penelope and I will sing."

Chaim smiled, relaxing the sadness in his thin face. He loved making music, whether with friends or professionals. "Gladly, Vic. But only a few songs. It's late and we go to California for a two-week tour tomorrow."

The atmosphere lightened. We went into the living room, where Chaim flipped through my music, pulling out Wolf's *Spanisches Liederbuch*. In the end, he and Max stayed with Lotty, playing and talking until three in the morning, long after Servino and Penelope's departure.

II

The detective business is not as much fun in January as at other times of the year. I spent the next two days forcing my little Chevy through unplowed side streets trying to find a missing witness who was the key to an eighteen-million-dollar fraud case. I finally succeeded Tuesday evening a little before five. By the time I'd convinced the terrified woman, who was hiding with a niece at Sixty-seventh and Honore, that no one would shoot her if she testified, gotten her to the state's attorney, and seen her safely home again, it was close to ten o'clock.

I fumbled with the outer locks on the apartment building with my mind fixed on a hot bath, lots of whiskey, and a toasted cheese sandwich. When the ground-floor door opened and Mr. Contreras popped out to meet me, I ground my teeth. He's a retired machinist with more energy than Navratilova. I didn't have the stamina to deal with him tonight.

I mumbled a greeting and headed for the stairs.

"There you are, doll." The relief in his voice was marked. I stopped wearily. Some crisis with the dog. Something involving lugging a sixty-pound retriever to the vet through snow-packed streets.

"I thought I ought to let her in, you know. I told her there was no saying when you'd be home, sometimes you're gone all night on a case"—a delicate reference to my love life—"but she was all set she had to wait and she'd a been sitting on the stairs all this time. She won't say what the problem is, but you'd probably better talk to her. You wanna come in here or should I send her up in a few minutes?"

Not the dog, then. "Uh, who is it?"

"Aren't I trying to tell you? That beautiful girl. You know, the doc's niece."

"Penelope?" I echoed foolishly.

She came out into the hall just then, ducking under the old man's gesticulating arms. "Vic! Thank God you're back. I've got to talk to you. Before the police do anything stupid."

She was huddled in an ankle-length silver fur. Ordinarily elegant, with exquisite makeup and jewelry and the most modern of hairstyles, she didn't much resemble her aunt. But shock had stripped the sophistication from her, making her dark eyes the focus of her face; she looked so much like Lotty that I went to her instinctively.

"Come on up with me and tell me what's wrong." I put an arm around her.

Mr. Contreras closed his door in disappointment as we disappeared up the stairs. Penelope waited until we were inside my place before saying anything else. I slung my jacket and down vest on the hooks in the hallway and went into the living room to undo my heavy walking shoes.

Penelope kept her fur wrapped around her. Her high-heeled kid boots were not meant for street wear: they were rimmed with salt stains. She shivered slightly despite the coat.

"Have—have you heard anything?"

I shook my head, rubbing my right foot, stiff from driving all day.

"It's Paul. He's dead."

"But—he's not that old. And I thought he was very healthy." Because of his sedentary job, Servino always ran the two miles from his Loop office to his apartment in the evening.

Penelope gave a little gulp of hysterical laughter. "Oh, he was very fit. But not healthy enough to overcome a blow to the head."

"Could you tell the story from the beginning instead of letting it out in little dramatic bursts?"

As I'd hoped, my rudeness got her angry enough to overcome her incipient hysteria. After flashing me a Lotty-like look of royal disdain, she told me what she knew.

Paul's office was in a building where a number of analysts had their practices. A sign posted on his door this morning baldly announced that he had canceled all his day's appointments because of a personal emergency. When a janitor went in at three to change a light-bulb, he'd found the doctor dead on the floor of his consulting room.

Colleagues agreed they'd seen Servino arrive around a quarter of eight, as he usually did. They'd seen the notice and assumed he'd left when everyone else was tied up with appointments. No one thought any more about it.

Penelope had learned of her lover's death from the police, who picked her up as she was leaving a realtor's office where she'd been discussing shop leases. Two of the doctors with offices near Servino's had mentioned seeing a dark-haired woman in a long fur coat near his consulting room.

Penelope's dark eyes were drenched with tears. "It's not enough that Paul is dead, that I learn of it in such an unspeakable way. They think I killed him because I have dark hair and wear a fur coat. They don't know what killed him—some dreary blunt instrument—it sounds stupid and banal, like an old Agatha Christie. They've pawed through my luggage looking for it."

They'd questioned her for three hours while they searched and finally, reluctantly, let her go, with a warning not to leave Chicago. She'd called Lotty at the clinic and then come over to find me.

I went into the dining room for some whiskey. She shook her head at the bottle. I poured myself an extra slug to make up for missing my bath. "And?"

"And I want you to find who killed him. The police aren't looking very hard because they think it's me.

"Do they have a reason for this?"

She blushed unexpectedly. "They think he was refusing to marry me."

"Not much motive in these times, one would have thought. And you with a successful career to boot. Was he refusing?"

"No. It was the other way around, actually. I felt—felt unsettled about what I wanted to do—come to Chicago to stay, you know. I have—friends in Montreal, too, you know. And I've always thought marriage meant monogamy."

"I see." My focus on the affair between Penelope and Paul shifted slightly. "You didn't kill him, did you—perhaps for some other reason?"

She forced a smile. "Because he didn't agree with Lotty about responsibility? No. And for no other reason. Are you going to ask Lotty if she killed him?"

"Lotty would have mangled him Sunday night with whatever was lying on the dining room table—she wouldn't wait to sneak into his office with a club." I eyed her thoughtfully. "Just out of vulgar curiosity, what were you doing around eight this morning?"

Her black eyes scorched me. "I came to you because I thought you would be sympathetic. Not to get the same damned questions I had all afternoon from the police!"

"And what were you doing at eight this morning?"

She swept across the room to the door, then thought better of it and affected to study a Nell Blaine poster on the nearby wall. With her back to me she said curtly, "I was having a second cup of coffee. And no, there are no witnesses. As you know, by that time of day Lotty is long gone. Perhaps someone saw me leave the building at eight-thirty— I asked the detectives to question the neighbors, but they didn't seem much interested in doing so."

"Don't sell them short. If you're not under arrest, they're still asking questions."

"But you could ask questions to clear me. They're just trying to implicate me."

I pinched the bridge of my nose, trying to ease the dull ache behind my eyes. "You do realize the likeliest person to have killed him is an angry patient, don't you? Despite your fears the police have probably been questioning them all day."

Nothing I said could convince her that she wasn't in imminent danger of a speedy trial before a kangaroo court, with execution probable by the next morning. She stayed until past midnight, alternating pleas to hide her with commands to join the police in hunting down Paul's killer. She wouldn't call Lotty to tell her she was with me because she was afraid Lotty's home phone had been tapped.

"Look, Penelope," I finally said, exasperated. "I can't hide you. If the police really suspect you, you were tailed here. Even if I could figure out a way to smuggle you out and conceal you someplace, I wouldn't do it— I'd lose my license on obstruction charges and I'd deserve to."

I tried explaining how hard it was to get a court order for a wiretap and finally gave up. I was about ready to start screaming with frustration when Lotty herself called, devastated by Servino's death and worried about Penelope. The police had been by with a search warrant and had taken away an array of household objects, including her umbrella. Such an intrusion would normally have made her spitting mad, but she was too upset to give it her full emotional attention. I turned the phone over to Penelope. Whatever Lotty said to her stained her cheeks red, but did make her agree to let me drive her home.

When I got back to my place, exhausted enough to sleep round the clock, I found John McGonnigal waiting for me in a blue-and-white outside my building. He came up the walk behind me and opened the door with a flourish.

I looked at him sourly. "Thanks, Sergeant. It's been a long day— I'm glad to have a doorman at the end of it."

"It's kind of cold down here for talking, Vic. How about inviting me up for coffee?"

"Because I want to go to bed. If you've got something you want to say, or even ask, spit it out down here."

I was just ventilating and I knew it—if a police sergeant wanted to talk to me at one in the morning, we'd talk. Mr. Contreras's coming out in a magenta bathrobe to see what the trouble was merely speeded my decision to cooperate.

While I assembled cheese sandwiches, McGonnigal asked me what I'd learned from Penelope.

"She didn't throw her arms around me and howl, 'Vic, I killed him, you've got to help me.'" I put the sandwiches in a skillet with a little olive oil. "What've you guys got on her?"

The receptionist and two of the other analysts who'd been in the hall had seen a small, dark-haired woman hovering in the alcove near Servino's office around twenty of eight. Neither of them had paid too much attention to her; when they saw Penelope, they agreed it might have been she, but they couldn't be certain. If they'd made a positive I.D., she'd already have been arrested, even though they couldn't find the weapon.

"They had a shouting match at the Filigree last night. The maitre d' was quite upset. Servino was a regular and he didn't want to offend him, but a number of diners complained. The Herschel girl"—McGonnigal eyed me warily—"woman, I mean, stormed off on her own and spent the night with her aunt. One of the neighbors saw her leave around seven the next morning, not at eight-thirty, as she says."

I didn't like the sound of that. I asked him about the cause of death.

"Someone gave him a good crack, across the side of the neck, close enough to the back to fracture a cervical vertebra and sever one of the main arteries. It would have killed him pretty fast. And as you know, Servino wasn't very tall—the Herschel woman could easily have done it."

"With what?" I demanded.

That was the stumbling block. It could have been anything from a baseball bat to a steel pipe.

The forensic pathologist who'd looked at the body favored the latter, since the skin had been broken in places. They'd taken away anything in Lotty's apartment and Penelope's luggage that might have done the job and were having them examined for traces of blood and skin.

I snorted. "If you searched Lotty's place, you must have come away with quite an earful."

McGonnigal grimaced. "She spoke her mind, yes . . . Any ideas? On what the weapon might have been?"

I shook my head, too nauseated by the thought of Paul's death to muster intellectual curiosity over the choice of weapon. When McGonnigal left around two-thirty, I lay in bed staring at the dark, unable to sleep despite my fatigue. I didn't know Penelope all that well. Just because she was Lotty's niece didn't mean she was incapable of murder. To be honest, I hadn't been totally convinced by her histrionics tonight. Who but a lover could get close enough to you to snap your neck? I thrashed around for hours, finally dropping into an uneasy sleep around six.

Lotty woke me at eight to implore me to look for Servino's killer; the police had been back at seven-thirty to ask Penelope why she'd forgotten to mention she'd been at Paul's apartment early yesterday morning.

"Why was she there?" I asked reasonably.

"She says she wanted to patch things up after their quarrel, but he'd already left for the office. When the police started questioning her, she was too frightened to tell the truth. Vic, I'm terrified they're going to arrest her."

I mumbled something. It looked to me like they had a pretty good case, but I valued my life too much to say that to Lotty. Even so the conversation deteriorated rapidly.

"I come out in any wind or weather to patch you up. With never a word of complaint." That wasn't exactly true, but I let it pass. "Now, when I beg you for help you turn a deaf ear to me. I shall remember this, Victoria."

Giant black spots formed and re-formed in front of my tired eyes. "Great, Lotty."

Her receiver banged in my ear.

III

I spent the day doggedly going about my own business, turning on WBBM whenever I was in the car to see if any news had come in about Penelope's arrest. Despite all the damaging eyewitness reports, the state's attorney apparently didn't want to move without a weapon.

I trudged up the stairs to my apartment a little after six, my mind fixed on a bath and a rare steak followed immediately by bed. When I got to the top landing, I ground my teeth in futile rage: a fur-coated woman was sitting in front of the door.

When she got to her feet I realized it wasn't Penelope but Greta Schipauer, Chaim Lemke's wife. The dark hallway had swallowed the gold of her hair.

"Vic! Thank God you've come back. I've been here since four and I have a concert in two hours."

I fumbled with the three stiff locks. "I have an office downtown just so that people won't have to sit on the floor outside my home," I said pointedly.

"You do? Oh—it never occurred to me you didn't just work out of your living room."

She followed me in and headed over to the piano, where she picked out a series of fifths. "You really should get this tuned, Vic."

"Is that why you've been here for two hours? To tell me to tune my piano?" I slung my coat onto a hook in the entryway and sat on the couch to pull off my boots.

"No. no." She sat down hastily. "It's because of Paul, of course. I spoke to Lotty today and she says you're refusing to stir yourself to look for his murderer. Why, Vic? We all need you very badly. You can't let us down now. The police were questioning me for two hours yesterday. It utterly destroyed my concentration. I couldn't practice at all; I know the recital tonight will be a disaster. Even Chaim has been affected, and he's out on the West Coast."

I was too tired to be tactful. "How do you know that? I thought you've been living with Rudolph Strayarn."

She looked surprised. "What does that have to do with anything? I'm still interested in Chaim's music. And it's been terrible. Rudolph called this morning to tell me and I bought an L.A. paper downtown."

She thrust a copy of the *L.A. Times* in front of me.

It was folded back to the arts section where the headline read AEOLUS JUST BLOWING IN THE WIND. They'd used Chaim's publicity photo as an inset.

I scanned the story:

Chaim Lemke, one of the nation's most brilliant musicians, must have left his own clarinet at home because he played as though he'd never handled the instrument before. Aeolus manager Claudia Laurents says the group was shattered by the murder of a friend in Chicago; the rest of the quintet managed to pull a semblance of a concert together, but the performance by America's top woodwind group was definitely off-key.

I handed the paper back to Greta. "Chaim's reputation is too strong—an adverse review like this will be forgotten in two days. Don't worry about it—go to your concert and concentrate on your own music."

Her slightly protuberant blue eyes stared at me. "I didn't believe Lotty when she told me. I don't believe I'm hearing you now. Vic, we need you. If it's money, name your figure. But put aside this coldness and help us out."

"Greta, the only thing standing between the police and an arrest right now is the fact that they can't find the murder weapon. I'm not going to join them in hunting for it. The best we can hope for is that they never find it. After a while they'll let Penelope go back to Montreal and your lives will return to normal."

"No, no. You're thinking Penelope committed this crime. Never, Vic, never. I've known her since she was a small child—you know I grew up in Montreal—it's where I met Chaim. Believe me, I know her. She never committed this murder."

She was still arguing stubbornly when she looked at her watch, gave a gasp, and said she had to run or she'd never make the auditorium in time. When I'd locked the door thankfully behind her, I saw she'd dropped her paper. I looked at Chaim's delicate face again, sad as though he knew he would have to portray mourning in it when the picture was taken.

IV

When the police charged Penelope late on Thursday, I finally succumbed to the alternating pleas and commands of her friends to undertake an independent investigation. The police had never found a weapon, but the state's attorney was willing to believe it was in the Chicago River.

I got the names of the two analysts and the receptionist who'd seen Servino's presumed assailant outside his office on Tuesday. They were too used to seeing nervous people shrinking behind partitions to pay much attention to this woman; neither of them was prepared to make a positive I.D. in court. That would be a help to Freeman Carter, handling Penelope's defense, but it couldn't undo the damage caused by Penelope's original lies about her Tuesday morning activities.

She was free on $100,000 bond. Swinging between depression and a kind of manic rage, she didn't tell a very convincing story. Still, I was committed to proving her innocence; I did my best with her and trusted that Freeman was too savvy to let her take the witness stand herself.

I got a list of Paul's patients, both current and former, from a contact at the police. Lotty, Max, and Greta were bankrolling both

Freeman and me to any amount we needed, so I hired the Streeter brothers to check up on patient alibis.

I talked to all of them myself, trying to ferret out any sense of betrayal or rage urgent enough to drive one of them to murder. With a sense of shameful voyeurism, I even read Paul's notes. I was fascinated by his descriptions of Greta. Her total self-absorption had always rubbed me the wrong way. Paul, while much more empathic, seemed to be debating whether she would ever be willing to participate in her own analysis.

"How did Paul feel about your affair with Rudolph?" I asked Greta one afternoon when she had made one of her frequent stops for a progress report.

"Oh, you know Paul; he had a great respect for what the artistic temperament and what someone like me needs to survive in my work. Besides, he convinced me that I didn't have to feel responsible—you know, that my own parents' cold narcissism makes me crave affection. And Rudolph is a much more relaxing lover than poor Chaim, with his endless parade of guilt and self-doubt."

I felt my skin crawl slightly. I didn't know any psychoanalytic theory, but I couldn't believe Paul meant his remarks on personal responsibility to be understood in quite this way.

Meanwhile, Chaim's performance had deteriorated so badly that he decided to cancel the rest of the West Coast tour. The Aeolus found a backup, the second clarinet in the Chicago Symphony, but their concert series got mediocre reviews in Seattle and played to half-full houses in Vancouver and Denver.

Greta rushed to the airport to meet Chaim on his return. I knew because she'd notified the local stations and I found her staring at me on the ten o'clock news, escorting Chaim from the baggage area with a maternal solicitude. She shed the cameras before de-camping for Rudolph's—she called me from there at ten-thirty to make sure I'd seen her wifely heroics.

I wasn't convinced by Greta's claims that Chaim would recover faster on his own than with someone to look after him. The next day I went to check on him for myself. Even though it was past noon, he was still in his dressing gown. I apologized for waking him, but he gave a sweet, sad smile and assured me he'd been up for some time. When I followed him into the living room, a light, bright room facing Lake Michigan, I was shocked to see how ill he looked. His black eyes had become giant holes in his thin face; he apparently hadn't slept in some time.

"Chaim, have you seen a doctor?"

"No, no." He shook his head. "It's just that since Paul's death I can't make music. I try to play and I sound worse than I did at age five. I don't know which is harder—losing Paul or having them arrest Penelope. Such a sweet girl. I've known her since she was born. I'm sure she didn't kill him. Lotty says you're investigating?"

"Yeah, but not too successfully. The evidence against her is very sketchy—it's hard for me to believe they'll get a conviction. If the weapon turns up . . ." I let the sentence trail away. If the weapon turned up, it might provide, the final caisson to shore up the state's platform. I was trying hard to work for Penelope, but I kept having disloyal thoughts.

"You yourself are hunting for the weapon? Do you know what it is?"

I shook my head. "The state's attorney gave me photos of the wound. I had enlargements made and I took them to a pathologist I know to see if he could come up with any ideas. Some kind of pipe or stick with spikes or something on it—like a caveman's club—I'm so out of ideas I even went to the Field Museum to see *if* they could suggest something, or were missing some old-fashioned lethal weapon."

Chaim had turned green. I felt contrite—he had such an active imagination I should have watched my tongue. Now he'd have night-mares for weeks and would wait even longer to get his music back. I changed the subject and persuaded him to let me cook some lunch from the meager supplies in the kitchen. He didn't eat much, but he was looking less feverish when I left.

V

Chaim's cleaning woman found him close to death the morning Penelope's trial started. Lotty, Max, and I had spent the day in court with Lotty's brother Hugo and his wife. We didn't get any of Greta's frantic messages until Lotty checked in at the clinic before dinner.

Chaim had gone to an Aeolus rehearsal the night before, his first appearance at the group in some weeks. He had bought a new clar-inet, thinking perhaps the problem lay with the old one. Wind in-struments aren't like violins—they deteriorate over time, and an active clarinetist has to buy a new one every ten years or so. Despite the new instrument, a Buffet he had flown to Toronto to buy, the re-hearsal had gone badly.

He left early, going home to turn on the gas in the kitchen stove. He left a note which simply said: "I have destroyed my music." The cleaning woman knew enough about their life to call Greta at Rudolph's apartment. Since Greta had been at the rehearsal—waiting for the oboist—she knew how badly Chaim had played.

"I'm not surprised," she told Lotty over the phone. "His music was all he had after I left him. With both of us gone from his life he must have felt he had no reason to live. Thank God I learned so much from

Paul about why we aren't responsible for our actions, or I would feel terribly guilty now."

Lotty called the attending physician at the University of Chicago Hospital and came away with the news that Chaim would live, but he'd ruined his lungs—he could hardly talk and would probably never be able to play again.

She reported her conversation with Greta with a blazing rage while we waited for dinner in her brother's suite at the Drake. "The wrong person's career is over," she said furiously. "It's the one thing I could never understand about Chaim—why he felt so much passion for that self-centered whore!"

Marcella Herschel gave a grimace of distaste—she didn't deal well with Lotty at the best of times and could barely tolerate her when she was angry. Penelope, pale and drawn from the day's ordeal, summoned a smile and patted Lotty's shoulder soothingly while Max tried to persuade her to drink a little wine.

Freeman Carter stopped by after dinner to discuss strategy for the next day's session. The evening broke up soon after, all of us too tired and depressed to want even a pretense of conversation.

The trial lasted four days. Freeman did a brilliant job with the state's sketchy evidence; the jury was out for only two hours before returning a "not guilty" verdict. Penelope left for Montreal with Hugo and Marcella the next morning. Lotty, much shaken by the winter's events, found a locum for her clinic and took off with Max for two weeks in Portugal.

I went to Michigan for a long weekend with the dog, but didn't have time or money for more vacation than that. Monday night, when I got home, I found Hugo Wolf's *Spanisches Liederbuch* still open on the piano from January's dinner party with Chaim and Paul. Between Paul's murder and preparing for Penelope's trial I hadn't sung since then. I tried picking out "In dem Schatten meiner Locken," but Greta was right: the piano needed tuning badly.

I called Mr. Fortieri the next morning to see if he could come by to look at it. He was an old man who repaired instruments for groups like the Aeolus Quintet and their ilk; he also tuned pianos for them. He only helped me because he'd known my mother and admired her singing.

He arranged to come the next afternoon. I was surprised—usually you had to wait four to six weeks for time on his schedule—but quickly reshuffled my own Tuesday appointments to accommodate him. When he arrived, I realized that he had come so soon because Chaim's suicide attempt had shaken him. I didn't have much stomach for rehashing it, but I could see the old man was troubled and needed someone to talk to.

"What bothers me, Victoria, is what I should do with his clarinet. I've been able to repair it, but they tell me he'll never play again—

surely it would be too cruel to return it to him, even if I didn't submit a bill."

"His clarinet?" I asked blankly. "When did he give it to you?"

"After that disastrous West Coast tour. He said he had dropped it in some mud—I still don't understand how that happened, why he was carrying it outside without the case. But he said it was clogged with mud and he'd tried cleaning it, only he'd bent the keys and it didn't play properly. It was a wonderful instrument, only a few years old, and costing perhaps six thousand dollars, so I agreed to work on it. He'd had to use his old one in California and I always thought that was why the tour went so badly. That and Paul's death weighing on him, of course."

"So you repaired it and got it thoroughly clean," I said foolishly.

"Oh, yes. Of course, the sound will never be as good as it was originally, but it would still be a fine instrument for informal use. Only—I hate having to give him a clarinet he can no longer play."

"Leave it with me," I said gently. "I'll take care of it."

Mr. Fortieri seemed relieved to pass the responsibility on to me. He went to work on the piano and tuned it back to perfection without any of his usual criticisms on my failure to keep to my mother's high musical standard.

As soon as he'd gone, I drove down to the University of Chicago Hospital. Chaim was being kept in the psychiatric wing for observation, but he was allowed visitors. I found him sitting in the lounge, staring into space while *People's Court* blared meaninglessly on the screen overhead. He gave his sad sweet smile when he saw me and croaked out my name in the hoarse parody of a voice.

"Can we go to your room, Chaim? I want to talk to you privately."

He flicked a glance at the vacant faces around us but got up obediently and led me down the hall to a Spartan room with bars on the window.

"Mr. Fortieri was by this afternoon to tune my piano. He told me about your clarinet."

Chaim said nothing, but he seemed to relax a little.

"How did you do it, Chaim? I mean, you left for California Monday morning. What did you do—come back on the red-eye?"

"Red-eye?" he croaked hoarsely.

Even in the small space I had to lean forward to hear him. "The night flight."

"Oh. The red-eye. Yes. Yes, I got to O'Hare at six, came to Paul's office on the el, and was back at the airport in time for the ten o'clock flight. No one even knew I'd left L.A.—we had a rehearsal at two and I was there easily."

His voice was so strained it made my throat ache to listen to him.

"I thought I hated Paul. You know, all those remarks of his about responsibility. I thought he'd encouraged Greta to leave me." He stopped to catch his breath. After a few gasping minutes he went on.

"I blamed him for her idea that she didn't have to feel any obligation to our marriage. Then, after I got back, I saw Lotty had been right. Greta was just totally involved in herself. She should have been named Narcissus. She used Paul's words without understanding them."

"But Penelope," I said. "Would you really have let Penelope go to jail for you?"

He gave a twisted smile. "I didn't mean them to arrest Penelope. I just thought—I've always had trouble with cold weather, with Chicago winters. I've worn a long fur for years. Because I'm so small people often think I'm a woman when I'm wrapped up in it. I just thought, if anyone saw me, they would think it was a woman. I never meant them to arrest Penelope."

He sat panting for a few minutes. "What are you going to do now, Vic? Send for the police?"

I shook my head sadly. "You'll never play again—you'd have been happier doing life in Joliet than you will now that you can't play. I want you to write it all down, though, the name you used on your night flight and everything. I have the clarinet; even though Mr. Fortieri cleaned it, a good lab might still find blood traces. The clarinet and your statement will go to the papers after you die. Penelope deserves that much—to have the cloud of suspicion taken away from her. And I'll have to tell her and Lotty."

His eyes were shiny. "You don't know how awful it's been, Vic. I was so mad with rage that it was like nothing to break Paul's neck. But then, after that, I couldn't play anymore. So you are wrong: even if I had gone to Joliet I would still never have played."

I couldn't bear the naked anguish in his face. I left without saying anything, but it was weeks before I slept without seeing his black eyes weeping onto me.

The Social Responsibility of Business Is to Increase Its Profits

MILTON FRIEDMAN

When I hear businessmen speak eloquently about the "social responsibilities of business in a free-enterprise system," I am reminded of the wonderful line about the Frenchman who discovered at the age of 70 that he had been speaking prose all his life. The businessmen believe that they are defending free enterprise when they declaim that business is not concerned "merely" with profit but also with promoting desirable "social" ends; that business has a "social conscience" and takes seriously its responsibilities for providing employment, eliminating discrimination, avoiding pollution and whatever else may be the catchwords of the contemporary crop of reformers. In fact they are—or would be if they or anyone else took them seriously—preaching pure and unadulterated socialism. Businessmen who talk this way are unwitting puppets of the intellectual forces that have been undermining the basis of a free society these past decades.

The discussions of the "social responsibilities of business" are notable for their analytical looseness and lack of rigor. What does it mean to say that "business" has responsibilities? Only people can have responsibilities. A corporation is an artificial person and in this sense may have artificial responsibilities, but "business" as a whole cannot be said to have responsibilities, even in this vague sense. The first step toward clarity in examining the doctrine of the social responsibility of business is to ask precisely what it implies for whom.

Presumably, the individuals who are to be responsible are businessmen, which means individual proprietors or corporate executives. Most of the discussion of social responsibility is directed at corporations, so in what follows I shall mostly neglect the individual proprietor and speak of corporate executives.

In a free-enterprise, private property system, a corporate executive is an employee of the owners of the business. He has direct responsibility to his employers. That responsibility is to conduct the business in accordance with their desires, which generally will be to make as much money as possible while conforming to the basic rules of society, both those embodied in law and those embodied in ethical custom. Of course, in some cases his employers may have a different objective. A group of persons might establish a corporation for an eleemosynary purpose—for example, a hospital or a school. The manager of such a corporation will not have money profit as his objective but the rendering of certain services.

In either case, the key point is that, in his capacity as a corporate executive, the manager is the agent of the individuals who own the corporation or establish the eleemosynary institution, and his primary responsibility is to them.

Needless to say, this does not mean that it is easy to judge how well he is performing his task. But at least the criterion of performance is straightforward, and the persons among whom a voluntary contractual arrangement exists are clearly defined.

Of course, the corporate executive is also a person in his own right. As a person, he may have many other responsibilities that he recognizes or assumes voluntarily—to his family, his conscience, his feelings of charity, his church, his clubs, his city, his country. He may feel impelled by these responsibilities to devote part of his income to causes which he regards as worthy, to refuse to work for particular corporations, and even to leave his job, for example, to join his country's armed forces. If we wish, we may refer to some of these responsibilities as "social responsibilities." But in these respects he is acting as a principal, not an agent; he is spending his own money or time or energy, not the money of his employers or the time or energy he has contracted to devote to their purposes. If these are "social responsibilities," they are the social responsibilities of individuals, not of business.

What does it mean to say that the corporate executive has a "social responsibility" in his capacity as businessman? If this statement is not pure rhetoric, it must mean that he is to act in some way that is not in the interest of his employers. For example, that he is to refrain from increasing the price of the product in order to contribute to the social objective of preventing inflation, even though a price increase would be in the best interest of the corporation. Or that he is to make expenditures on reducing pollution beyond the amount that is in the best interests of the corporation or that is required by law in order to contribute to the social objective of improving the environment. Or that, at the expense of corporate profits, he is to hire "hardcore" unemployed instead of better qualified available workmen to contribute to the social objective of reducing poverty.

In each of these cases, the corporate executive would be spending someone else's money for a general social interest. Insofar as his actions in accord with his "social responsibility" reduce returns to stockholders, he is spending their money. Insofar as his actions raise the price to customers, he is spending the customers' money. Insofar as his actions lower the wages of some employees, he is spending their money.

The stockholders or the customers or the employees could separately spend their own money on the particular action if they wished to do so. The executive is exercising a distinct "social responsibility," rather than serving as an agent of the stockholders or the customers or the employees, only if he spends the money in a different way than they would have spent it.

But if he does this, he is in effect imposing taxes, on the one hand, and deciding how the tax proceeds shall be spent, on the other.

This process raises political questions on two levels: principle and consequences. On the level of political principle, the imposition of taxes and the expenditure of tax proceeds are governmental functions. We have established elaborate constitutional, parliamentary, and judicial provisions to control these functions, to assure that taxes are imposed so far as possible in accordance with the preferences and desires of the public—after all, "taxation without representation"—was one of the battle cries of the American Revolution. We have a system of checks and balances to separate the legislative function of imposing taxes and enacting expenditures from the executive function of collecting taxes and administering expenditure programs and from the judicial function of mediating disputes and interpreting the law.

Here the businessman—self selected or appointed directly or indirectly by stockholders—is to be simultaneously legislator, executive, and jurist. He is to decide whom to tax by how much and for what purpose, and he is to spend the proceeds—all this guided only by general exhortations from on high to restrain inflation, improve the environment, fight poverty and so on and on.

The whole justification for permitting the corporate executive to be selected by the stockholders is that the executive is an agent serving the interests of his principal. This justification disappears when the corporate executive imposes taxes and spends the proceeds for "social" purposes. He becomes in effect a public employee, a civil servant, even though he remains in name an employee of a private enterprise On grounds of political principle, it is intolerable that such civil servants—insofar as their actions in the name of social responsibility are real and not just window-dressing—should be selected as they are now. If they are to be civil servants, then they must be selected through a political process. If they are to impose taxes and make expenditures to foster "social" objectives, then political machinery must be set up to guide the assessment of taxes and to determine through a political process the objectives to be served.

This is the basic reason why the doctrine of "social responsibility" involves the acceptance of the socialist view that political mechanisms, not market mechanisms, are the appropriate way to determine the allocation of scarce resources to alternative uses.

On the grounds of consequences, can the corporate executive in fact discharge his alleged "social responsibilities"? On the one hand, suppose he could get away with spending the stockholders' or customers' or employees' money. How is he to know how to spend it? He is told that he must contribute to fighting inflation. How is he to know what action of his will contribute to that end? He is presumably an expert in running his company—in producing a product or selling it or financing it. But nothing about his selection makes him an expert on inflation. Will his holding down the price of his product reduce inflationary pressure? Or, by leaving more spending power in the hands of his customers, simply divert it elsewhere? Or, by forcing him to produce less because of the lower price, will it simply contribute to shortages? Even if he could answer these questions, how much cost is he justified in imposing on his stockholders, customers and employees for this social purpose? What in his appropriate share and what is the appropriate share of others?

And, whether he wants to or not, can he get away with spending his stockholders,' customers' or employees' money? Will not the stockholders fire him? (Either the present ones or those who take over when his actions in the name of social responsibility have reduced the corporation's profits and the price of its stock.) His customers and his employees can desert him for other producers and employers less scrupulous in exercising their social responsibilities.

This facet of "social responsibility" doctrine is brought into sharp relief when the doctrine is used to justify wage restraint by trade unions. The conflict of interest is naked and clear when union officials are asked to subordinate the interest of their members to some more general social purpose. If the union officials try to enforce wage restraint, the consequence is likely to be wildcat strikes, rank-and-file revolts and the emergence of strong competitors for their jobs. We thus have the ironic phenomenon that union leaders—at least in the U.S.—have objected to government interference with the market far more consistently and courageously than have business leaders.

The difficulty of exercising "social responsibility" illustrates, of course, the great virtue of private competitive enterprise—it forces people to be responsible for their own actions and makes it difficult for them to "exploit" other people for either selfish or unselfish purposes. They can do good—but only at their own expense.

Many a reader who has followed the argument this far may be tempted to remonstrate that it is all well and good to speak of government's having the responsibility to impose taxes and determine expenditures for such "social" purposes as controlling pollution or training the hardcore unemployed, but that the problems are too urgent to wait on the slow course of political processes, that the exercise of social responsibility by businessmen is a quicker and surer way to solve pressing current problems.

Aside from the question of fact—I share Adam Smith's skepticism about the benefits that can be expected from "those who affected to trade for the public good"—this argument must be rejected on grounds of principle. What it amounts to is an assertion that those who favor the taxes and expenditures in question have failed to persuade a majority of their fellow citizens to be of like mind and that they are seeking to attain by undemocratic procedures what they cannot attain by democratic procedures. In a free society, it is hard for "good" people to do "good," but that is a small price to pay for making it hard for "evil" people to do "evil," especially since one man's good is another's evil.

I have, for simplicity, concentrated on the special case of the corporate executive, except only for the brief digression on trade unions. But precisely the same argument applies to the newer phenomenon of calling upon stockholders to require corporations to exercise social responsibility (the recent G.M. crusade, for example). In most of these cases, what is in effect involved is some stockholders trying to get other stockholders (or customers or employees) to contribute against their will to "social" causes favored by the activists. Insofar as they succeed, they are again imposing taxes and spending the proceeds.

The situation of the individual proprietor is somewhat different. If he acts to reduce the returns of his enterprise in order to exercise his "social responsibility," he is spending his own money, not someone else's. If he wishes to spend his money on such purposes, that is his right, and I cannot see that there is any objection to his doing so. In the process, he, too, may impose costs on employees and customers. However, because he is far less likely than a large corporation or union to have monopolistic power, any such side effects will tend to be minor.

Of course, in practice the doctrine of social responsibility is frequently a cloak for actions that are justified on other grounds rather than a reason for those actions.

To illustrate, it may well be in the long-run interest of a corporation that is a major employer in a small community to devote resources to providing amenities to that community or to improving its government. That may make it easier to attract desirable employees, it may reduce the wage bill or lessen losses from pilferage and sabotage or have other worthwhile effects. Or it may be that, given the laws about the deductibility of corporate charitable contributions, the stockholders can contribute more to charities they favor by having the corporation make the gift than by doing it themselves, since they can in that way contribute an amount that would otherwise have been paid as corporate taxes.

In each of these—and many similar—cases, there is a strong temptation to rationalize these actions as an exercise of "social responsibility." In the present climate of opinion, with its widespread aversion to "capitalism," "profits," the "soulless corporation" and so on, this is one way for a corporation to generate goodwill as a by-product of expenditures that are entirely justified in its own self-interest.

It would be inconsistent of me to call on corporate executives to refrain from this hypocritical window-dressing because it harms the foundations of a free society. That would be to call on them to exercise a "social responsibility"! If our institutions and the attitudes of the public make it in their self-interest to cloak their actions in this way, I cannot summon much indignation to denounce them. At the same time, I can express admiration for those individual proprietors or owners of closely held corporations or stockholders of more broadly held corporations who disdain such tactics as approaching fraud.

Whether blameworthy or not, the use of the cloak of social responsibility, and the nonsense spoken in its name by influential and prestigious businessmen, does clearly harm the foundations of a free society. I have been impressed time and again by the schizophrenic character of many businessmen. They are capable of being extremely far-sighted and clear-headed in matters that are internal to their businesses. They are incredibly shortsighted and muddle-headed in matters that are outside their businesses but affect the possible survival of business in general. This short-sightedness is strikingly exemplified in the calls from many businessmen for wage and price guidelines or controls or income policies. There is nothing that could do more in a brief period to destroy a market system and replace it by a centrally controlled system than effective governmental control of prices and wages.

The short-sightedness is also exemplified in speeches by businessmen on social responsibility. This may gain them kudos in the short run. But it helps to strengthen the already too prevalent view that the pursuit of profits is wicked and immoral and must be curbed and controlled by external forces. Once this view is adopted, the external forces that curb the market will not be the social consciences, however highly developed, of the pontificating executives; it will be the iron fist of government bureaucrats. Here, as with price and wage controls, businessmen seem to me to reveal a suicidal impulse.

The political principle that underlies the market mechanism is unanimity. In an ideal free market resting on private property, no individual can coerce any other, all cooperation is voluntary, all parties to such cooperation benefit or they need not participate. There are no "social" values, no "social" responsibilities in any sense other than the shared values and responsibilities of individuals. Society is a collection of individuals and of the various groups they voluntarily form.

The political principle that underlies the political mechanism is conformity. The individual must serve a more general social interest—whether that be determined by a church or a dictator or a majority. The individual may have a vote and a say in what is to be done, but if he is overruled, he must conform. It is appropriate for some to require others to contribute to a general social purpose whether they wish to or not.

Unfortunately, unanimity is not always feasible. There are some respects in which conformity appears unavoidable, so I do not see how one can avoid the use of the political mechanism altogether.

But the doctrine of "social responsibility" taken seriously would extend the scope of the political mechanism to every human activity. It does not differ in philosophy from the most explicitly collectivist doctrine. It differs only by professing to believe that collectivist ends can be attained without collectivist means. That is why, in my book *Capitalism and Freedom*, I have called it a "fundamentally subversive doctrine" in a free society, and have said that in such a society "there is one and only one social responsibility of business—to use its resources and engage in activities designed to increase its profits so long as it stays within the rules of the game, which is to say, engages in open and free competition without deception or fraud."

Corporations and Moral Responsibility

RICHARD T. DEGEORGE

The corporation is a special kind of entity. In 1819, Chief Justice Marshall, in *Dartmouth College v. Woodward*, defined it as follows: "A corporation is an artificial being, invisible, intangible, and existing only in contemplation of law. Being the mere creature of law, it possesses only those properties which the charter of creation confers upon it, either expressly, or as incidental to its very existence. These are such as are supposed best calculated to effect the object for which it was created." It can act, hold property, and be sued. A major aspect of corporations, and one of the primary reasons for which they are established, is that they have only limited liability. This shelters corporate shareholders or owners from personal liability. Those who invest in a corporation can lose only the amount of money they invest. Their personal assets cannot be attached.

Moral responsibility is usually both ascribed to and assumed by individuals. Does it make any sense to speak of the moral responsibility of nations, or corporations, and of other formal organizations?[1] If it does make sense to do so, do we mean the same thing by the term *moral responsibility* in these cases as we do when referring to human individuals?

If we start from ordinary usage, people clearly do refer to the actions of some nations as immoral, they speak of the moral responsibilities of rich nations vis-à-vis poor ones; they claim that corporations that sell unsafe or harmful products act immorally. Yet a strong position has been adopted by such people as Milton Friedman[2] and by such organizational theorists as Herbert Simon,[3] who seem to hold that corporations and other formal organizations are not moral entities. According to this view, they are legal beings, at best. They can be held legally liable, and they can be bound by laws, but only human beings are moral agents and only human beings have moral responsibility. Some people may speak as if corporations or businesses had moral obligations, but they are simply confused. Moreover, the view continues, when individuals work for a company, they act for the company and in the company's name. When so acting, their actions are part of the actions of the firm; hence, they should not be evaluated from a moral point of view. When they act contrary to the interests of the firm or when they break the law, steal from the company, or embezzle funds, then they act in their own right and are properly judged from a moral point of view. The conclusion is that businesses are not moral agents, have no moral responsibilities, and should not be morally evaluated.

This view, which I shall call the Organizational View, is a variant of the Myth of Amoral Business. It was developed in part as a reaction to a number of moral demands made by environmentalists and consumer groups concerning the social responsibility of business. Milton Friedman's reaction to such claims is to assert that the business of business is to make profits and that social reform, welfare, and the like are the proper concern not of business but of government.

The Organizational View has been widely attacked, yet it cannot be dismissed out of hand. It makes the valid point that organizations, corporations, and nations are not moral entities in the same sense as individual human beings. Therefore, if we are to consider them as moral agents, we must be careful how we use our terms, and make clear what we mean by them.

The argument against the claim that formal organizations are not moral beings is fairly simple. Morality governs the action of rational beings insofar as they affect other rational beings. Formal organizations— for instance, corporations—act. Ford Motor Company produces cars; it also builds factories, hires and fires people, pays them wages, pays taxes, recalls defective models, and so on. Not only do businesses act, they act rationally according to a rational decision-making procedure. Because their rational actions affect people, these actions can be evaluated from a moral point of view. If it is immoral for an individual to discriminate, it is also immoral for a corporation to discriminate. If it is praiseworthy for an individual to give to charity, it is praiseworthy for a business to give to charity. If it is wrong for people to steal, it is wrong for businesses to steal. Actions can be morally evaluated whether done by an individual or by an entity such as a company, a corporation, or a nation. The alternative would be to say that although murder is wrong for individuals, it is not morally wrong for businesses, or that although exploitation of one person by another is morally wrong, exploitation of a person by a corporation is morally neutral. This is clearly unacceptable, because murder, stealing, exploitation, and lying are wrong whether done by a human being, a corporation, or a nation; the action is wrong whoever the perpetrator of the action is.

The dispute does not end here, however, for part of the point of the Organizational View is that formal organizations do not act. Neither do corporations, clubs, companies, or nations. People within them act, but the organization itself is nothing more than a formal structure. It does not do anything. People within it do whatever it is that gets done. Obviously, there is something correct about the assertion that only people act and that formal organizations do not act. Yet, as we noted previously, we often speak of firms and nations as acting. Who is correct? How do we decide?

The answer to both questions can be found through a closer analysis of our use of language. When we say, "Ford makes cars," we do not mean that the cars are made by magic; we know that no car will get made unless someone makes it. A great many people, using a variety of tools and machines, contribute to making a Ford car. Yet we can use the name *Ford* to mean all of the people and their relations and activities together. We know that there are workers and managers, a president of the firm, a board of directors, and shareholders. Yet without any knowledge of who does what within the firm, we can speak of Ford making cars. This is a perfectly understandable statement, made from outside the corporation and referring to it as a whole. If Ford recalls defective cars, someone must make the decision to recall them, and either the same person or other people must send out the notices. They act not in their own names but as employees or agents of the firm.

In our ordinary use of English it is proper and common to use the name of a firm to refer to all those associated with it, to refer to the products that those associated with it produce, or to refer to the entity that is liable to suit. Therefore, when we make a moral judgment about the actions of a firm or of a nation, we need not know who within the firm is the person or persons responsible. We can hold the firm as such responsible, from a moral as well as from a legal point of view. But granted that we can make moral judgments about the actions of a firm or nation, why should we? The answer can be found in what we wish to accomplish by such judgments. In making moral judgments about the actions we attribute to a firm or nation, we do many things. We express our emotions, evaluate an action, and encourage other people to react to the action as we do. In expressing our moral evaluation we either praise or blame. When we morally condemn an action, we might wish to encourage others to impose moral sanctions, or bring pressure to bear to rectify the wrong or to change the policy in question.

One method of doing this is a consumer boycott, such as the one that California migrant workers sponsored on lettuce at Safeway stores, or that the INFACT coalition sponsored against Nestlé.[4] A boycott attempts to bring pressure on a company to change what is seen as an immoral practice or policy. Those who call a boycott may not know who within the company is responsible for the questionable practices, and may not care. A boycott may result in a cutback in production by the company, with a consequent laying off of workers who are not involved in setting policy or implementing it in any way. A boycott is called, however, not to lay off particular people but to change the company's policy. From the outside, it is a matter of indifference who is responsible

for the practice and who carries it out. The intent is to identify the
practice as immoral, to call it to people's attention, and to unite them
to create moral pressure to stop the practice.

A similar analysis can be applied to nations. When the United
States condemned the Iraqi invasion of Kuwait, spokesmen for the
United States did the condemning. Although we say that Iraq invaded
Kuwait, we obviously mean that Iraqi soldiers invaded it. We see them
as agents receiving orders from the heads of government. But the heads
of government do not themselves physically invade. In some cases, we
distinguish what the leaders of a country do from what the ordinary
people do; in other cases, we do not. If one country blockades another,
members of the armed forces of the one country prevent the exporta-
tion or importation of goods from or to the other country. One country
may declare war on another and does so through its government; but
war is not declared only against certain people in that country. Just as
in talking about a business, the collective term serves many functions,
and no nation acts unless people act for it.

The issue is not whether an action can correctly be attributed to
a corporation (or formal organization or nation), or whether it should
more appropriately be attributed to the person or people within the corporation who make the decisions in question and carry them out. At-
tribution of an action, and so of moral responsibility for that action, to
a corporation is intelligible, and from a practical point of view may be
effective. Nor is the issue one of deciding whether we should ascribe responsibility to *either* the corporation *or* to the individuals within it.
There is no need to choose. We can ascribe responsibility to the corporation only; to the corporation, as well as one or more of the individuals within it; or only to an individual or individuals within the
corporation.[5] To whom we ascribe responsibility depends on the facts of
the particular case in question.

The assumption of responsibility, however, must always be by individuals, whether they assume it for themselves or, by virtue of their
position, for the corporation. Moral responsibility for a corporation's actions may be assumed by the members of the board of directors, the
president, various levels of management, or by the workers. Each person may hold himself morally responsible for doing his job, and he may
hold others morally responsible for doing theirs; or moral responsibility
may be refused by some or all of them.

Moral charges made from the outside, and moral responsibility
ascribed to a corporation or nation from the outside, may be rejected,
rebutted, refuted, or ignored. This happens when no one within the
corporation or nation accepts the responsibility ascribed to it.

Corporations are not human beings. The differences between
human individuals and corporations, other formal organizations, and

nations are significant from a moral point of view and from the point of view of moral responsibility. A corporation as such has no conscience, no feelings, no consciousness of its own.[6] It has a conscience only to the extent that those who make it up act for it in such a way as to evince something comparable to conscience. Because a corporation acts only through those who act for it, it is the latter who must assume moral responsibility for the corporation. It may not always be clear who within the corporation should assume this responsibility.

When harm is unjustly done to an individual by a firm, the firm has the moral obligation to make reparation to the individual. For example, it matters little whether the particular person who systematically paid women employees less than men for the same work is still with the firm. If the women deserve compensation for past injustice, the firm has the moral obligation to make it good. Someone who had nothing to do with perpetrating the past injustice but who is now employed by the firm may have the moral obligation to take action to make up for past wage discrimination. If a firm is morally responsible for wrongs done, it is morally obliged to make good those wrongs. But exactly who must do what within the firm can often only be appropriately decided by an analysis of individual cases.

We can and do use moral language with respect to the actions of businesses, formal organizations, and countries. But in any analysis, as we shift from individual human beings to organizational entities, we should be aware of the differences in meaning and application of the terms we use.

Insofar as corporations act intentionally, they can be held morally responsible for their actions. They are thus moral actors. But because corporations are not ends in themselves, they are not moral persons. Hence, we can morally evaluate the ends for which a corporation is established. Because corporations are not human beings, they cannot claim the moral rights of human beings—the right to life or continued existence, for example. The attempt to attribute all the rights of human persons to corporations results from a confusion about the moral status of corporations.

Because the moral status of corporations is different from the moral status of human beings, the moral obligations of corporations are different from the moral obligations of human beings. The difference hinges on the fact that corporations are limited, and organized for only certain purposes. The fact that a corporation does exist and has been established for certain purposes is no guarantee that it should exist or that its purposes are morally justifiable. But as long as the ends for which corporations are formed are not immoral, and as long as the means by which those ends are pursued are not immoral, corporations are not bound by a large range of moral rules that bind natural persons.

As is true of all other moral actors, corporations are bound not to harm others. This negative injunction is a major restraint on corporations. But the positive obligations of corporations depend on their ends, their particular situations, their legal status, and the sociopolitical environment in which they are organized and operate. Because corporations are not human persons, the injunction to produce the greatest amount of good applies differently to individual persons with a full range of activities open to them and to a corporation with very great restrictions on its purpose and its appropriate activities. Because corporations are not moral persons, it is doubtful whether we can expect them to act from moral motives. What we can expect is that they not do what is morally prohibited. We can praise them for doing what is in accord with the moral law, and blame them for what is a violation of it. Corporations lack the interiority characteristic of human individuals; therefore, their actions, not their motives, are the proper object of moral evaluation. Corporations are neither machines nor animals. They are organizations run by human beings and, as such, have a moral status that makes them amenable to moral evaluation, even though they are not moral persons per se.

Moral Responsibility Within the Corporation

Corporations are the result of free agreements, even if most owners do not know what management does. They purchase stock, knowing that they will not have control and knowing that they will gain or lose, depending on how effectively management runs the corporation. They know that the corporation may be sued, they know it may make a profit or suffer losses, and they know in general how such things happen. Shareholders agree to invest money, and they understand what this means. The shareholders of the corporation are legally represented by the board of directors, whose job it is, among other things, to look out for the interests of the shareholders. The board of directors oversees management. Management has the task of organizing the corporation in such a way that it can effect its end—make and market a product profitably.[7]

In a large corporation, responsibility falls ultimately on the board of directors. The board members are the legal overseers of management. *The members of the board are responsible to the shareholders* for the selection of honest, effective managers, and especially for the selection of the president of the corporation. They may also be responsible for choosing the executive vice-president and other vice-presidents. They are morally responsible for the tone of the corporation and for its major policies; they can set a moral tone or they can condone immoral practices. They can and should see that the company is managed honestly and that the interests of the shareholders are cared for instead of ignored by management.

Board members are also responsible for agreeing to major policy decisions and for the general well-being of the corporation. The members are morally responsible for the decisions they make, as well as for the decisions they should make but fail to make. To be effective in their roles as protectors of the interests of the shareholders and judges of the performance of management, they should be separate from management. Members of the board cannot be objective in their evaluation of management if they are also members of management. If the president and the chairman of the board are one and the same person, for instance, we can hardly expect the board to be as objective as it should be in fulfilling its responsibility vis-à-vis management. Nor can we expect impartial evaluation of management if the board is composed of people appointed or recommended by management because of mutual ties. We can also not expect a board to be effective if it is not informed by management of what management is doing, if the board does not have access to all information about the firm it thinks necessary, and if its members do not have the time to investigate what should be investigated.

The increasing incidence of corporate takeovers raises special problems for boards of directors. Whatever the complications, the board is morally and legally responsible for the interests of the shareholders, and must resist the temptation to act out of personal interest and advantage, which might be to the detriment of the shareholders.

Management is responsible to the board. It must inform the board of its actions, the decisions it makes or the decisions to be made, the financial condition of the firm, its successes and failures, and the like. Management is responsible, through the board, to the shareholders. It is responsible to the shareholders for managing the firm honestly and efficiently. Management is *not* morally responsible for maximizing profits, for increasing the worth of the company's stock, or for higher quarterly sales or profits. Although these are all reasonable goals at which management may aim, shareholders have no right to any of these; if management acts as best it can within its proper moral and legal bounds, it cannot, strictly speaking, be faulted for not achieving them. If managers fail to produce as the board thinks they should, they may be fired or replaced. But that is different from their fulfilling or not fulfilling their moral obligations. Shareholders know that a corporation's stock may decrease as well as increase in value, and that profits may increase or decline. They should also know that profit maximization cannot morally override a firm's moral and legal obligations. Although shareholders may desire short-term profits, they have no right to them, and managers should manage for the long-term benefit of the firm as well as for short-term results.

Management is responsible for setting the moral tone of the firm. Unless those at the top insist on ethical conduct, unless they punish unethical conduct and reward ethical conduct, the corporation as a whole will tend to function without considering the moral dimensions of its actions.

Management is also responsible to the workers. It both hires them and provides for the conditions of work. In hiring workers it has the obligation to engage in what have become known as fair employment practices. These include following equitable guidelines and not discriminating on the basis of sex, race, religion, or other non-job-related characteristics. Once a worker is hired, there is a continuing obligation of fairness in evaluation, promotion, and equitable treatment. These are moral matters, which may or may not be specified in contracts but are implied in the hiring of one person by another. It is not moral for management to ignore unsafe working conditions. For instance, it should not endanger workers by failing to provide screening from dangerous machines, where appropriate; by not supplying goggles for work where fragments may cause blindness; by not supplying adequate ventilation; and, in general, by ignoring the needs of workers as human beings.

Employers are not free to set any terms they wish as conditions of employment. They have a moral obligation to employees even if these are not spelled out in contracts or by government regulations. Government regulations, such as those imposed by the Occupational Safety and Health Act (OSHA), make explicit many of the conditions employers are morally as well as legally obliged to fulfill with respect to the safety and health of their employees. The OSHA regulations are sometimes inappropriate for certain firms, or are based on codes inappropriate to particular enterprises. Where inappropriate, the regulations can and should be changed. But if employers had lived up to the moral obligation to provide adequate conditions of safety and health for their employees, there would have been no need for OSHA regulations.

Workers, in turn, are responsible for doing the jobs for which they are hired. This obligation is captured in the dictum "a fair day's work for a fair day's pay." Failure to live up to this obligation is reasonable ground for discharge. From a moral point of view one's job can never legitimately involve either breaking the law or doing what is unethical, even if one is ordered to do so. But within the guidelines of one's job description, employees are expected to carry out their jobs as instructed by those above them. They are hired for specific tasks that they are expected to fulfill to the best of their ability—carefully, skillfully, and on time.

Corporations are responsible to their suppliers and competitors for fair treatment. Corporations deal with other firms as well as with the general public. They may buy raw or semifinished materials, parts, or a variety of supplies from others. In their dealings they are responsible for acting fairly, both in supplying and in receiving goods and services. If bidding is used, the bidding should be fair for all. If prices are agreed upon, they should be honored. If specifications are set, they should be met. If payment by a certain date is agreed upon, it should be adhered to. All this is fairly obvious, yet not always observed. The temptations for cutting corners, for cost-overruns, for manipulating bids, and for seeking and receiving preferential treatment are ever-present, and an ethical firm needs to guard constantly against them through a clearly stated and enforced company policy.

Fairness to one's competitors is also required. In a competitive situation no firm has any obligation to help a competing firm, and frequently competition involves gaining greater market share at a competitor's expense, hiring better workers and managers than one's competitor, charging less for similar products, producing better products, and the like. All of this is morally acceptable. If, as a result of fair competition, a competing firm goes out of business, the successful firm has no moral responsibility to the failing one. The key word, however, is *fair*. Fairness precludes lying about one's competitor or the competitor's products; it precludes stealing trade secrets, sabotage, or other direct intervention in the competitor's firm. Fairness in dealing with one's competitor also precludes colluding with competing firms, price fixing, manipulating markets, and in other ways acting to undermine fair competition at the public's expense.

The corporation is responsible to the consumer for its products. The goods produced should be reasonably safe. This means that the ordinary user is exposed to only a certain acceptable risk level that is known by the user, when using the product. For example, people do not expect to get shocked or electrocuted when they plug in an electrical appliance. They do not buy such appliances expecting to take that risk. A product that shocks or electrocutes them when plugged in is defective, causes harm to the consumer, and violates the contract involved in the purchase of the product. Goods must be as advertised or labeled, and the labeling should be adequate, so the buyer knows what he or she is buying. Because adequate knowledge is one of the ingredients of a fair transaction, it is the obligation of the manufacturer to inform the purchaser of those significant qualities that the purchaser cannot observe for himself or herself. For instance, the kind of material a garment is made of is pertinent, as is the horsepower of a vehicle. Also, goods should be reasonably durable; they should not fall apart on first use. Warranties should be clear and honored. The customer buys a product for a certain price. He should know what he is getting, and he has a moral right to have certain expectations fulfilled. Obviously, there are various grades of goods. Some are more expensive than others and may be correspondingly safer, more durable, more reliable, more attractive, and made of better quality components than cheaper products. For any transaction to be fair the consumer must have adequate information and his or her reasonable expectations must be fulfilled by a product, or there must be adequate notice that the ordinary expectation in the given case will not be fulfilled. Damaged goods can be sold if marked as damaged. "Seconds" may be sold as seconds, but to sell them as "first quality" is immoral.

These few examples do not exhaust the responsibilities of corporations to consumers. We have not questioned the morality of built-in obsolescence; of purposeful lack of standardization, which locks a consumer into a certain line of products; of failure to develop certain products; or of preventing the production of items that would benefit the consumer but hurt a particular industry or manufacturer. But we have illustrated enough of the moral responsibility of a corporation to consumers to indicate where its moral obligations in this area lie, and how they can be ascertained.

Finally, *the corporation is morally responsible for its actions to the general public or to society in general.* In particular, it has the moral obligation not to harm those whom its actions affect. We can group these obligations under three major headings. The first can be called its obligation not to harm the environment that it shares with its neighbors. It has the obligation not to pollute the air and water beyond socially acceptable levels, and also to control its noise pollution. It is obliged to dispose of toxic and corrosive wastes so as not to endanger others. It must reclaim and restore the environment to a socially acceptable level, if its operation despoils the environment.

The second group of moral obligations to the general public concerns the general safety of those who live in an area affected by a company's plant. A company has no right to expose those people living near it to a health risk from possible explosion or radiation. Some jobs involve a high risk, and those who knowingly take this risk are paid accordingly. But a plant has no right to expose its neighbors, even its distant neighbors, to dangers without their consent. Similarly, a corporation has an obligation to the general public for the safety of its products. For instance, substandard tires endanger not only those who purchase them but also those whom the purchaser may kill or injure in an accident that the tires may cause.

The third set of responsibilities to the public concerns the location, the opening, and the closing of plants—especially in small communities and one-industry towns. These actions affect not only the corporation and its workers but also the communities in which the plants are located. Plant openings can affect a community positively or negatively, just as closings can. A corporation must consider, from a moral point of view, the impact of its actions on the community in these matters. This is not to say that plants can never morally be closed or opened. In both opening and closing a plant, a corporation has the obligation to minimize the harm, and so to consider a variety of strategies to achieve this end.

The opening of a plant may involve a large commitment on the part of the community in which it is located. The community, for example, may have to add sewer lines, increase its fire and police department staff, and add to its social services personnel. Developers build houses for the increased employment the plant makes available. Businesses spring up to provide support services. Schools may be built to educate the children of the workers. The city or county begins to count on the increased tax base the plant represents. All of this results from the new plant. The corporation does not always ask that all this happen; but it at least expects that its workers will be provided housing and services in response to market demand.

The community may thus be said to provide indirect support to the plant. The corporation should, therefore, not ignore the community's contribution to its operation when it considers closing the plant. It may have no legal duty to consider the community with which it has been associated; but morally, it does have an obligation to consider the effects of its action and to minimize the harm its closing will cause the community.

If we ask who has the obligation to do all this, the answer is, the corporation. Management has the major role to play. Yet both the members of the board and the individual workers may find, on occasion, that they have the moral responsibility to take certain actions to satisfy the corporation's responsibility to the general public.

Since the corporation has responsibility to a great many constituencies, it is not accurate to claim that a corporation owes allegiance only to the owners or shareholders of the firm. Nor is it clear from a moral point of view that the interests of the shareholders always take precedence over other interests. For instance, the moral obligations of the firm to ensure the safety of workers, the environment, and consumers properly take precedence over increasing profits.

All those to whom the corporation has any moral obligations are collectively referred to as stakeholders in the corporation. A *stakeholder analysis*[8] consists of weighing and balancing all of the competing moral demands on a firm by each of those who have a claim on it, in order to arrive at the firm's moral obligation in any particular case. The stakeholder approach has the strength of forcing us to consider carefully all the obligations involved, for instance, in a plant closing, instead of just looking at the closing from the point of view of profitability, and so from the point of view of the shareholders. The stakeholders in a plant closing include not only shareholders but also workers, suppliers, consumers, the local community, and possibly others. A stakeholder analysis does not preclude the interests of the shareholders overriding the interests of the other stakeholders affected, but it ensures that all affected will be considered. The stakeholder approach is compatible with utilitarian and deontological approaches, as well as with using second-order moral judgments. It simply requires that all those whose interests are involved get fair consideration.

A firm that wishes to operate morally will establish structures that encourage and facilitate ethical action on the part of all members of the firm. It will establish channels and procedures for accountability up, down, and laterally. It will develop input lines whereby employees, consumers, shareholders, and the public can make known their concerns, demands, and perceptions of the firm's legitimate responsibilities. Finally, it will develop appropriate mechanisms for anticipating and resolving ethical issues—whether the firm uses ombudsmen, ethical hot-lines, a corporate ethics office, an ethics committee, or other means for achieving those ends.

Corporate Culture and Moral Firms

In dealing with human individuals we speak of their moral character. Do firms, other formal organizations, and nations have moral character? Some people maintain that a firm that takes its moral responsibilities seriously, tries to be fair in dealing with its employees and customers, takes into consideration the effects of its actions, and so on, is correctly called a moral firm. It can be said to have a moral character, in a sense analogous to that used with respect to individuals. Its character is formed by its habitual actions in the past. It develops within it certain structures and patterns of acting. It molds those who join it into thinking and acting in certain ways. Tradition develops; pride in the policies of the firm takes root; and each member of the firm helps to form and to mold the others in the firm in conformance with its tradition. In this sense, then, a firm or a nation can be called moral or immoral, can be said to have a moral or an immoral character, and can be thought of as having, or as not having, a conscience. But the sense is only analogous; it is not identical with the meaning of these terms when used with respect to individual persons.

We can, however, properly speak of a *corporate culture*, and this may either foster or inhibit moral action on the part of its members. Corporate culture is analogous to the culture of a society, people, or nation. It includes the ambiance of the corporation, its values, beliefs, and practices; the relation of the people within the corporation to one another, and their feelings toward the firm; the history of the corporation; and the extent to which the present members identify with the history and tradition of the corporation in the past and present. Some firms have a strong corporate culture, unique and distinctive. Employees who join the firm are inculturated into it when hired by the firm. Such inculturation—which can take several years—may involve learning something of the firm's history, becoming familiar with its ideals and practices, and perhaps taking part in special activities of the firm. Some firms go so far as to have company songs; many have formal and informal meetings to discuss the firm's outlook, problems, or ideals. A company's culture may be consciously formed or may develop spontaneously. And part of a firm's culture may include a positive or a negative approach to moral issues and moral actions, both by individuals in the firm and by the firm itself, when dealing with employees, customers, and other firms.

Although a firm's corporate culture is established over time, it is both initially and continuously responsive, especially to direction from the top. Top management sets the tone that the rest of the firm follows. Those who do not agree with the tone and do not fit in usually do not stay long. It is possible for the top management to insist on morality throughout the firm. It can expect moral conduct on the part of all its employees, and establish a pattern—eventually a tradition—of moral action on the part of the firm and its officers. Not surprisingly, there is great loyalty and job satisfaction among employees who work for a firm that does not fire employees in times of cyclical downturns, and employees take pride in a firm that operates morally. Corporate excellence is not identical with corporate morality because competent management is also necessary. But it is doubtful that corporate excellence is compatible with corporate immorality, or with a corporate culture that condones or encourages its employees to act either immorally or amorally in their roles for the firm.

A moral firm, or a firm that acts with integrity, lives up to and fulfills its responsibilities. It helps its employees to act responsibly by clarifying their responsibilities, and it encourages them to assume their responsibilities. Only when all those within a firm assume appropriate moral responsibility can the full moral responsibility of a firm be met. Ultimately, moral responsibility, and morality itself, must be self-imposed and self-accepted.

NOTES

1. The contemporary discussion of the moral status of corporations and formal organizations began with John Ladd's "Morality and the Ideal of Rationality in Formal Organizations," *The Monist* 54 (1970), pp. 488–516. An excellent collection of articles on the topic is Hugh Curtler (Ed.), *Shame, Responsibility and the Corporation* (New York: Haven Publishing Corp., 1986). See also

Peter A. French, *Collective and Corporate Responsibility* (New York: Columbia University Press, 1984).

2. Milton Friedman, "The Social Responsibility of Business Is to Increase Its Profits," *New York Times Magazine*, September 13, 1970.
3. Herbert A. Simon, *Administrative Behavior*, 2nd ed. (New York: The Free Press, 1965).
4. For details on the Nestlé boycott, see Chapter 10 of Richard T. DeGeorge's *Business Ethics* 4th ed. (Upper Saddle River, N.J.: Prentice Hall, 1982).
5. For discussions of collective responsibility, see Larry May, *The Morality of Groups* (Notre Dame, Ind.: University of Notre Dame Press, 1987); and Peter A. French (Ed.), *Individual and Collective Responsibility* (Cambridge: Schenkman Publishing Co., 1972).
6. See Kenneth E. Goodpaster and John B. Matthews, Jr., "Can a Corporation Have a Conscience?," *Harvard Business Review* (January–February 1982), pp. 132–141.
7. For two critical discussions of moral responsibility within the corporation, see S. Prakash Sethi, *Up Against the Corporate Wall*, 5th ed. (Englewood Cliffs, N.J.: Prentice-Hall, 1991); and Christopher D. Stone, *Where the Law Ends: The Social Control of Corporate Behavior* (Prospect Heights, Ill.: Waveland Press, 1991, reissue).
8. For discussions of stakeholder analysis, see R. Edward Freeman, *Strategic Management: A* Stakeholder Analysis (Boston: Pittman, 1984); and Kenneth Goodpaster, "Business Ethics and Stakeholder Analysis," *Business Ethics Quarterly* 1 (January 1991), pp. 53–72.

The Duty to Treat Patients with AIDS and HIV Infection

ALBERT R. JONSEN

The father of modern surgery, Ambroise Pare, once reflected on the danger of caring for persons infected with plague. "[Surgeons] must remember," he wrote, "that they are called by God to this vocation of surgery: therefore they should go to it with high courage and free of fear, having firm faith that God both gives and takes our lives as and when it pleases Him."[1] These reflections of a sixteenth-century Frenchman, expressed in religious terms, may seem foreign to our times, but they remind us of a question that seems to haunt physicians, surgeons, and other providers of health care perennially: at what danger or cost to myself must I carry out my work? Throughout history, many have answered as did Pare: something morally compelling about being a healer, whether divinely given or not, requires one to take even great risks in caring for the sick. Others, although they rarely assert so in writing, seem to have viewed their work more prosaically and felt no greater or lesser obligation than any decent person who must balance the risks of living against the goods of livelihood.[2]

The AIDS epidemic revives that perennial question in vivid ways. The sudden appearance of a lethal infection, the rapid spread of infection to more than a million Americans, the death of thousands of those infected, and the expected death of many more have thrust American health care providers into an epidemic that caught them unprepared. Remarkably, the scientific unpreparedness ceded to a rapid mobilization of several biomedical disciplines—virology, immunology and epidemiology—leading to identification of the causative agent and the modes of transmission. Clinical care developed more slowly, but research on therapies and preventative interventions is now intense. The social, ethical, and psychological unpreparedness lingers on, however, being met by sporadic and incomplete responses.[3]

Among the lingering issues is the troubling question of the duty to treat the HIV-infected person. Because this question is a contemporary version of the perennial question stated above, it will never be definitively answered; still, professional providers of care must form their consciences honestly and firmly. Failure to do so can lead to deterioration of care, discrimination, and distrust between patients and providers.

Although most physicians, nurses, and technicians in American health care seem to have accepted the duty to provide suitable care even in the face of risk, the constant stresses arising from the perception of risk to self and from the difficulties of caring for AIDS patients can erode the general dedication to serve. The erosion may appear in a variety of ways. Subtle evasion of certain forms of interaction with patients and the discovery of excuses and exceptions, sometimes cloaked with pseudoscientific rationales, can lead to a deterioration of quality of care. Even the most dedicated providers can find their ability to care eroded by the constant exposure to perceived risks. Questions arise regularly about the desirability of screening all patients, or all surgical and obstetrical patients, or anyone seeking elective surgery. It is asked whether the physician has the right to refuse to perform certain risky procedures that might not be strictly necessary for the patient. There are continuing reports of an anecdotal nature about providers actually refusing needed care and about inappropriate referrals and transfers of patients suspected of HIV infection. Occasionally, refusals of care are reported to government agencies or advocacy groups as complaints of discrimination.

Relatively few physicians and nurses have encountered these patients up until now, because AIDS has been concentrated in large metropolitan areas. But in the next decade these patients will begin to appear throughout the American health care system. Many physicians and nurses will see them for the first time. The lessons already learned in the major centers of the epidemic must be communicated to those professionals who will be called to care for patients in the near future. The special features of health care outside major metropolitan areas must also be taken into consideration in designing policies and programs.

At the center of all educational efforts stands the fundamental moral question, is it ethically permissible for a provider of health care to refuse to care for a patient with AIDS or who has positive test results for antibody to HIV?

This is a question of conscience, a question posed by an individual to himself or herself in order to decide how his or her conduct should reflect certain values and principles. It is a deeply personal question, but it goes beyond personal choice to the acceptance or rejection of values and principles beyond the private self and deriving from social, cultural, and religious sources that surround the individual. Answering it expresses the willingness to be identified with and by a certain course of action and to bear the burdens of being so identified. Thus, I will say little about the legal obligations to treat, although the question of conscience might sometimes involve the legal, insofar as each person must decide whether or not to obey the law.[4] In this essay I define the duty to treat as a moral rather than a legal obligation.

This particular question of conscience is not familiar for most modern health professionals. They generally go about their work, caring for the patients that come into their hands in various ways, rarely having to ask themselves, "Do I have a duty to treat this person?" Occasionally, the question will arise in a peculiar circumstance, such as the extremely noncompliant patient or the very demanding and difficult patient. Occasionally, the question will occur as a matter of policy, such as the decision to provide uncompensated care to indigent patients. In general, however, physicians take it for granted that they have duties to care for patients that they, or their institutions, have accepted. Nurses assume that they have the duty to care for the patients to whom they are assigned.

So, the problem of conscience with regard to patients with HIV infection is particularly difficult because it is unfamiliar to those struggling to resolve it. They may be unclear about the terms of the problem, about the reasons it is a problem, and about the principles that might be used to reflect upon it. I will attempt to state the terms of the problem. Ultimately, resolution depends on the conscientious judgment of individuals.

Reasons for the Problems

The problem of conscience has at least four salient components: the perception of serious risk, the influence of prejudice, the burden of caring for AIDS patients, and the presumption of professional freedom of choice. Some professionals will be bothered by all of these components; others by only one or two of them. Any review of the problem must consider them all.

Health providers are at risk of infection when they are engaged in providing medical and nursing care to persons with HIV infection. The virus can be transmitted from an infected to an uninfected party even before any symptoms of AIDS are recognized. The modes of transmission of the virus are well understood: exposure to the blood and bodily fluids of an infected person, usually through sexual intercourse, the sharing of drug needles, or transfusion of infected blood. The fetus can be infected by maternal blood. Health professionals are at risk of exposure by accidental punctures or cuts incurred while caring for patients or by contact with hemorrhage through spills or splashes of blood. A small number of health professionals are known to have been infected in this way. Serious efforts have been made to quantify the risk of infection for providers of care, and in general, the risk is apparently low—in the range of 0.4 percent after exposure to infected blood by sharp needle injury. The risk after exposure to infected blood in other ways (for example, contact with mucous membranes or nonintact skin) "is probably considerably less and cannot be measured with existing data."[5] Health professionals, particularly those whose work puts them into frequent contact with patient's blood and fluids, may know the statistical facts about their risks but may remain deeply concerned. Their concern has two sound bases: even low risks are real, and the low risk has a serious outcome—lethal disease.

Formation of one's conscience must take account both of facts, in the form of statistics and other data, and of fears and apprehensions. While it is often difficult and sometimes impossible to dispel fears and apprehensions entirely (some professionals, of course, seem immune to them), still a conscientious judgment about a duty to treat in face of risk must ask whether the risks, as well as the fears, are reasonable. We shall return to this consideration.

A second component in the problem of the duty to treat is the peculiar epidemiology of the disease—namely, prevalence among homosexual men and abusers of intravenously injected illicit drugs. Both of these groups are viewed in a negative light by American society: the former because many deeply disapprove of their sexual preferences; the latter because they are involved in a criminal and destructive activity. Both are the object of what sociologists call stigmatization. This term designates a complex social and psychological process whereby certain persons are perceived as without social value and even as threatening to the dominant society. They are marked (hence, the word *stigma*, which in derivation evokes the branding of a criminal) for exclusion from certain social benefits and interactions. The stigma goes far beyond the actual features of the stigmatized and creates a negative social image that extends into all aspects of judgment about them, making it difficult to be objective about their behavior and their needs.

Health professionals have long honored an ethic of objectivity about their patients; they try not to allow their personal opinions about the values, lifestyle, and morality of their patients to influence their professional judgments about the patients' health care needs. Yet, this honored ethic sometimes comes under stress. Some professionals may find certain persons so repugnant that they will not accept them as patients or, if they must serve them, do so reluctantly and sometimes negligently. This latter course is rightly condemned as unethical, even when the former may be implicitly tolerated. Stigmatization influences the judgments of individuals in more subtle ways than overt dislike and frank prejudice. Professionals may disvalue the stigmatized in ways they hardly recognize. Even when professionals believe they are not prejudiced, they may perceive and treat stigmatized persons differently from others. For example, providers who have never seriously balked at the risk of infection from hepatitis B (which still causes a number of deaths each year) are fearful of the risk of HIV infection (which has yet to cause the death of an exposed provider). This makes one wonder whether submerged prejudices enhance the apprehension of danger.[6]

In addition to the perception of risk and the problem of prejudice, health professionals may find the care of AIDS patients a demanding task. The disease itself is devastating, no cure is presently available, and death is the inevitable outcome. Many patients come largely from groups with whose life-style the health professional may be unfamiliar and even unsympathetic. On the other hand, the patients are predominantly young adults whose lives are cut short; some of these have great promise. Such patients as the female partners of intravenous drug users, infants born infected, and unknowing recipients of transfusions of infected blood inspire particular compassion. With these patients, the provider of care may be deeply sympathetic, even emotionally identified. In general, caring for AIDS patients imposes notable stress on professionals. The psychological phenomenon known as burnout is all too familiar to those who have dedicated themselves to the care of these patients.[7] This phenomenon itself, or the anticipation of it, may be a component in the problem of conscience.

Thus, as health professionals are exposed to increasing numbers of persons who are infected with HIV, their sense of responsibility toward these patients may be influenced by their perception of the risks involved in caring for such patients, their overt prejudices and covert complicity with stigma, and the stresses they actually experience, or expect to experience, in dealing with AIDS patients.

A final component cannot be discounted—namely, the strong value that Americans of all sorts, including health professionals, place on freedom of choice. There has long been, in the United States, a reluctance to force one person to provide services to another against his or her will. The Principles of Ethics of the American Medical Association state that a physician may choose those whom he or she wishes to serve.[8] American law does not require physicians to provide services to any particular patient, unless some special relationship already exists.[9] Nurses are in a different situation, since they are usually employees of hospitals and are rarely given the opportunity to select their patients. Still, the right to refuse to care for a particular patient, either by not accepting that person as a patient or by discharging oneself from responsibility in a recognized way, is deeply embedded in the ethos of American medicine. It is difficult to challenge this ethos by stating that physicians or other providers have an obligation that prohibits them from exercising such a presumed moral right.

The Sources of Obligation

How does one go about forming one's conscience? Does one do so merely by deciding whether or to what extent one wishes to participate in so problematic a business? Formation of conscience, I believe, is more than an expression of personal preference. It is an exercise in which one tests personal preferences against the importance of what one is asked to do. For the pious Ambroise Pare (whose motto was, "I dressed his wounds but God cured him"), a divine vocation to surgery was the measure of importance. But in an era when such faith is rare, measures of importance must be discovered, and they must be such as to persuade many, if not all, of the concerned parties that caring for the sick without discrimination and regardless of personal risk and inconvenience is intimately bound up with the profession and the work of health care.

This conclusion may not attain the stance of an absolute moral principle. Indeed, philosophers may cavil at designating it a moral principle at all, since the inference from importance to moral imperative is not strictly logical. Still, whether we call it important or imperative, the work of caring for the seriously ill even under adverse circumstance for the provider cannot be casually dismissed. Individuals should exempt themselves only for the most serious reasons, and public policies should not sanction practices that undermine such commitment.

The discovery of importance requires a careful look at the nature of the work of health care. That look should begin with an inquiry into the history and tradition of this work with a view to answering the questions: Have those who engaged in health care in the past considered it important to undertake their work in the face of personal danger and inconvenience? If so, how seriously did they take this task? Are there circumstances in which a physician may refuse to respond to a person's need? Was caring for the sick at danger to oneself considered an ethical duty and were those who refused or refrained judged unethical practitioners?

Scholars have reviewed the evidence that might indicate whether physicians in many times and cultures have acknowledged a moral duty to treat the sick even at risk to themselves and contrary to their inclinations. The historical record is mixed. First, the problem is raised only occasionally. When it is, the distinction between actual behavior and the affirmation of a duty is not often made. Still, it appears that, as long as a distinct and self-defined class of healers has existed in our culture, they have faced the perennial problem in some form or another. The problem of caring for strangers and enemies was sometimes debated; the problem of caring for those who could not pay has been an enduring issue. In times of epidemic disease, physicians have fled the dangers (but have felt compelled to excuse themselves, as Galen and Sydenham did), and physicians have stayed to face death. In such times, the populace has seemed to expect their healers, physical and spiritual, to remain with them, and no lack of criticism of those who did not can be found in the records. The persistence of the question is, at least, a hint that a moral issue lurks in the background. At the root of this question may be a basic fact about medicine and health care: its providers present themselves as helpers in a time of need, and the public believes that offer. If providers withdraw the offer when the needy actually seek their proffered help, they seem deceitful. Deceit is always a moral matter.[10]

In the United States, the role of the physician has long been identified with a willingness to serve in times of personal danger. This willingness derived, it seems, sometimes from courage and dedication and sometimes from opportunism.[11] Still, in the epidemics of cholera, yellow fever, influenza, and polio that ravaged the United States in the last century and in the first half of this century, the record of physician service in time of danger is notable. This record has been an important ingredient in the positive reputation of medicine and of physicians.

So important was this ingredient that the American Medical Association (AMA) compromised its strong stand in favor of the rights of physicians to choose whom they would serve by making an exception in time of epidemic. The original version of its Code of Ethics (1847) contained the passage, "when pestilence prevails, it is their duty to face the danger and to continue their labors for the alleviation of suffering, even at jeopardy to their own lives."[12]

That passage was eliminated in 1957, when the threat of epidemics seemed over, but when AIDS appeared, the Judicial Council of the AMA reaffirmed the physicians' duty: "A physician may not ethically refuse to treat a patient whose condition is within the physician's realm of competence . . . neither those who have the disease [AIDS] nor those who have been infected with the virus should be subject to discrimination based on fear or prejudice, least of all by members of the health care community."[13] Almost all major organizations of physicians and other providers have issued similar statements in recent years.

The statements of professional organizations, however solemn, do not themselves create an ethical duty.[14] These statements must rest on an ethical principle independent of the contingent preferences and politics of their members. Similarly, even if the long tradition of Western medicine includes the acknowledgment by physicians and the expectation of the public that the sick must be served, the very relevance of that tradition might be questioned: does the fact that people once held such a belief mean that we today must also hold it? At the same time, the evidence of history and the declarations of professionals testify to the importance of the idea of service, even when dangerous or inconvenient. The idea persists, surfaces in time of dispute, and is rarely, if ever, challenged or openly refuted. Is it possible to go deeper than proclamations and traditions?

In the recent literature on the subject of professional responsibility, philosophers, physicians, and historians have sought to go deeper. They have attempted to articulate a basic principle that applied to the very work of providing help to the sick. Some have found it in the nature and character of the physician's role, still others in the reciprocal obligations between society and the profession.[15] The former line of argument suggests that undertaking the profession implies a commitment to certain virtues associated with medicine and healing and among these is the duty to care for the sick. The second line of argument stresses the implicit contract between a profession to which society grants a monopoly on the healing arts and the society whose needs it serves. A short article by Edmund Pellegrino states the case in favor of a strong obligation most comprehensively. He suggests that three things specific to medicine impose an obligation that subordinates the physician's self-interest to a duty of altruism. First, medical need itself constitutes a moral claim on those who are equipped to help because illness renders the patient uniquely vulnerable and dependent. Physicians invite trust from those in a position of relative powerlessness. Second, the physician's knowledge is not proprietary, since it is gained under the aegis of the society at large for the purpose of having a supply of medical personnel. Those who acquire this knowledge hold it in trust for the sick. Third, physicians in entering the profession, enter a covenant with society to use competence in service of the sick. These three reasons, Pellegrino argues, support the conclusion that physicians, collectively and individually, have a moral obligation to attend the sick.[16] There are, then, multiple reasons—tradition, the solemn declarations of professionals, the nature of the profession itself and its virtues, the conditions of the sick and their relationship to providers, the expectations of society as a whole, and its social contract with professions—to support the affirmation that service to the sick at risk and inconvenience to oneself is a matter of great importance. All of these reasons, as John Arras points out in an excellent article,[17] are open to some critical comment, but taken together they converge to the same point, namely that there appears to be a stringent and serious moral obligation, closely bound up with the very profession of being a physician or other provider of health care.

At the same time, all commentators allow that even this stringent and serious obligation has certain limitations and exceptions. The ethical principle of attending the sick cannot be interpreted as an obligation on the physician to respond to any and every request for help; that would be physically impossible and financially ruinous for the practitioner. Providers do not present themselves to society (to use the terms in the title of a paper by George Annas)[18] as saints, whose personal lives are totally subordinated to a higher ideal, but as healers with an important but limited skill. They offer to help, but they and the society recognize their finitude.

Thus, if there is such a principle, it must be limited in some way. Some limitations are generally accepted without question. Most obvious among these are the choice of a specialty, the selection of a geographical area, the establishment of a practice, and the determination of prices for service. Under special circumstances, such as the dearth of physicians in an area or specialty, even these generally accepted limitations might be questioned. Certain other limits that a physician might set on his or her service are ethically dubious, such as serving only the rich or persons of one race or religion. These sorts of limits make a mockery of the overall principle, since being rich or white or Catholic, for example, have nothing to do with medical need.

The most problematic sort of limitation would be the exclusion of certain sorts of genuine, treatable medical needs because the physician finds something unacceptable about the need or the needy. For example, the disease renders the patient physically repugnant, the disease is associated with behavior the physician considers immoral, or—and this is the case with AIDS—the disease is dangerous to the physician. Refusing service for the first two reasons is clearly reprehensible. But is personal risk a reasonable excuse from service?

Until quite recently, physicians regularly exposed themselves to serious risk when they treated patients with infectious diseases. Even when the principle of accepting risk in order to help those in need is acknowledged, however, certain rules of thumb guide its application. Those rules are the familiar ones defining the circumstances in which a person has a moral obligation to aid another person who is in danger: the reasonableness of the risk, the feasibility of help, the urgency of the need, and the absence of less risky alternatives.

The reasonableness of the risk in caring for patients with AIDS is the question in this case. Reasonableness refers to such things as evidence that the activity is actually dangerous, the probability that harm will occur, and the magnitude of the harm for oneself and for others. Each of these elements must be assessed in light of the best available information and the best common sense about the situation at hand.

In the ordinary course of life, activities are usually designated as high risk because the *frequency* of adverse events is high. We engage almost unthinkingly in many activities in which the adverse affects rarely occur but may be very serious, indeed lethal, when they do, such as driving to work and engaging in sports activities. In the case of AIDS, the frequency of the adverse event, seroconversion after accidental occupation exposure, is very low.[19] At the same time, the magnitude of the harm is great: there is strong probability that infection will proceed to disease and that disease will lead to death.

Thus, the moral quandary: Should I undertake an action that I have a presumed duty to perform, if the action has a low probability of resulting in harm to me (and others, for example, my spouse) of great magnitude? In general, one could respond to that quandary by reflecting that a life ruled by the strategy of avoiding the low probabilities of even great harm would be a paralyzed life. Usually, however, our reflection on this question turns to the importance of the work to be done or the activity to be performed. We ask ourselves whether "it's worth it."

One way of asking whether some activity is worth the risk is to reflect on certain features of the actual case in question. These features are included in the traditional "rules of rescue," namely, the urgency and feasibility of helping and the existence of alternatives. The seriousness of the obligation to which physicians are held can be mitigated by demonstrating cases in which the medical intervention is not urgent, such as a request for cosmetic surgery only to enhance one's image, a procedure that is unlikely to benefit the patient, such as inserting a shunt to dialyse a patient whose death is imminent under any circumstances, or a medical intervention that would be as useful as a surgical one. In some situations a plausible case might be made that an intervention be omitted. The rationale is that the intervention is actually not needed at this time or under this form. It does not constitute a rescue in any significant sense. But it is obvious that in such cases, psychological, and emotional factors can distort this judgment by exaggerating the sense of danger, magnifying perceived risks, or trivializing the need or urgency of treatment. Scrupulous honesty and courage are indispensable adjuncts to such evaluation. Excusing oneself from so serious an obligation as service to those one is professionally committed to serve cannot be done lightly. These sorts of cases are debatable, and the best approach to their resolution is debate or, at least, open discussion with the patient and one's colleagues.

A question less dramatic than actual refusal to treat is the proposal to require an HIV antibody test of all patients or of all surgical patients. In addition to the problems about the behavior of the test in low-risk populations and about interpretation of the test, it is crucial to ask what decisions might be faced and what procedures initiated on the basis of information gained by that test. Are there specific maneuvers that might be modified if the patient is antibody-positive? For example, would the surgeon staple rather than suture, use a different technique for hemostasis, proceed more slowly and cautiously, pass instruments differently? If there are safer procedures that could be employed in the more dangerous (to the surgeon) situation, what increase in risk to the patient can be tolerated? Clearly, such reasoning might be part of a rational approach to care. If reasonable modification might decrease the risk to the operator without increasing risk to the patient, voluntary preoperative testing might be justified. In the absence of any practical modification of procedure, information about the patient's infective state could lead to unjustified refusal of needed care.

The point of the preceding discussion is to demonstrate the stringency of the physician's duty to treat by examining the allowable exceptions. Even when exceptions and limitations to the duty to treat are admitted, they are limited and narrow. If made more generous and wide, these exceptions would evacuate the obligation itself of all meaning. I conclude, then, that there is a strong imperative on physicians to respond to the need of the sick and that the imperative does allow certain limitations, but that a refusal to serve based on fear of disease, burden of care, or inconvenience is not easy to justify. Only the most sound and serious reasons, together with scrupulously honest reasoning, may excuse a refusal to provide to the HIV-infected patient any service that would be rendered to noninfected patients with similar needs. Even then, the justification of such a refusal holds only in the particular cases in which the facts meet the ethical tests mentioned above. Policies that allow providers easy outs or designate broad classes of refusable patients or services should be repudiated. . . .

The refusal or reluctance of one surgeon here and one nurse there may seem insignificant, but the occasional refusal, once tolerated, establishes a new and perverse principle in health care: individuals may ethically ignore those in need of care. Such a principle fosters the perception that medicine is in no way different from a business, setting up shop where safe profits can be made. Admitting into medicine a principle that would allow the health professionals to rescue themselves from caring for sick persons because that care might cause them harm, especially at a time of major crisis and challenge, hovers on the verge of massive hypocrisy. It says to society the equivalent of, "Believe in medicine and its powers; yet do not expect medical practitioners to use those powers when they are needed, but only when it is safe and practical for them to do so."

This perception is a serious threat to the reputation of the profession and all of its practitioners. Refusing treatment in specific cases casts a shadow on the most precious value of medicine, its commitment to service. A London apothecary who stayed to treat patients during the plague in London in 1665 wrote eloquently about those who deserted their charges. His words are worth recalling even today: "Every man that undertakes to be of a profession or takes upon him any office must take all parts of it, the good and the evil, the pleasure and the pain, the profit and the inconvenience altogether and not pick and choose, for the ministers must preach, captains must fight and physicians attend the sick."[20]

NOTES

1. C. E. A. Winslow, *The Conquest of Epidemic Disease: A Chapter in the History of Ideas* (Madison: University of Wisconsin Press, 1980), 118.
2. D. W. Amundsen, "Medical Deontology and Pestilential Disease in the Middle Ages," *Journal of the History of Medicine and Allied Sciences* 32 (1977), 402–421.
3. C. F. Turner, H. G. Miller, L. E. Moses, eds., *AIDS: Sexual Behavior and Intravenous Drug Use* (Washington, D.C.: National Academy Press, 1989), chapters 6, 7.
4. G. Annas, "Not Saints but Healers: A Health Care Professional's Legal Obligation to Treat," *American Journal of Public Health* 78 (July 1988), 844–849; T. Brennan, "Occupational Transmission of HIV," in Lawrence O. Gostin, ed., *AIDS and the Health Care System* (New Haven, Conn.: 1990), Chapter 10.
5. D. M. Bell, "HIV Infection in Health Care Workers," in *AIDS and the Health Care System*, chapter 8; J. R. Allen, "Health Care Workers and the Risk of Transmission," *Hastings Center Report* (April 1988), 2–4.

6.   J. A. Kelly, J. S. St. Lawrence, S. Smith, et al., "Stigmatization of AIDS Patients by Physicians," *American Journal of Public Health* 77 (July 1987), 789–791.
7.   R. M. Wachter, "The Impact of AIDS on Medical Residency Training," *New England Journal of Medicine* 314 (1986), 177–179.
8.   AMA Council on Ethical and Judicial Affairs, *Current Opinions*, 1986, Principle VI, 9.11.
9.   Annas, supra note 4.
10. Amundsen, supra note 2; D. W. Amundsen, R. L. Numbers, *Caring and Curing: Health and Medicine in the Western Religious Traditions* (New York: Macmillan, 1987).
11. D. M. Fox, "The Politics of Physicians' Responsibility in Epidemics: A Note on History," *Hastings Center Report* (April 1988), 5–9.
12. *Code of Ethics of the American Medical Association, 1847.* (Philadelphia: Turner Hamilton, 1871), 32.
13. AMA Council on Ethical and Judicial Affairs, "Ethical Issues Involved in the Growing AIDS Crisis," *Journal of the American Medical Association* 259 (1988), 1360–1361.
14. B. Freedman, "Health Professions, Codes and the Right to Refuse HIV Infected Patients," *Hastings Center Report* (April 1988), 20–24.
15. A. Zuger, S. H. Miles, "Physicians, AIDS, and Occupational Risk: Historical Traditions and Ethical Obligations," *Journal of the American Medical Association* 258 (1987), 1924–1928; E. Emmanuel, "Do Physicians Have an Obligation to Treat Patients with AIDS?" *The New England Journal of Medicine* 318 (1988), 1686–1688; J. D. Arras, "The Fragile Web of Responsibility: AIDS and the Duty to Treat," *Hastings Center Report* (April 1988), 10–20; L. M. Peterson, "AIDS: The Ethical Dilemma for Surgeons," *Law, Medicine & Health Care* 17 (1989), 139–144; L. Walters, "Ethical Issues in Prevention and Treatment of HIV Infection and AIDS," *Science* 239 (1988), 597–603; E. Pellegrino, "Altruism, Self-Interest and Medical Ethics," *Journal of the American Medical Association* 258 (1988), 1939–1940.
16. Pellegrino, supra note 15.
17. Arras, supra note 15.
18. Annas, supra note 4.
19. Bell, supra note 5.
20. W. Boghurst, *Limographia*, edited by J. F. Payne (London, 1894), 61.

EXERCISES

Paretsky:

1.   Has V. I. reached the best solution, according to you? Why or why not?
2.   What values does V. I.'s decision enact? Show how it enacts them.
3.   Explain several meanings of the term *responsibility* as argued for by some of the story's characters. How does V. I. understand her responsibility to her work and to others (professionally or otherwise)?

4. What is the relationship between responsibility and intention? For example, can you be responsible for something that you did not intend to happen?
5. Returning to the terms of chapter 3, do you think V. I. is more of a separatist or a holist? Be sure to define these terms in your answer, and give concrete examples from the story to substantiate your answer.

Friedman:

1. What, according to Friedman, are the responsibilities, not exclusively the moral ones, of business? When answering this question, explain why these are the sole responsibilities of business.
2. What, according to Friedman, are the responsibilities of corporate executives? What does Friedman mean by the principal versus agent distinction?
3. Give an example of the kind of behavior of business that Friedman would be against. Do you find this perspective persuasive? Why?
4. When a corporation attempts to spend money for the greater social interest, what are the political questions raised on the level of principle and consequences? Are these really just questions for Friedman?
5. Do you think that business today uses the cloak of social responsibility for its own benefit, social, financial, or otherwise? Is it possible for business to have a positive impact on society? If so, what is the impact? If not, why?

DeGeorge:

1. Explain what DeGeorge means by the Organizational View. Do you think it is fair to attribute this view to Friedman?
2. Give an example of the kind of action DeGeorge would hold a corporation morally accountable for. Would you also hold a corporation responsible for this kind of action? Why?
3. What does DeGeorge mean when he holds that there is no need to choose between ascribing responsibility to either corporations or to individuals?
4. Discuss the different ways in which management, corporations, and workers are responsible, according to DeGeorge. Do you think this is an appropriate or overwhelming list of responsibilities?
5. DeGeorge stresses the role of corporate culture in determining what kind of excellence, moral or otherwise, a corporation will achieve. Is this a plausible statement? Articulate the reasons for DeGeorge's statement and then assess their plausibility.

Jonsen:

1. What is Jonsen's conclusion, and how does he argue for it? What values does he employ, and what sort of theory does he use? Do you agree with his conclusion? Why or why not?

2. How do you think Jonsen's discussion relates to beneficence and non-maleficence enacted specifically by medical professionals?
3. How are the Rule of Reasonable Care, the Rule of Proportionality, and the Rule Against Paternalism relevant or not relevant to Jonsen's argument? Explain.
4. Discuss how both the Jonsen article and the Paretsky short story consider whether there are limits to a professional's responsibility. Are there such limits, in general, or in this case? If so, what are they?
5. Do you think that there are occupations other than medicine that have a greater responsibility to enact beneficence or nonmaleficence? Which occupations and why? Or, why do you think that no occupations fit within this category?

Selected Bibliography

Professional Ethics in General:

APPELBAUM, DAVID, and SARAH VERONE LAWTON. *Ethics and the Professions.* Englewood Cliffs, N.J.: Prentice Hall, 1990.

BAUMRIN, BERNARD, and BENJAMIN FREEDMAN, eds. *Moral Responsibility and the Professions.* New York: Haven Publications, 1983.

BAYLES, MICHAEL D. *Professional Ethics.* Belmont, Calif.: Wadsworth, 1981.

BEABOUT, GREGORY R., and DARYL J. WENNEMANN. *Applied Professional Ethics.* Lanham, Md.: University Press of America, 1994.

CALLAHAN, JOAN C. *Ethical Issues in Professional Life.* New York: Oxford University Press, 1988.

CAMPBELL, DENNIS M. *Doctors, Lawyers, Ministers: Christian Ethics in Professional Practice.* Nashville, Tenn.: Abingdon, 1982.

FLORES, ALBERT, ed. *Professional Ideals.* Belmont, Calif.: Wadsworth, 1988.

FREIDSON, ELIOT, ed. *The Professions and Their Prospects.* Beverly Hills, Calif.: Sage Publications, 1971.

GOLDMAN, ALAN H. *The Moral Foundations of Professional Ethics.* Savage, Md.: Rowman and Littlefield, 1980.

GOODE, WILLIAM J., ROBERT K. MERTON, and MARY JANE HUNTINGTON. *The Professions in American Society.* New York: Russell Sage Foundation, 1957.

GORLIN, RENA A., ed. *Codes of Professional Responsibility.* Washington, D.C.: Bureau of National Affairs, 1986.

KOEHN, DARYL. *The Ground of Professional Ethics.* New York: Routledge, 1994.

KULTGEN, JOHN. *Ethics and Professionalism.* Philadelphia, Penn.: University of Pennsylvania Press, 1988.

LEBACQZ, KAREN. *Professional Ethics: Power and Paradox.* Nashville, Tenn.: Abingdon Press, 1985.

LYNN, KENNETH S. *The Professions in America.* Boston, Mass.: Beacon Press, 1963.

MOORE, WILBERT E. *The Professions: Roles and Rules.* New York: Russell Sage Foundation, 1970.

Professional Ethics in Specific Professions:

Business

BOATRIGHT, JOHN R. *Cases in Ethics and the Conduct of Business.* Englewood Cliffs, N.J.: Prentice Hall, 1995.

CAUSEY, DENZIL Y. *Duties and Liabilities of Public Accountants.* Third edition. Mississippi State, Miss.: Accountant's Press, 1986.

DONALDSON, THOMAS, and PATRICIA WERHANE. *Ethical Issues in Business.* Fourth edition. Englewood Cliffs, N.J.: Prentice Hall, 1993.

GOODPASTER, KENNETH E. *Ethics in Management: Harvard Business School Case Studies.* Boston, Mass.: Harvard Business School, 1984.

HOFFMAN, W. MICHAEL, and JENNIFER M. MOORE. *Business Ethics: Readings in Corporate Morality.* New York: McGraw-Hill, 1983.

HOSMER, LaRUE TONE. *The Ethics of Management.* Second edition. Homewood, Ill.: Irwin, 1991.

ROBISON, WADE L., MICHAEL S. PRITCHARD, and JOSEPH ELLIN. *Profits and the Professions: Essays in Business and Professional Ethics.* Clifton, N.J.: Humana Press, 1983.

SNOEYENBOS, MILTON, ROBERT ALMEDER, and JAMES HUMBER, eds. *Business Ethics: Corporate Values and Society.* Second edition. Amherst, N.Y.: Prometheus Books, 1992.

WINDAL, FLOYD W. *Ethics and the Accountant: Text and Cases.* Englewood Cliffs, N.J.: Prentice Hall, 1990.

Computer

ERMANN, M. DAVID, MARY B. WILLIAMS, and MICHELE S. SHAUF. *Computer, Ethics, and Society.* Second edition. New York: Oxford University Press, 1997.

FORESTER, TOM, and PERRY MORRISON. *Computer Ethics.* Cambridge, Mass.: MIT Press, 1990.

JOHNSON, DEBORAH G. *Computer Ethics.* Second edition. Englewood Cliffs, N.J.: Prentice Hall, 1993.

KLING, ROB, ed. *Computerization and Controversy: Value Conflicts and Social Choices.* Second edition. New York: Academic Press, 1996.

PARKER, DONN B., SUSAN SWOPE, and BOB BAKER. *Ethical Conflicts in Information and Computer Science, Technology, and Business.* Wellesley, Mass.: QED Information Sciences, 1990.

SPINELLO, RICHARD A. *Case Studies in Information and Computer Ethics.* Englewood Cliffs, N.J.: Prentice Hill, 1997.

Criminal Justice

ELLISTON, FREDERICK A. *Police Ethics: Source Materials.* Washington, D.C.: Police Foundation, 1985.

ELLISTON, FREDERICK A., and MICHAEL FELDBERG, eds. *Moral Issues in Police Work.* Totowa, N.J.: Rowman and Allanheld, 1985.

GOODMAN, DEBBIE J. *Enforcing Ethics: A Scenario-Based Workbook for Police and Corrections Recruits and Officers.* Englewood Cliffs, N.J.: Prentice Hall, 1998.

HEFFERNAN, WILLIAM C., and TIMOTHY STROUP, eds. *Police Ethics: Hard Choices in Law Enforcement.* New York: John Jay Press, 1984.

KLEINIG, JOHN, ed. *Handled with Discretion: Ethical Issues in Police Decision Making.* Lanham, Md.: Rowman & Littlefield, 1996.

———. *The Ethics of Policing.* New York: Cambridge University Press, 1996.

Education

CAHN, STEVEN M. *Saints and Scamps: Ethics in Academia.* Totowa, N.J.: Rowman and Littlefield, 1986.

PAYNE, STEVE L., and BRUCE H. CHARNOV, eds. *Ethical Dilemmas for Academic Professionals.* Springfield, Ill.: C. C. Thomas, 1987.

RICH, JOHN M. *Professional Ethics in Education.* Springfield, Ill.: C. C. Thomas, 1984.

ROBINSON, G. M., and J. MOULTON. *Ethical Problems in Higher Education.* Englewood Cliffs, N.J.: Prentice Hall, 1985.

STRIKE, KENNETH A., and JONAS SOLTIS. *The Ethics of Teaching.* New York: Teachers College, 1985.

STRIKE, KENNETH A., JONAS SOLTIS, and P. LANCE TERNASKY. *Ethics for Professionals in Education: Perspectives for Preparation and Practice.* New York: Teachers College, 1993.

Engineering

FLORES, ALBERT, ed. *Ethical Problems in Engineering.* Troy, N.Y.: Rensselaer Polytechnic Institute, 1980.

JOHNSON, DEBORAH G. *Ethical Issues in Engineering.* Englewood Cliffs, N.J.: Prentice Hall, 1991.

LAYTON, EDWIN T., JR. *The Revolt of the Engineers: Social Responsibility and the American Engineering Profession.* Second edition. Baltimore, Md.: Johns Hopkins University Press, 1986.

MARTIN, MIKE W., and RONALD SCHINZINGER. *Ethics and Engineering.* New York: McGraw-Hill, 1983.

SCHAUB, JAMES H., and KARL PAVLOVIC. *Engineering Professionalism and Ethics.* New York: John Wiley & Sons, 1983.

UNGER, STEPHEN H. *Controlling Technology: Ethics and the Responsible Engineer.* New York: Holt, Rinehart, and Winston, 1982.

WEIL, VIVIAN. *Report of the Workshops on Ethical Issues in Engineering.* Chicago, Ill.: Center for the Study of Ethics in the Professions, 1980.

Government/Public Policy

BOWIE, NORMAN E. *Ethical Issues in Government.* Philadelphia, Penn.: Temple University Press, 1981.

BOWMAN, JAMES S., and FREDERICK A. ELLISTON. *Ethics, Government, and Public Policy: A Reference Guide.* New York: Greenwood Press, 1988.

FRENCH, PETER A. *Ethics in Government.* Englewood Cliffs, N.J.: Prentice Hall, 1983.

GUTMAN, AMY, and DENNIS THOMPSON, eds. *Ethics and Politics: Cases and Comments.* Chicago, Ill.: Nelson-Hall, 1984.

LEWIS, CAROL W. *The Ethics Challenge in Public Service: A Problem-Solving Guide.* San Francisco, Calif.: Jossey-Bass, 1991.

TIMMINS, W. M. *A Casebook of Public Ethics and Issues.* Pacific Grove, Calif.: Brooks/Cole, 1990.

TONG, R. *Ethics in Policy Analysis.* Englewood Cliffs, N.J.: Prentice Hall, 1986.

Journalism/Media

CHRISTIANS, CLIFFORD G., KIM B. ROTZOLL, and MARK FACKLER. *Media Ethics: Cases and Moral Reasoning.* Fourth edition. New York: Longman, 1995.

COHEN, ELLIOTT D. *Philosophical Issues in Journalism.* New York: Oxford University Press, 1992.

FINK, CONRAD C. *Media Ethics.* Englewood Cliffs, N.J.: Prentice Hall, 1994.

GOODWIN, H. EUGENE. *Groping for Ethics in Journalism.* Second edition. Ames, Iowa: Iowa State University Press, 1987.

KLAIDMAN, STEPHEN, and TOM L. BEAUCHAMP. *The Virtuous Journalist.* Oxford: Oxford University Press, 1987.

MERRILL, JOHN C., and S. JACK ODEL, eds. *Ethics and the Press.* New York: Hastings House, 1983.

OLEN, JEFFREY. *Ethics in Journalism.* Englewood Cliffs, N.J.: Prentice Hall, 1988.

PATTERSON, PHILIP, and LEE C. WILKINS, eds. *Media Ethics: Issues and Cases.* Third edition. New York: McGraw-Hill, 1997.

Law

DAVIS, MICHAEL, and FREDERICK A. ELLISTON, eds. *Ethics and the Legal Profession.* Amherst, N.Y.: Prometheus Books, 1986.

ELLISTON, FREDERICK A., and JANE VAN SCHAICK. *Legal Ethics: An Annotated Bibliography and Resource Guide*. Littleton, Colo.: Fred B. Rothman & Co., 1984.
GREENAWALT, KENT. *Conflicts of Law and Morality*. Oxford: Oxford University Press, 1987.
HAZARD, GEOFFREY C. *Ethics and the Practice of Law*. New Haven, Conn.: Yale University Press, 1978.
KIPNIS, KENNETH. *Legal Ethics*. Englewood Cliffs, N.J.: Prentice Hall, 1986.
LUBAN, DAVID, ed. *The Good Lawyer: Lawyers' Roles and Lawyers' Ethics*. Totowa, N.J.: Rowman and Allanheld, 1983.
SCHRADER, DAVID E. *Ethics and the Practice of Law*. Englewood Cliffs, N.J.: Prentice Hall, 1988.
SIMON, WILLIAM H. *The Practice of Justice: A Theory of Lawyers' Ethics*. Cambridge, Mass.: Harvard University Press, 1998.

Library

HAUPTMAN, ROBERT. *Ethical Challenges in Librarianship*. Phoenix, Ariz.: Oryx Press, 1988.
LANCASTER, F. W. *Ethics and the Librarian*. Chicago, Ill.: University of Illinois Graduate School, 1991.
LINDSEY, JONATHAN A., and ANN E. PRENTICE. *Professional Ethics and Librarians*. Phoenix, Ariz.: Oryx Press, 1985.

Medicine

BEAUCHAMP, TOM L., and JAMES F. CHILDRESS. *Principles of Biomedical Ethics*. Fourth edition. New York: Oxford University Press, 1994.
BEAUCHAMP, TOM L., JAMES F. CHILDRESS, and L. B. MCCULLOUGH. *Medical Ethics: The Moral Responsibilities of Physicians*. Englewood Cliffs, N.J.: Prentice Hall, 1984.
BRODY, BARUCH A., and H. TRISTAM ENGELHARDT. *Bioethics: Readings and Cases*. Englewood Cliffs, N.J.: Prentice Hall, 1987.
GOROVITZ, SAMUEL. *Doctors' Dilemmas*. New York: Macmillan, 1982.
RESNICK, DAVID M. *Professional Ethics for Audiologists and Speech Language Pathologists*. San Diego, Calif.: Singular Publishing, 1993.
RODWIN, MARC A. *Medicine, Money, and Morals: Physicians' Conflicts of Interest*. New York: Oxford University Press, 1993.
WORTHLEY, JOHN A. *The Ethics of the Ordinary in Healthcare: Concepts and Cases*. Chicago, Ill.: Health Administration Press, 1997.

Ministry

BOYAJIAN, JANE A., ed. *Ethical Issues in the Practice of Ministry*. Minneapolis, Minn.: United Theological Seminary of the Twin Cities, 1984.

GULA, RICHARD M. *Ethics in Pastoral Ministry*. Mahwah, N.J.: Paulist Press, 1996.

JERSILD, PAUL. *Making Moral Decisions: A Christian Approach to Personal and Social Ethics*. Minneapolis, Minn.: Fortress Press, 1990.

MALONY, H. NEWTON, THOMAS L. NEEDHAM, and SAMUEL SOUTHARD. *Clergy Malpractice*. Philadelphia, Penn.: Westminster Press, 1986.

NOYCE, GAYLORD B. *Pastoral Ethics: Professional Responsibilities of the Clergy*. Nashville, Tenn.: Abingdon Press, 1988.

TAYLOR, THOMAS F. *Seven Deadly Lawsuits: How Ministers Can Avoid Litigation and Regulation*. Nashville, Tenn.: Abingdon Press, 1996.

WIEST, WALTER E., and ELWYN A. SMITH. *Ethics in Ministry: A Guide for the Professional*. Minneapolis, Minn.: Fortress Press, 1990.

WIND, JAMES P., J. RUSSELL BURCK, PAUL F. CAMENISCH, and DENNIS P. McCANN. *Clergy Ethics in a Changing Society: Mapping the Terrain*. Louisville, Ky.: Westminster John Knox Press, 1991.

Nursing

APPLEGATE, MINERVA, and NINA ENTRENKIN. *Case Studies for Students: A Companion to Teaching Ethics in Nursing*. New York: National League for Nursing, 1984.

BENJAMIN, MARTIN, and JOY CURTIS. *Ethics in Nursing*. Third edition. Oxford: Oxford University Press, 1991.

CARROLL, MARY ANN, HENRY G. SCHNEIDER, and GEORGE R. WESLEY. *Ethics in the Practice of Nursing*. Englewood Cliffs, N.J.: Prentice Hall, 1985.

CURTIN, LEAH, and M. JOSEPHINE FLAHERTY. *Nursing Ethics: Theories and Pragmatics*. Bowie, Md.: Robert Brady, 1982.

JAMETON, ANDREW. *Nursing Practice: The Ethical Issues*. Englewood Cliffs, N.J.: Prentice Hall, 1984.

PENCE, TERRY. *Ethics in Nursing: An Annotated Bibliography*. Second edition. New York: National League for Nursing, 1986.

Psychology/Counseling

ANDERSON, ROBERT M., TERRI L. NEEDELS, and HAROLD V. HALL. *Avoiding Ethical Misconduct in Psychology Specialty Areas*. Springfield, Ill.: Charles C. Thomas Pub. Ltd., 1998.

CARROLL, M. A., H. G. SCHNEIDER, and G. R. WESLEY. *Ethics in the Practice of Psychology*. Englewood Cliffs, N.J.: Prentice Hall, 1985.

HUBER, CHARLES H. *Ethical, Legal, and Professional Issues in the Practice of Marriage and Family Therapy*. Second edition. Englewood Cliffs, N.J.: Prentice Hall, 1993.

JACOB-TIMM, SUSAN, and TIMOTHY S. HARTSHORNE. *Ethics and Law for School Psychologists*. Third edition. New York: John Wiley & Sons, 1998.

KEITH-SPIEGEL, PATRICIA, and GERALD P. KOOCHER. *Ethics in Psychology: Professional Standards and Cases*. Second edition. New York: Oxford University Press, 1998.

MARSH, DIANE T., and RICHARD D. MAGEE. *Ethical and Legal Issues in Professional Practice with Families*. New York: John Wiley & Sons, 1997.

STEIN, RONALD H. *Ethical Issues in Counseling*. Amherst, N.Y.: Prometheus Books, 1989.

Social Work

BULLIS, RONALD K. *Clinical Social Worker Misconduct: Law, Ethics, and Interpersonal Dynamics*. Chicago, Ill.: Nelson-Hall, 1995.

HUGMAN, RICHARD, and DAVID SMITH. *Ethical Issues in Social Work*. New York: Routledge, 1995.

LUM, DOMAN, ed. *Social Work and Health Care Policy*. Totowa, N.J.: Rowman and Littlefield, 1982.

REAMER, FREDERICK G. *Ethical Dilemmas in Social Service*. Second edition. New York: Columbia University Press, 1993.

RHODES, MARGARET L. *Ethical Dilemmas in Social Work Practice*. Boston, Mass.: Routledge and Kegan Paul, 1986.

ROTHMAN, JULIET CASSUTO. *From the Front Lines: Student Cases in Social Work Ethics*. Needham Heights, Mass.: Allyn & Bacon, 1997.

WELLS, CAROLYN C., and KATHLEEN M. MASCH. *Social Work Ethics Day to Day: Guidelines for Professional Practice*. White Plains, N.Y.: Longman, 1988.

Other

ANDERSON, ALBERT. *Ethics for Fundraisers*. Bloomington, Ind.: Indiana University Press, 1996.

BAILEY, DIANA M., and SHARON L. SCHWARTZBERG. *Ethical and Legal Dilemmas in Occupational Therapy*. Philadelphia, Penn.: F. A. Davis Co., 1994.

BISSELL, LECLAIR, and JAMES E. ROYCE. *Ethics for Addiction Professionals*. Second edition. Center City, Minn.: Hazelden, 1994.

BURD, RACHEL. *Graphic Artists Guild Handbook: Pricing & Ethical Guidelines*. Ninth edition. New York: Graphic Artists Guild, 1997.

Ethics for the Insurance Professional. Second edition. Chicago, Ill.: Dearborn Trade, 1996.

FLIGHT, MYRTLE. *Law, Liability, and Ethics: For Medical Office Professionals*. Third edition. Albany, N.Y.: Delmar Publishers, 1997.

LONG, DEBORAH H. *Doing the Right Thing: A Real Estate Practitioner's Guide to Ethical Decision Making*. Second edition. Scottsdale, Ariz.: Gorsuch Scarisbrick Pub., 1998.

Credits and Permissions

Chapter 3

Case 3: Conflicts in a Social Worker's Social Conscience. From: *Ethical Issues in the Professions*, by Windt/Appleby/et al., © 1989. Adapted with permission of Prentice Hall, Inc., Upper Saddle River, N. J.

Chapter 4

The Fate of Baby Joe. From: *Principles of Biomedical Ethics, Fourth Edition*, by Tom L. Beauchamp and James F. Childress, © 1979, 1983, 1989, 1994 by Oxford University Press, Inc. Used with permission of Oxford University Press, Inc.

The dilemma of a TV anchor and journalist. Reprinted with permission of Knight-Ridder/Tribune Information Services.

Ibid. Reprinted with permission of Knight-Ridder/Tribune Information Services.

Chapter 5

Case 4: Client Access to the Psychologist's Records. From: *Ethics in Psychology: Professional Standards & Cases*, by Patricia Keith-Spiegel and Gerald P. Koocher, © 1985 by McGraw-Hill Companies. Used by permission of the McGraw-Hill Companies.

Chapter 6

Georgine's dilemma. From: *Principles of Biomedical Ethics, Fourth Edition*, by Tom L. Beauchamp and James F. Childress, © 1979, 1983, 1989, 1994 by Oxford University Press, Inc. Used with permission of Oxford University Press, Inc. From *Utilitarianism: For and Against*, by J.J.C. Smart and Bernard Williams, © 1973 by Cambridge University Press. Used with permission of Cambridge University Press.

Abdul Khan and the security system. From: *Computer Ethics*, 2/E, by Johnson, Deborah, © 1994. Adapted with permission of Prentice Hall, Inc., Upper Saddle River, N.J.

The Unhappy Social Worker. Adapted from: Vincent Barry, *Personal and Social Ethics: Moral Problems with Integrated Theory*, © 1978 by Wadsworth Publishing Co., Belmont, Calif. Used with permission.

Case 1: The Boss Who Will Cover for You. From: *Case Studies in Business Ethics*, 2/E, by Donaldson/Gini, © 1990. Adapted with permission of Prentice Hall, Inc., Upper Saddle River, N.J.

Case 2: The Observant Pharmacist. From: *Human Values in Health Care: The Practice of Ethics*, by Richard A. Wright, © 1990 by McGraw-Hill Companies. Used with permission of the McGraw-Hill Companies.

Chapter 7

Yolanda Biltmore's Dilemma. Adapted from: Vincent Barry, *Personal and Social Ethics: Moral Problems with Integrated Theory*, © 1978 by Wadsworth Publishing Co., Belmont, Calif. Used with permission.

Case 1: Professional Integrity and Academic Tenure. From: *Ethical Issues in the Professions*, by Windt/Appleby/et al., © 1989. Adapted with permission of Prentice Hall, Inc., Upper Saddle River, N.J.

Case 2: Lying for Business Reasons. From: *Ethics and the Professions*, by Applebaum/Lawton, © 1990. Reprinted with permission of Prentice Hall, Upper Saddle River, N.J.

Readings on Integrity and Respect for Persons

Whistleblowing and Employee Loyalty. Used with permission of author.

Lying and the Law. Used with permission of author.

"On Duties of Virtue Toward Other Men ..." by Kant. From: *The Metaphysics of Morals* by Immanuel Kant, translated and edited by Mary Gregor, © 1991, Cambridge University Press. Reprinted with permission of Cambridge University Press.

Chapter 9

Alan Nelson, vineyard owner. Reprinted with permission of the *Wall Street Journal*, © 1998 Dow Jones & Company, Inc. All Rights Reserved Worldwide.

Chapter 10

Readings on Justice and Compassion

Readings on Beneficence and Nonmaleficence and Responsibility

Index